DOLLARS FOR LIFE

MARY ZIEGLER

Dollars for Life

THE ANTI-ABORTION MOVEMENT AND THE FALL OF THE REPUBLICAN ESTABLISHMENT

Yale
UNIVERSITY PRESS
NEW HAVEN & LONDON

Published with assistance from the foundation established in memory of William McKean Brown.

Yale University Press books may be purchased in quantity for educational, business, or promotional use. For information, please e-mail sales.press@yale.edu (U.S. office) or sales@yaleup.co.uk (U.K. office).

Set in Scala & Sans Scala type by IDS Infotech, Ltd., Chandigarh, India.
Printed in the United States of America.

Library of Congress Control Number: 2021951004
ISBN 978-0-300-26014-4 (hardcover : alk. paper)

A catalogue record for this book is available from the British Library.

This paper meets the requirements of ANSI/NISO Z39.48-1992 (Permanence of Paper).

10 9 8 7 6 5 4 3 2

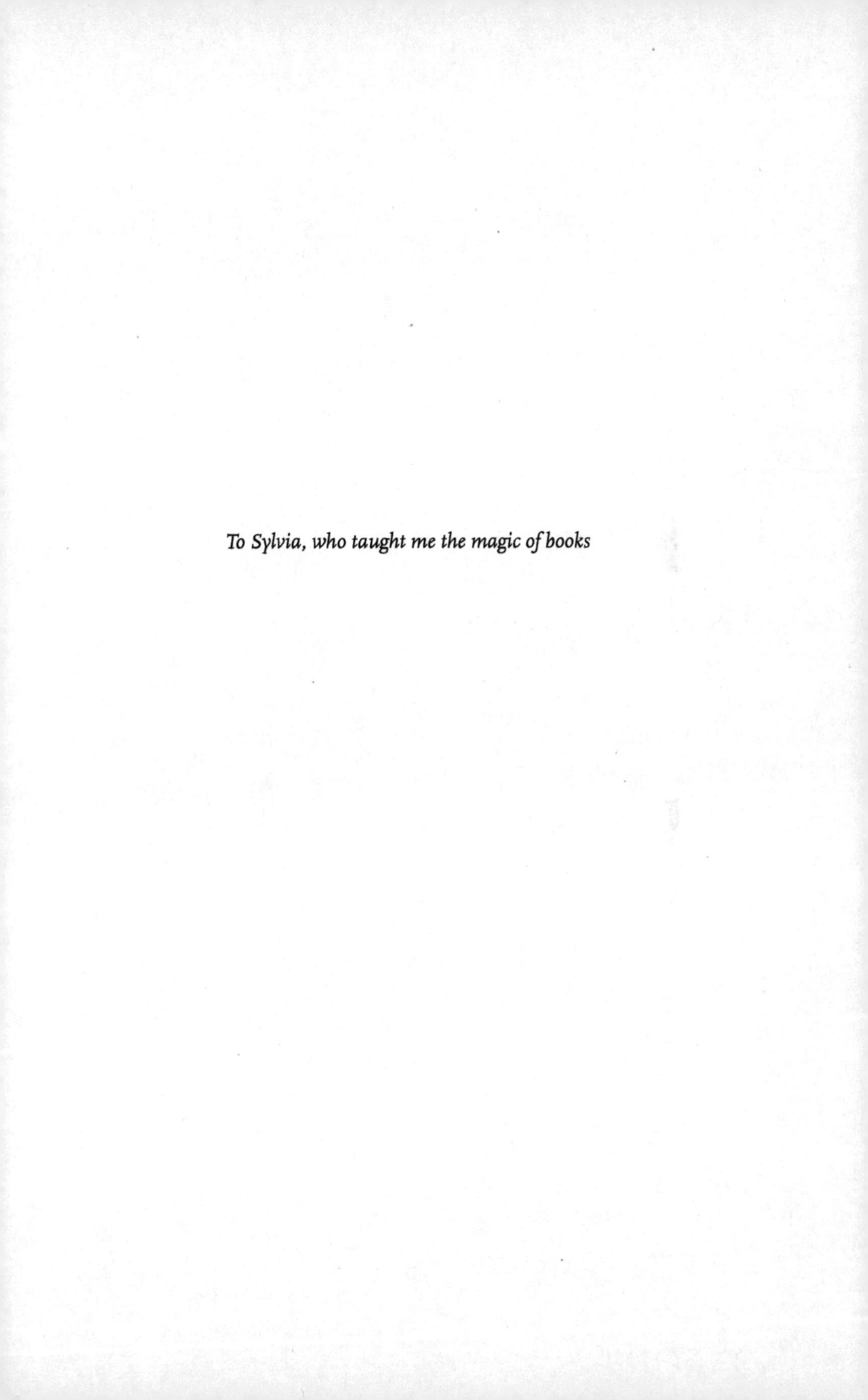

To Sylvia, who taught me the magic of books

CONTENTS

PREFACE

IN JANUARY 2021, THE DEMISE OF *Roe v. Wade* seemed imminent, but few were paying attention. This should not have been a surprise. That month, the United States had its highest number of deaths in the COVID-19 pandemic to date and one of the highest per capita COVID death rates in the world. After being voted out of office in November, Donald Trump mounted an unprecedented and ongoing campaign to overturn the 2020 presidential election. Alleging a massive conspiracy, Trump brought dozens of lawsuits, pressured state legislators and other officials, and urged Congress and the vice president to refuse to certify the election results. This campaign culminated in an invasion of the U.S. Capitol that killed five people. For a time, even anti-abortion leaders seemed focused on other things. James Bopp Jr., one of the movement's most prominent lawyers, filed and later withdrew lawsuits challenging the election results in four key states. Two months after Election Day, Janet Folger Porter, a firebrand known for pushing early bans on abortion, promised supporters that God would find a way for Trump to win. Democracy in the United States was in crisis, and the country's caustic abortion politics seemed to have faded into the background.[1]

Yet the American anti-abortion movement contributed far more to the rise of Donald Trump and the transformation of the GOP than we often think. Scholars have traced how an ascendant form of Christian nationalism—the belief that the United States was and always should be a Christian nation—was needed for Trump to edge out Hillary Clinton in 2016. But the influence of the anti-abortion movement went much further, and it had everything to do with money in U.S. politics.[2]

Political scientists and historians of the religious right have told part of the story of the fascinating partnership between abortion foes and Republican leaders. Their studies often suggest that while pro-lifers became dependent on the GOP, the Republican Party did not fundamentally change its priorities. Some assert that the GOP co-opted the religious right, gaining its votes while offering little but speeches in return.[3]

By focusing on the pro-life movement and its complex relationship with the broader religious right, this book shows that partnership with the movement had consequences for the GOP that went well beyond abortion. Anti-abortion operatives helped make control of the Supreme Court a deciding issue for conservative voters who had no legal background. And to gain control of the Supreme Court, abortion foes joined and ultimately helped to lead a growing fight against campaign finance laws, persuading many social conservatives and GOP leaders to oppose them as well.

These shifts to a focus on judicial nominations and money in politics helped the GOP score electoral victories it might not otherwise have managed. But in the long term, the changes in campaign finance rules that the anti-abortion movement helped to achieve came at a terrible price for the Republican establishment—and had important consequences for the functioning of American democracy.

Of course, other factors helped to gut the establishment as well. To begin with, the GOP had long courted the kind of voters whose loyalty Trump later captured. For decades, Republicans had fueled whites' anxieties about immigration and demographic change. Christian nationalism—and some evangelical Protestants' investment in a masculine populism—did not begin with Trump. In the past, however, Republican politicians had effectively managed these forces. GOP voters had fallen in love with populists before, but the establishment had found a way to sideline them.[4]

Gradually, however, the Republican establishment grew less able to marginalize insurgents. Americans increasingly disliked those in the opposing political party, and this negative partisanship triggered a surge in partisan loyalty. Whomever their own party nominated, polarized voters did not cross party lines because they viewed the opposing party's candidate as unacceptable. Some of these changes affected both parties; negative partisanship became common among Democrats, and politicians on the left became more ideologically homogenous (and more progressive) than they once were. Democrats have relied on independent expenditures, dark money, and super PACs (political action committees) to fund their campaigns, and at times have outraised and outspent the opposition. And Democrats on occasion played a part in pushing more money into politics, passing laws like the 2014 Continuing Appropriations Act, which significantly raised the contribution limits that applied to political party committees. But partisan polarization has been asymmetric. The GOP veered sharply to the right on issues from climate change to immigration, and the party has proven more willing to play constitutional hardball than the opposition, holding up Supreme Court nominations and routinely forcing government shutdowns.[5]

The destruction of the GOP establishment had as much to do with the rise of conservative media as with negative partisanship. Before the rise of outlets like Newsmax and the Fox News Channel, establishment Republicans enjoyed superior access to the press. But conservative media gave insurgents a platform and encouraged voters to reject the establishment for its willingness to compromise.[6]

If the rise of conservative media helps to explain the transformation of the GOP, changes to the rules of campaign spending also gutted the Republican establishment. Because the Republican Party tended to benefit disproportionately from a surge in outside spending—and attracted most of the top-dollar donors behind it—changes to campaign finance rules often had a greater influence on the balance of power within the GOP. In the past, when charismatic populists like Pat Buchanan ran for the GOP presidential nomination, the Republican establishment used its campaign spending advantage to crush them. But after the rules of campaign finance were changed by *Citizens United v. Federal Election Commission* (2010) and *SpeechNow.org v. Federal Election Commission* (2010), nonparty outside spending—money independent of candidates, campaigns, and parties—soared. Republican insiders ran some of the nominally "outside" spending groups, but the party itself did not control them, and many had agendas quite different from those of the conventional GOP leadership. Issue-based and ideological groups had always been able to push their own candidates, but they could never hope to dominate the party. In the old world of campaign finance rules, when populists ran for office, the Republican establishment spent them out of the race. In the world of *Citizens United,* populists had more than enough to win.[7]

How did the abortion debate come to revolutionize the broader struggle over money in politics? The story has many characters, but James Bopp Jr. stands out. A proud Hoosier, Bopp was a passionate conservative before he ever worked a day on abortion politics. He was a state prosecutor in Indiana when Congress passed crucial amendments to the Federal Election Campaign Act in 1974, a major overhaul of campaign finance inspired by President Nixon's Watergate scandal. By the late 1970s, Bopp had become the general counsel for the National Right to Life Committee (NRLC), the largest national anti-abortion group. At first, he and other anti-abortion lawyers viewed campaign finance laws as no more than a nuisance, but by the mid-1980s, they saw these laws as a lasting headache and began arguing that campaign finance limits were unconstitutional.

This shift came because the anti-abortion movement had embraced a new mission: control of the Supreme Court. In the 1970s and early 1980s, conservative attorneys in groups like the Federalist Society mobilized to influence the courts, forming professional networks that would find promising judicial nominees, influence legal norms, and legitimize conservative legal arguments. At first, pro-lifers mostly stayed out of this work. Instead, for a decade after *Roe v. Wade*, the 1973 decision recognizing a right to abortion, abortion foes promoted a constitutional amendment banning the procedure and worked to elect candidates who pledged their support for such an amendment. One of Bopp's colleagues at NRLC, Dr. John Willke, a pro-life celebrity known for his anti-abortion slideshows, led efforts to make pro-life voters into a significant swing vote. When the GOP became the only party endorsing the "human life amendment," most leading pro-life groups cast their lot with the Republicans.

By the mid-1980s, however, abortion foes recognized that even if Republicans controlled Congress, the human life amendment would never pass. Desperate for a new strategy, they focused on changing the composition of the Supreme Court in the hope that it would overrule *Roe*. Allying with the GOP became more important than ever: Republican presidents could select nominees skeptical of *Roe*, and Republican senators could confirm them. Rather than try to influence legal elites, pro-life leaders set about convincing grassroots activists, even those with no knowledge of the law, that control of the Court was essential.

In 1992, however, a Supreme Court transformed by Republican presidents defied expectations by preserving abortion rights. The Court's decision in *Planned Parenthood of Southeastern Pennsylvania v. Casey* convinced many in the pro-life establishment that their movement lacked real influence over the GOP. Despite the presence of Antonin Scalia and Clarence Thomas on the Court, right-to-lifers felt that Republican presidents still too often gravitated to consensus nominees who could sail through Congress—the kind of judges who shied away from overturning a major precedent like *Roe*. Bopp argued that the movement needed the freedom to spend more on political speech if abortion foes expected more influence—or more say in Supreme Court nominations. He asserted that deregulating campaign finance would help pro-life candidates win—and that if right-to-lifers helped Republicans raise and spend more money, the anti-abortion movement would prove its worth to the GOP.

From the mid-1990s onward, groups like NRLC brought abortion foes into a broader coalition committed to deregulating money in politics. Champions of civil liberties, GOP powerbrokers, advocacy group staffers, and small-government libertarians worked together to deregulate campaign finance. It was far from inevitable that the Republican Party would unite against campaign finance reform. To be sure, business interests that backed the GOP had historically denounced campaign limits, and the GOP often enjoyed a fundraising edge that made it favor more campaign spending rather than less. Nevertheless, in the 1990s, Republicans felt tremendous pressure to embrace campaign finance reforms that many saw as an effort to clean up elections. They also supported campaign limits that hurt union-backed urban Democratic machines. Anti-abortion lawyers gave a crucial boost to the efforts of other Republican insiders, hoping to convince social conservatives and party leaders that opposing campaign finance limits was a matter of principle.

A decades-long attack on campaign finance rules in the courts also helped to cement a conservative political consensus about the issue. In the 1990s, Bopp and his colleagues reframed campaign finance rules as the kind of government overreach that genuine conservatives had to oppose. After the 2002 passage of the Bipartisan Campaign Reform Act, they had begun to focus on donor secrecy and corporate campaign spending, honing a message that would unite business and social conservatives.

By the mid-2000s, however, other conservative attorneys and movements sometimes took the lead in major campaign finance cases and pursued a different tactical plan than the one favored by right-to-life litigators. And some of the changes to campaign finance rules did not reflect the strategy of any litigator or movement, beginning instead with the reasoning of a new conservative Supreme Court majority. But even when other conservative movements dictated strategy, right-to-lifers understood more than enough about what changed campaign finance rules could mean for the Republican Party: the new laws gave conservative movements a chance to take power away from the GOP establishment.

As anti-abortion groups made campaign finance a priority, NRLC leaders also retooled their strategy to dismantle abortion rights. Larger anti-abortion groups would shift to promoting abortion restrictions that enjoyed the most popular support, and these restrictions, in turn, would increase public approval of both the GOP and the anti-abortion cause. Helping the GOP outraise and outspend the opposition would give abortion foes more allies in the White House and Congress. More GOP leaders in office created more opportunities to transform the Court and overturn *Roe*. This plan of attack helped produce a series of Supreme Court decisions, including *Gonzales v. Carhart* (2007) and *Citizens United v. Federal Election Commission* (2010).

But leading anti-abortion groups did not always successfully harness their movement's energy. Clinic blockaders, Catholic absolutists, and other grassroots activists contended that dependence on the GOP had made the pro-life movement unable to demand social change. These activists also questioned the wisdom of relying on a Court that had hesitated to dismantle abortion rights. Many within the right-to-life movement also questioned the value of investing so much in the rules of campaign finance. At first, when Bopp and his allies focused on narrow challenges to rules that hobbled the anti-abortion movement, such as limits on voter information guides or nonprofit corporations, few right-to-lifers objected. But by the 1990s, when NRLC made opposition to all campaign finance laws a priority, many anti-abortion leaders rebelled. Some, like rightwing icon Phyllis Schlafly, argued that focusing on campaign finance needlessly divided the movement and hurt political allies whom it needed to pass abortion restrictions. Others, like anti-abortion activist Judie Brown, saw the emphasis put on campaign finance as a sign that their colleagues in NRLC cared more about the success of Republican candidates than about advancing the rights of the unborn. Still others questioned whether Bopp's strategy would help the pro-life movement gain influence in the GOP as much as it would expand the power of large corporations and major donors.

The GOP establishment initially found nothing to dislike in the dominant pro-life strategy. The promise of controlling the Court could unite a fractious coalition and turn out voters who might otherwise not care about a particular race. The fight to deregulate campaign finance also suited the GOP hierarchy. Activists like Bopp helped the Republican Party perfect fundraising techniques from super PACs to "dark money" organizations.

But changes to campaign finance rules ultimately helped to shatter the traditional GOP hierarchy. Of course, other forms of spending can also boost extreme candidates; at times, small donors, who tend to sometimes be on their party's radical flanks, have banded together to influence the GOP or the Democratic Party. In 2020, for example, small donors offered a lifeline to politicians, like Georgia representative Marjorie Taylor Greene, who opposed certification of the 2020 election results. But small donors at times became apathetic, and outside spending organizations, which provided an attractive vehicle for professional activists and major donors, often had more staying power. It is true that the party establishment, too, benefited from the new super PACs and nonprofits. But so did issue-based organizations, many of which looked to remake the GOP. With a surge in outside spending, the GOP establishment had less control over the flow of campaign dollars. Already weakened by conservative media and negative partisanship, the establishment no longer had the tools to put down a populist insurgency.[8]

By 2021, the price of a populist GOP had become clear. Donald Trump attracted new voters to the GOP, but he drove at least as many away. Having lost control of both the Senate and the White House, conservative movements, including the pro-life movement, could no longer be sure that the decline of the GOP establishment was much of a victory. The traditional GOP hierarchy was in shambles, but movement conservatives had not taken up the reins. Instead, Trump had remade the party in his own image.

Activists like James Bopp believed that campaign finance limits would handicap democracy in the United States. But the relationship between money and democracy has always been complex. While increased spending on political speech often improved voter participation and turnout, the changes wrought by *Citizens United* also harmed democracy. By empowering those who viewed compromise as a dirty word, the new rules of campaign finance fueled partisan gridlock that made it hard for anyone to govern. The demise of the establishment removed a crucial obstacle to Trump's takeover of the party. When he tried to overturn the election, a weakened establishment did little to stand in his way.

The GOP establishment had hoped to emerge from the abortion conflict unscathed. Abortion itself was merely one issue—and to the establishment, far from the most important—in a broad right-wing agenda. Abortion foes had helped the party by convincing rank-and-file Republican voters that control of the Supreme Court should be on their minds on Election Day. But to many Republican leaders, the justices they nominated and confirmed were often more valuable for other reasons, such as limiting environmental and workplace regulation, than for their opposition to abortion. The party leadership ignored the anti-abortion movement when it was convenient to do so. It was no surprise that pro-life leaders would try to gain more leverage. Their campaign to unleash political spending, however, had consequences they most likely did not anticipate. In their efforts to reinvent the Republican Party, abortion foes changed how American democracy works.

ACKNOWLEDGMENTS

I COULD NOT HAVE COMPLETED THIS BOOK without the support of many people. Thanks to the library staffs at Harvard University, Catholic University, Columbia University, Duke University, the Concordia Seminary of the Lutheran Church Missouri Synod, the George H. W. Bush Presidential Library and Museum, the William J. Clinton Presidential Library and Museum, the Gerald Ford Presidential Library and Museum, the University of California, Berkeley, the Sisters for Life Convent, Smith College, the Southern Baptist Historical Society, the Phyllis Schlafly Center Archives, and the Wilcox Collection at the University of Kansas.

Many wonderful people have shared comments on the ideas advanced in the book. David Courtwright, Don Critchlow, Darren Dochuk, David Garrow, Linda Gordon, Amanda Hollis-Brusky, Laura Kalman, Ken Kersch, Kevin Kruse, Kristin Luker, Ken Mack, and Steve Teles offered invaluable help with the framing of the project. Others closely read parts of the manuscript, often more than once, including Aziza Ahmed, Dale Carpenter, David Cohen, Deborah Dinner, Michele Goodwin, Joanna Grossman, Sophia Lee, Andrew Lewis, Michael Morley, Rachel Rebouché, Dan Sharfstein, Ann Southworth, Nat Stern, Karen Tani, Joshua Tate, and Daniel K. Williams.

I thank my editor at Yale University Press, Bill Frucht, for taking such care with the book, and my agent, Chris Calhoun, for his advocacy of my work. Others at Yale University Press, including Karen Olson, have been unfailingly helpful. Katrina Miller and the library staff at Florida State have done more than I could have asked to keep the project on track. I also thank my tremendous research assistants, Matt Michaloski, Sahara Williams, Bradyn Shock, Savannah Harden, and Rachelle Hollinshead, for helping me sort through a ridiculous amount of archival material. I am grateful to James Bopp Jr. for access to his archive.

Finally, I thank my husband, Dan, my daughter, Layla, and my mom and dad, all of whom made this book possible. My grandmother Sylvia died of COVID-19 while I was finishing the book. She was the person who first taught me the wonder of books. I only wish that she could have read this one.

ABBREVIATIONS

ACLJ	American Center for Law and Justice
ACLU	American Civil Liberties Union
ACU	American Conservative Union
ALEC	American Legislative Exchange Council
ALI	American Law Institute
ALL	American Life League
AUL	Americans United for Life
BCRA	Bipartisan Campaign Reform Act
CBN	Christian Broadcasting Network
CPAC	Conservative Political Action Conference
CPC	crisis pregnancy center
FEC	Federal Election Commission
FECA	Federal Election Campaign Act
GOPAC	GOP Action Committee
GRL	Georgia Right to Life
HLA	Human Life Amendment
JFC	joint fundraising committee
LAPAC	Life Amendment PAC
MCCL	Minnesota Citizens Concerned for Life

MCFL	Massachusetts Citizens for Life
MCFL	*Federal Election Commission v. Massachusetts Citizens for Life*
NARAL	National Abortion Rights Action League (formerly National Association for the Repeal of Abortion Laws)
NCPAC	National Conservative Political Action Committee
NIFLA	National Institute of Family and Life Advocates
NOW	National Organization for Women
NRLC	National Right to Life Committee
NRCC	National Republican Congressional Committee
NRSC	National Republican Senatorial Committee
OAN	One America News Network
PAC	political action committee
RMIC	Republican Majority Issues Committee
RNC	Republican National Committee
RNC-Life	Republican National Coalition for Life
SBC	Southern Baptist Convention

1

The Fall of Personhood

JAMES BOPP JR.'S HOMETOWN, Terre Haute, Indiana, was not the kind of place where people talked about abortion. In the 1950s and 1960s, the place seemed to be a slice of Americana, with a historic downtown, a leafy university campus, and loads of manufacturing jobs. James, the oldest of five children and the only boy, was the son, grandson, and nephew of local prominent doctors. His mother, a homemaker and leading member of the Women's Auxiliary of the Vigo County Medical Society, helped plan picnics, modeled local fashions at shows hosted by a statewide sorority, and co-hosted talks about the threat of socialism abroad. Bopp's father, an anesthesiologist, competed in the annual golf tournament at the local country club. James Bopp Sr. believed that abortion violated physicians' Hippocratic Oath, and he had trouble imagining that anyone he knew would perform one.[1]

Yet in 1950, when James Jr. was two years old, Indiana newspapers reported on the arrest of Mrs. Floyd Ruhl, a thirty-seven-year-old housewife who had been performing illegal abortions in her home. Ten years later, they picked up the story of twenty-eight-year-old Virginia Stott, a mother of three on probation for possession of abortion instruments. Stott did not give up abortion after her first brush with the law. In 1960, she again faced criminal charges after a client died in her home. It seemed that women like Ruhl and Stott would continue to land in prison—deservedly so, many felt. But cracks were beginning to show in what seemed to be a national consensus on abortion. By 1967, states across the country were reconsidering their criminal abortion laws.[2]

The United States had long regulated abortion, but until the late nineteenth century, some jurisdictions allowed abortion before quickening, the point at which fetal movement could be detected. That changed partly through the work of Dr. Horatio Storer, a Boston-born, Harvard-educated doctor often viewed as the father of modern gynecology. Beginning in the 1850s, he steered the American Medical Association into a physician's crusade. He insisted that life began at fertilization—and that abortion, even early in pregnancy, was murder. The campaign had far-reaching effects. By the end of the nineteenth century, virtually every state had criminalized abortion except in cases in which a woman's life was at risk.[3]

The criminal law for which Storer fought failed to eliminate abortions. An 1888 exposé run by the *Chicago Times* found dozens of doctors ready to perform abortions or refer patients to someone who would. Doctors might have been willing to run the risk because abortion prosecutions were so rare—usually occurring only when a patient died. Even then, as few as 25 percent of prosecutions resulted in a conviction. Nevertheless, in the early twentieth century, abortion, like pregnancy, was quite dangerous. Maternal mortality rates were high: more than 800 per 100,000 in 1920 compared to only 17.8 per 100,000 in 2017. Because doctors routinely failed to follow proper sterilization protocols, most abortion-related deaths occurred because of post-surgical infections. By the 1930s, however, the rate of abortion-related mortality had begun to dip: dropping roughly 32 percent from 1927 to 1933 and a further 44 percent between 1933 and 1939. More abortion doctors properly sterilized equipment, and antibiotics such as penicillin became more widely available.[4]

During the Great Depression, the abortion rate spiked for almost all women, regardless of race or class. Married women felt they could not afford more children. Cash-strapped couples postponed marriage but not sex. Demand for abortion soared, and as more patients terminated pregnancies, more faced complications and hospitalization, even as abortions themselves were becoming somewhat safer. With hospitalizations on the rise, it was no longer possible to deny that abortions were still happening, whatever the law said.[5]

Prosecutors began cracking down on abortion providers. In the past, the government had primarily targeted incompetent practitioners who killed their patients. But after World War II, law enforcement tried to break up "abortion rackets," going after respected physicians as well as underground practitioners. This newfound interest in abortion cases came at a time when obstetric progress made it harder to justify abortion as necessary to save a woman's life. The spread of penicillin and the growing use of Cesarean sections made fewer pregnancies life-threatening.[6]

Obstetricians responded to the crackdown by forming therapeutic abortion committees that would have to sign off on any procedure performed. By 1950, many non-Catholic hospitals had set up such committees. A group of physicians writing in Michigan that year noted that these committees were meant to "protect the physician" from prosecutors.[7] Legal abortions decreased: one study found that the rate of abortions per live births fell from 5.3 per 1,000 in 1943 to 2.9 in 1953, a decline of 43 percent.[8]

Not all physicians agreed on when an abortion qualified as lifesaving: some committees began authorizing procedures for women claiming to be suicidal. A survey of California physicians found that 80 percent would authorize abortion in such cases. Mental health justifications spread rapidly. Catholic physicians saw this admission as a sign that therapeutic committees interpreted a life-of-the-patient exception too leniently. For other physicians, however, the spread of mental health indications signaled that there was something wrong with the law.[9]

Reform and Its Discontents

One of these doctors, Alan Guttmacher, the head of the obstetrics department at prestigious Mt. Sinai Hospital in New York, helped to lead a movement to reform criminal abortion laws. Few obstetricians had such impeccable credentials. A longtime champion of access to birth control, he had deep ties to the eugenics cause and the fight for global population control; he had served as vice president of the American Eugenics Society and held prominent positions in the Association for Voluntary Sterilization, a group that promoted sterilization as a tool to curb demographic growth. Guttmacher was also one of the first to call for new laws on the termination of pregnancy. His reform movement rallied around a blueprint offered by an elite legal body, the American Law Institute (ALI), a group of judges, lawyers, and professors who proposed improvements to the law.[10]

In 1959, the ALI contended that the medical profession was "in revolt" against abortion laws, and that the law should be changed to codify what leading practitioners were already doing. It proposed that abortion be authorized in cases of rape, incest, fetal abnormality, and certain threats to a woman's health. By the mid-1960s, a reform movement had taken shape, with New York at its epicenter. Jimmye Kimmey, a transplant from Texas, took up abortion politics while working as a photographer. A devout Episcopalian, she saw abortion as a human right. Kimmey's colleague Lawrence Lader, a New York–based author, came from serious money, got a Harvard education, and became a magazine writer. Lader's life seemed more glamorous than political; he frequented the Harvard Club, and his wife, Joan, was an internationally famous opera star. Lader became interested in the abortion issue while researching a book on Margaret Sanger, the founder of Planned Parenthood. In 1966, after it hit the shelves, he announced that he would help women seek access to abortion.[11]

Guttmacher, Kimmey, and Lader worked with the Association for the Study of Abortion (ASA), a reform group founded in 1964. With roughly twenty members, mostly in New York, the organization sponsored research on abortion and worked to educate the public on the issue. By 1967, states were taking up the ALI model. The momentum for abortion law reform was undeniable.[12]

An organized opposition, initially launched from local Catholic dioceses, formed as soon as legislatures began taking the ALI bill seriously. Because it denounced contraception as well as abortion, however, this early movement failed to grow beyond its Catholic base. That fact was not lost on the Catholic theologians leading the Family Life Division of the National Conference of Catholic Bishops. In 1967, the Church laid out plans for a separate secular organization to spearhead the fight. To lead it, Catholic officials turned to a left-leaning young priest, James McHugh, who had worked to bring sex education into Catholic schools. McHugh advised the nation's bishops to drop all mention of birth control. He also convinced his colleagues to give him $50,000 to form a national pro-life group, the National Right to Life Committee, to oversee the fight against the ALI bill.[13]

McHugh held up a handful of state pro-life groups as a model of how the anti-abortion movement could reverse the tide of reform. The men who led

New York State Right to Life were mostly conservative lay Catholics. Ed Golden, a self-described hard hat, had founded the group in 1965 but soon found allies in a pair of law professors, Robert Byrn of Fordham and Charles Rice of Notre Dame. Rice made no apologies for his conservatism. Frustrated that the New York Republican Party continued to field liberals like Nelson Rockefeller, he had helped to launch the state's populist, small-government Conservative Party. During state legislative races, the Conservative Party put up pro-life signs and collaborated with Golden's group to defeat politicians who supported legal abortion. But no matter how conservative Golden and his colleagues were, New York State Right to Life pursued support from both parties. As Golden explained, "To our way of thinking, any legislator who doesn't respect human life . . . is unfit, . . . whether he is a Democrat, a Republican, or an independent."[14]

Minnesota Citizens Concerned for Life (MCCL), another successful anti-abortion group, would have felt even less comfortable aligning with the GOP. While Golden's group prided itself on taking political "scalps," MCCL spotlighted crisis pregnancy centers, facilities intended to discourage patients from having abortions. And while Charles Rice worked with the Conservative Party to elect William F. Buckley's brother James to the U.S. Senate, the pro-life power couple leading MCCL, Fred and Marjorie Mecklenberg, were Protestant and relatively progressive. In the early 1970s, Fred even organized a birth control clinic at the University of Minnesota.[15]

The Limits of Reform

Neither Golden nor the Mecklenbergs were lawyers. But they saw their movement as a constitutional struggle, built around a right to life rooted in the Declaration of Independence. Senator James Buckley, the standard-bearer for New York's Conservative Party, was an outspoken critic of civil rights legislation in the late 1960s yet, like many abortion foes, he and Rice claimed the mantle of the civil rights movement, equating unborn children with Black Americans who had once been enslaved. This argument had the strategic benefit of marking a clear break from the religious rhetoric that once made it hard for the movement to expand. The language of rights resonated with homemakers, doctors, and blue-collar workers who believed there could be no compromise on abortion. If there was a fundamental right to life, as activists like Golden and the Mecklenbergs believed, middle-ground legislation such as the ALI bill was unacceptable.[16]

Neither major party staked out a consistent position on abortion. In 1967, Colorado became the first state to approve an ALI bill after it was introduced by a freshman Democrat, Representative Dick Lamm, endorsed by an overwhelmingly Republican legislature, and signed by a Republican governor. Republican governors in Delaware, Oregon, and New Mexico did the same, as did Richard Nixon's future vice president, Governor Spiro Agnew of Maryland, and Governor Ronald Reagan of California. Democratic politicians likewise held a variety of positions on abortion. The ALI bill struck many as a reasonable compromise, leading politicians to hope that by passing it, they could make the issue go away.[17]

But the ALI bill hardly resolved the abortion conflict. If anything, the reform bills of the late 1960s increasingly frustrated the movement that had fought for them. It was not hard to understand why those who had fought for abortion access were losing patience. In Colorado, doctors performed at most four hundred abortions the first year after reform. California granted fewer than five hundred requests (including only eleven to women from out of state). Hospitals were generally unwilling to perform the procedure. Getting a legal abortion was expensive, averaging between $600 and $700 in California, with some procedures costing as much as $1,800. To establish mental health grounds in California, a patient had to get a recommendation from her own doctor, an independent practitioner, and a psychiatrist before a therapeutic committee could even convene.[18]

The limitations of reform statutes helped inspire a movement to repeal abortion laws outright. Professionals were still prominent in the repeal movement, but the movement's leaders now included feminists and population controllers who had no fear of controversy. The National Organization for Women (NOW), a liberal feminist organization, endorsed the repeal of abortion laws at its November 1967 meeting in Washington, DC. Some in the organization opposed the measure, arguing that it would prompt an exodus of Catholic feminists and damage NOW's "newspaper image" by linking the organization to a controversial issue. But most members believed they needed to change the terms of debate. As one explained her vote: "So far, not a thought has been given to women, who are the most concerned with the question of abortion."[19]

The organizers of NOW framed abortion as a right for women, not just another health procedure. Two of those leaders, Lana Clarke Phelan and Pat Maginnis, had advocated for repeal well before it became fashionable to do so. Phelan had grown up in poverty in Florida, married at fifteen, and had a dangerous illegal abortion in Tampa's Ybor City just a few months after the birth of her first child. By the early 1960s, she had settled into a comfortable middle-class life in Long Beach, California, working as a legal secretary and living with her second husband, a police officer. The daughter of a large and struggling Catholic family, Maginnis, like Phelan, grew up during the Depression. She swore off marriage and children, trained to become a surgical technician, and later joined the Women's Army Corps. After she was caught fraternizing with a Black soldier, she was deployed to Panama as a punishment. Working in the pediatric and obstetric wards of a military hospital there, she was radicalized by the shabby treatment given to women who were admitted after botched abortions. She and Phelan were both committed to teaching women how to terminate their own pregnancies.[20]

Betty Friedan, NOW's leader, had become a feminist celebrity after her 1963 manifesto, *The Feminine Mystique*, became a best seller. Like Maginnis and Phelan, she made no apologies for thinking of abortion as a civil right for women. In 1969, Friedan helped to launch the National Association to Repeal Abortion Laws (NARAL), a single-issue group that would change the repeal movement.[21]

NARAL included not only feminists but also those worried about international population growth. Having taken shape after World War II with the backing of philanthropists like John D. Rockefeller III, the movement to curb world population growth was by the 1960s a major bipartisan force that had helped to launch major domestic and international family planning programs. Some population controllers saw their movement as a Cold War initiative to prevent developing nations from embracing Communism. Others had once promoted eugenic measures, including compulsory sterilization laws, that had since become unacceptable. Still others saw population control as a way of protecting the environment or liberating women.

Not all population controllers espoused the repeal of abortion laws (or the legalization of any abortions). But Rockefeller gave significant financial support to repeal efforts, and the leaders of organizations like Zero Population Growth considered abortion repeal a valuable tool.[22]

The repeal movement made the party politics of abortion even more complex. Population-control programs often had a bipartisan appeal, and so did women's rights proposals. The differences between the parties on women's rights in the 1960s were slender and shrinking. When Congress began working in earnest toward the ratification of an Equal Rights Amendment (ERA) constitutionalizing protections against sex discrimination, both parties backed the effort.[23]

The repeal movement did not automatically alienate either party. In 1969, Gallup found that 46 percent of Republicans (compared with only 35 percent of Democrats) wanted to repeal criminal abortion laws for the first twelve weeks of pregnancy. In California, Ronald Reagan, already beloved by conservatives, signed an abortion reform bill into law. Arizona senator Barry Goldwater, another conservative icon, endorsed legalization. At Stanford University, the president of the university chapter of Young Americans for Freedom, a conservative youth organization founded in 1960, Harvey Hakari Jr., proclaimed the organization's support for new abortion laws.[24]

The Democrats were hardly more welcoming to pro-lifers. In 1970, when New York repealed its criminal abortion law, it was with ample support from liberal Democrats. Conservative Democrats had steered reform bills through state legislatures in the South, and liberal Democrats were the most visible supporters of repeal in much of the North and West.[25]

Reform battles had largely unfolded in state legislatures, with both sides debating the justifications for legal abortion—and sniping at one another about whether legalization would make their state an "abortion mecca." The repeal movement launched a parallel campaign in state and federal courts, arguing that the Constitution recognized a federal right to abortion. Lader, Friedan, and their colleagues believed that abortion was a natural extension of a right to privacy that the Supreme Court had already recognized. At least at the beginning, pro-lifers did not worry too much about the shift of action into the courts. NRLC's leaders hoped the courts would stop repeal in its tracks—and maybe even recognize a right to life.[26]

The Meaning of a Right to Privacy

In 1966, when Larry Lader proclaimed his commitment to the abortion rights cause, it was possible for perhaps the first time to find judicial precedents that would support a right to abortion. A year earlier, in *Griswold v. Connecticut*, the Supreme Court had struck down a Connecticut law preventing any use of contraception. In practical terms, *Griswold* seemed unlikely to change much. Connecticut's law had been the only one like it in the nation, and even there authorities had seldom enforced it. It was also possible to interpret *Griswold* narrowly. William Douglas's majority opinion emphasized the unique importance of marriage in the nation's culture. Lawyers could read *Griswold* as a decision only about the constitutional importance of marriage and nothing more.[27]

Yet the case had more explosive potential. The majority held that a constitutional right to privacy encompassed the use of birth control. If there was a right to use birth control, it might apply to single as well as married persons—and birth control might not be the end of the matter. Abortion, like contraception, involved decisions about whether to have children. If constitutional privacy covered the right to prevent a pregnancy, might it not also protect the right to end one?[28]

By the late 1960s, abortion rights attorneys were insisting that state abortion laws violated the right to privacy. In courts from Connecticut to California, judges began holding that *Griswold*'s privacy right encompassed the decision to end a pregnancy. In the early 1970s, however, anti-abortion lawyers eagerly went to court themselves. Before *Roe*, pro-lifers' attitude toward the courts made a close partnership with movement conservatives hard to imagine. While pro-lifers looked to the courts to protect a constitutional right to life, movement conservatives often viewed the Supreme Court as the enemy.[29]

A Pro-Life Court?

Republican frustration with the Supreme Court reached back more than a decade. Under the stewardship of Eisenhower nominee Earl Warren, the Court had issued controversial decisions on a range of topics, invalidating de jure school segregation, recognizing new rights for criminal defendants, and holding that school prayer undercut the separation of church and state. By the late 1960s, opposing the liberal Supreme Court helped bring together conservatives who disagreed deeply on specific issues.[30]

Anti-Communists had had Warren in their crosshairs since the "Red Monday" of June 1957, when the Court—in decisions announced on the same day—sided with the government in four major cases involving alleged Communist subversion. It overturned the convictions of "lower-tier" Communist leaders, sided with a diplomat accused of disloyalty, held that an investigation into alleged subversive activities violated the Constitution's due process clause, and drew a sharp line between advocacy of Communism and action. The backlash was swift. Within months, conservatives in Congress had introduced hundreds of anti–Supreme Court bills. Robert Welch Jr., the Massachusetts businessman who led the John Birch Society, called for the resignation of Chief Justice Earl Warren. Billboards demanding Warren's impeachment sprang up along roadways across the country. The conservative press expressed outrage at what many viewed as the Court's treason. "The boys in the Kremlin may wonder why they need a 5th column in the United States so long as the Supreme Court is so determined to be helpful," the *Chicago Tribune* observed.[31] Red Monday helped catalyze complaints that the justices acted as "politicians rather than lawyers."[32]

The Warren Court angered traditionalists as much as anti-Communists. In *Engel v. Vitale* (1962), it voted 6-1 that New York had violated the establishment clause by making students begin each school day with a nondenominational prayer (two justices did not take part in the decision). A year later, in *School District of Abington Township v. Schempp* (1963), the Court held that state law could not require the reading of biblical passages or the recitation of a prayer even if students could be excused with a written note from their parents. Some conservatives saw *Schempp* and *Engel* as a nonissue; some libertarians approved of what they saw as the separation of church and state. While Catholics tended to oppose *Schempp* and *Engel*, conservative evangelical leaders, eager to draw distinctions between public schools and Catholic parochial schools, often endorsed both decisions despite their misgivings. But other traditionalists saw *Schempp* and *Engel* as declarations of war. The same went for *Griswold*. Charles Rice wrote a book denouncing the decision. William F. Buckley's

National Review skewered the Supreme Court. Republicans in Congress proposed constitutional amendments to permit school prayer. Many school districts simply continued conducting prayers as if nothing had happened.[33]

Other decisions made the Warren Court an election issue for conservatives. In the late 1960s, some federal courts recognized that many school districts had failed to achieve integration and began ordering the busing of students. Busing infuriated white parents from Jackson, Mississippi, to Boston, Massachusetts. The Court also created new procedural protections for criminal defendants, including rights to counsel and so-called *Miranda* warnings, which gave suspects the right to be silent or request counsel. These decisions came down as crime rates were spiking. On the presidential campaign trail in 1968, Richard Nixon argued that the Court had given the "green light" to the nation's "criminal elements."[34]

Not all pro-lifers saw the Court as a problem. Even right-leaning abortion foes hoped that liberal Supreme Court doctrine would help the unborn. Between 1967 and 1972, a group of anti-abortion lawyers asked state and federal courts to recognize fetal rights under the Fourteenth Amendment of the Constitution. They could point to recent state judicial decisions on fetal personhood. Conventionally, the law had not treated anyone as a rights-holding person until birth, but in the 1940s, in cases involving personal injury or inheritance, courts had begun recognizing the interests of unborn children. "The law is presumed to keep pace with the sciences and medical science certainly has made progress since 1884," the district court for the District of Columbia explained in a 1946 decision. By 1967, virtually every state sometimes treated fetuses as persons. In the 1960s, New Zealand physician William Liley pioneered successful neonatal treatments. A growing group of anti-abortion lawyers framed fetal personhood as a biological fact.[35]

The anti-abortion movement forged its own court-centered strategy, drawing on several lines of Warren Court jurisprudence. Starting with its landmark school desegregation decision, *Brown v. Board of Education* (1954), the Court had shown new solicitude for marginalized minorities, especially Black Americans, and under the equal protection clause of the Fourteenth Amendment, it had begun to closely scrutinize any law that classified people by race. By the late 1960s, the justices had also struck down some laws that discriminated against illegitimate children. Invoking the idea of equal protection under the law, employers and universities were launching race-based affirmative action programs to help racial minorities. The Equal Protection Clause applied to "persons" within the jurisdiction of specific states, and abortion foes insisted that the authors of the clause intended to include fetuses or unborn children within the category of "persons" protected by the amendment. Leaders of the anti-abortion movement believed the Court might see the unborn as another embattled minority.[36]

Other pro-lifers hoped to leverage the Supreme Court's new anxiety about rights for criminal defendants. David Louisell, a conservative from Duluth, Minnesota, who found himself profoundly out of place in the counterculture of 1960s Berkeley, was a law professor at the University of California specializing in the law of evidence and civil procedure. Louisell opposed abortion, and because of his professional interests, found himself attracted to procedural protections for fetal life. If the liberal Supreme Court protected certain rights for criminal defendants, Louisell argued, it might do the same for unborn children. He planned to argue that unborn children counted as rights-holding persons under the Fourteenth Amendment. "Appointment of a guardian [ad litem] to represent the fetus," he wrote with his Berkeley colleague John Noonan, "would seem feasible and would be the minimum starting point for any attempt at due process."[37]

Others, like attorney Dennis Horan, believed the Court might recognize a right to life in the due process clause of the Fourteenth Amendment. But whereas Louisell focused on what lawyers call procedural due process—the procedures required before the government could meddle with life, liberty, or property—Horan experimented with arguments that the Constitution (and international human rights law) implied the existence of a fundamental right to life. Horan was a personal-injury lawyer for whom the pro-life movement was a family affair: his brother-in-law was a founding member of NRLC, and his wife and sister-in-law worked in the movement. Like his family members, Horan believed the Court might back a right to life. After all, the justices had recognized an implied right to privacy in *Griswold*. Horan believed that a right to life was even more basic: without life, other constitutional rights were meaningless. In his view, it all boiled down to hard science. Biology proved fetal personhood, and the constitutional analysis flowed from there.[38]

By the early 1970s, pro-life lawyers were taking these arguments to court. Horan created a blueprint in the Illinois case of *Doe v. Scott.* When the ACLU challenged the constitutionality of the state's abortion prohibition in 1969, Horan intervened and asked that his brother-in-law, Dr. Bart Heffernan, be appointed a guardian for all unborn children in the state. Heffernan told the press that the case would persuade the "Supreme Court to define the rights of the unborn in the area of abortion, just as it has in property law, tort cases, and equity."[39]

Anti-abortion attorneys across the country rushed to copy Horan's tactics.[40] In December 1971, law professor Robert Byrn filed two suits. In the first, a Queens judge granted his petition to be named guardian for the fetus of a woman scheduled to have an abortion in a local hospital. In a separate suit, Byrn requested an injunction blocking all abortions in municipal hospitals in New York City, and asked to be named guardian for all unborn children affected by those procedures. "The purpose of the guardianship," he told the press, "is to allow the unborn children to assert their constitutional rights in court."[41]

Byrn became a hero to other anti-abortion lawyers. The press could not get enough of him. Reporters often hinted that he was eccentric, a forty-year-old bachelor who shared an apartment with his mother, a massive man with an easy smile and an office festooned with pro-life buttons. But Byrn also drew the spotlight because of his perspective on litigation. He hoped, "through the courts, to restore the [abortion] law the way it was before."[42] In January 1972, a Queens judge blocked abortions in the city, reasoning that a fetus was "a living human being." But Byrn soon suffered setbacks: the New York Appellate Division reversed the January ruling, reasoning that Americans disagreed about when life began—and that Byrn could not impose his view on everyone else (or override the conclusions about personhood drawn by the state legislature). The New York Court of Appeals affirmed Byrn's defeat.[43]

Other losses followed. In 1972, a federal district court in Pennsylvania had rejected a lawsuit like the one brought by Byrn, and between 1969 and the spring of 1972, courts in Washington, DC, Wisconsin, Georgia, Illinois,

Florida, and New Jersey all struck down state laws prohibiting most abortions. Several relied on the idea that existing laws were impermissibly vague: no sensible doctor could know ahead of time which abortions were allowed. But attorneys like Byrn did not worry too much, since the U.S. Supreme Court had already rejected similar arguments. In January 1971, in *United States v. Vuitch*, abortion rights attorneys argued that the Washington, DC, law—which permitted abortion only in cases of a threat to a patient's health or life—did not clearly inform doctors when they might be criminally liable. Upholding the law, the Court held that the law's definition of "health" covered both physical and mental wellness, and that the law was clear enough for doctors to understand.[44]

Byrn and his colleagues did not feel any more hopeless after the Court struck down a Massachusetts contraception ban in 1972. That case, *Eisenstadt v. Baird*, involved a state law that limited unmarried citizens' access to birth control; married couples could get contraceptives to prevent pregnancy or sexually transmitted infections, but unmarried people could do so only to prevent disease. The Court held that the law violated the equal protection clause because it cut off access to a fundamental right for only one group of people without good reason. Justice William Brennan explained that if "the right to privacy means anything, it is the right of the individual, married or single, to be free from unwarranted governmental intrusion into matters so fundamentally affecting a person as the decision whether to bear or beget a child." Abortion rights attorneys—correctly, it turned out—saw *Eisenstadt* as a sign of what was to come in abortion cases. It was easy to apply Brennan's statement to abortion, which likewise involved the "decision whether to bear or beget a child."[45] Byrn, Horan, and their allies were not so sure that the Supreme Court would see it that way. Besides, courts in Louisiana, North Carolina, Maryland, and Vermont had turned away constitutional challenges to prohibitions on abortion.[46]

It was not clear who was winning in the political arena either. There were hopeful signs for the anti-abortion movement. Voters in Michigan and North Dakota defeated referenda that would have legalized abortion. Abortion foes managed to win enough votes in the New York State legislature to reverse the state's abortion policy, only to see Republican governor Nelson Rockefeller veto the bill. As the 1972 election season got under way, abortion opponents felt their campaign had made progress. Before that year, President Nixon had been a vocal supporter of family planning and had allowed federal dollars to pay for abortions on U.S. military bases. Now, under political pressure and seeking reelection, Nixon reversed course and condemned abortion. On the campaign trail, he delighted in mocking his eventual opponent, South Dakota senator George McGovern, for embracing the "3 As": acid, abortion, and amnesty. Despite Nixon's taunting, McGovern hardly embraced abortion rights. He enraged feminists by picking a known abortion opponent, Thomas Eagleton, as his running mate in an effort to win over Catholic voters and put the abortion issue behind him.[47]

But if neither party embraced abortion rights, neither did they endorse a right to life. In 1972, Gallup found that more than 60 percent of respondents thought the decision to have an abortion should be "left solely to the woman and her doctor."[48]

Armed with new poll data, proponents of abortion hoped to repeal many more abortion bans. Abortion foes, heartened by wins in Michigan, North Dakota, and even New York, believed the tide had turned in their favor. By 1973, both movements had defined their cause as a constitutional mission. When the Supreme Court stepped in, each side hoped to deliver a knockout blow.

Roe v. Wade

The Supreme Court had had *Roe* and its companion case, *Doe v. Bolton*, on its radar for some time. The justices had heard oral arguments on the case once already, in December 1971. *Roe* challenged the constitutionality of a Texas law banning all abortions unless a woman's life was in jeopardy. *Doe* involved a version of the ALI therapeutic abortion law on the books in Georgia. After that first round of argument, Justice Harry Blackmun, a Nixon nominee, was inclined to write a narrow opinion striking down the Texas law as unconstitutionally vague. But some of his more liberal colleagues pressed for a more sweeping ruling. The Court ordered that the case be reargued in fall 1972.[49]

Anti-abortion lawyers brought the full arsenal of constitutional arguments that their movement had developed over the past decade.[50] In a brief for Americans United for Life, Charles Rice relied on the equal protection clause—and on the Supreme Court's tradition of recognizing implied rights.[51] Dennis Horan, who had desperately wanted the Court to take his own abortion case, submitted a brief that carefully combed through scientific and legal evidence supporting fetal personhood.[52]

Pro-life lawyers felt the makeup of the Court would work in their favor. Richard Nixon, an opponent of abortion, had already reshaped the Court by replacing Earl Warren with Warren Burger, an outspoken critic of his predecessor. By 1971, Nixon had added three more justices: Harry Blackmun, William Rehnquist, and Lewis Powell. If he opposed abortion, perhaps his Supreme Court picks would do the same.[53]

From *Roe* to Watergate

In January 1973, James Bopp found himself miles away from two events that would shape the rest of his career. Early that month, criminal proceedings began against Nixon administration associates accused of breaking into the Democratic National Committee headquarters at the Watergate office building in Washington, DC. The ensuing investigation would bring down the president and see many leading White House figures grappling with grave criminal charges.[54]

Well before the break-in, both parties had expressed concern about the soaring cost of national elections, and the scandal shone a light on the spending practices that had helped Nixon secure reelection. Nixon shelled out twice as much for his 1972 reelection campaign as he had spent in 1968; the total spent by the Democratic nominee, George McGovern, was four times what Hubert Humphrey had spent four years earlier. In 1971, Nixon had signed into law the Federal Election Campaign Act (FECA), which tightened disclosure requirements for candidates, parties, and other political actors, but he was not really that committed to cleaning up campaign spending. By 1974, investigators had traced $780,000 in illegal contributions to his campaign from thirteen corporations. His fall from grace sparked new interest in regulating how money shaped U.S. politics.[55]

In January 1973, not long after Nixon's associates went to trial, the Supreme Court handed down its decision in *Roe* and its companion case.

Bopp, then a twenty-four-year-old law student, turned on the car radio on his way back from class. News reporters announced that the U.S. Supreme Court had struck down most of the nation's restrictions on abortion. For Bopp, time seemed to stand still. It seemed unthinkable that the procedure was now legal across the country. But the moment passed; he drove home and did his reading for the next day's classes.[56]

Bopp imagined that after graduation he would spend his life in Terre Haute. He loved the town, but he had grown up believing that everything good about it could easily change—Hoosiers had long ago christened it the Sin City of the Midwest. In the 1970s, Terre Haute was a Democratic stronghold, as famed for its underworld gambling syndicate as for its homespun values.[57]

Bopp had been fascinated by politics since elementary school. One of his clearest childhood memories was of standing on a boulevard a few houses from his home, watching a parade for Republican presidential candidate Dwight Eisenhower. As a teenager, he greatly admired Arizona senator Barry Goldwater, and he served as vice president of the Vigo County Teenage Republicans. At Indiana University in Bloomington, Bopp had been a leading member of the campus chapter of Young Americans for Freedom, represented fraternities and sororities in the student senate and then became its president, lost a race for student body president, and helped with production at the *Alternative*, a conservative newspaper that ultimately became the *American Spectator*.[58]

Bopp had planned to be a doctor like his father, but he soon realized that he understood almost nothing his organic chemistry professor was saying. Instead, he attended the University of Florida's law school, although by graduation time he could not wait to leave swampy Gainesville behind. In the summer of 1973, shortly after graduation, he interviewed in the nation's capital for a job with the Nixon administration's Environmental Protection Agency, but then drove back to Indiana, with no desire to see Washington ever again. Abortion was not uppermost on his mind. He planned to use his law degree to help the conservative movement.[59]

The details of the *Roe* decision only deepened the shock experienced by Bopp and others like him. The Court struck down both the Texas and Georgia laws, invalidating most states' abortion statutes. Harry Blackmun wrote the 7-2 majority opinion holding that the constitutional right to privacy was broad enough to encompass the decision to terminate a pregnancy. *Roe* framed abortion as a decision about family and reproduction. "The detriment that the State would impose upon the pregnant woman by denying this choice altogether is apparent," Blackmun wrote. He stressed that the right to abortion was not absolute—and did not entirely resemble the civil right that feminists like Betty Friedan had expected. According to the majority, the right belonged to physicians as much as to women. Nevertheless, *Roe* created significant protection for abortion access. In analyzing future abortion regulations, courts would apply a trimester framework. In the first trimester, states would have little latitude to regulate abortions. In the second trimester, they could regulate only to advance an interest in protecting maternal health. Only after viability, the point at which survival outside the womb became possible, did the state's interest in protecting fetal life become compelling.[60]

Abortion foes were even more dismayed by the Court's analysis of personhood. Blackmun acknowledged that if the Fourteenth Amendment defined unborn children as persons, the case for abortion rights would "collapse"—unborn children would have rights to due process and equal protection. Abortion foes had relied on biological evidence that human life began at fertilization, but in addressing the personhood issue, *Roe* did not highlight this evidence. Instead, the Court focused on the text of the Constitution. Other constitutional provisions, Blackmun wrote, applied the word *person* only to those who had been born; therefore, the framers of the Fourteenth Amendment must have adopted a similar definition. *Roe* likewise rejected the argument that the government had a compelling interest in protecting life from the moment of fertilization. Leading religious and medical figures disagreed about when life began. If there was no consensus on the issue, the state could not write its own view into the law.[61]

In the short term, *Roe* did little to change the partisan politics of abortion. Richard Nixon had gradually moved toward a pro-life position, but the Watergate scandal forced him out of office nineteen months after the Court decision. In the run-up to the next presidential election, Nixon's vice president, Gerald Ford, did everything he could to avoid the abortion issue. His rival Ronald Reagan had signed California's abortion reform into law, but political calculations changed his mind. In 1976, Reagan took up the pro-life banner, but the party was hardly united on the issue. Ford's interim vice president, Nelson Rockefeller, was a prominent supporter of abortion rights. The Democratic Party was just as fractured: home both to liberal feminists like Representative Shirley Chisholm of New York, the "unbought and unbossed" advocate who had worked closely with NARAL, and to outspoken pro-lifers like Missouri senator Thomas Eagleton.[62]

Nevertheless, *Roe* did frame the abortion issue in terms that would make it easier for pro-life attorneys to join the conservative legal movement. The decision attracted more than its share of scholarly criticism—some of which was to be expected. Some legal scholars had mocked the *Griswold* decision for finding a right to privacy in the "penumbras" of the Constitution's text. *Roe*, which recognized a related privacy right found nowhere in the text of the Constitution, seemed to invite similar attacks. Right-to-life scholars were also quick to denounce the decision. Robert Byrn's 1973 law review article on *Roe*, "An American Tragedy," hardly surprised anyone. But some who endorsed abortion rights found the decision unconvincing. While supporting the legalization of abortion, Yale law professor John Hart Ely published a biting critique of Blackmun's majority opinion. Ely took the Court to task for creating a new constitutional right without relying on constitutional text, history, or any other conventional source of interpretation. Robert Bork, a former member of the Nixon administration and future conservative star, agreed with Ely's analysis, testifying before Congress in 1981 that *Roe* was "an unconstitutional decision, a serious and wholly unjustifiable judicial usurpation of state legislative authority."[63]

Neither pro-lifers nor conservatives saw an alliance between their movements as inevitable. Some conservatives defined themselves as libertarians and supported the outcome of *Roe*. Others wanted to keep their distance from what they considered a toxic issue. Pro-lifers, for their part, did not consistently see themselves as conservatives. Still, the widespread academic criticism of *Roe* made a difference. If critics as different as Ely and Bork could label *Roe* an activist decision, conservative political operatives could easily follow suit. It mattered less if conservatives agreed on abortion policy (or wanted to talk about abortion at all). Equating *Roe* with judicial activism gave them a way to unify around the issue.

Campaign Spending on Abortion

In the mid-1970s, James Bopp defined himself as a conservative above all else. It was no surprise that a conservative giant, M. Stanton Evans, helped bring him into the abortion fight. When Bopp was in college, Stan, as his friends called him, would host twenty to thirty conservatives for dinner each month on the second floor of an Italian restaurant in downtown Indianapolis. At meetings of the Beer and Pizza Marching Society, Evans would hold court while everyone traded ideas, talked strategy, and ate slices washed down by large amounts of beer. Bopp could not help but be starstruck by the man. Stan Evans had been a founding member of Young Americans for Freedom, the managing editor of the conservative journal *Human Events*, the editor of the *Indianapolis News*, a staff writer for *National Review*, head of the American Conservative Union (ACU), a prominent conservative advocacy organization, and a frequent commenter on *CBS News*.[64]

After Bopp returned from Gainesville with a law degree, Evans helped him land a job in the Indiana attorney general's office, later introduced him to NRLC's fledgling Indiana affiliate, and convinced him to become the organization's lawyer. As a young lawyer in Indianapolis, Bopp attended Evans's weekly luncheons (much smaller than the meetings of the Beer and Pizza Marching Society), where he chatted up the players in Indiana's GOP. Ironically, the lunches gave him his first campaign finance gig, representing Bob Bales, a Republican state representative from Danville. Bales was campaigning for a congressional seat in Indiana's Sixth District, a chunk of land sandwiched between Indianapolis and Cincinnati. Bopp argued that the county GOP had violated federal election law by leaving his client off its slate of candidates. He lost.[65]

Bopp's friend Stan Evans hated campaign finance rules.[66] By 1976, he had had enough of President Gerald Ford, whom he considered soft on Communism. In that year's GOP primary, Evans's ACU spent tens of thousands of dollars on radio ads promoting Ford's opponent, Ronald Reagan. In some of the spots, Evans mocked the "Ford team," a group of people whom Evans described as sympathetic to "every leftist cause imaginable," from legalizing marijuana to decriminalizing homosexuality. But he felt that campaign finance laws tied him down.

ACU wanted to give Reagan money directly, rather than just running ads and disclaiming any formal connection with the former California governor. Decades before Bopp turned his attention to campaign financing, ACU and *Human Events* joined *Buckley v. Valeo* (1976), a landmark lawsuit against Congress's campaign finance reform, the Federal Election Campaign Act. Evans, along with New York senator James Buckley, scored a partial victory, but fights about campaign finance and the Constitution raged on. At the time, Bopp did not see *Buckley* as particularly momentous. He had his hands full with the abortion issue.[67]

2

Controlling the Court

LESS THAN A MONTH AFTER *Roe v. Wade* was decided, the leaders of state anti-abortion organizations, religious conservatives, and other major pro-life groups gathered in Washington, DC, to discuss strategy. The mood at the meeting matched the gloom outside. John Willke had come to Washington from Cincinnati, Ohio, leaving behind six children and a busy medical practice. Before joining the anti-abortion movement, Willke had traveled widely as a Catholic sex educator, and when he and his wife, Barbara, turned their attention to abortion, they had crisscrossed the nation presenting a slideshow of graphic pictures of aborted fetuses. Willke had lost count of the number of converts these slideshows had made. At the February 1973 strategy meeting, he agreed with the quickly emerging consensus on what the anti-abortion movement should do next: work to pass a constitutional amendment. Congress had already circulated several proposals. One prohibited the government from denying any person, from the moment of conception, either due process or equal protection of the law. A second defined the word *person* to include "all human beings, including their unborn offspring."[1] Most of those attending the meeting believed that Americans would demand such an amendment if they understood what abortion truly involved. Many had joined the cause after watching slideshows said to depict real abortions.[2]

What consumed many in the anti-abortion movement was not the strategy for passing an amendment but choosing the right one. The movement had no shortage of lawyers, and each seemed to believe he or she knew how to write the perfect constitutional amendment while the rest of the movement's lawyers hadn't the faintest idea how to begin. Some of these attorneys were newcomers to the movement. After the Court decided *Roe,* Nellie Gray, a career woman and a Democrat, had abruptly left her job at the U.S. Department of Labor to found March for Life, an annual protest of legal abortion in America. Others, like Robert Byrn and Dennis Horan, were movement veterans. Everyone agreed on the importance of banning abortions, whether performed by private citizens or government employees. They also favored only an amendment that would make abortion unconstitutional nationwide while opposing alternative proposals that let each state set its own policy. Other details, however, proved more divisive. Gray, for example, opposed an exception for abortions that were necessary to save a woman's life. Horan responded that without such an exception, no amendment would pass.[3]

To abortion rights supporters, pro-lifers' talk of a constitutional amendment seemed delusional. The leaders of groups like the Planned Parenthood Federation of America and the renamed National Abortion Rights Action League believed such an amendment was doomed. A majority in the Senate seemed to support legal abortion. Several states had reformed their abortion laws before *Roe* and might vote against a constitutional abortion ban. Pro-lifers, who thought that a constitutional amendment was only a matter of time, seemed to be living in another world.[4]

Pro-lifers did not invest particularly heavily in the 1974 midterm elections. Many believed instead that the key to success was public education. The Willkes had won over thousands of grassroots activists with their slideshows, and if the national media carried something similar, pro-lifers thought, voters (and therefore politicians) would take their side. Anti-abortion groups launched their own publications. NRLC began its newsletter, *National Right to Life News,* less than a year after *Roe* came down. J. P. McFadden, the former business manager for *National Review,* single-handedly created an entire pro-life media ecosystem.[5]

The conservative media also showed sympathy for the pro-life cause. Before *Roe,* William F. Buckley Jr. had suggested that in light of a global population explosion, legal abortion might be acceptable for non-Catholics. After 1973 he changed his tune: *National Review* began blasting *Roe.* Stan Evans's *Human Events,* which had previously danced around the issue, published a piece by firebrand North Carolina senator Jesse Helms arguing that abortion was "murder—and no other face can be put upon it."[6]

For pro-lifers, however, mainstream media coverage was far more crucial than the sympathy of commentators like Buckley or Evans. Some movement members found little to love in *National Review* or *Human Events.* Besides, conservative media leaders were in financial freefall—and increasingly looking to influence legacy media outlets rather than compete with them. As production costs rose in the 1970s, paid circulation for *Human Events* dropped more than 40 percent. In the early 1970s, *National Review* likewise reported hefty financial losses. Rather than start new publications, ambitious conservative commentators tried instead to find a niche in mainstream media outlets.[7]

That process got under way in the late 1960s after Richard Nixon and his vice president, Spiro Agnew, made media bias a major political topic. Agnew, a sometime moderate who had pushed for abortion reform, recast himself as a pull-no-punches conservative. He seemed to relish the role, especially when it came to the press. In one speech—written by future *New York Times* columnist William Safire—he argued that the press was as unaccountable as it was biased, controlled by a "closed fraternity of privileged men, elected by no one." Agnew's speech struck a chord, even with many who opposed his politics. The mainstream media had long held itself out as an arbiter of truth, dedicated to factual accuracy. Agnew presented an alternative vision of journalistic integrity: one centered on balance. Even progressive editorialists seemed attracted to Agnew's view. Newsrooms began hiring conservative commentators.[8]

While some pro-lifers saw ongoing conservative hostility to their cause, William F. Buckley's brother James felt the movement's true enemies dominated the liberal media. James Buckley still had the crew cut from his navy days, a famous name, and a telegenic smile that was perfect for politics. In 1970 he had run for the U.S. Senate on a third-party ticket, representing New York's Conservative Party, and managed a narrow win in a three-way Senate race by appealing to disaffected middle-class voters in the outer boroughs and upstate with the slogan: "Isn't It Time *We* Had a Senator?" In a race against two liberal opponents, he received 39 percent of the vote—enough to win the seat.[9]

Buckley quickly became one of the pro-life movement's champions. Shortly after *Roe,* he and six other senators introduced a constitutional amendment banning abortion. He also argued that the media made the movement's job harder. In 1975, his special assistant, Bill Gribbin, filed a complaint with the nonpartisan National News Council arguing that the *New York Times* consistently mentioned the religion of pro-lifers while saying nothing about the religious convictions of abortion rights supporters. The council did not ultimately censure the *Times,* and anyway, pro-lifers felt they had bigger problems with the media. Willke and his colleagues believed Americans would care about abortion if they saw and understood what the procedure involved but, citing decency standards set by the Federal Communications Commission (FCC), broadcasters often refused to show graphic images of abortion. The FCC also applied its Fairness Doctrine, which required broadcasters to present controversial issues in what regulators viewed as a balanced way. When pro-lifers purchased ad time in local markets, broadcasters refused to run the ads on the grounds that neither local television stations nor pro-choice groups could afford to air "opposing-view" ads for counterbalance.[10]

Some pro-lifers saw running for office as a way to force the media to educate the public about abortion. In New York in 1974, Barbara Keating, a thirty-five-year-old war widow living in Larchmont, launched a long-shot bid for the Senate against Republican incumbent Jacob Javits. Keating had found solace working with conservative mothers and homemakers horrified by the idea of abortion. No one in Keating's group entertained any illusions about her chances in the race, given that Javits was something of a political institution and his primary competitor, Ramsey Clark, the former attorney general under Lyndon B. Johnson, had become famous for his promotion of civil rights and his opposition to the Vietnam War. If Javits came across as grumpy and abrupt, Clark had a crusader's lonely air. Keating saw her campaign as a public education tool. She conducted her campaign with folksy humor. At one debate, she poked fun at both Javits and Clark as remote establishment figures by quoting the song *Ol' Man River:* "He must know something; he don't say nothing; he just keeps rolling along." All of Keating's jokes served a purpose. Pro-lifers believed that images of fetal life—and of real abortions—would sway undecided voters, but the media's refusal to run pro-life advertisements, especially graphic ones, created an unfair handicap that an election campaign could remedy. "While educational materials can be barred by the media," Keating observed, "the political commercials of a candidate cannot."[11]

Keating, who never planned to win any election (and didn't), was one of several activists working to get anti-abortion voters to the polls. In 1974, John Willke put a target on Democrat John Glenn, the former astronaut, who was leading his nearest competitors for an Ohio Senate seat by up to 80 points in the polls. But Glenn favored abortion rights, and so Willke launched a get-out-the-vote campaign, urging right-to-lifers to pick Glenn's opponent, Republican Ralph Perk, the mayor of Cleveland. Going after such a popular frontrunner seemed unwise, but the point was not to defeat him. Instead, the Willkes wanted to see how many anti-abortion voters they could find—and if those voters could swing an election. John and Barbara put out a voter guide detailing candidates' positions on abortion. Recruits distributed the guide door to door.[12]

Glenn, of course, won his race. It was not even close. But John Willke felt triumphant. He told NRLC that abortion foes had narrowed Glenn's margin of victory and urged his colleagues to pay more attention next election season. "Since the entire direction of our national ethic on protection of human life is in the hands of legislators," he contended, "we must simply select ones who are pro-life."[13]

Like his colleagues, Willke had to navigate a new world of election laws ushered in by the passage of the Federal Election Campaign Act. At first, pro-life groups mostly piloted programs centered on political advertising and voter guides. Other conservatives, like Paul Weyrich, invested in political action committees. A midwesterner and son of a German immigrant, Weyrich had started his career working in radio news, but politics was his true love. While working for Barry Goldwater's 1964 presidential campaign, he came to believe that liberals had engineered a takeover of most institutions, and the only way to fight back was to learn from the opposition. Later, as the press secretary for Senator Gordon Allott, a Republican from Colorado, Weyrich got to know an aide of Joseph Coors Sr., the patriarch of the Coors brewing dynasty. Between 1973 and 1974, Weyrich persuaded Coors to pour money into two of his pet projects: a think tank to be called the Heritage Foundation, and a PAC, the Committee for the Survival of a Free Congress.[14]

Weyrich also had a parallel project. In 1973, with support from the conservative Scaife Foundation, he co-founded the Conservative Caucus of State Legislators, a group that would write model legislation for the people the Committee for the Survival of a Free Congress helped elect. Within a few years, the group had a new name, the American Legislative Exchange Council (ALEC), and a reputation for promoting socially conservative legislation in state legislatures across the country. The Heritage Foundation would come up with conservative ideas, the Committee for the Survival of a Free Congress would find promising conservative candidates, and ALEC would provide those candidates with legislation to sponsor.[15]

The last leg of Weyrich's four-legged stool was money. Fielding the right candidates and writing model legislation would not matter if conservatives did not have the campaign dollars to win elections. In Weyrich's view, conservatives were losing the money race, and badly. Since 1948, liberals had relied on the National Committee for an Effective Congress, a political action committee, to help elect progressive candidates. Weyrich planned to create a conservative alternative. PACs, political committees designed to help elect a candidate or advance an ideological cause, had existed since the 1940s, but Weyrich hoped to use them to vastly outspend his competitors, all without violating the law.[16]

Until the 1974 amendments to the Federal Election Campaign Act, campaign finance law had been murky and largely ineffective. During the administrations of Theodore Roosevelt and William Howard Taft, scandals took down the once-revered life insurance industry, exposing fraudulent business practices and insider trading. Investigation into wrongdoing by the "big three" life insurance companies revealed that corporations had contributed to Theodore Roosevelt's 1904 presidential campaign. In 1907, majorities in both parties passed the Tillman Act, legislation prohibiting banks and federally chartered corporations from making contributions to federal, state, or local elections and barring all corporations from making contributions to presidential or congressional elections. Another scandal inspired lawmakers to act in 1925. Albert Fall, the secretary of the interior, had leased oil-rich government land at Teapot Dome, Wyoming, to big companies without competitive bidding.

Subsequent investigations revealed that one of the lease recipients, oilman Harry F. Sinclair, had contributed $260,000 to the Republican National Committee in 1923, but the massive sum had not been made publicly known because the law at the time required reporting only in election years. The 1925 Federal Corrupt Practices Act, which mostly codified existing campaign finance rules, closed the Teapot Dome loophole by requiring political committees to make annual reports in nonelection years. More reforms followed during the Great Depression. Passed in 1939, the Hatch Act, named after a little-known Democratic senator from New Mexico, was rumored to be the brainchild of Franklin Delano Roosevelt's vice president, John Nance Garner. The act prohibited most federal workers from participating in or contributing to federal elections for Congress or the White House. A year later, the ban was extended to state and local workers who worked on federally financed projects. Anti–New Deal Republicans and southern Democrats favored the Hatch Act—which they believed would hurt New Dealers—and the GOP also backed a law to extend the Tillman Act's ban on direct corporate contributions to include contributions by unions, especially after the labor movement pumped money into Roosevelt's 1936 campaign. Republicans justified the extension as a wartime expedient in 1944, and unions responded by forming the first PACs. The ban on direct spending by unions became permanent through the 1947 Taft-Hartley Act.[17]

Before 1974, however, Republicans and Democrats circumvented campaign finance law by forming multiple (often ambiguously named) committees supporting the same candidate, making it impossible to tell who was giving what to whom. Besides, everyone knew that there was almost never a penalty for failing to abide by disclosure rules: in 1968, 107 congressional candidates and twenty fundraising committees for Republican Richard Nixon had not filed a single disclosure report, and in 1970, the Justice Department announced that it would not pursue charges against any of them. By the 1970s, driven by the cost of television and radio advertising, election spending skyrocketed, with the total cost of federal campaigns rising from $155 million in 1956 to $300 million by 1968.[18]

In 1971, Congress responded with more stringent disclosure requirements. The Watergate scandal prompted a much more significant change.[19] The 1974 amendments to the Federal Election Campaign Act limited contributions to candidates or campaigns; placed a ceiling on the overall amount each contributor, candidate, PAC, or party could spend; created a system for publicly financing elections; and established a new agency, the Federal Election Commission (FEC), to enforce the law.[20]

When he challenged the constitutionality of the new federal law, Senator James Buckley joined former senator Eugene McCarthy. Each had a personal interest in killing campaign finance restrictions. Because it set up a system of public financing that tended to give much larger sums to the candidates of major parties (and used past vote totals to determine preelection funding), FECA threatened third-party runs like the one Buckley had successfully engineered in 1970. McCarthy, who had run and lost in the 1968 and 1972 primaries as an antiwar Democrat, had since left the Democratic Party and was now running as an independent. Civil libertarians working with the New York Civil Liberties Union agreed that limits on the money spent on political speech could function the same way as limits on political speech itself, and they opposed FECA. Stan Evans's *Human Events* and American Conservative Union joined the case because he and his fellow conservatives were fed up with the Republican establishment. "When 'our people' get to the point where they can do us some good," he said tartly, "they stop being 'our people.' " Limits on campaign spending, he believed, only served the interests of a Republican establishment he increasingly wanted to destroy. Establishment figures like President Ford had connections, name recognition, and easy access to the press. Evans thought eliminating FECA was critical if conservative insurgents were ever going to have the kind of war chest needed to challenge Ford and others like him.[21]

The government defended FECA before the Supreme Court as a necessary check on corruption. A group of seasoned attorneys led the attack on FECA: Brice Clagett, Joel Gora of the ACLU, Yale law professor Ralph Winter, and his former student John Bolton, a young Baltimore native. Winter had already played a leading role in questioning the wisdom of FECA, publishing several pamphlets (including one with Bolton) for the conservative American Enterprise Institute questioning the constitutionality of campaign finance limits. During the *Buckley* litigation, Clagett, Winter, and Bolton elaborated on the argument that political money was speech. Voters sent a powerful message about what they thought about candidates or causes when they cut a check. As Clagett argued, "To limit expenditures and contributions is to limit in every sense the speech they make possible."[22]

The broader pro-life movement did not participate in Buckley's suit. At its 1975 convention, NRLC remained preoccupied with a constitutional amendment to ban abortion. In addition to James Buckley's proposed amendment, attendees held out hope for one proposed a year earlier by Senator Jesse Helms, a Republican from North Carolina. Before running for office, Helms had been a conservative commentator for Raleigh's WRAL TV, arguing that the civil rights movement was full of Communists.[23] He had been in the Senate for only a year when *Roe* came down, and he fought fiercely for an amendment to ban abortion as soon as the idea hit the Senate floor. Whereas James Buckley could play the smiling military hero, Helms was a hell-raiser who spat at the idea of compromise. But even with allies like Buckley and Helms, those at the 1975 NRLC Convention understood that the Senate was slow to act. NRLC leaders thought the solution was more effective lobbying. Mildred Jefferson, the organization's charismatic new president, convened a group of thirty activists with experience in state legislatures to train rank-and-file activists in the best lobbying techniques. The first Black graduate of Harvard Medical School, Jefferson was a brilliant speaker and a walking billboard for the pro-life movement's claim to represent all Americans. Like many in her movement, she saw both litigation and incremental abortion restrictions as "peripheral and secondary." It was an amendment or nothing.[24]

Campaign Finance and Political Speech

Right-to-lifers also seemed indifferent to a growing constitutional conflict over campaign finance. In *Buckley v. Valeo*, the DC Circuit Court of Appeals had rejected most of the constitutional arguments made against FECA. The result in the Supreme Court was far less clear. In January 1976, in an unsigned opinion, the Court first decided that campaign finance limits could be the same as direct limits on political speech. Of course, the relationship between speech and conduct could be anything but straightforward. If someone burned an effigy of Gerald Ford, everyone knew that it meant something very different from simply building a bonfire on the beach. The government insisted that election spending was just functional—closer to a beach bonfire than to burning an effigy. But the Court rejected this argument. It reasoned that election spending involved a mixture of speech and conduct.[25]

The Court further reasoned that the goal of FECA had everything to do with limiting expression. Congress had tried to equalize "the relative ability of all voters to affect electoral outcomes by placing a ceiling on expenditures for political expression by citizens and groups." Worrying that the wealthy had more say than most Americans because they could afford to cut politicians a check, lawmakers created campaign finance rules to help ensure that politicians reacted to the will of the majority, not the wishes of those with the most money. As the Court saw it, however, lawmakers could not equalize speech in the political marketplace by pushing out some speakers or limiting their spending.[26]

Primarily, however, the Court insisted that limits on campaign spending could be the functional equivalent of direct limits on political speech. "A restriction on the amount of money a person or group can spend on political communication during a campaign," the Court reasoned, "necessarily reduces the quantity of expression by restricting the number of issues discussed, the depth of their exploration, and the size of the audience reached." This was especially true when the electorate increasingly relied on radio, television, and other mass media for information. Even printing and distributing the "humblest handbill" required money.[27]

The Court then turned to the constitutionality of specific aspects of FECA. The majority upheld a $1,000 limit on contributions to individual candidates or campaigns, reasoning that the cap served a crucial governmental interest in preventing corruption or its appearance. The Court especially focused on what it called quid pro quo corruption—when large donors dumped huge sums into candidates' coffers and expected victorious politicians to reward them. The justices reasoned that by targeting large contributions, Congress had tailored its law to address the greatest risks of corruption. The more money a donor gave, the more she might expect a politician to give her something in return. The Court also upheld limits on contributions made by political committees and caps on how much a donor could contribute per year.[28]

But the majority opinion reached quite a different conclusion about FECA's expenditure limits. The Court considered three provisions: a $1,000 limit on expenditures "relative to a clearly identified candidate," restrictions on expenditures made by a candidate from his or her personal or family funds, and limitations on overall expenditures made by candidates for public office. As FECA defined it, "expenditures" included all spending intended to influence a federal election beyond contributions to specific candidates or campaigns.[29]

When considering the "relative to a clearly identified candidate" provision, the Court worried that the standard was vague enough to sweep in lobbying and other political speech outside the campaign context. To resolve this problem, the Court interpreted the provision to apply only to what the justices called express advocacy—"communications that, in express terms advocate the election or defeat of a clearly identified candidate for federal office." In a footnote, the Court listed several examples of express advocacy, such as ads using words or phrases like "vote for," "elect," "support," "cast your ballot for," "Smith for Congress," "vote against," "defeat," and "reject."[30]

But even interpreted to apply only to express advocacy, the Court held that the "clearly identified candidate" provision was unconstitutional. The justices reasoned that it substantially burdened donors' freedom of expression. The government argued that the provision was needed to prevent wealthy donors from circumventing contribution limits. The Court was not persuaded. The justices reasoned that expenditures coordinated with campaigns—as opposed to independent expenditures—were "treated as contributions rather than expenditures under the Act." Independent expenditures, by contrast, often provided "little assistance to the candidate's campaign." "The absence of prearrangement and coordination of an expenditure with the candidate or his agent," the Court reasoned, "not only undermines the value of the expenditure to the candidate, but also alleviates the danger that expenditures will be given as a *quid pro quo* for improper commitments from the candidate."[31]

The Court struck down FECA's other expenditure limits for similar reasons. It made no sense, the justices stated, to stop candidates from using personal funds or family money on independent expenditures when "the use of personal funds reduces the candidate's dependence on outside contributions, and thereby counteracts the coercive pressures and attendant risks of abuse to which the Act's contribution limitations are directed." The Court rejected the overall expenditure limit in equally unequivocal terms, reasoning that "the First Amendment denies government the power to determine that spending to promote one's political views is wasteful, excessive, or unwise."[32]

The opinion then addressed FECA's disclosure requirements. Political committees had to keep detailed records of contributions and expenditures, subject to periodic audit or field investigation by the FEC; political committees, candidates, and campaigns all had to file quarterly reports. FECA further required any individual (other than a candidate) or any group (other than a political committee) to meet certain reporting requirements if they made contributions or expenditures of at least $100 to anyone but political candidates or their campaigns. Those challenging the law argued that it was overbroad, violating the rights of third parties, independent candidates, and donors who made token contributions. The challengers also asserted that FECA could not constitutionally require disclosure when it came to protected independent expenditures. To address this concern, *Buckley* interpreted the disclosure requirements to apply only to individuals or groups that made expenditures "that expressly advocate the election or defeat of a clearly identified candidate." Interpreted in this way, the law was constitutional—and protected the government's important interests in preventing corruption and informing the electorate.[33]

Finally, the Court upheld FECA's new system of public election financing. The law created different pots of public money for presidential conventions, primaries, and general elections. In general elections, a major-party candidate opting into public financing would receive a lump sum—a little under $22 million in 1976—in return for refusing private contributions. Candidates who accepted public funding (and refused private contributions) could also receive matching funds during primaries if they raised at least $5,000 in each of twenty states. James Buckley argued that the public funding rules violated the equal protection clause of the Fifth Amendment by discriminating against third parties. FECA gave the two major parties more money, denied funds to any candidate receiving less than 5 percent of the vote in the last election, and used prior vote levels to set funding for the next race. The majority saw no reason for concern. Third parties could receive some public money so long as they hit the 5 percent threshold and, unlike major parties, they faced no cap on independent expenditures.[34]

Right-to-Lifers and the Race for the White House

After *Buckley*, the failure of Ronald Reagan's insurgent candidacy for the 1976 Republican presidential nomination and the stalling of an anti-abortion constitutional amendment began to convince pro-life activists that they had invested too little in national elections. In making a bid for the 1976 Democratic presidential nomination, Ellen McCormack, one of Barbara Keating's colleagues in a New York pro-life group, tried to copy Keating's strategy at the national level. Born to Irish Catholic parents in the Bronx, McCormack had married a man she met at a dance, had four children, and supported her husband's progress in the New York Police Department. Like many colleagues, McCormack felt she could not remain silent after seeing an anti-abortion slideshow. New to politics, she had not even held a position at her local parent-teacher association before she decided to seek the Democratic nomination for president. The point was not to win but, like Keating before her, to "bring to as many as 100 million people visual information about the life of the unborn child and the reality of abortion."[35]

NRLC and Americans United for Life (AUL) were still working to convince major-party candidates to endorse a human life amendment. Gerald Ford, who had assumed the presidency after Nixon's resignation, did his best to dodge the abortion issue. Already damaged by the Watergate scandal and his pardon of Nixon, he wanted no additional controversy. Ford's wife, Betty, was an outspoken proponent of legal abortion. But Reagan, armed as always with his rugged good looks and infectious optimism, forced his hand; the former California governor and movie star was happy to talk about abortion.[36]

Even with Reagan breathing down his neck, Ford refused to back the kind of amendment that Buckley or Helms proposed. When a pro-life delegation led by Nellie Gray sought an audience with him, Ford stalled for months before finally agreeing to meet in March 1976. The meeting left Gray and her delegation deeply unsatisfied. Ford would not fully commit to an amendment banning all abortions. Democratic candidates were even less forthcoming. Most primary candidates, including Jimmy Carter, the eventual nominee, declared themselves personally opposed to abortion, and Carter announced plans to fund "alternatives to abortion," including increased spending on birth control. But Carter was more outspoken than Ford in opposing an outright constitutional ban. Neither party's presumptive nominee seemed willing to give right-to-lifers what they wanted.[37]

Within the anti-abortion movement, the mood darkened further when the Senate voted in June 1976 to table all the amendments before it. Jesse Helms used a parliamentary maneuver to force a vote on his own version of the human life amendment. But he was not a miracle worker. Following a heated three-hour debate, the Senate voted 47-40 to table his amendment. NRLC leaders concluded that lobbying would no longer be enough. The group pledged to take down the "deadly dozen" senators who had voted to table the amendment.[38]

Nothing about the 1976 presidential race reassured pro-life leaders. That August, *National Right to Life News* complained that Jimmy Carter would not return the calls of anti-abortion delegates to the Democratic National Convention. Carter, who made a great show of his lack of pretension and loved to wear the denim he sported on his peanut farm, had risen to power in the Georgia Democratic Party by opposing segregation and endorsing some forms of affirmative action. He refused to support an anti-abortion amendment. Many thought he was plotting to sideline anti-abortion Democrats. According to one rumor, someone at the 1976 Democratic National Convention had turned down the loudspeakers whenever a pro-lifer took the microphone.[39]

The GOP was only slightly less hostile. Although he edged out Reagan, Ford recognized that right-leaning activists embraced Reagan's message, including on the abortion issue. He selected Senator Bob Dole, a Kansas Republican who vocally supported the Human Life Amendment (HLA), as his vice president. At the 1976 convention, Ford's backers had hoped to keep abortion out of the GOP platform, but Reagan and Dole both lobbied for an anti-abortion plank. Dole eventually brokered a compromise in which the platform expressed support for the "efforts of those who seek a constitutional amendment to restore protection for the right to life for unborn children." Some NRLC members celebrated, but Ford quickly backed away from any anti-abortion stand. He interpreted the compromise plank to endorse a states' rights amendment—a measure that would allow but not require states to criminalize abortion. Virtually no anti-abortion group favored that proposal. Neither NRLC nor other anti-abortion groups had given up on an alliance with the Democratic Party. *National Right to Life News* described the 1976 election as a blessing in disguise that awakened pro-life Democrats to "the abortion philosophy that was creeping into their party leadership."[40]

A Post-*Buckley* Election

The first post-*Buckley* elections proceeded as the lawmakers who passed FECA might have intended. They had hoped that its contribution limits—set at $1,000 for individuals and $5,000 for committees—would limit the influence of ultra-wealthy donors. Before FECA, newspapers had carried stories about donors like W. T. Duncan, a real estate developer from Bryan, Texas, who gave $257,000 of his own money to Richard Nixon. The "Malibu Mafia," a group of wealthy liberal donors who met at the beachside home of economist Stanley Sheinbaum, had filled George McGovern's coffers in 1972. One member of that group, Max Palevsky, had personally given hundreds of thousands of dollars to McGovern's failed campaign. In 1976, when Palevsky contributed to Jimmy Carter's campaign, the law limited him to $1,000.[41]

When the 1976 race was over, reformers felt so optimistic that they proposed extending the public financing system to congressional races too. Political parties seemed pleased with the control over spending that the new law afforded them. The GOP had bridled at the limits imposed by FECA because it had generally outspent the Democrats for decades. But Republicans liked the fact that FECA gave the party more financial pull. With direct contributions reduced, most congressional candidates had to rely more on parties for everything from voter registration to polling. "The law tends to weaken the influence of individuals," explained Mark Siegel, the executive director of the Democratic National Committee, "and strengthen the influence of institutions, such as the party."[42]

Conservatives, many of whom had little love for the party establishment, were not as happy. Stan Evans's American Conservative Union had seen unlimited campaign spending as the linchpin of its mutiny against incumbent Gerald Ford. Wealthy conservative donors like Charles Koch, the chief executive of the eponymous Koch Industries who had helped to finance the Libertarian Party's litigation in *Buckley v. Valeo*, wanted to use campaign spending to promote more conservative candidates. After the Supreme Court announced its decision in *Buckley*, ACU spent $110,000 on ads for Reagan in seven states, helping him clinch several surprise victories in Republican primaries. The radio commercials featured Evans himself warning that a vote for Ford was a vote for "liberal politics as usual." But Reagan struggled to raise enough to depose the incumbent. His campaign got into the black only after Ford had already won the nomination.[43]

Reagan loyalists believed that he would have prevailed had the rules been different. David Keene, the southern regional director for Reagan's campaign, objected to the law's new contribution limits. Still in his early thirties, Keene had already made a big name for himself in conservative circles. As a college student in the 1960s, he had been the national leader of Young Americans for Freedom. He dipped a toe into electoral politics, running unsuccessfully in 1969 for the state senate in Wisconsin and even gaining Richard Nixon's endorsement before deciding he would fare better behind the scenes. He worked as a staffer for both Spiro Agnew and James Buckley before joining Reagan's 1976 campaign.[44]

Keene believed conservatives had not done enough to tap the resources already available to them, particularly when it came to PACs. Most PACs had steered clear of any apparent violation of the new maze of campaign rules. Political commentators had expected corporations to solicit their employees for $5,000 contributions (the limit for committees in 1976), which could be bundled and sent to candidates. A 1976 survey found that only 28 percent of the 176 corporate PACs formed since November 1975 had managed to raise more than $1,000 in bundled contributions. Ford's running mate, Bob Dole, had tried to shame corporations into stepping up, but to no avail. The few PACs that did get involved in 1976 primarily contributed to incumbents, especially Democrats in the House of Representatives.[45]

Issue-based conservative PACs, however, soon built a fearsome reputation. The National Conservative PAC, a group founded in 1975 by activists John Terry Dolan, Roger Stone, and Charles Black, loomed largest. Stone's first political memory involved lying to his elementary school class in 1960 about Richard Nixon. A supporter of John F. Kennedy, he told his classmates that Nixon wanted to make everyone go to school on Saturday. Eight years later, he dropped out of college to volunteer for Nixon's presidential campaign. Stone specialized in opposition research—gathering intelligence about political opponents—and while working for Nixon, he hired someone to spy on Hubert Humphrey's campaign. Dolan also worked for the Nixon campaign, but both men ended up with grievances against the Republican establishment. Stone lost his job working for Senator Bob Dole after the press portrayed him as one of Nixon's dirty tricksters. Dolan felt that he had been robbed of the top position at the College Republican National Committee, an auxiliary arm of the Republican National Committee, by RNC chairman George H. W. Bush.[46]

The beauty of the National Conservative PAC (NCPAC) was that it let Dolan and Stone target their enemies without breaking the law. NCPAC took advantage of *Buckley*'s holding on independent expenditures, pooling money from donors to fund attack ads. David Keene, who had taken work consulting for conservative PACs after Reagan's 1976 campaign folded, thought issue-based groups like NCPAC could spend their way into a more influential role in the Republican Party. Presidential candidates felt they had no practical choice but to accept public financing and abide by related fundraising limits. Even congressional candidates fell under FECA's contribution caps. Keene suggested that PACs' independent expenditures could help to defeat moderate Republicans, a goal that greatly appealed to Dolan and his colleagues. With the 1978 midterms looming, he announced plans to take down six such politicians. "In a Republican primary," Dolan quipped, "you can always beat a liberal."[47]

Returning to the Courts

James Bopp certainly had no love for the candidates NCPAC attacked, but his focus was the pro-life movement. He was back in Terre Haute, and the town was thriving. It hosted big factories that made everything from steel and aluminum to medicine and records. The Honey Creek Shopping Mall, with thirty-five stores from Sears to Orange Julius, was barely a decade old. Larry Bird, the "hick from French Lick," had just left Terre Haute's Indiana State University for the National Basketball Association. The antiabortion movement was a different story. There may have been no progress yet, but Bopp still pinned his hopes on a constitutional amendment.[48]

He also wondered if his movement had given up on the courts too quickly. He helped to launch the Legal Action Project and invited other antiabortion lawyers to take up cases that would help the cause while the constitutional amendment fight dragged on.[49] His first client, Doretta Ince of Oregon, had been told by her partner, William Bates, to get an abortion after she got pregnant because he did not want to pay child support. Ince refused, and following the birth of her child, Bates refused to pay. As Bopp told his colleagues, Bates argued that "the father should have an equal right to have his child aborted." Ince prevailed in the Oregon state courts, and in 1977, Bopp represented her in the U.S. Supreme Court, which refused to hear Bates's appeal. The win energized the Legal Action Project's backers, and Bopp urged his colleagues to take up similar cases.[50]

He also joined other attorneys trying their hand at writing abortion laws. He drafted a model law passed in Cocoa Beach, Florida, for example, that required abortion clinics to meet exacting standards. Whereas Bopp argued that the law protected women's health, abortion rights supporters believed that the ordinance would make abortions more expensive or force clinics to close. Abortion providers sued, and Bopp represented one of the city commissioners defending the suit.[51]

Attorneys affiliated with AUL also deepened their involvement in litigation. Dennis Horan helped recruit young pro-life attorneys in the Chicagoland area, as did Victor Rosenblum, a liberal constitutional law professor at Northwestern. While Horan met young lawyers at talks he gave throughout the city, Rosenblum converted some of his students to the cause. Together with Bopp, AUL lawyers submitted amicus curiae briefs to the Supreme Court throughout the 1970s, including *Planned Parenthood of Central Missouri v. Danforth* (1976) and three 1977 cases: *Maher v. Roe, Poelker v. Doe,* and *Beal v. Doe.*[52]

The outcome of these cases convinced attorneys like Bopp and Horan that the Supreme Court held out more promise for change than many had expected. In *Danforth*, the Court upheld a Missouri informed consent requirement. In *Maher*, *Beal*, and *Poelker*, it rejected a challenge to laws banning the use of public money or facilities for abortion; the Supreme Court would later uphold a federal ban on Medicaid reimbursement, the Hyde Amendment. After these decisions, anti-abortion lawyers invested further in litigation, believing the courts might whittle away abortion rights while the fight for an HLA continued.[53]

With little support from large national organizations, some pro-lifers also worked to replicate the 1976 success of New Right PACs. In 1977, three former Democrats, Paul Brown, Robert Sassone, and Sean Morton Downey Jr., founded the Life Amendment PAC (LAPAC) to support pro-life candidates, and Paul Weyrich gave them space at the offices of the Committee for the Survival of a Free Congress. Brown, a career Kmart employee, was married to a pro-life activist, but he had not been particularly interested in politics for much of the 1970s. Downey, the son of a show business family, had protested the war in Vietnam and joined Martin Luther King's March on Washington in 1963. A union Democrat and attorney, Sassone worried that abortion would undermine the security of the nation. The three planned to put on a show—and make the anti-abortion movement a central story in the 1978 election. Brown was fond of political stunts, but the leaders of LAPAC had serious intentions: making enough of an impact to convince politicians that pro-life voters could swing a close race.[54]

The leaders of LAPAC and NCPAC saw Iowa as an important opportunity, given its large base of evangelical Protestant voters. Working closely with Iowa Right to Life, Stone, Dolan, and direct-mail guru Richard Viguerie pledged to take down incumbent Democratic senator Dick Clark. Viguerie shared NCPAC's ambition to purge the GOP of moderates. His goal, he explained, was to replace establishment Republicans with "leverage conservatives"—"men who can influence policy and help elect other conservatives." The Iowa race struck him as a perfect opportunity. He sent over seven hundred thousand pieces of direct mail in support of Roger Jepsen, an evangelical Protestant father of six and former lieutenant governor. Jepsen had a reputation for contradicting himself on the campaign trail and flip-flopping on key issues. But even though his primary opponent was widely considered more electable, Jepsen pulled off an upset. In the general election, helped by the collaboration between NCPAC and abortion foes, Jepsen managed a shocking win.[55]

For many, the message sent by Jepsen's win was unmistakable: pro-life evangelicals, his presumed core constituency, could decide an election. In 1978, Paul Weyrich helped the Reverends Robert Grant and Richard Zone found Christian Voice, an advocacy group for conservative Christians, and gave the group office space at the Heritage Foundation. A year later, he persuaded the Reverend Jerry Falwell to organize the Moral Majority, another group that brought conservative evangelical voters to the polls. Within a few years, Falwell's organization had a budget in excess of $3 million.[56]

Pro-life organizations also believed elections would make the difference for an HLA. Carolyn Gerster based her run for the NRLC leadership in 1978 on a pledge to launch a voter identification project similar to the one that helped Jepsen in Iowa. Her opponent, Mildred Jefferson, was unquestionably the pro-life movement's most charismatic speaker, but Gerster brought her own touch of glamour to the race. An internist in Paradise Valley, Arizona, Gerster had lived a version of the American dream. Arriving in Arizona on a Greyhound bus in 1932, the sickly daughter of a single mother, Gerster had graduated from college at seventeen, become a physician, married a doctor, and raised her five sons in a sprawling Spanish-style home surrounded by golf courses and stately saguaro cacti, in the same neighborhood as Barry Goldwater's hilltop haunt. In the end, Jefferson's charisma did not matter. She had made enemies in NRLC, many of whom accused her of spending the organization to death. In 1979, the group had a six-figure debt and had not paid its general counsel's bill for months. When Gerster beat her, Jefferson quit NRLC and founded her own organization, Right to Life Crusade.[57]

Her departure worsened the financial crisis. NRLC could not use its own direct-mail list because its fundraiser, Bothell, Inc., claiming the organization had breached its contract, had obtained a court order enjoining the list's use. Meanwhile, Jefferson used Bothell (and the NRLC mailing list) for her new organization, alienating potential donors. Gerster promised to lift NRLC out of a crisis by prioritizing "effective lobbying (with emphasis on citizens' lobbying), expansion of our Legal Action Project and (probably most important) implementation of the Voter I.D. Project towards the goal of identifying every registered pro-life voter by 1980." Her commitment would help to bring NRLC into an alliance with the Republican Party that would change both.[58]

Into the Election Conflict

NARAL, the nation's largest single-issue pro-choice group, gave NRLC a crash course in campaign finance law. NARAL had organized its own PAC in 1977, and following Jepsen's 1978 victory in Iowa, the organization stepped up its fight against its pro-life counterparts. Most of NARAL's focus at its 1979 national convention was about how to succeed in electoral politics.[59]

Starting that spring, NARAL filed complaints against NRLC with the Federal Election Commission.[60] NARAL argued that LAPAC was a connected PAC of NRLC and thus could solicit contributions only from NRLC members, not the general public. But NARAL alleged that LAPAC constantly (and illegally) asked the public for money, sending direct mailers and selling tickets. Next, NARAL argued that NRLC's voter identification project, which sought to identify and mobilize anti-abortion voters, constituted unlawful in-kind corporate contributions of information to anti-abortion candidates. The group's remaining complaints focused on alleged campaign finance violations of either LAPAC or state affiliates of NRLC.[61]

The FEC complaint against NRLC created panic in an already struggling organization. Carolyn Gerster worried about fallout from the FEC's request to inspect the list of voters already located by the group's voter identification project. If the FEC made their names public, anti-abortion donors might fear potential stigma and distance themselves from the cause. The financial cost of defending the FEC charges could have been equally disturbing. "NARAL has apparently launched an attempt to cripple the NRLC," Gerster complained in NRLC's newsletter, "and force it to divert its resources to its defense rather than the pursuit of a human life amendment."[62]

At first, tangling with election law mostly encouraged anti-abortion groups to look harder for allies. NRLC founded its own PAC in 1979, making Sandra Faucher the group's first PAC director. A lifelong Democrat, Faucher had honed her electoral skills in Maine and had long seen herself as a champion of equality for women. She resented the discrimination she experienced while working as a secretary at a law firm. But the GOP's stand on abortion eventually led her to become a Republican. She worked to elect GOP candidates, who received roughly 80 percent of the group's early expenditures. As important, NRLC tried to pick winners. The PAC always resisted the pleas of pro-lifers who argued that some purist candidate was perfect, which often meant "perfectly unelectable."[63]

As the 1980 election season began, NRLC leaders still saw a constitutional amendment as their main mission. While the group planned to work on the presidential election, congressional races commanded more attention. "We have definitely found Congress to be more important to our political aspirations than the executive branch," Faucher explained.[64] In any case, the presidential politics of abortion remained uncertain. Throughout his presidency, Jimmy Carter had tried to take a middle ground on abortion, opposing a constitutional amendment but also condemning Medicaid funding for the procedure. Carter's Republican challengers had a wide range of positions. Representative John Anderson of Illinois, a candidate who supported abortion rights, ran competitively in early primaries and quickly became a media darling. George H. W. Bush, another strong contender, had a long record of promoting family-planning legislation and opposed a constitutional amendment outlawing abortion. Only Ronald Reagan, who had announced his support for the HLA in 1975, seemed likely to lead the charge for constitutional change. As spring primaries continued, Reagan built on a victory in New Hampshire and steamrolled his opponents in the southern primaries. As the presumptive nominee, he looked like he could reconfigure abortion politics.[65]

Don Devine, Reagan's deputy director for policy and analysis, had made the candidate's position on abortion a major selling point. He claimed, for example, that the abortion issue helped Reagan beat Bush by a 7-1 margin in key primary states (and ended Anderson's bid for the Republican nomination). In the general election, anti-abortion voters were similarly key to Reagan's election strategy. "There has been significant erosion in the Democratic coalition that elected Jimmy Carter in 1976," explained a confidential strategy paper written by Reagan's campaign. Some blue-collar Catholics and conservative evangelical Protestants would more willingly turn their backs on the Democratic Party for a candidate who denounced legal abortion.[66]

Reagan's nomination presented an unprecedented opportunity for anti-abortion organizers. NRLC launched the Pro-Life Impact Committee to influence the GOP platform. At the Republican National Convention in Detroit's Joe Louis Arena, forty-one volunteers handed out pro-life buttons and brochures to attendees. When the convention began, Reagan expected to preserve the 1976 platform's relatively weak stance on abortion. NRLC leaders fought for something more but did not know if Reagan would deliver. James Bopp worked with Phyllis Schlafly, the conservative anti-feminist icon, and Carl Anderson, a senatorial aide to Jesse Helms, to draft platform language endorsing a right to life. Then right-to-lifers lobbied the Republican National Committee platform committee to stake out a right-to-life position.[67]

Their efforts met with surprising success. In addition to a stronger endorsement of a constitutional abortion ban, the platform "pledge[d] the appointment of new justices on the Supreme Court who respect traditional family values and the sanctity of all human life." On July 11, 1980, Willke wrote an exultant letter to members of his group, but he also called their attention to the work ahead. "The passage of a Human Life Amendment ultimately depends . . . on the votes of public officials," he noted. "Therefore, the election of pro-life candidates has become crucial to the pro-life movement."[68]

Few expected Reagan to win as easily as he did. Carter secured 41 percent of the vote and carried only six states and the District of Columbia. The Republican Party gained thirty-four seats in the House and twelve in the Senate, taking control of the latter chamber for the first time since 1954. *National Right to Life News* proclaimed that "the pro-abortionists were left in shambles."[69] It seemed that alliance with the GOP would finally pay off.[70]

PACs like the one run by NRLC helped achieve what Willke called "Fantasy Island come true."[71] While both Reagan and Carter participated in the public funding system, Reagan also tapped into a new source of money. After FECA passed, critics argued that voters had unplugged from elections and become more reluctant to vote. In 1979, Congress responded with a new provision to increase voter turnout. Under the new law, national parties could spend unlimited amounts on building local and state parties, which could then pay for everything from phone banks to bumper stickers (in 1979, the Federal Election Commission also ruled that national parties could raise state-regulated money as long as they spent it on state elections). These funds—labeled soft money—soon came to fuel attack ads in federal campaigns. But in 1980, Reagan raised only $10–15 million in soft money, while PACs spent a record $131 million on the campaign. For the first time, almost as much of that money—much of it coming out of the pockets of right-wing small donors—went to Republicans as to Democrats. Ideological PACs seemed set to place more power in the hands of conservatives: six of the top ten PACs by dollars spent—and all of the top three—identified with the New Right. PAC money meant that parties—which could give relatively large sums under FECA—no longer had a clear edge in campaign fundraising. In turn, conservative activists displeased with the establishment had more financial leverage.[72]

But as much as pro-lifers celebrated the 1980 election, there remained formidable obstacles to a constitutional amendment. Many GOP politicians had come to power because of other issues, and the anti-abortion movement could not assemble a majority of lawmakers to back an abortion ban. Having influence on the federal government was no bad thing, but within a few years, pro-lifers were so divided about how to use their power that the quest for a constitutional amendment died forever.

The Anti-Abortion Civil War

Even after their successes in 1980, NRLC leaders recognized that pro-lifers lacked the votes in Congress to pass a constitutional amendment. Willke estimated that the movement was missing fifteen to twenty votes in the Senate and forty in the House.[73] Stephen Galebach, a young attorney at the Christian Legal Society, published an article in the *Human Life Review* arguing that Congress already had the authority to pass a federal statute recognizing fetal personhood and functionally banning abortion. Galebach had the kind of biography Ronald Reagan loved: he had been a platoon commander in the marines and the president of the Yale Republican Club before earning a degree from Harvard Law School. His proposal caught the attention of Jesse Helms, who introduced what he called the Human Life Bill in January 1981. The bill declared that unborn children were legal, rights-holding persons from the moment of conception.[74]

Some abortion opponents did not think Galebach's bill went far enough. A later Congress could just repeal a statute, whereas a constitutional amendment would last. Paul Brown's wife, Judie, was one of the skeptics. Paul had been transferred around the country as he climbed the corporate ladder at Kmart, and in each new town, Judie had taken pro-life work where she could find it. As a Catholic wife and mother, she hardly saw herself as the person to lead a social movement. But she quickly rose at NRLC, eventually becoming Mildred Jefferson's executive director. A conservative like Jefferson, Brown welcomed an alliance with the GOP. But Jefferson's abrupt departure in 1978 crystallized some of Brown's doubts about the direction NRLC was taking. To avoid alienating potential allies, NRLC remained silent on every issue but abortion. Brown opposed contraception and sex education as well, and her colleagues' silence on the issues struck her as cowardly. She wondered if the GOP was telling the pro-life movement what to do.[75]

Pragmatists like Bopp and Willke thought Brown had it backward: abortion opponents needed a dose of practical advice, not more idealism. For the Human Life Bill to pass, Congress had to have the constitutional authority to enact it. Helms invoked the Fourteenth Amendment, which guaranteed citizens equal protection and due process of law. Pro-lifers had long argued that fetuses counted as "persons" under this amendment, and Helms tried to make the same point. However, the Court did not allow Congress to define new rights, and in *Roe v. Wade*, the Supreme Court had rejected arguments for fetal personhood. Even legal commentators who saw *Roe* as wholly without merit questioned the viability of the Human Life Bill.[76]

The O'Connor Controversy

The Supreme Court returned to the spotlight in June 1981 when Justice Potter Stewart, one of the seven justices who had voted in *Roe* to recognize a right to choose, announced his retirement. Reagan had floated the idea of nominating the first woman to the Court, and Representative John Rhodes Jr. of Arizona, a longtime friend of Barry Goldwater's, recommended Sandra Day O'Connor, a judge on the Arizona Court of Appeals. O'Connor had previously served as a Republican state legislator. Rhodes described her

"Republican credentials" as "impeccable." She was also tough, having spent much of her childhood on a ranch without heat or running water. As an adult, she had survived the rough-and-tumble (and very male) world of Arizona politics. Being the first woman on the Supreme Court seemed unlikely to faze her. Pro-lifers saw the nomination as a betrayal. Carolyn Gerster denounced O'Connor, believing that as a state lawmaker, she had stymied Arizona pro-lifers' efforts to restrict abortion in the state. Gerster was livid that a president who proclaimed his love of the unborn child had picked O'Connor to sit on the nation's highest court.[77]

Gerster was not the only one who was angry. After Reagan announced O'Connor's nomination, pro-lifers inundated the White House with calls and letters. Willke threatened to undermine O'Connor's nomination. Gerster herself hand-delivered a letter to the White House detailing O'Connor's record on abortion.[78]

Reagan did not back down but sent a harshly worded letter about Gerster to another pro-life activist. The letter leaked, and NRLC leaders rallied to Gerster's defense. At the end of August, more than thirty pro-life groups held an anti-O'Connor rally in Dallas. Some, thinking her confirmation was a given, were careful not to take a direct stand. The editors of the *National Right to Life News* had hoped that Reagan had not understood O'Connor's record but now began to worry that he did simply did not care.[79]

O'Connor did face some questioning about abortion, a marked change from past judicial nomination hearings (John Paul Stevens, confirmed unanimously in December 1975, did not have to answer a single question about *Roe*). In her Senate testimony, she restated her personal opposition to abortion "as a method of birth control" but refused to weigh in on *Roe*, saying she did not want to prejudge a case that might come before the Court. Willke and Gerster testified against the nominee, but to little effect. The Senate vote to confirm her was unanimous.[80]

While embarrassed by this outcome, NRLC leaders nevertheless spun the episode as a step in the right direction. "We were able to raise abortion as a serious issue with respect to Supreme Court nominations," Willke argued, "and that is progress of a sort."[81]

It seemed that O'Connor had put the administration in a no-win situation. On one hand, Reagan wanted to placate new GOP voters concerned about taxes and economic growth who might also be alienated by overtly pro-life judges. On the other hand, his coalition included social conservatives who expected the administration to keep its word about judicial nominations. After the confirmation, Reagan's advisors suggested a strategy that might turn this dilemma into a political coup and unite the Republican coalition. "Whatever one may think of . . . the merits of abortion itself," wrote Michael Uhlmann, a special assistant to the president, "the intensity of right-to-lifers on the issue of judicial power should not be underestimated." But, he continued, promising to nominate pro-lifers might alienate other prospective Republican voters. "It does not follow that a pro-lifer must be nominated. It does follow, I think, that the nominee's record on the issue be examined with special scrutiny and that the nominee regard *Roe v. Wade* and its progeny as most unwise assertions of judicial power." The dust-up over O'Connor's nomination turned out to be a blessing in disguise. Reagan staffers recognized how much some GOP voters cared about judicial nominations and saw that the promise of controlling the Supreme Court could solidify some voters' commitment to the GOP.[82]

Hatch versus Helms

Meanwhile, NRLC leaders celebrated an apparent consensus about what an ideal constitutional amendment would entail. A gathering of lawyers and professors had endorsed a "unity amendment" that right-to-lifers would promote if they gained enough votes in Congress, but unity was the last thing pro-lifers would find. In October 1981, Utah senator Orrin Hatch introduced a constitutional amendment allowing but not requiring the states and Congress to ban abortion. Hatch was an attorney in his early thirties who had never held elective office when he decided to run for the Senate in 1976, launching a long-shot campaign against Frank Moss, Utah's seemingly unbeatable Democratic incumbent. Hatch, who was fond of calling himself a "non-politician," had picked the right time to campaign as an outsider. Howard Phillips, the chairman of the Conservative Caucus, claimed that the New Right "organizes discontent," and he recognized Hatch's ability to tap into the anger of middle-class white Americans. One group Hatch planned to organize was voters angry about legalized abortion.[83]

Hatch's proposal was a far cry from the Unity Amendment so many right-to-lifers favored. The Hatch Amendment would allow states to criminalize abortion, but nothing in the proposal required anyone to do anything. If the Hatch Amendment were law, states like New York or California (which often accounted for the vast majority of abortions nationwide) could keep the procedure legal, accessible, and publicly funded. Nevertheless, anti-abortion pragmatists saw the Hatch Amendment as a satisfactory short-term solution. In a memo on the subject, James Bopp acknowledged that while it stopped far short of what many pro-lifers wanted, it addressed pro-lifers' most immediate concern—stopping the courts from striking down promising bans or restrictions. Willke, the NRLC president, also asserted that Hatch's proposal would appeal to more Republicans, Democrats, and independents than Helms's Human Life Bill because it would "defer rather than face the hard questions of personhood, conception, and rape."[84]

But rather than win universal support, the Hatch Amendment touched off a war inside the anti-abortion movement and even within NRLC, where it was denounced by roughly half the board. In December 1981, when NRLC endorsed the amendment, Judie Brown's American Life League (ALL) came out against it.[85] "Very few who have fought these many years," Brown wrote, "want to support an amendment to the Constitution which 'regulates the killing' and which gives legislatures and the Congress the 'right to choose' to regulate or not." She thought that by relying on the GOP, pro-lifers had forfeited the ability to make any real demands on politicians.[86]

To many in the movement, these concerns rang true.[87] Willke responded by reiterating that the Human Life Bill could be struck down by federal judges. The only way to save lives, he argued, was to remove the courts' jurisdiction or pass something that the Supreme Court would uphold. Helms was not convinced. In March, he introduced a new version of the Human Life Bill. A panel advanced the proposal, but Helms could not muster the votes to overcome an August filibuster. NRLC leaders tried to build a consensus in favor of the Hatch Amendment, but the divide within the pro-life movement only deepened. Hatch announced that he would postpone debate until after the midterm election in the hope of winning more votes.[88] But the picture for abortion opponents only grew worse after the 1982 midterm election. Democrats, many of whom vowed to vote against anti-abortion laws, picked up twenty-six seats in the House and one in the Senate.[89]

By June 1983, leaders of the pro-life movement could not help but be despondent. That month, Congress rejected the Hatch-Eagleton Amendment, a revised version of Hatch's original proposal, by a vote of forty-nine to fifty with one abstaining. Even with an ally in the White House and considerable GOP success, pro-lifers had not advanced a constitutional amendment coming from Congress. Their partnership with the GOP looked like it might have been a waste.[90]

A New Justification for Aligning with the GOP

With the pro-life civil war raging, the Reagan administration began looking for an exit strategy. Reagan staffer Edwin Harper summarized widespread concern that conflict within the pro-life movement could only hurt the president. "It would neither be appropriate nor wise for the Administration to support one legislative vehicle over another," he wrote, since neither seemed likely to succeed. The administration's most important task was to "make sure that any subsequent defeat of anti-abortion legislation on Capitol Hill is not placed on the doorstep of the White House." But Reagan's team did not want to lose the abortion foes' support. Gary Bauer, a deputy undersecretary for planning and budget at the Department of Education, proposed low-cost steps the administration could take to appease anti-abortion activists. A Southern Baptist from Kentucky, Bauer had quit his job in 1980 to campaign for Ronald Reagan; after the election he became the assistant director for opposition research at the Republican National Committee, where his job was to dig up dirt on Democratic leaders. The *New York Times* would later quip that Bauer's height—just five foot six—made him hard to notice. But his aggression and self-confidence more than made up for his short stature. Unlike some in the administration, Bauer was deeply opposed to abortion and believed that both the traditional family and the nation's Judeo-Christian values were under attack. He made it his mission to convince Reagan that he could please anti-abortion voters without losing any of the younger voters flocking to the GOP.[91]

Bauer knew that the Supreme Court was considering a challenge to an anti-abortion ordinance in Akron, Ohio. Many leading academics and attorneys in the pro-life movement had a hand in drafting the ordinance, and James Bopp was helping to defend it in court. Bauer urged the administration to submit an amicus brief supporting Akron. He recognized that the Court would likely invalidate all or part of the law, but winning was beside the point. "No matter what the court decides," he wrote to Counselor to the President Edwin Meese III, "we will have taken a position right-to-life advocates will applaud." The promise of controlling the Court—or even influencing the justices—would please pro-lifers even if Reagan himself did nothing to ban abortion. Meese set staffers to work framing an argument that could appeal to every member of the Reagan coalition.[92]

The administration would improve on Bauer's recommendation. Reagan called for *Roe* to be overruled while saying nothing explicit about abortion at all. Instead, he framed *Roe* as the kind of judicial activism that all conservatives denounced—activism that had produced bad Supreme Court decisions on everything from protecting criminal defendants to banning school prayer. Striking down the Akron law would be activism as well, because it would deny the city the power "to regulate the hows and whens of abortion within its own jurisdiction." As the administration framed it, the issue was the abuses committed by the judiciary—and by a federal government that had grown too big.[93]

For their part, NRLC leaders desperately needed a new justification for their reliance on the Republican Party. NRLC's PAC had spent $110,000 to elect anti-abortion candidates and to launch effective voter identification projects in states without strong anti-abortion movements, especially across the South. All that effort had brought the organization no closer to an anti-abortion constitutional amendment. A poll commissioned by Ohio Right to Life, an NRLC affiliate, showed that most Americans still opposed a constitutional abortion ban. Relying on the GOP seemed pricey and pointless: NRLC was $175,000 in debt, with little to show for it.[94]

After the Supreme Court announced its decision in *City of Akron v. Akron Center for Reproductive Health*, anti-abortion lawyers believed that they had identified a new justification for partnering with the GOP. A 6-3 majority struck down the Akron ordinance, including provisions in which pro-life lawyers had invested a great deal, on the ground that the law impermissibly burdened women's abortion rights.[95]

But Sandra Day O'Connor, much reviled in pro-life circles, wrote a dissent that criticized the very framework of *Roe v. Wade*. O'Connor reasoned that the trimester framework could not be viewed as either "legitimate or useful." As time went on, the date of viability would move up, and experts would change the standard of care for abortion providers. She laid out an alternative: unless a regulation caused a severe or absolute obstacle to women seeking an abortion, the Court should uphold it.[96]

O'Connor's dissent helped to put control of the Supreme Court at the heart of the relationship between the GOP and the anti-abortion movement. In January 1984, as Reagan plotted his reelection strategy, the White House pitched the Supreme Court as the main reason social conservatives should vote Republican. White House talking points had the president tell pro-life leaders that "even though we are having such difficulty with members of the Congress on this issue, I think we should not be discouraged. One sure way eventually to overturn the *Roe v. Wade* decision is by improving the United States Supreme Court. I am sure you all have read Justice O'Connor's dissent in the Akron cases. Let's work to make sure the next several new Justices share our views."[97]

NRLC leaders used the idea of controlling the Court to justify their movement's reliance on the GOP. "The stakes are tremendous," Bopp and Willke wrote in a 1984 fundraising letter. "If President Reagan wins reelection, he will appoint at least two and maybe even three new Supreme Court justices." Why should abortion opponents care about the composition of the Court? NRLC's answer was simple: "The five oldest Supreme Court justices all voted in favor of the fatal 1973 *Roe v. Wade* decision." Their departures would offer an opportunity to mold a radically different Court.[98]

Other conservatives already recognized the importance of controlling the Court. Conservative attorneys created professional organizations, law school programs, and public interest law firms aimed at influencing both the Court's membership and its decisions. The Federalist Society, founded to create a conservative legal elite, was launched in 1982. It grew out of a three-day conference at Yale Law School spearheaded by a group of friends who had met as Yale undergraduates. Steven Calabresi, Lee Liberman (later Lee Liberman

Otis), and David McIntosh came to the same conclusion when attending law school: either their classmates were uniformly liberal, or those with conservative perspectives were afraid to step forward. The three hoped to create an intellectual home for conservative lawyers. While the Federalist Society was new in the early 1980s, there were already prominent conservative jurists with a vision of how the courts should change. At the top of that list were Antonin Scalia, Robert Bork, and many of the speakers at the group's founding conference. By making the Court a primary issue, anti-abortion lawyers hoped to join this broader conservative legal movement. But they had a unique approach to changing the law. The Federalist Society sought to make legal conservatism respectable—to groom a generation of judges, professors, and high-powered lawyers—and to promote compelling conservative ideas. NRLC and AUL lawyers did not initially concern themselves as much with the legal elite—or have much luck influencing them. Instead, Bopp and Willke believed the way for pro-lifers to influence the Court was for grassroots advocates to make control of the judiciary a priority.[99]

From PACs to Soft Money

In 1984, the pro-lifers advancing this goal scrambled to understand a new campaign finance landscape. The dominance of conservative PACs like NCPAC could not go unchallenged for long. The once-mighty Life Amendment PAC, which had brought down several major incumbents in 1978, had only $261 to its name in 1984.[100] Between 1980 and 1984, citizen PACs like NCPAC learned that they faced structural limitations too. All PACs had record-keeping and compliance requirements that could complicate campaign spending. Moreover, after *Buckley*, contribution limits meant that ideological PACs had to mobilize an army of small donors. When NCPAC and its allies could promise motivated donors a shot at taking over Congress and the White House, donors happily opened their wallets. But after 1980, many small donors felt that they had already gotten their wish and saw no reason to spend any more. By 1984, most New Right PACs were drowning in debt. Outside spending actually decreased that year, from over $13 million in 1980 to a little more than $11.5 million in 1984. While pro-life PACs bucked the trend, ideological PACs struggled, and the party establishment gained influence.[101] Soft money quickly dwarfed PAC spending: the Republican Party alone spent about $15.6 million in soft money in 1984. The roughly $22 million of soft money raised by both parties was almost double the total of outside spending that year.[102]

To navigate the new campaign finance landscape, NRLC's PAC laid out a more sophisticated election strategy, publishing a handbook, *Margin of Victory*, that offered advice to pro-life candidates, putting out flyers and voter guides in Spanish as well as English, and funding political ads in key races. Control of the Court was the clear goal of these efforts. Asked what NRLC wanted most, Sandra Faucher answered: "to re-elect the pro-life class of 1980 and maintain a pro-life majority in the Senate."[103]

Pro-Life Nonprofits

Pro-life groups hoped that the 1984 election season would prove the importance of anti-abortion voters to the GOP. But anti-abortion groups operated as nonprofit corporations, and at least since the passage of the Tillman Act in 1907, Congress had viewed corporate election spending as particularly dangerous. Corporations could build massive war chests, and unlike wealthy individuals, they could live forever (and never stop accumulating money). Congress thought businesses could buy results that had almost nothing to do with what most voters thought. One of the provisions in place to check corporate campaign finance prohibited corporations from making contributions or independent expenditures from their own treasury funds "in connection with" any federal election.[104]

An NRLC affiliate, Massachusetts Citizens for Life (MCFL), got in trouble after it put out a special election edition of its newsletter. Urging readers to "vote pro-life," the guide detailed the views on abortion of roughly four hundred candidates running for federal office. Candidates with "a 100% pro-life voting record" were rewarded with photos.[105] After receiving a complaint, the FEC concluded that MCFL had paid for the special edition with its own money and thereby violated the law. In 1984, a Massachusetts district court held that the FEC could not constitutionally regulate MCFL's voter guide. While regulators appealed, Bopp filed a separate suit against the FEC based on the agency's decision to impose "substantial restrictions on corporations publishing voter guides."[106]

As he waited to see what would come next in *Massachusetts Citizens for Life*, Bopp could only be gratified by the results of the 1984 election. Reagan carried every state but Minnesota and the District of Columbia. The GOP also defended its Senate majority and picked up sixteen seats in the House. Despite this dominance, the GOP entered a period of soul-searching. Reagan had united a diverse group of conservatives but could not run again, and the Republican National Committee now had to worry about how to keep the coalition from collapsing after the president's departure.[107]

At the RNC's June 1986 meeting, some members argued that the abortion issue itself threatened to tear the party apart. Reagan had benefited from demographic changes that were only becoming more obvious as the 1980s progressed. The number of voters between twenty-five and forty-four increased sharply, as did the suburban population around Sunbelt cities like Atlanta and Orlando. Many of these baby boomers had voted for the GOP in 1984, but they appeared divided on social issues. Prosperous young professionals had chosen Reagan *despite* his position on *Roe*, while conservative Christians supported the president largely *because* of his stand on social issues. Business conservatives seemed to have the greatest influence, even within organizations founded by New Right operatives. Consider the shift in priorities of Paul Weyrich's ALEC. By the mid-1980s, ALEC boasted a $3 million budget and corporate board members from Procter and Gamble to Eli Lilly. These corporate partners pushed it away from social issues. Between 1976 and 1979, a majority of ALEC's bills had addressed issues like abortion. But by the mid-1980s, ALEC spent most of its energy on business-friendly initiatives—everything from building private prisons to fighting clean-air regulations—while less than 5 percent of its model legislation tackled social issues. The group's shifting agenda reinforced the idea that GOP voters did not agree, especially on abortion. Reversing *Roe* might shatter an already fragile coalition.[108]

Distinguishing Nonprofits

In 1986, James Bopp took note when the Supreme Court finally issued its decision in *Federal Election Commission v. Massachusetts Citizens for Life* (*MCFL*). A year earlier, in *Federal Election Commission v. National Conservative*

PAC, the Court had struck down part of FECA that limited the independent expenditures of political committees. In *MCFL*, the Court held that federal bans on the independent expenditures of some nonprofits were unconstitutional too. The Court acknowledged that corporations had been the bogeymen of campaign finance debates for decades. Yet most nonprofits, including pro-life groups, were corporations, and Bopp's client argued that some corporations posed no threat at all. The justices ultimately agreed.[109]

Massachusetts Citizens for Life first argued that the disputed provision applied only to what *Buckley* described as "express advocacy"—and that its guide did not qualify as such. The Court agreed that the contested provision of FECA, section 441b, applied only to express advocacy but found that MCFL's guide clearly fell within the prohibited category. *MCFL* noted that the disputed guide not only "urges voters to vote for 'pro-life' candidates, but also identifies and provides photographs of specific candidates fitting that description." Even if the precise meaning of express advocacy was unclear, MCFL's guide certainly qualified.[110]

Nevertheless, *MCFL* concluded that section 441b could not constitutionally apply to the pro-life group's independent expenditures. The Court first concluded that FECA burdened the group's political speech. Because MCFL was incorporated, the only way it could make independent expenditures was through a PAC, but PACs faced onerous disclosure and record-keeping requirements. Moreover, they could solicit contributions only from their members. If a grandmother working with MCFL hosted a bake sale or raffle, the FEC would brand her an outlaw if she opened the event to her entire neighborhood. These limits on corporate speech, the Court concluded, made "engaging in protected speech a severely demanding task."[111]

Yet no compelling interest justified this burden, the Court continued, at least when it came to nonprofit corporations like MCFL. Regulating corporate election spending served a useful purpose in reducing "the effect of aggregated wealth on federal elections" and curbing "the political influence of those who exercise control over large aggregations of capital." But MCFL did not resemble the corporations that distorted election results. Issue-based groups raised money on the strength of their ideas. MCFL did not exist to amass wealth or make a profit for shareholders. *MCFL* exempted certain nonprofits from limits that stopped corporations from spending their own money on independent expenditures in federal elections.[112]

MCFL was a big win, but it did not give the anti-abortion movement everything it needed when it came to campaign finance. To begin with, *MCFL* protected only a subset of nonprofits—those with bigger war chests, or that ran for-profit businesses, might receive less protection from the courts. The Court in *MCFL* also said almost nothing about other issues that mattered to anti-abortion organizations—particularly, what their PACs could do and when they could run attack ads without bringing regulators down upon them.

Most rank-and-file right-to-lifers hardly noticed *MCFL*. But a smaller group of lawyers thought it would be easier to challenge campaign finance laws that hobbled their movement before pro-life organizations got in trouble, not after. When bringing constitutional challenges, pro-life lawyers initially focused on laws that affected them most, particularly regulations on political ads and nonprofit spending. Over time, however, the abortion wars would lead pro-lifers like Bopp to mount a much larger and far more controversial effort to dismantle the rules governing money in politics.

3
The Price of a Nominee

FOR MUCH OF THE 1980s, it was easy for Ronald Reagan to tell his anti-abortion supporters what they wanted to hear when he could not actually do much about *Roe*. But as the decade wound down, abortion politics began to feel less humdrum. While a solid five votes still stood in the way of any abortion restriction in the Court's most recent decision, *Thornburgh v. American College of Obstetricians and Gynecologists* (1986), the Supreme Court majority in favor of abortion rights had shrunk. The outcome in *Thornburgh* made the 1988 presidential election even more important to the anti-abortion movement. The next president would likely choose at least one new justice.[1]

In 1981, with his nomination of Sandra Day O'Connor, Reagan had hoped to win praise across the ideological spectrum and ensure a smooth confirmation. But since then, Reagan's attorney general, William French Smith, had been replaced by Edwin Meese III, the former counselor to the president. A native Californian, Meese had worked with Reagan since 1966 and was intensely loyal both to the president and his conservative ideology. He was a big man with a big personality, a bulldog convinced that the judiciary had lost its way. As attorney general, Meese went on the road to popularize originalism, a method of constitutional interpretation requiring a judge to focus on the original intentions of the Constitution's framers (or the original public meaning of the text). His ascent also signaled a shift in the administration's approach to judicial nominations. With Meese in charge, the administration would use nominations to rally conservative voters.[2]

Reagan planned to pick a sitting justice to replace Burger as chief justice. The choice came down to O'Connor and William Rehnquist, a conservative stalwart selected by Richard Nixon. Meese and his allies admired Rehnquist but were less trusting of O'Connor, who sometimes sided with the liberal justices. Rehnquist accepted the job, opening a spot for an associate justice.[3]

In choosing his replacement, the administration applied what it had learned from the O'Connor nomination. Administration insiders like Meese wanted a justice who would change the course of constitutional interpretation, and they recognized the extent to which judicial selections could energize pro-life and other conservative activists. As White House communications director Patrick Buchanan explained in a July 1985 memo to Don Regan, Reagan's chief of staff: "Given the cruciality of the Supreme Court to the Right to Life movement, the School Prayer movement, the anti-pornography movement, etc.—all of whom provide the Republicans with decisive Presidential margins—the significance of this . . . nomination is hard to exaggerate."[4]

Reagan had to choose between two conservatives from the DC Circuit Court of Appeals, Antonin Scalia and Robert Bork. In meetings about the vacancy, White House attorneys laid out the principles used to narrow down the president's selection. "The ideal candidate for this President to nominate to the Supreme Court," read one internal memo, "would be: 1. Conservative; 2. Intelligent; 3. Likely to exercise strong leadership on the Court; 4. Have predictable, well-formed views; 5. Easily confirmable; 6. A politically popular choice; 7. A good speaker and leader outside the Court; 8. Young and in good health; 9. Unlikely to quit." Moreover, they needed a judge with an existing plan of attack. "Unfortunately, the Court does not merely decide cases: it also decides which cases to decide, and it writes opinions which govern the way future cases are decided in the Supreme Court and elsewhere. Thus, the ideal justice will have given some thought to which cases he will want the Court to pick and what language to include in opinions—the better to shape the law."[5] Meese and some other advisors apparently considered Bork the slightly stronger choice, but Reagan became enamored of Scalia because of his youth and Italian American heritage (he would be the first Italian American justice on the Court). The president thought Scalia would stand up for "conservative principles on the Court."[6]

If Reagan saw Scalia as a different kind of nominee, many court watchers were not expecting a radical change. Some noticed the traits that would define much of Scalia's career: his sarcasm, his intellect, the hard-line views that earned him the nickname "Ninopath" from colleagues on the DC Circuit Court of Appeals. In August 1987, Eleanor Smeal of the National Organization for Women testified before the Senate that Scalia's confirmation would be "disastrous." Beverly LaHaye, a best-selling conservative Christian self-help author and founder of Concerned Women for America, a conservative evangelical nonprofit, gave Scalia a glowing recommendation. But across the ideological spectrum, many did not see Scalia's confirmation as hugely consequential. William Rehnquist, Reagan's pick for chief justice, faced blistering scrutiny over whether he had intimidated Black and Latinx voters while working as a GOP activist in Phoenix in the late 1950s and early 1960s—and whether he had overseen an unconstitutional army surveillance program of political groups during his time in the Nixon administration. Scalia's confirmation, by contrast, was smooth sailing. Democratic insiders predicted that Scalia would be too stubborn to win over his colleagues—a doppelganger of the famously difficult outgoing chief justice, Warren Burger, who had often ended up in dissent. Representative Barney Frank, a Democrat from Massachusetts, suggested that if Reagan substituted Scalia for Burger, few would notice the difference. Burt Neuborne of the American Civil Liberties Union thought that the Supreme Court's voting patterns would "remain stable." Even as some thirty-three senators voted against Rehnquist's confirmation, few progressives seemed to see a fight against Scalia as worth the trouble. The nominee dodged questions about *Roe*, and with little debate, in September 1986, the Senate voted unanimously to confirm him.[7]

It was the next opening that framed control of the Court as a central election issue. In the summer of 1987, Justice Lewis Powell announced his retirement. Any Supreme Court vacancy was major news, but Powell's looked like a game changer. He had not been the Court's most liberal member on abortion, but he had joined *Roe* and had written the Court's recent decision in *Akron I*, striking down an anti-abortion ordinance in its entirety. More important, his departure meant that there was no longer an obvious majority in favor of abortion rights.[8]

Sooner than many would have expected, however, the nomination of Robert Bork, the judge picked to succeed Powell, went down in flames. To "bork" became a verb meaning to campaign—by implication, unfairly—to defeat an ideologically unsympathetic nominee. Certainly, the politicization of Supreme Court nominations began much earlier, with nominations made by Richard Nixon and Lyndon Johnson. Nevertheless, political observers saw Bork's nomination as a watershed. Whether the nominee himself or the campaign to defeat him was to blame remains to this day in the eye of the beholder; but both sides agree that after Bork, Supreme Court nominations became more obviously polarized along partisan lines. National elections would simply determine which party called the tune.[9]

The Bork Controversy

The importance of Bork's nomination was not lost on anyone inside the White House. "During the next four months, no Presidential initiative will have higher priority than the confirmation of Robert Bork," Arthur B. Culvahouse, Reagan's chief counsel, wrote in an internal memo. Liberals' response to Bork drove home the importance of the nomination. Hundreds of left-leaning organizations formed a Block Bork Coalition intent on labeling the nominee an extremist who could not be trusted with the Constitution. The National Abortion Rights Action League alone vowed to spend $1 million to defeat him.[10]

NARAL had obvious reasons to oppose the nominee: Robert Bork was among the most prominent critics of *Roe v. Wade*. A former marine, he came across as stern and imposing, but in private he could be witty and easygoing. For conservatives, his brilliance had already made him a giant, and not only on social issues: his work on antitrust enforcement, for instance, was and remains profoundly influential. He had written a well-known critique of *Griswold v. Connecticut*, the 1965 decision striking down a ban on married people's use of contraception that formed a major part of the foundation for the Court's holding in *Roe*. Reagan fully understood how Bork was likely to vote on abortion and partly chose him on that basis. As a staffer wrote, Bork "would not hesitate to overturn constitutional aberrations such as *Roe v. Wade*."[11]

While devising their confirmation strategy, administration officials got wind of the tactical plan that Senate Democrats expected to use. Joe Biden, the chair of the Senate Judiciary Committee, was rumored to be the architect of the anti-Bork campaign. "Biden will construct the case for rejecting Bork," wrote a staffer, "around the claim that if a President makes ideology the controlling factor in a nomination, then the Senate can reject the nominee for the same reasons." The White House set out to prove that Bork was not an ideologue but a judge who saw how partisan the Supreme Court had already become.[12]

Conservative activists understood perfectly well what Bork might mean to the Court. *National Right to Life News* praised him as "one of America's most distinguished constitutional scholars" but predicted that his confirmation battle would be bloody. As one NRLC editorial explained, "Those who oppose Bork do so mostly on the ground of his 'ideology.' " Despite the scare quotes, the organization's own fundraising material emphasized the results that Bork would deliver if confirmed to the Court. A September 1987 NRLC fundraising letter asserted that his confirmation would mean "a pro-life majority on the Supreme Court."[13]

The early conservative legal movement had not focused on social issues, so it was no surprise that before 1987, social conservatives had not found a Supreme Court nominee who had their full confidence. Bork was the first to have their unified support. Until 1987, the Southern Baptist Convention (SBC), the world's largest Baptist denomination, had never officially embraced a judicial nominee, but that year, the group's leaders asked James Bopp if the SBC would risk its tax-exempt status if it formally endorsed Bork. The SBC ultimately made the endorsement. So did both the American Conservative Union and the National Right to Work Committee, a group that advocated for anti-union legislation. Christian Voice, a religious right organization, sent supporters a letter for them to send members of Congress. "Since the 1930s," the letter read, "this country has been burdened by a liberal majority on the Supreme Court. No longer will I stand for it."[14] NRLC likewise coordinated a letter-writing campaign. "Concerning *Roe v. Wade*," NRLC explained, "Bork has described it as 'unconstitutional' because there is no basis in the Constitution for the Supreme Court to deny states the power to restrict or prohibit abortion."[15]

The White House wanted to energize social conservatives and pro-lifers without casting Bork as an ideologue. Administration officials did this by stressing that Bork was a mainstream jurist precisely because he rejected *Roe.* White House talking points repeated that Bork questioned "whether there is a right to abortion in the Constitution." But the administration emphasized that Bork was not opposed to abortion so much as judicial activism. The issue was not whether abortion was right or wrong but "whether it should be the court, or the people through their elected representatives, that should decide our policy on abortion."[16]

Within the Senate, however, the administration's strategy seemed to create the worst of all possible worlds. The White House had apparently admitted that Bork's presence would radically change the outcome of cases like *Roe,* yet it did not fully defend Bork's positions on their own terms. It was fine to call Bork a mainstream jurist. But when members of Congress attacked his views, the White House did not have an effective response. After Bork failed to get enough votes in committee, the White House pushed for a full Senate vote, but on October 23, 1987, lawmakers voted down the nomination 58-42.[17]

Ironically, that failure convinced both GOP leaders and pro-life activists that the Supreme Court could be a winning election issue. Bork symbolized different things to different constituencies: hostility to unions, a brake on progressive federal legislation, and an end to legal abortion. In part, conservatives were reacting to the fierce opposition, but Bork himself also made a difference. He helped make social conservatives' causes respectable among conservative legal elites. Even in defeat (or perhaps because of it), Bork proved that control of the Court motivated conservative voters who agreed on little else.

Anthony Kennedy and the 1988 Presidential Election

With the 1988 election season under way, Reagan looked for another Bork, but one without the kind of track record that Democrats could use as a bludgeon. He first chose Douglas Ginsburg, a sharp young protégé of Ed

Meese with a sterling résumé. But when Ginsburg withdrew after admitting to having used marijuana, Reagan settled on Anthony Kennedy, a fifty-one-year-old judge on the Ninth Circuit Court of Appeals.[18]

Kennedy, who been on Reagan's short list for years, struck many as humble and calm. The son of a lobbyist and a schoolteacher, he had worked for a time under Meese when Reagan was the governor of California. In a memo to White House Counsel Peter Wallison, a staffer described Kennedy as "one of the more conservative members of the Ninth Circuit." But some of Kennedy's opinions alarmed Reagan staffers. *Beller v. Middendorf* (1980) involved navy regulations that prohibited same-sex anal or oral sex. While upholding the regulations, Kennedy's opinion had favorably cited *Roe* as a decision protecting "certain private decisions intimately linked with one's personality." One staffer commented, "This easy acceptance of privacy rights as something guaranteed by the Constitution is really very distressing."[19]

After Ginsberg's nomination collapsed and the administration quickly announced Kennedy as the next selection, some conservatives immediately revolted. Judie Brown of American Life League, long a skeptic of strategies centered on control of the Court, denounced him publicly. Conservative activist Don Feder complained that Kennedy appeared "to be struck from the O'Connor mold: no sweeping judicial philosophy, decisions on a case-by-case basis, undue regard for dangerous precedents, a man who probably will be with the president on crime control, but more often than not on the opposite side on abortion and the other social questions."[20]

The administration tried to pitch Kennedy to these voters as a stealth conservative. After announcing the nomination, White House lawyers put together talking points stressing that Kennedy was "popular with colleagues of all political persuasions," partly because of his "reputation for being fair, openminded and scholarly." The talking points did not completely abandon the rhetoric of judicial activism. The White House presented Kennedy as a judge who would "not . . . substitute his own personal preferences as to desirable social policy." But on specific substantive areas, the talking points said next to nothing other than presenting Kennedy as a fair judge who was generally tough on crime.[21]

John Willke, Bopp, and other NRLC leaders maintained what they called "guarded optimism" about the nomination. Partly because he was hard to pin down, Kennedy easily won over the Senate, which unanimously voted to confirm him on February 3, 1988.[22]

Kennedy's confirmation forced the contenders for the GOP nomination for president to describe their own vision for the future of the High Court. Senator Bob Dole, an establishment mainstay with an anti-abortion record, was in the running, as was Representative Jack Kemp of New York, another favorite of the pro-life movement. Kemp was an ebullient campaigner who delighted in paradoxes. He was a devout believer in supply-side economics who favored affirmative action as a remedy for racial inequality as well as big tax cuts and big spending. Kemp and Dole both faced obstacles. Dole's dour personality could be a liability, and Kemp was trying to move from the House of Representatives to the White House, a feat not managed since James Garfield did it in 1880. Vice President Bush had thrown his hat in the ring as well.[23]

Arguably the most attention went to the candidacy of Pat Robertson, the head of the $230-million-a-year Christian Broadcasting Network (CBN). Robertson, born into a prominent Virginia political family, for a time led the life you might expect of a young southern aristocrat: military service without front-line combat, four years at the genteel Washington and Lee University, where he claimed his real major was the girls attending nearby schools. He graduated near the top of his class at Yale Law School, but after failing the bar exam on his first attempt, he had a religious conversion. He started CBN in 1960, was ordained as a minister in the Southern Baptist Convention in 1961, and founded CBN University (later Regent University) in 1977. For Protestant evangelicals, Robertson was a major celebrity. Those who watched Robertson's *700 Club* had given Republican candidates an undeniable boost in 1980 and 1984, but by 1988, Robertson was not alone in being frustrated with the slow pace of change. As one GOP consultant framed it, evangelicals had grown tired of excuses made by establishment candidates and decided to "go out and do it themselves." The televangelist's candidacy showed how easily the Republican coalition could fall apart once Reagan's name was no longer on the ballot.[24]

Promising to select a nominee in the Bork mold could strengthen Vice President Bush's candidacy. Bush presented himself as Reagan's successor but could not quite get Republicans to believe he was as socially conservative as some of his competitors. Reagan reminded some voters of John Wayne—manly, honest, and authoritative—but as the conservative media consultant Roger Ailes put it, Bush was no John Wayne. He was a military veteran, a ferociously hard worker, unusually courteous, a lover of stability, and a believer in American exceptionalism. But he was too much an establishment figure for the anti-abortion movement to see him as a reliable ally, especially since he had a long track record of supporting family planning. As NRLC explained in a 1988 memo, he had backed only two of the constitutional amendments that still symbolized the anti-abortion cause, while his main competitors, Kemp and Robertson, had endorsed every single one.[25]

Bush's run helped to crystallize a new approach to politics that would come to define the movement. In Reagan, anti-abortion voters hoped to have a champion of their views. But after eight years, NRLC leaders had more practical ambitions. The goal was control of the Supreme Court, and the only way to achieve that was to pick a winner. Focusing on short-term success was the best way forward, even if that meant backing candidates with imperfect records. As David N. O'Steen, the group's executive director, explained in a confidential memo: "We cannot afford to let a pro-abortion president appoint a justice."[26]

But by 1988, judicial nominations had become as important to many grassroots conservatives as they already were to rank-and-file abortion foes. Anthony Kennedy may have been the one on the Supreme Court, but it was Bork who loomed large in the minds of grassroots conservatives, not least when it came to *Roe*. Already perhaps the leading figure among the conservative legal elite, Bork had used *Roe* as the prime example of judicial error since well before his nomination. After he became a household name—and that name had even become a verb—elite conservatives felt more comfortable following suit. For their part, grassroots conservatives saw Bork as a martyr who had learned the hard way that the Supreme Court had already become partisan.

The Road to *Webster*

With Kennedy on the bench, anti-abortion groups began looking for a case that could directly test the justices' opposition to *Roe*. James Bopp and a young attorney he had hired, Richard Coleson, stumbled on another strategy when a man asked for help blocking his ex-girlfriend from having an abortion. A decade earlier, the Court had invalidated a law requiring a woman to get her husband's written consent before terminating a pregnancy. Bopp and Coleson tried a different approach, asking the Court to balance the facts of each individual case. The two lawyers argued that some women simply did not have good enough reasons for having an abortion: some did not want to gain weight or spend less time with their boyfriends. And some men, Bopp and Coleson insisted, had strong justifications for wanting a pregnancy to continue, such as an emotional bond with an unborn child. The two urged courts to decide on a case-by-case basis rather than merely recognizing a right to abortion.[27]

As the odds of *Roe*'s demise went up, GOP leaders became uneasy. The 1988 Republican National Convention offered worrying signs of division. In Georgia, George H. W. Bush won the primary, but Pat Robertson's supporters made a bid to control the state's party machinery and sent delegates favoring the televangelist to the Republican National Convention. In Michigan, where Bush also won the primary, a coalition of Kemp and Robertson supporters banded together to challenge every state delegate, arguing that Bush supporters had violated state rules. The national convention gave every appearance of unity, but divisions festered below the surface. A Georgia delegate described his socially conservative colleagues as "the people who brought you the Spanish Inquisition and the Salem witch trial." Roger Stone, then a Kemp consultant, argued that a strong anti-abortion position would alienate voters of color.[28]

Fortunately for the GOP hierarchy, Bush had soft money to help him overcome any internal divisions. Since 1979, parties had been able to spend unlimited amounts of money on party building. This so-called soft money quickly boosted federal candidates, particularly those running attack ads. After the 1984 election, Common Cause, a government watchdog organization, had filed a complaint with the FEC to check the flow of soft money. Insisting that both Democrats and Republicans illegally funneled money to state parties to influence federal elections, Common Cause advocated for new regulations, but the FEC rejected the proposals. In 1987, after Common Cause went to court, Judge Thomas Flannery ordered the FEC to tighten the rules on soft money, but throughout 1988, the agency sat on its hands. Both parties rushed to take advantage. Joan Kroc, heiress to the McDonald's fast-food fortune, gave a record $1 million in soft money to the Democratic National Committee. The two parties racked up an unprecedented number of donations in excess of $100,000. In the primary season, Bush's lavish fundraisers, complete with ice sculptures and champagne, helped him outpace his rivals. Real estate mogul Donald Trump hosted an event that raised $500,000 for Bush in one night at the Plaza Hotel. Tobacco companies, construction firms, hotel chains, and other corporations, from makeup giant Revlon to cookie maker Nabisco, all poured money into Bush's campaign. Having long dismissed GOP leaders as squishy moderates, Charles and David Koch, the brothers behind an eponymous energy conglomerate, began spending their fortune on political candidates like Bush. By September 1987, Bush had raised $9.4 million, nearly as much as the $11 million amassed by the rest of the GOP primary field. The money allowed him to hire the best staffers and launch operations in all fifty states. NRLC leaders also got behind Bush. Despite their reservations about his record, he stood the best chance of determining who would sit on the Supreme Court.[29]

The Activists Speak

If Bush's wishy-washy position on abortion caused consternation, a rebellion inside the anti-abortion movement led by Randall Terry's Operation Rescue raised more pressing concerns. A devout evangelical Protestant, Terry grew up in Rochester, New York. Family on his mother's side was progressive and even feminist. He dropped out of high school four months before graduation and went on the road hoping to become a rock star, then bounced between flipping burgers, pumping gas, and selling tires. He was born again on the side of a road in Rochester, graduated from Bible college in 1981, and began protesting at local abortion clinics a few years later. He had been watching people in groups like NRLC and did not like what he saw. The anti-abortion establishment, he believed, expected too much from politicians. While these groups focused on overturning *Roe*, Terry insisted that the goal was "not to change the law, but to change hearts, in practical obedience to God in faith." He was convinced that politicians would not do anything about abortion unless right-to-lifers forced their hand—by protesting, getting arrested, clogging the courts, and making it unbearable to keep the status quo in place. "We are obliged to . . . treat murder like murder," a pamphlet asserted. He began an organized effort to blockade abortion clinics in 1987; nearly two hundred blockades unfolded in 1988 alone, resulting in over five thousand arrests. By the summer of 1988, Operation Rescue was stealing headlines from established anti-abortion groups by protesting the 1988 Democratic National Convention in Atlanta—law enforcement ultimately arrested twelve hundred people outside Atlanta's Omni Coliseum. These arrests and those prompted by the blockades brought media coverage, which facilitated fundraising and recruiting. Operation Rescue had launched a new era in pro-life activism and seemed set to become a permanent feature of abortion politics.[30]

Despite the challenge raised by Operation Rescue, that fall brought good news for established pro-life groups like NRLC. George H. W. Bush won the White House, and Republicans made modest gains in the House of Representatives. By the end of the race, soft money and independent expenditures allowed Bush to raise $54 million beyond the $46 million in public financing guaranteed to the Republican and Democratic nominees. Many expected Bush to make several more Supreme Court nominations. Although the president-elect had not made control of the Court his primary issue, he had vowed to select candidates who "did not legislate from the bench." The plan to undo *Roe* seemed to be working brilliantly.[31]

The *Webster* Backlash

Before the Supreme Court heard arguments in the Missouri case *Webster v. Reproductive Health Services* in April 1989, anti-abortion attorneys met to hash out a strategy. Larger groups like NRLC anticipated their first success in a major abortion case. Bopp and Burke Balch, the director of NRLC's department of state legislation, wrote of the most likely outcomes in *Webster*, "The Court could effectively overturn *Roe v. Wade* either by saying there is no constitutionally protected right to abortion and saying that laws banning or restricting abortion will be upheld as long as they are rational, or perhaps by saying that the state has a compelling interest in the unborn child from conception." New organizations joined to litigate *Webster*. Focus on the Family, a group started by psychologist and televangelist James Dobson, coordinated strategy with Bopp. So did evangelical lawyers working with Christian Advocates Serving Evangelism, a group founded the previous year to defend conservative Christians' freedoms of speech and religion.[32]

But unity in the pro-life movement went only so far. Many, like those flocking to Operation Rescue, saw no point in trying to shape the Supreme Court or please the GOP. In Operation Rescue's newsletter for January 1989, Terry urged blockaders not to "pin hope in *Roe v. Wade* being overturned" because "overturning *Roe v. Wade* will not make child killing illegal."[33] Terry's arguments had made political inroads. That March, the Republican Study Committee, a group of 136 conservative congressmen, considered declaring a national day of rescue to officially recognize the work of blockaders. Jerry Falwell described blockades as the pro-life movement's best chance to criminalize abortion. Operation Rescue credibly claimed to be the movement's future.[34]

But *Webster* certainly suggested that NRLC's investment in controlling the Supreme Court would soon pay off. By a 5-4 margin, the Court upheld all the disputed parts of the Missouri statute: a preamble stating that life begins at conception, a prohibition on the use of public money or facilities for abortion, and a measure related to fetal viability, the point at which survival is possible outside the womb. *Roe* had held that the state's interest in protecting fetal life did not become compelling until viability. Prior to that point, under *Roe*, states could not ban abortion.[35] Missouri had created a presumption of fetal viability at twenty weeks. But *Roe* concluded that viability did not occur until the twenty-fourth week—and reasoned that doctors, not lawmakers, should determine when a pregnancy was viable. *Webster* suggested that the very concept of viability—and *Roe*'s trimester framework—were incoherent. Anthony Kennedy and Antonin Scalia, the Court's newest members, expressed profound doubt about *Roe*'s validity. *Webster* sent a clear message: many on the Court believed *Roe* was fundamentally unsound.[36]

Bopp and Coleson felt that the movement had already won. "We argue that *Roe* is de facto largely overruled," Rich Coleson wrote.[37] Confident about its chances, NRLC championed a law that would outlaw abortion "as a method of birth control." The statute made abortion legal only in cases of rape, incest, fetal abnormality, and threats of "severe and long-lasting health damage." NRLC leaders believed the law would not damage the

GOP because the organization's internal polling suggested that Americans approved of legal abortion only under certain circumstances.[38]

But other established pro-life groups recognized that their movement had an image problem that did the GOP no favors. The National Conference of Catholic Bishops commissioned Wirthlin, a conservative pollster, to survey public attitudes toward abortion. Americans United for Life did its own internal polling. The results suggested that Americans thought pro-lifers were "against women . . . [and] against the democratic process." The pro-life movement could be a liability to the GOP.[39]

After *Webster*, some GOP leaders no longer hid their worries about the wisdom of a partnership with the pro-life movement. Mary Matalin, the chief of staff for the new chairman of the Republican National Committee, Lee Atwater, acknowledged that the abortion issue could cost her party with young women. Michele Davis, the executive director of the Republican Governors Association, described herself as "hugely concerned" about *Webster*'s effect on forthcoming elections.[40]

Atwater publicly admitted that the abortion issue could hurt his party. He fancied himself something of a rebel. He liked cigars, played guitar in a rock band, and had built a political brand in South Carolina with hard-edged campaigns. George H. W. Bush tapped him to manage his 1988 presidential campaign, and the South Carolinian lived up to his reputation for controversy. Atwater pushed the line that Bush's opponent, Massachusetts governor Michael Dukakis, was soft on crime. An independent pro-Bush group ran an ad invoking the story of Willie Horton, a Black inmate from the state who tortured a young man and sexually assaulted his partner while on weekend furlough. Because Atwater rarely missed a chance to tie Dukakis to Horton, he was accused of race-baiting. Hard-nosed tactics aside, Atwater shared his colleagues' doubts about aligning with the anti-abortion movement. Although Bush did not officially change his own stand on abortion, the president began to stress that Republican voters and candidates could hold any position they liked. "I want to make sure that everyone feels comfortable as Republicans, regardless of their position on abortion," he told the press. Election results in 1989 only heightened anxieties. Democrats won gubernatorial races in Virginia and New Jersey partly by stressing reproductive rights.[41]

In the following year, however, so much went well for established pro-life groups that fears of a split with the GOP barely registered. There already seemed to be enough justices to guarantee that *Roe v. Wade* would be overturned, and in 1990 and 1991, President Bush filled two new openings. At the same time, Operation Rescue began to struggle under the burden of debt, fines, and court costs. Randall Terry himself spent a year in prison before stepping down as the organization's leader. To escape legal liability, Operation Rescue disbanded and relaunched as Operation Rescue National, but the new group never recaptured the allure of Terry's original. Conservative evangelicals loved the spectacle of clinic blockades and the feeling of stopping an abortion in real time. But for many, the threat of jail time and hefty fines broke the spell. Those who remained were more radical; some were attracted to the idea of violence against abortion clinics and providers.[42]

It seemed that Bopp's vision of the anti-abortion movement would prevail. Pro-lifers had reshaped the Court, and now they simply had to wait for a decision undoing abortion rights. When a series of scandals put campaign finance reform back on the agenda, most pro-life groups took little notice. Abortion foes had little time for anything but the fight against *Roe*.

A Revived Campaign Finance Push

For over a decade, groups on both sides of the abortion debate had had no choice but to learn something about campaign finance. As their activists dived into electoral politics, each movement accused the other of breaking the rules, triggering rounds of investigations and lawsuits. In the late 1980s, however, Bopp decided to take the fight to campaign finance reformers.[43]

With a decade under his belt as the NRLC general counsel, Bopp had come to see legal limits on campaign spending as restrictions on political speech—and a major infringement of Americans' liberty. Others, like Ralph Winter and even Stan Evans, had made these arguments, but Bopp, too, began to think that incumbents and liberal media organizations thrived in part because they were exempt from spending limits, while advocacy groups had to wade through a maze of regulations and lawsuits. Worse, while the Supreme Court had recognized that some limits on spending for political speech violated the First Amendment, bureaucrats were still trying to stop Americans from expressing themselves. In his view, spending on political speech was at the core of the First Amendment, and the "First Amendment is not a loophole." Throughout the late 1980s and early 1990s, he primarily challenged laws limiting the spending of nonprofit, issue-based corporations like his own.[44]

In 1985, he filed suit with Sandra Faucher, the head of the NRLC PAC. Faucher wanted to send out two surveys detailing the abortion positions of candidates for state and federal office. The FEC had introduced regulations interpreting section 441b of FECA, which prohibited corporations from making contributions or expenditures "in connection with" a federal election. The FEC took the position that corporations could not use independent expenditures for "partisan voting guides," a term that the FEC defined to include guides that "suggest or favor any position on the issues covered" or "indicate any support or opposition to any candidate or political party." Bopp's case on Faucher's behalf turned on the meaning of "express advocacy"—clear pleas to vote for or against specific candidates. He argued that in *MCFL*, the Supreme Court had allowed the government to limit corporate independent expenditures only if they fell in this category. The Federal Election Commission argued that *MCFL* had not adopted an express advocacy test—and that the Constitution allowed the government to regulate voter guides if they expressed an "editorial opinion" or "favored a position." With that definition, Faucher was stuck: any pro-life voter guide favored a position that a candidate adopted.[45]

While the district court considered Bopp's arguments, a financial debacle ramped up interest in election spending limits. Also known as thrifts, savings and loans (S&Ls), originally formed to help working-class people purchase homes, specialized in accepting savings at interest and making loans, mostly for home mortgages. After World War II, commercial banks and thrifts competed for customers by offering higher interest rates on savings accounts. To stamp out rate wars, Congress set fixed savings rates. But by the 1970s, thrifts began to struggle with these regulations, especially because customers could turn to more financially appealing money market funds. At the same time, the economic slowdown meant that fewer Americans qualified for home loans, putting further pressure on S&Ls. In 1980 and 1982, in an effort to let S&Ls outgrow their problems, Congress passed laws to deregulate the industry. Weaker thrifts tried to save themselves by making riskier investments. Poor oversight, fraud, and conflicts of interest ultimately decimated the industry. Of the 3,234 savings and loan associations in business in the early 1980s, 1,043 collapsed between 1986 and 1995, costing taxpayers roughly $132 billion.[46]

The S&L crisis cast a long shadow over the campaign finance debate. In 1989, one thrift, Lincoln Savings and Loan, fell apart at a cost of $3.2 billion. It soon emerged that Charles Keating Jr., the head of Lincoln, had made significant contributions to the campaigns of four Democratic senators (Donald Riegle, John Glenn, Alan Cranston, and Dennis DeConcini) and one Republican (John McCain). In 1987, the Federal Home Loan Bank Board was set to investigate Lincoln, but the five senators, later called the "Keating Five," made the investigation go away. By 1989, the Keating Five scandal had campaign finance reform back on the political agenda.[47]

Mitch McConnell, a young Republican senator from Kentucky, helped lead the fight against campaign reform. Even his friends admitted that McConnell did not have much charm. Some thought he looked alarmed even when nothing was wrong. His opponents compared him to a "warmed-over vanilla milkshake." The press called him a man "with the natural charisma of an oyster." But McConnell knew what he was good at. And he was better than good, he was brilliant: a cunning, disciplined strategist who did not mind being the bad guy. Years later, he would step up to the lectern at a press conference and announce that Darth Vader, the archvillain of the *Star Wars* franchise, had arrived.[48]

In his youth, McConnell was a moderate Republican, the kind of person who urged his classmates to march with civil rights leader Martin Luther King Jr., and a supporter of both abortion rights and campaign finance reform. In a 1973 op-ed, he called money in politics "a cancer." But his long-shot bid for the Senate in 1984 changed his mind (he later claimed that he was simply distancing himself from the Watergate scandal and had opposed campaign finance regulations all along). McConnell often said he would not have stood a chance if he not been able to raise and spend as much as he wished. He believed the same was true of any challenger in an election. McConnell would work closely with James Bopp on campaign finance in the decades to come. Nevertheless, NRLC leaders certainly felt a chill wind blowing after the Keating Five scandal. Trying to loosen any campaign finance rules would be that much harder.[49]

Yet even with the Keating Five scandal in the news, Sandra Faucher's Maine Right to Life Committee got good news in court. In June 1990, the district court in *Faucher v. Federal Election Commission* held that the FEC's regulations violated Faucher and Maine Right to Life's freedom of speech. Bopp had offered an expansive interpretation of the Court's 1986 decision in *Federal Election Commission v. Massachusetts Citizens for Life*, another case on ideological nonprofits and their voter guides. There, the Court had focused on the fact that MCFL was a nonprofit corporation—it had no shareholders, had never functioned as a business or union, and operated only to advance political ideas. Bopp insisted that *MCFL* also turned on the *kind* of speech at issue. He argued that under *MCFL*, bans on corporations' independent expenditures applied only to express advocacy. If Maine Right to Life engaged in issue advocacy, the FEC could not constitutionally prevent it from getting its material to voters. A district court accepted this argument. The FEC appealed, but few in NRLC were paying attention, especially after President Bush nominated David Souter to the Supreme Court.[50]

Two Visions of the Ideal Nominee

The Souter nomination promised to create a more conservative judicial majority. Souter would replace William Brennan, arguably the Court's leading liberal and a consistent vote for abortion rights. When Bush consulted Senator Bob Dole about potential nominations, Dole warned that if the president picked a hard-line abortion opponent, the confirmation hearings would be a "bloodbath." Souter, by design, was a cipher. A lifelong bachelor who lived alone on his family farm, he was famously taciturn. He had served as the New Hampshire attorney general before joining the Superior Court of New Hampshire and later the New Hampshire Supreme Court. In January 1990, John Sununu, the White House chief of staff and a former governor of New Hampshire, recommended Souter for the First Circuit Court of Appeals, which he joined that May. Just weeks later, Bush nominated him for the Supreme Court.[51]

Bush had also considered Clarence Thomas, a judge on the DC Circuit Court of Appeals, but thought that he could make a stronger case for Thomas after he gained more experience on the bench. Anyway, Souter seemed perfect: "bright, scholarly, non-political, a strict constructionist, and the right age." Perhaps most important, as one staffer predicted, "Congress would not reduce [the nomination] to a partisan battle." Souter was not outspoken about anything, much less abortion. By October, when his confirmation hearings began, he had still been on the court of appeals for less than six months and had virtually no paper trail. Sununu vouched for Souter with conservatives, but the administration framed the nominee as a quality jurist whom most members of Congress could approve. "The President did not use any litmus test, nor did any single issue dominate his decision," White House talking points explained. No one could prove Souter was an ideologue, much to the administration's delight.[52]

While senators on both sides of the aisle seemed favorably inclined toward Souter, the nominee made it even harder to predict how he would vote. In his Senate testimony, he said he had not made up his mind on *Roe v. Wade*. He declined to give a full-throated defense of judicial restraint and praised the jurisprudence of his liberal predecessor, Brennan.[53]

This performance clearly pleased senators, but it prompted social movements across the ideological spectrum to rail against the very idea of a consensus nominee. Roger Craver, a prominent progressive direct-mail fundraiser, sent out over three hundred thousand pieces of mail urging opposition to Souter. The National Organization for Women posted red "Stop Souter" signs throughout Washington, DC, and joined other abortion rights organizations in a "Do or Die Day" of lobbying and protest. Pro-life groups were no happier. Howard Phillips of the National Conservative PAC chided Souter for not criticizing *Roe*. NRLC leaders, who generally trusted Bush, stayed silent. Reaction to the nomination suggested that the rules of the game had changed. No longer would conservatives quietly accept an inoffensive centrist. Movements now wanted only judges who would be their champions. For the time, however, political leaders could not be bothered about what interest groups demanded. Only nine senators voted against Souter.[54]

Ironically, the confirmation only heightened Republican officeholders' anxiety about an alliance with the pro-life movement. With Souter replacing Brennan, the Court seemed to have more than enough votes to overturn *Roe*, and GOP leaders worried that winning that fight would lead voters to punish their party. In the winter of 1990, at the RNC mid-year meeting, Atwater and Bush kept emphasizing a "big tent" approach that welcomed Republicans with any position on abortion. Some religious right leaders resented the party's new angle. "We would not go around saying that our party is big enough for people who want to raise federal income taxes," quipped Gary Bauer. Generally, however, pro-choice Republicans felt they were gaining the upper hand in the party.[55]

In April 1990, Ann Stone, a conservative fundraiser, founded Republicans for Choice. Like her ex-husband, Roger, Ann Stone was used to being ostracized. She grew up wearing dollar dresses, one of three children raised poor by a single mother in Stratford, Connecticut, and had become a Republican in elementary school. She met Roger in college and learned the direct-mail business from Richard Viguerie before turning thirty. Less than a decade later, she was a direct-mail millionaire, but many of her former conservative allies looked at her like she had horns. In 1989, when Lee Atwater suggested she start a pro-abortion rights PAC, Stone was more than game. She did not mind a little controversy. Republicans for Choice laid out a three-year plan to change the party's abortion platform. Two hundred GOP lawmakers signed on to the organization's advisory board, and Stone pledged to raise $3 million for pro-choice Republican candidates.[56]

Established pro-life groups initially seemed unconcerned. In part, groups like NRLC had their hands full with the Supreme Court. In 1990 the Court decided two cases involving abortion rights for minors, *Hodgson v. Minnesota* and *Ohio v. Akron Center for Reproductive Health* (known as *Akron II*). In *Hodgson*, it upheld a Minnesota law requiring minors to notify both parents before having an abortion. In *Akron II*, it rejected a challenge to an Ohio parental-involvement law. The language of both decisions suggested that the Court no longer considered abortion a fundamental right. Rather than having to justify interfering with a protected liberty, the government had to explain whether, as Kennedy's opinion put it, the state had chosen a "rational way to further [its] ends." Kennedy seemed to use the language of "rational basis," the least protective form of judicial review, which applied when a law did not affect any constitutional rights at all.[57]

Some in the religious right still worried about the GOP's loyalty. In the fall of 1990, Gary Bauer and a group of like-minded activists met in DC's Washington Square Hotel to form a competitor to Republicans for Choice. Since leaving the Reagan White House, Bauer had led the Family Research Council, the newly formed political arm of televangelist James Dobson's political powerhouse Focus on the Family. Vowing "to keep the Republican Party principled on the fundamental issues of life," the meeting attendees planned for a group that was pro-life, single issue, and Republican. The stakes seemed high: as Bauer and his colleagues wrote, "The Republican Party is the only vehicle through which conservatives can govern America."[58]

The new organization, christened the Republican National Coalition for Life (RNC-Life), planned to exploit gaps in campaign finance rules. Because RNC-Life would not primarily raise money for candidates or campaigns, its organizers did not think they were bound by the Federal Election Campaign Act's contribution limits. Instead, the group's leaders would work to influence the party's platform and control the selection of delegates to the Republican National Convention. From the beginning, Bauer and his colleagues had viewed NRLC and its allies with skepticism. Like NRLC, RNC-Life attached great significance to the GOP's official position on abortion. But those behind RNC-Life viewed NRLC's emphasis on electability as suffering from a severe drawback: the moderate candidates it supported would discard the pro-life movement when it suited them. For their part, NRLC leaders saw RNC-Life's focus on the platform as misguided. As Bopp and his colleagues saw it, the GOP platform could be pristine, but that wouldn't matter if abortion foes did not control the Senate and the White House.[59]

While groups like RNC-Life found a way to get around federal campaign finance limits, Bopp deepened his involvement in campaign finance litigation. In March 1991, the First Circuit Court of Appeals sided with him in *Faucher*. The district court had accepted Bopp's argument that *MCFL* permitted bars on corporate independent expenditures only when a corporation engaged in express advocacy. The First Circuit Court of Appeals agreed that the FEC did not have the authority to pass the new regulations and allowed Faucher to put out her voter guide.[60]

Bopp publicized the win within NRLC and celebrated when the Supreme Court declined the FEC's appeal. For the most part, however, campaign finance seemed like a side issue when Justice Thurgood Marshall, another liberal mainstay, announced his retirement. President Bush quickly nominated Clarence Thomas, who had been on the short list for the nomination ultimately awarded to Souter. Thomas had held several positions in the Reagan administration, serving as the assistant secretary for civil rights at the Department of Education before becoming chairman of the Equal Employment Opportunity Commission (EEOC). Bush had nominated him to serve on the DC Circuit Court of Appeals the year before. A Catholic former Black nationalist who still at times admitted to admiring Malcolm X, Thomas believed racism was an intractable feature of American life. From the outset, the Bush administration downplayed Thomas's record on substantive issues. Bush called his life "a very stirring testament to what people can do when they refuse to take no for an answer."[61]

But no matter how much the administration dodged, Thomas's views could not be hidden. He was a regular on the conservative conference circuit, frequently speaking at events hosted by the Heritage Foundation and the Federalist Society, and his lectures identified him as an outspoken supporter of what supporters called a color-blind Constitution. This perspective on the equal protection clause of the Constitution required judges to closely scrutinize (and often invalidate) any racial classification, especially affirmative action programs. Pro-choice groups also insisted that Thomas would work against them. At a June 1987 speech before the Heritage Foundation, the nominee had called *Roe* "a coup against the Constitution."[62] He had gone out of his way to compliment an article published in the conservative magazine *American Spectator* that compared legal abortion to both slavery and the Holocaust. For the leaders of NARAL and NOW, it was not hard to read between the lines.[63]

Nor did anti-abortion groups have any trouble predicting how Thomas would vote. In August, NRLC praised the administration for refusing to settle "on a 'compromise' candidate." Gary Bauer helped launch Concerned Citizens to Confirm Clarence Thomas, a group of conservative organizations that planned to lobby and influence the media on Thomas's behalf. By September, conservative groups ranging from the American Conservative Union to Young Americans for Freedom had endorsed the nominee. Two political action committees, the Conservative Victory Fund and Citizens United, bankrolled a pro-Thomas advertising campaign attacking prominent Democratic senators who opposed the nominee. The campaign revealed that some conservatives cared far more about the Thomas nomination than they did about the goodwill of the Bush administration or the Republican National Committee. The president worried that the ads, which included extremely personal attacks on prominent members of the Senate, would damage the administration's reputation. When the president requested that the ads be stopped, Floyd Brown, the chairman of Citizens United, refused. "What [Bush's advisors] don't understand," Brown explained, "is how bitter people are about Bork."[64]

Conservative support for Thomas intensified after the press leaked accusations made by Anita Hill, an employee who had worked under him at the EEOC. Hill planned to testify that Thomas had repeatedly sexually harassed her while the two worked together, but after her story went public, GOP leaders launched an all-out attack. Utah senator Orrin Hatch accused Hill of acting at the behest of "slick lawyers" from liberal interest groups intent on destroying Thomas's chances of joining the Court. But Hill's accusation was not made in a vacuum. The *Los Angeles Times* reported that other women stood ready with stories of harassment eerily similar to Hill's. Ultimately, the hearings ended without anyone but Hill testifying (the other witnesses, Angela Wright, Sukari Hardnett, and Rose Jourdain, later claimed that Biden's committee had no interest in hearing from them; Biden maintained that the three ultimately decided not to testify).[65]

The Senate confirmed Thomas in a historically close vote, 52-48. The opposition to his nomination made him more of a hero to anti-abortion leaders. NRLC organized a petition demanding that the FBI investigate the source of the Hill leak. As far as *Roe* was concerned, NRLC proclaimed, Thomas's "good Christian upbringing would not fail him when the time came to vote."[66]

It was like a reprise of the Bork battle, but this time, movement conservatives had won. It would be decades before another Republican president nominated anyone so controversial, but the contrast between Bush's two nominees had lasting resonance for the leaders of established anti-abortion groups, especially after the Supreme Court defied expectations by saving abortion rights in *Planned Parenthood of Southeastern Pennsylvania v. Casey* (1992). If the Court had had more justices like Thomas, few imagined that

Casey would have come out the same way. For a decade after that decision, anti-abortion leaders would look for a way to guarantee that GOP presidents picked more justices like Clarence Thomas. That quest brought them to the center of battles over money in politics.

Abortion, Money, and the 1992 Race

The Court agreed to hear *Casey*, a major abortion case, after Thomas was already confirmed. Conservative groups met in January 1992 to strategize about how to argue the case. Those present included leaders of right-leaning organizations like the Heritage Foundation as well as those from newer conservative Christian groups like the American Center for Law and Justice. *Casey* addressed the constitutionality of a Pennsylvania law that contained several restrictions on abortion access, including a waiting period and measures on informed consent, spousal notification, and parental involvement. The Court theoretically could uphold the statute without addressing the central question of abortion rights, but many at the conference focused on arguments for reversing *Roe* outright. NRLC was optimistic, putting out a 1992 fundraising letter that predicted "a major pro-life victory in the Pennsylvania case."[67]

The idea that the Court might overrule *Roe* frightened the Bush administration. Lee Atwater had died of cancer in 1991, but his concerns about the abortion issue lived on. Federalist Society co-founder Lee Liberman, a close advisor of the president's, laid out the administration's view that *Casey* would likely be a disaster for Bush. A constitutional amendment banning abortion, she wrote, was a "loser" for the GOP. Yet Bush and other Republicans relied on pro-life and conservative voters, and without *Roe* as a shield they would have difficulty keeping that constituency if they did not demand sweeping penalties for abortion. Worst of all, as Liberman saw it, would be an ambiguous decision that neither overturned *Roe* nor left abortion rights intact. Such a ruling would be "very dangerous" because it would require the president to talk directly about what abortion law should look like—and he would be "buffeted from the right and the left." Republicans had made control of the Supreme Court a formidable election issue, but by 1992, Bush and the GOP establishment had begun to regret that decision. The promise of conservative judicial nominations had brought together factions with deep disagreements. But the prospect of transforming the Court could motivate the opposition too.[68]

The 1992 Democratic primary signaled that the Court would be a central concern for left-leaning voters. Two of the frontrunners, Bill Clinton and Jerry Brown, had experience as state governors. The third prominent candidate, Paul Tsongas, was a senator from Massachusetts. At a winter NARAL gathering, the Democratic candidates tried to outdo one another in their support for abortion rights. Outgoing, with a voracious intellect, and almost always hoarse from too much talking, Clinton presented himself as a new kind of Democrat, a social liberal not afraid to cut taxes or reform welfare. The former Arkansas governor went out of his way to defend abortion rights, describing *Roe* as "the most fundamental decision in American jurisprudence."[69]

Bush, meanwhile, faced a primary challenge from conservative commentator Patrick Buchanan. Although to the right of the president on virtually every issue, Buchanan drew particular attention to his pro-life record and hostility to immigration. He had shuttled between politics and journalism, working for Richard Nixon and Ronald Reagan and writing a newspaper column. He always loved to get a reaction and delivered his populist stump speeches with a puckish grin. Buchanan needled the GOP establishment, called Bill Clinton a cross-dresser, and used "*New York Times*" as an insult. He made extreme conservatism fun—and that made him dangerous for Bush.[70]

At the start of the year, Buchanan seemed to be gaining on the president, especially in New Hampshire. To defuse the threat posed by Buchanan, Bush sought to reassure social conservatives. He named Oklahoma senator Don Nickles, one of the strongest abortion opponents in Congress, to head the Republican platform committee. Well before the party held any debate on the subject, Nickles let on that it would not change its abortion plank. Partly because of Buchanan, Bush moved closer to pro-lifers.[71]

Campaign finance rules also helped Bush and the GOP establishment. Buchanan had no shortage of enthusiastic small-dollar donors. But the GOP hierarchy was fully behind Bush and gave him access to a wealthier set of supporters. By February, he already had $9 million in his campaign fund. Buchanan reported a little over $20,000. By the end of the primary campaigns Buchanan had raised at least $7.2 million, but Bush had accumulated far more. The GOP establishment proved especially adept at new fundraising strategies. Bush had once inveighed against a strategy called bundling—corporations, wealthy individuals, and others solicited a large number of contributions (capped at $1,000) and then gave them to a candidate. But by 1992 he was threatening to veto a Democratic bill banning bundling if it landed on his desk. The practice had proved profitable for the Republican and Democratic Party leadership. Throughout the 1992 election season, companies like IBM and Goldman Sachs hosted million-dollar bundling events for both parties.[72]

Bush and the GOP leadership used soft money to bury Buchanan. The President's Dinner, an event launched by GOP congressional committees, invited donors to write big checks for the privilege of dining with Bush. In theory, the money went to party building in the states. In reality, it freed up funding for attack ads. Bush also announced Team 100, an initiative to recruit GOP donors who would contribute at least $100,000. By September, nearly 250 had signed up. By November 1992, the national Democratic and Republican Parties together had raised a total of $70 million in soft money, with state parties adding some $50–60 million more. Buchanan disappeared beneath this tidal wave of spending. Party leaders had wanted him to exit the race—and thanks to Bush's fundraising success, they got their wish.[73]

NRLC leaders were not sad to see Buchanan go. He had impeccable antiabortion credentials, but in 1992, it was unimaginable to them that someone like Pat Buchanan would win the presidency. His candidacy was a distraction that could only damage the GOP and make it harder to press for abortion bans after *Roe* was gone. The leaders of groups like NRLC felt vindicated in their reliance on the GOP. The party had put in place a Supreme Court that everyone thought was destined to reverse *Roe*. But when it issued its decision in *Casey* that June, the outcome would seriously damage the relationship between the pro-life movement and the Republican Party.

Casey and Its Aftermath

The *Casey* decision was one of the most widely anticipated Supreme Court rulings in decades, but few correctly predicted its details. In a 5-4 decision, the Court declined to reverse *Roe*. Joined by John Paul Stevens and Harry Blackmun, three Republican-nominated justices, David Souter, Anthony Kennedy, and Sandra Day O'Connor, wrote an opinion saving it.[74] While looking to analogous precedents, O'Connor, Kennedy, and Souter described the abortion liberty as "unique." Here, their opinion echoed arguments suggesting that abortion touched on concerns about equal treatment as well as autonomy.[75] As the three explained: "The ability of women to participate equally in the economic and social life of the Nation has been facilitated by their ability to control their reproductive lives."[76]

But the opinion did not leave *Roe* unscathed. The 1973 decision had invalidated all abortion restrictions in the first trimester, allowed second-trimester regulations only to protect a woman's health, and permitted the state to advance an interest in fetal life only after viability. The plurality (Justices Stevens and Blackmun declined to join this section of the opinion) saved the right to choose abortion before viability but undid the trimester framework, instead adopting the undue burden test, under which courts would invalidate any law that had the "purpose or effect of placing a substantial obstacle in the path of a woman seeking an abortion of a nonviable fetus." In applying this standard, the plurality upheld all the disputed provisions of the Pennsylvania law but one, a spousal notification provision.[77]

The ruling came as an ugly shock to pro-lifers. Wanda Franz, the recently named leader of NRLC, pronounced herself "enraged." Within months, Guy Condon, the president of AUL, resigned and renounced any strategy focused on political leaders and judges. Franz worried that if the pro-life movement lost its ally in the White House, it would take "a decade to recover."[78]

With the support of clashing social movements, Bush and Clinton again put the Supreme Court at the center of the election. Both candidates, however, had to contend with a surprisingly strong challenge mounted by independent candidate Ross Perot. Perot touted unusual policies, from electronic direct democracy to a balanced budget. Having made a fortune in the data-processing industry, he opted out of the public financing system and could therefore spend as much of his own money as he wished. Perot was pro-choice but stressed that he would abide by whatever the Supreme Court said. At the time *Casey* came down, Perot had pulled roughly even with the leading candidates, and in June, he briefly held the lead.[79]

Clinton emphasized his likely Supreme Court nominations—and the strength of his pro-choice commitments—as a point of differentiation. "You have four judges plainly committed to repeal *Roe vs. Wade*, three others nibbling around the edges and a brave Justice Blackmun saying he doesn't know how much longer he can hang on," Clinton stated. "This is one of the things this presidential election is about." He promised to apply a "litmus test" and select only judges who believed that *Roe* was rightly decided. Bush similarly tried to use the Court to energize his base. In a speech before the Knights of Columbus, he vowed to stock the Court with judges who would undo abortion rights.[80]

That August at the Republican National Convention, Bush again promised new judges. Hoping to win over disenchanted Buchanan voters, he also gave his erstwhile rival a prominent speaking slot. Gary Bauer's RNC-Life had already launched a fifty-state delegate selection strategy to dictate who voted on the Republican platform.[81] All of this effort almost turned out to be unnecessary. The president wanted to leave the strict 1988 abortion plank untouched. Several members of the platform subcommittee took extra precautions, presenting technical amendments that shut down debate on the abortion plank before it started. Buchanan became the face of the convention. He railed against radical feminism, criticized working mothers, and denounced efforts to make condoms available in high school. Angela "Bay" Buchanan, Pat's sister and campaign manager, rhapsodized that the platform was identical to the one Pat would run on if he made another try in 1996. Ralph Reed, a young aide to Pat Robertson, gleefully proclaimed that the GOP had delivered "a platform you can take to any church on any Sunday morning."[82]

In New York at the Democratic convention, Clinton similarly emphasized abortion—and control of the Supreme Court. Women sporting "Pro-Choice, Pro-Clinton" shirts and signs filled Madison Square Garden. Many of the featured speakers were pro-choice women, including Representative Pat Schroeder of Colorado, one of Congress's strongest supporters of abortion rights. "It does make a difference who is president," said the keynote speaker, Texas representative Barbara Jordan. "A Democratic president would appoint a Supreme Court Justice who protects liberty, rather than burdens liberty."[83]

NARAL reinforced this message in a national media campaign. The organization's fifteen-second spots emphasized that there was "a single flickering flame—one Supreme Court justice" standing "between us and the darkness." *USA Today* framed the Supreme Court as one of the defining issues of the election. "One changed vote," the paper editorialized, "one new justice, could push the court right or left, or anchor it in the center."[84]

On Election Day, Perot made a strong showing, winning over 18 percent of the vote. Clinton still carried thirty-two states and the District of Columbia and beat Bush by nearly 6 points in the popular vote.[85]

Pro-life groups, already reeling from the verdict in *Casey*, were devastated. While the GOP had strengthened its relationship with the pro-life movement in the lead-up to the 1992 election, voters had rebuked the party. NRLC analyses insisted that the economy, not abortion, had been the major issue, but other pro-lifers began to feel that politicians served no purpose for their movement. Too easily, it seemed, Republicans betrayed their commitments, or else lost.

James Bopp had already come to see campaign finance reform as disastrous. He believed that limits on spending privileged big government at the expense of liberty, protected incumbents from grassroots movements, and made it hard for advocacy organizations to function. Now he grew convinced that pro-lifers' loss in *Casey* was related to campaign finance rules too. The Republican Party opposed abortion, but Bush and even Reagan had never made the issue a priority. Bush had relied on his war chest to push past Buchanan, but pro-lifers had played at most a small role in his fundraising success. In Bopp's view, the anti-abortion movement needed more influence over who won GOP primaries. Judicial nominations would follow from that.

But Bopp was no longer content with piecemeal challenges. After founding his own law firm in 1992, he wanted to take down all campaign finance restrictions. He believed that the more Republicans could spend, the more of them would win, and a bulletproof Republican majority might be willing to confirm judges to overturn *Roe*. And if right-to-lifers led the fight against campaign finance regulation, the anti-abortion movement might prove its worth to a GOP establishment that was beginning to see the abortion issue as a liability. Building influence was no simple thing, but if abortion foes spent more on elections, and if the pro-life movement helped the GOP raise as much money as party leaders wished, that would be a good start.

4
The Big-Money Party

THE RELATIONSHIP BETWEEN THE GOP AND the pro-life movement had been troubled throughout the 1990s, but *Casey* laid bare a deeper division. Haley Barbour, who had won a bruising contest for the leadership of the Republican National Committee, shared Lee Atwater's skepticism about the party's relationship with the pro-life movement. Barbour came to the RNC as one of the best-known lawyer-lobbyists in the nation's capital, and his leadership of the party opened a new chapter for the organization. In the decades since Eisenhower won the presidency in 1952—during which Republicans had controlled the executive branch for all but twelve years—the RNC had largely been an extension of the White House. The wide-open leadership fight that Barbour joined in response to George H. W. Bush's loss in 1992 was almost unprecedented. When he emerged victorious, Barbour pledged to focus on the economy. He urged his colleagues to downplay abortion and welcome pro-choice voters. "We're a broad, mainstream, and diverse party," he said, "and we can't give people the impression that if you don't agree . . . on everything, you're not welcome."[1]

To be fair, Barbour and other RNC leaders understood that Bush's loss stemmed from more than the abortion issue. The president had also been hurt by the slow economy, together with dissatisfaction with the DC establishment. "The electorate is unhappy with the status-quo," reported the pollster Market Strategies. "And in many respects, this unhappiness made it impossible for the President to compete."[2]

But other autopsies confirmed that Bush had hurt himself by emphasizing abortion. To overcome a primary challenge from Pat Buchanan, he had made the issue central to the 1992 convention. Pollster David Hansen found that "the charge that the Republican Convention hurt the President outright, by portraying the Republican Party as too captive of extreme conservative forces, is confirmed by the survey data." While the abortion issue had seemingly cost him only about 1 percent of the national vote, Hansen stressed that the GOP base had not responded to Bush's call to arms. He concluded that "people may be trending away from seeing themselves as pro-life."[3]

In 1993, four prominent senators announced the formation of the Republican Majority Coalition, a PAC meant to change the party's image and challenge pro-life leaders for dominance of the party. Most of the founders of the group, like Pennsylvania senator Arlen Specter, were pro-choice, but other GOP leaders understood the call to make the party more inclusive. Senator John McCain, a steady opponent of abortion, argued for a focus on economic rather than social issues. Barbour announced a National Policy Forum, a series of town halls in which differences on abortion and other controversial issues could be hashed out. The goal was clearly not to reaffirm the party's existing stand on abortion. Party leaders seemed to want the issue to go away.[4]

The Christian Coalition, an increasingly powerful organization of evangelicals that had risen from the ashes of Pat Robertson's 1988 presidential campaign, opposed any change to the party's official position. Ralph Reed, the group's young leader, had come to the Christian Coalition through a series of coincidences. Raised Methodist, Reed was never particularly religious but had long been committed to Republican politics. He campaigned for Gerald Ford before graduating from high school, planned Republican rallies as a student at the University of Georgia, and became the executive director of the College Republicans in 1983. Washington, DC, of all places, was the site of his religious awakening. One night in 1983, while sitting at a Washington bar, he felt a calling to go back to church. The next morning, he drove to services at the Evangel Assembly of God Church in Camp Springs, Maryland. Six years later, he was finishing a doctorate in history at Atlanta's Emory University when he ran into Pat Robertson at George H.

W. Bush's inauguration. Robertson told him about the Christian Coalition and asked him to help launch it. Reed was the perfect choice. Pat Robertson could come across as awkward and doctrinaire. Ralph Reed was composed and almost hip.[5]

Under Reed's leadership, the Christian Coalition downplayed the abortion issue to broaden its base. A growing group of right-to-lifers saw political strategies as potentially pointless; they gravitated to crisis pregnancy centers (CPCs), organizations intended to discourage women from ending their pregnancies. While supporters of abortion rights argued that CPCs deceived patients looking for medical care or abortion services, right-to-lifers contended that CPCs aided pregnant women in desperate need of help. Heartbeat International grew out an existing network of CPCs. Care Net was founded by an evangelical organization that had focused on lobbying. The National Institute of Family and Life Advocates defended CPCs against lawsuits and criminal prosecutions. National Institute of Family and Life Advocates (NIFLA) leader Thomas Glessner believed that the courts and politicians would become less important to the movement's future. He told editors of *Human Events* magazine that CPCs "could virtually halt abortions without changing the law."[6] Even the Alliance Defense Fund (later the Alliance Defending Freedom), a major funder of conservative Christian litigation founded in 1993 by leading evangelicals, initially did nothing to help those who planned to use the courts to decimate abortion rights.[7]

Groups like AUL and NRLC believed the Supreme Court still would overturn *Roe* if the movement played its cards right. James Bopp focused on a passage in the *Casey* plurality suggesting that if the justices reversed *Roe* "under fire," it would damage the Court's reputation. NRLC attorneys read *Casey*'s focus on legitimacy as a signal that the Court paid attention to popular attitudes about abortion. "The most pressing need," Bopp wrote, "is to recapture public opinion on this issue."[8] Thus began a new chapter in pro-life incrementalism. For years, NRLC leaders had argued that most Americans would oppose abortion if only they understood what it really entailed. Bopp acknowledged that the public did not yet support an abortion ban, and so NRLC promoted laws that a majority would already endorse, regardless of how peripheral those statutes were to the pro-life cause. AUL adopted a similar tactic.[9]

Casey also helped to push some abortion foes more fully into the war against campaign finance laws. NRLC leaders saw *Casey* as proof that the Republican establishment felt perfectly comfortable using and then ignoring anti-abortion voters. As a matter of electoral politics, GOP leaders were not convinced that siding with the pro-life movement made sense. If right-to-lifers took the lead in fighting campaign finance limits, Republican leaders might see new value in their partnership. The more pro-lifers could spend on political speech, the more politicians might listen to them. Besides, the Republican Party remained the only realistic vehicle for control of the Supreme Court. Helping pro-life Republicans outraise and outspend the competition would mean better odds of controlling the Court and reversing *Roe*.

But much like the court-centered strategy, a battle against election spending limits profoundly divided the anti-abortion movement. Prior to the mid-1990s, few had criticized Bopp for litigating the issues that were the most central to anti-abortion activists, such as voter guides and limits on ideological nonprofits. After all, a wide variety of anti-abortion groups spent plenty on campaign speech themselves. Phyllis Schlafly, for example, had been embroiled in a campaign finance controversy in 1997. For conservatives, Schlafly was a living legend. She cultivated an image as the classic American homemaker, slim and elegant in pearls, responsible for six healthy children. She rocketed to stardom after the distribution of millions of copies of her book, *A Choice Not an Echo*, in support of Barry Goldwater's 1964 presidential run. In the 1970s, Schlafly became a household name. She launched a campaign to defeat the Equal Rights Amendment to the Constitution, a measure that would have prohibited discrimination on the basis of sex. Although Schlafly herself was a successful lawyer and political activist, she championed the cause of traditional women who believed that equality would destroy their way of life. By the early 1980s, the ERA was dead, and Schlafly claimed responsibility.[10]

By the 1990s, Schlafly had hit retirement age. She held court at Eagle Forum headquarters in a gracious brick building in Clayton, Missouri, where she kept an archive of material on her career. She knew historians would be interested. But if Schlafly was reflecting on her legacy, she was not finished with politics yet. In 1997, she had been dragged into a controversy surrounding Triad Management Services, a DC consulting firm run by Oliver North, the former Marine Corps colonel who had been embroiled in the Iran-Contra scandal, an illegal weapons sale to the Islamic Republic of Iran in exchange for the release of American hostages in Lebanon. In the mid-1990s, Triad worked by locating conservative donors and advising them on how to max out donations under existing campaign finance rules. Some donors contributed to their preferred candidates and then gave money to Schlafly's Eagle Forum, which did the same thing. In 1997, the FEC argued that Triad was a PAC and therefore subject to disclosure requirements, but Triad refused to file the required report. The matter dragged on for nine years. Schlafly wanted the freedom for her organization to raise and spend money as she wished without the kind of controversy that surrounded the Triad affair.[11]

But James Bopp was proposing something entirely different: an all-out war on campaign finance limits, one that would be made a top priority for the right-to-life movement. Schlafly questioned how much influence social conservatives would gain by deregulating campaign finance. She thought that big corporations and wealthy donors might benefit more from looser campaign finance rules than anyone else. Nor was it clear to Schlafly that GOP leaders would be any more likely to ban abortions if right-to-lifers helped them build on their fundraising advantage. Other GOP constituencies, from libertarian litigators to corporations, did just as much or more to challenge campaign finance limits—and might receive just as much credit from the Republican establishment if campaign finance rules were looser. Most important, fights about money in politics seemed likely to divert scarce resources to something that had precious little to do with abortion. Fighting campaign finance laws would make enemies of any politician who favored reform, no matter what that candidate thought about the right to life, while the abortion issue itself was pushed to the side.[12]

New Possibilities

Bill Clinton's election marked a turning point in struggles over both campaign spending and abortion. Clinton was the most strongly pro-choice president elected since *Roe v. Wade* was decided (Jimmy Carter, the only other Democrat elected in that period, had never been more than a lukewarm supporter of abortion rights). And unlike Bush, Clinton had not pledged to veto any campaign finance bill that came before him. Ideas about how to change campaign finance rules certainly flew around in the aftermath of the 1992 election. Clinton proposed outlawing soft money. Members of Congress responded with a proposed ban on political action committees.[13]

As the pressure for reform grew, Bopp redoubled his efforts to convince NRLC to fight all campaign finance restrictions. In 1993, he persuaded his colleagues to join a newly minted coalition opposed to campaign finance limits. Its founders, attorneys William J. Olson and Mark Weinberg, had cut their teeth leading an earlier group, the Coalition for a Free Marketplace of Ideas, that opposed tougher tax regulations on advocacy groups. Olson, a big personality who loved to share quotes from Ronald Reagan and the Bible, ran a law office in the tony suburb of Vienna, Virginia, where he kept a treasured photo of himself as a young man with Richard Nixon. He specialized for a time in postal litigation, but campaign finance intrigued him, and he became a repeat player in the campaign finance debate. His new umbrella group, christened the Free Speech Coalition, included organizations ranging from NRLC to EMILY's List, a PAC that raised money for pro-choice women running for office. By the time Olson got involved, the fight to stop campaign finance regulations was well under way, and it was not a partisan cause. Groups like the American Enterprise Institute had criticized campaign finance reform since the 1970s. In the late 1980s and early 1990s, wealthy donors like Charles and David Koch had begun to put their money into the fight for looser campaign finance limits. Many outside groups believed that their ability to spend determined whether anyone in Washington would take them seriously. Major unions like the AFL-CIO opposed campaign finance limits, as did the ACLU. Conservative groups, including the National Rifle Association and the Chamber of Commerce, also joined the cause.[14]

In 1993, Olson recognized that his beloved GOP was not a reliable ally in the fight against campaign finance reform. It was true that the Republican Party had historically been more likely to oppose campaign finance limits because the GOP had long raised and spent more than the opposition.

Starting in the early decades of the twentieth century, wealthy families, major corporations, and other moneyed interests generally favored the GOP. In the late 1980s and early 1990s, the most outspoken opponents of campaign finance reform, like Kentucky senator Mitch McConnell, were Republicans. But both parties were opportunistic. The GOP enthusiastically backed anything that hurt the opposition. In the early 1990s, for example, the Republicans favored limits on PACs because even business-related ones primarily donated to Democratic incumbents. Polls suggested that voters in both parties liked the idea of campaign finance reform. It was far from inevitable that it would become a partisan issue. It also seemed that reform efforts had stalled indefinitely. A year earlier, a Democratic Congress had passed a campaign finance bill, but Bush vetoed it. Following Clinton's election, Democrats retained control of the House, but a majority opposed the leading proposal, a ban on PACs. Members of the Congressional Black Caucus insisted that nonwhite candidates relied on PAC money to mount competitive campaigns, especially when they represented low-income communities.[15]

But even if the push for reform at the national level was at a standstill, the same was not true of the states. In Minnesota, lawmakers had introduced regulations encouraging candidates to rely on public funding, limiting contributions, and imposing disclosure requirements on groups that made independent expenditures. Challenging these regulations gave Bopp a new perspective on campaign finance litigation. For some time, he had used the legal status quo—particularly the Supreme Court's landmark decision in *Buckley v. Valeo*—to defend anti-abortion ads and voter guides. Following the Minnesota case, *Day v. Holahan*, he believed he could do better than *Buckley*.[16]

The case that sparked this ambitious strategy began the same year the Free Speech Coalition opened its doors, when the Minnesota Education Association, a teachers' union, challenged Minnesota's campaign finance law. Bopp's client, Minnesota Citizens Concerned for Life, wanted to sue too. Federal law prohibited corporations like MCCL from contributing directly to candidates or making independent expenditures from their own treasuries. The law did allow corporations to form a political action committee, but PACs could be difficult to set up and operate. In the 1986 case *Federal Election Commission v.*

Massachusetts Citizens for Life, the Supreme Court had held that the federal ban on corporate campaign spending did not constitutionally apply to nonprofits' independent expenditures. But Minnesota argued that MCCL was not the kind of group the Court had in mind. It made money from a small side enterprise and accepted corporate contributions—both factors the *MCFL* decision had mentioned as potentially disqualifying. But this argument did not worry Bopp. "It is not a corporation's ability to amass a great amount of wealth per se that gave the state a compelling interest to regulate," wrote Karen Sayon, an attorney at Bopp's firm. "Rather, it was a corporation's ability to amass a great amount of wealth unrelated to its political purposes." In other words, Bopp argued, a nonprofit could raise as much money as it wanted so long as the reason donors donated was to support the organization's cause.[17]

In striking down several of Minnesota's regulations in 1994, the Eighth Circuit Court of Appeals went further than Bopp's firm requested. In addition to reasoning that MCCL qualified as a protected nonprofit under the *MCFL* decision, the court also held that Minnesota's contribution limit was unconstitutionally low. *Buckley v. Valeo* had created a distinction between contributions, money given to a candidate or campaign, and expenditures, which encompassed most other forms of election spending. Even though *Buckley* gave states more room to regulate contributions, the Eighth Circuit still thought Minnesota had gone too far. The state had imposed a $100 cap on contributions to political committees or funds, an amount, the court said, that was too low to "allow meaningful participation in protected political speech and association." It also struck down a state system of public fundraising for candidates.[18]

Bopp thought *Day* had opened new possibilities. In the 1980s, he had focused on campaign finance restrictions that most troubled his movement. By 1993, however, he had concluded that almost all campaign finance restrictions harmed anti-abortion groups. In *Day*, for example, he argued that almost all such limits stopped "most non-profit corporations from making any election related expenditures," while the state's public funding scheme "penalized independent expenditures made by pro-life organizations." In Bopp's view, campaign finance rules almost always helped Democratic incumbents and media conglomerates while silencing conservatives like him.[19]

Soft Money and Electioneering

However exciting *Day* might have been, Bopp and the rest of the Free Speech Coalition did not feel good about the politics of campaign finance in the mid-1990s. Scandal swirling around the 1994 midterm election intensified the calls to limit money in politics. Republicans took over the House for the first time since the early 1950s, but Democrats attacked the legality of GOPAC, an organization founded in 1978 to elect Republicans to state and local office in Georgia. By the late 1980s, Newt Gingrich, who became the new House Speaker in 1994, had taken the helm at GOPAC, which began billing itself as "the Republican Party's preeminent education and training center." Before 1991, GOPAC claimed that it didn't use its funds to help federal candidates and thus had neither registered with the FEC nor been subject to relevant disclosure rules. But the FEC argued that GOPAC had been heavily involved in federal campaigns prior to that time; for example, during Gingrich's 1990 run for Congress, the FEC claimed that GOPAC had funneled $250,000 into the congressman's campaign. Although Gingrich was ultimately found not to have violated federal campaign finance law, the GOPAC controversy made Gingrich a symbol of campaign spending. He had been in Congress since the late 1970s, but he had only recently raised his profile. In 1994, his trademark white mop of hair and easy grin were everywhere. He was pioneering a new brand of political combat, full of name-calling, sharp partisan divisions, and made-for-TV moments. After leading the GOP to a historic win, he was an easy choice for *Time* magazine's Man of the Year. Under Gingrich's leadership, soft money poured into the GOP's coffers—$11.5 million to the Senate and House campaign committees between January 1993 and October 1994. Soft money seemed to be the story of the campaign: the parties raised over $80 million of it, breaking the record set in 1992, a presidential election year.[20]

In the aftermath of the 1994 election, Republicans gained a more durable fundraising advantage. For years, they had had better access to wealthy donors and therefore fared better in the race for soft money. Since the early 1980s, however, PACs had primarily donated to Democrats because of that party's apparent stranglehold on the House. Almost immediately after the 1994 election, the positions flipped: PACs aggressively courted Republican members of Congress. To some extent, this shift simply reflected that a new party controlled the House. But because they often represented business or industry, many PACs felt more at home with politicians opposed to regulations and taxation that could hurt corporate bottom lines. As Republicans profited from the flow of political money, the chances grew for a clearer partisan split on campaign finance.[21]

Nevertheless, some prominent Republicans sponsored reform proposals. Pat Buchanan called for reform while prepping for another run at the White House. So did third-party candidate Ross Perot. Republicans also initially found themselves divided by a major piece of campaign finance legislation. In 1995, Senators John McCain, Republican of Arizona, and Russ Feingold, Democrat of Wisconsin, proposed an overarching reform, the Bipartisan Campaign Reform Act (BCRA), a version of which (Shays-Meehan) was also filed in the House. McCain became James Bopp's nemesis in the battle over money in politics. A former navy pilot and POW during the Vietnam War, McCain had established himself as a maverick who sometimes bucked GOP orthodoxy, a self-proclaimed wiseass who did not worry much if he aggravated party leaders. Campaign finance was one of his causes. Skeptics questioned whether his motives were entirely pure. Less than a decade earlier, McCain had been one of the Keating Five senators embroiled in the savings and loan scandal. Whatever his intentions, in 1995, he joined Feingold in proposing a major change in the rules of election spending. Their bill initially had four primary goals: banning soft money, eliminating or heavily restricting PACs, limiting spending on certain political ads, and granting free television time to candidates who were willing to limit spending.[22]

Right away, Bopp and NRLC lobbyist Doug Johnson saw the bill as a dire threat to the pro-life movement. Johnson was something of a legend in Washington. Known for his thick glasses and rumpled suits, he refused to wine and dine lawmakers but was nevertheless remarkably effective—especially when it came to campaign finance. In a letter to members of the Senate, Johnson argued that BCRA would end political speech for everyone but the news media and wealthy individuals. He was particularly worried about the new definition of "express advocacy" written into BCRA. The law, Johnson warned, would define the term "so broadly that citizen groups other than PACs would be effectively prohibited from informing the public about candidates' positions."[23]

It was far from clear that the GOP would answer Johnson's plea to vote down BCRA. For more than a century, Republicans had enjoyed a fundraising advantage over the Democrats—and had generally been more hostile to campaign finance restrictions. But in the 1990s, the GOP's position was less clear. In September 1995, Haley Barbour—worried that opposing campaign finance reform would damage Republican candidates—sounded the alarm when Ross Perot started a tour to promote reform. Many Republican freshmen in Congress had made campaign pledges to back reform, and Perot pushed them to make good on that promise. Barbour convened a meeting of House and Senate Republicans to warn of the dangers of inaction. Republicans in the House, including Representatives Linda Smith of Washington, Lindsey Graham of South Carolina, and Sam Brownback of Kansas, pushed a bill banning out-of-state donations, PAC contributions, and taxpayer-paid mailings during campaigns.[24]

This move by Smith, Graham, and Brownback showed how far support for some kind of campaign finance legislation reached within the GOP. Smith came from Washington State's apple country, and in high school, she had worked part-time in an orchard to help her mother, stepfather, and five siblings make ends meet. As an adult, she considered herself a liberal Democrat until a tax hike on businesses hurt her new enterprise, and she embraced Ronald Reagan. She made opposition to taxes her calling card, but she picked up support from the Christian right based on her opposition to gay rights. By the time she won her congressional seat as a write-in candidate, she commanded the support of a group called Linda's Army: anti-tax activists, gun enthusiasts, property rights zealots, abortion opponents, and small-government devotees. Lindsey Graham's early life was as rough as Smith's. He grew up in the back of the Sanitary Café, a pool hall in the town of Central, South Carolina. His parents died fifteen months apart while he was in college, and he raised his younger sister while attending classes at the University of South Carolina. A natural trial lawyer with a flair for drama, he got into politics after years of active duty as an air force attorney. Like Linda Smith, Graham hated taxes and legal abortion. Brownback, early in his career, presented himself as the second coming of Bob Dole, a moderate Republican who understood midwestern values.[25]

All three swept into office in the Republican wave of 1994. But they were not outliers. Many of the new conservatives in Congress favored campaign finance reform. Incumbents seemed reluctant to change a system that filled their coffers, but opposing reform on the merits was a different thing. Conservative groups like the National Rifle Association and the Christian Coalition had pushed for a filibuster of the McCain-Feingold bill, but many other social conservatives had remained on the sidelines. Ross Perot labeled opponents of reform dirty fat cats, and polls suggested that voters agreed with him. Republicans could hardly shut him up by condemning McCain-Feingold.

Bopp, Johnson, and others within NRLC set out to make the GOP a more reliable voice on campaign finance. Corporations, wealthy families, and business groups had often condemned campaign finance limits, but social conservatives were a different story. Activists like Phyllis Schlafly and Gary Bauer took advantage of openings in campaign finance rules to raise and spend more, but Schlafly's supporters did not always see campaign finance as a priority because the spending of wealthy donors and major corporations dwarfed the fundraising power of social conservatives. Bopp, Johnson, and their allies hoped to make the fight against campaign finance rules a matter of principle—a worthy battle for anyone who favored liberty over expanding government power.[26]

Colorado Republican

In 1996, the Supreme Court gave NRLC leaders an obvious reason to invest in campaign litigation. *Colorado Republican Federal Campaign Committee v. Federal Election Commission* began in 1993 when Jan Witold Baran, a veteran of Republican politics, led the defense of a Republican campaign committee in Colorado against FEC charges that a 1986 attack ad had violated reporting and spending limits. Baran's path to campaign finance work seemed natural. Something of a political junkie, Baran had skipped classes at Vanderbilt Law School to work for the campaigns of both Richard Nixon and Tennessee senator Howard Baker. He had not planned to make law or politics a permanent gig. After graduation, he moved to Washington, DC, with the dream of opening a restaurant. But an offer came that convinced him to quit the restaurant business for good. The Federal Election Campaign Act had just passed, and the GOP asked Baran to help the party understand the emerging field of campaign finance law. Once he got started, he never really stopped. He served as the general counsel for George H. W. Bush's 1988 campaign and for the RNC between 1989 and 1992, but campaign finance became his calling. In *Colorado Republican,* he had a chance to give Republicans even more freedom to raise and spend.[27]

The group Baran defended, the Colorado Republican Federal Campaign Committee, got itself into trouble by spending $15,000 on radio ads against Democratic representative Tim Wirth during his run for the Senate. Under FECA, the committee could spend up to a certain amount on expenditures coordinated with a political party, but the committee had already assigned all of its 1986 limit to the National Republican Senatorial Committee. While the committee maintained that its ad was just a voter education tool (and thus did not create a legal problem), Colorado Democrats argued that because the ad counted as a coordinated expenditure, the committee had violated the law. Under *Buckley*, coordinated expenditures qualified as contributions, subject to spending limits and reporting requirements that the committee had failed to meet. After the FEC filed suit, the committee prevailed in district court, but a federal appeals court sided with the FEC.[28]

Colorado Republican came down in 1996, shortly before Bopp and Baran became founding members of the Federalist Society's Free Speech and Election Law Practice Group. By then, the Federalist Society was unquestionably the leader of the conservative legal movement. In 1996, the group boasted a membership of eighteen thousand and had chapters on 150 law school campuses; and by 1997, it had a budget of $2.5 million. The Scaife and Olin Foundations provided support (others, like the Bradley Foundation and the Koch family, would later follow suit). Within the legal elite, the Federalist Society's attention to campaign finance signaled that the issue had arrived. The Federalist Society also provided a platform for talented lawyers to polish arguments against campaign finance reform. Bradley Smith, a professor at Capital University School of Law, worked with the practice group and quickly became an intellectual hero to many opponents of campaign finance. So did Allison Hayward, a young lawyer who had just completed a clerkship with the conservative judge Danny Boggs of the

Sixth Circuit Court of Appeals. Lawyers like Hayward, Bopp, and Smith would provide the movement against campaign finance limits with intellectual firepower. But social conservatives and Republican voters would not uniformly oppose campaign finance reform just because key members of the Federalist Society had spoken out.[29]

Nor did the emerging conservative media fuel much opposition. Rush Limbaugh had become a conservative celebrity in the early 1990s, and talk radio exploded as the decade continued: the number of talk radio stations increased from roughly three hundred in 1989 to between eight hundred and over one thousand in 1994. Limbaugh did oppose a lobbying reform, but the recently founded Fox News Channel largely deferred to the Republican leadership on campaign finance. The owner of Fox News, Rupert Murdoch, had planned to create a right-of-center news network since 1985. In 1996, he launched a twenty-four-hour news channel. He hired Roger Ailes, a former GOP strategist and NBC executive, to run it after Ailes left his job at America's Talking (now MSNBC). The network fulfilled Murdoch's promise to create a conservative alternative to CBS and CNN, but Fox News did not take a consistent position on campaign finance before the GOP did.[30]

In the mid-1990s, neither the GOP nor conservative media reliably opposed campaign finance regulations. Campaign finance reform could fit into conservative politicians' favorite narratives. A politician like Lindsey Graham might relish the chance to cast himself as a champion of heartland voters hurt by liberal big money. Other politicians put party before all else and concluded that some spending limits might be useful in hobbling the Democrats. Some social conservatives like Schlafly, who were not always connected to wealthy donors, wondered if looser campaign finance rules would primarily benefit wealthy donors rather than unborn babies. Groups like NRLC set out to convince all conservative Christians to oppose campaign finance limits.

A New Breed of Abortion Restriction

NRLC also wanted to convince self-interested politicians of the value of restricting abortion. Anti-abortion incrementalism was not new. For decades, groups like NRLC had chosen restrictions almost exclusively on the basis of what would both erode *Roe* and survive in federal court. But an equally important consideration came to the fore in the mid-1990s: abortion restrictions had to enjoy public support (or at least appear to). Anti-abortion lawyers believed the Court would not reverse *Roe* if the justices thought the public would strongly oppose such a move. Popular restrictions could make it easier for anti-abortion Republicans to win their races, so that they could later put the right kind of judges on the Court. And if GOP leaders questioned the value of an alliance with the anti-abortion movement, popular restrictions could change their minds.

In 1993, a Minnesota NRLC affiliate got a transcript of a talk given by Dr. Martin Haskell at a meeting of the National Abortion Federation, a gathering of abortion providers. Haskell described a relatively uncommon technique, "intact dilation and extraction," whereby a provider would remove a fetus in one pass rather than several. Minnesota abortion foes found the procedure disturbing and used it to argue against a federal law protecting abortion rights. In 1995, NRLC began promoting a ban on the procedure, which it renamed "partial-birth abortion." NRLC graphically described the procedure as one in which "the person performing the abortion vaginally delivers a living fetus before killing the fetus and completing the delivery."[31]

After the GOP took control of the House of Representatives in the 1994 midterm elections, Doug Johnson worked with Representative Charles Canady of Florida to introduce a bill banning the procedure. The bill struck Johnson as a perfect example of the new pro-life incrementalism: a ban on "partial-birth abortion" would win voters' support, convince more Americans that they were pro-life, and make an alliance with abortion opponents look politically profitable for the GOP. At a January 1995 NRLC board meeting, Johnson detailed a strategy to prove that public attitudes had shifted. Rather than expect politicians to favor strong abortion bans, pro-lifers would "try to highlight issues which will shape public opinion to become more sympathetic to our views and policies, forcing the opposition to defend extreme and unpopular positions." In the short term, NRLC would emphasize laws that would "force the [Clinton] administration to 'show its hand' by vetoing popular legislation, thus alienating large segments of the voters, or else alienating his pro-abortion voting block by allowing some abortion-regulating legislation to become law." Bopp and Johnson still favored outright bans and believed that the Court would one day reverse *Roe*. But that effort would take time. Johnson hoped that in the short term, partial-birth abortion bans would increase public opposition to abortion, strengthen pro-life candidates, and hasten the end of *Roe v. Wade*.[32]

Partial-birth abortion cases were only a part of the campaign to influence the GOP. NRLC leaders also attacked campaign finance limits that they believed had made it harder to elect pro-life candidates or influence anyone in office. Bopp challenged a New Hampshire law capping independent expenditures at $1,000, a West Virginia statute that presumed voter guides to be express advocacy if they were distributed within sixty days of an election, and federal regulations broadening the category of express advocacy.[33] Wins in such cases helped establish that anti-abortion groups had the skill and sophistication to help the GOP. So did the emphasis on abortion restrictions, like prohibitions on partial-birth abortion, that enjoyed more public support than an outright ban.[34]

At first, other pro-life groups mostly approved of the growing focus on partial-birth abortion and campaign finance, but there were clear signs of trouble. Judie Brown's American Life League tried to mobilize opposition to NRLC's plan. The passage of time had not made Brown any friendlier to a court-centered strategy. Her three children were grown, so she had more time to invest in her cause. She had been reluctant to give up on Operation Rescue, and in 1994, when Congress passed a federal law protecting access to abortion clinics, Brown sued to stop it. Between 1993 and 1994, however, anti-abortion fanatics murdered two abortion doctors. One of the murderers, Paul Hill, was a member of Operation Rescue. Some in the organization approved of what Hill had done. By 1996, Randall Terry had quit leading Operation Rescue to focus on his radio show and his hatred of Bill Clinton.[35]

Brown had to find another alternative to NRLC's strategy of controlling the Court. She found the fight for a ban on partial-birth abortion especially offensive. Such a ban would not stop anyone from getting an abortion, she thought; at best, it would force patients to use a different method. Brown also believed that the bans sent an unacceptable message: that the value of life in the womb was relative. ALL circulated a "unity pledge" asking pro-lifers to oppose any exceptions to abortion bans and to condemn the partial-birth abortion campaign.[36] Brown also saw no point to NRLC's focus on campaign finance. NRLC leaders argued that looser campaign finance rules meant more influence for pro-life PACs and nonprofits, which would mean more pro-life candidates in office, better judges on the courts, and better odds of reversing *Roe*. Brown believed instead that NRLC was currying favor with the Republican Party—and helping Republicans win—without any proof that doing so would protect the unborn. As it was, Brown thought that the right-to-life movement could demand very little of the GOP. Helping Republicans raise more money would do nothing to change that balance of power.

Brown's unity pledge attracted the support of Focus on the Family and what remained of Operation Rescue. Phyllis Schlafly's Republican National Coalition for Life was also lukewarm on NRLC's strategy on partial-birth abortion. As Schlafly wrote to Doug Johnson: "I am concerned that grassroots people and the media might perceive support for this bill as a move away from our goal of legal protection and toward the incremental regulation of abortion." Internally, Schlafly's group used much harsher language. But for the time being, NRLC successfully headed off a larger rebellion. The National Conference of Catholic Bishops invested heavily in a partial-birth abortion ban. And NRLC effectively promoted the strategy on partial-birth abortion, together with opposition to campaign finance limits, at secret sessions of a coalition known as Life Forum.[37]

Life Forum meetings were begun in 1989 to repair cracks in the anti-abortion movement. By 1996, the gatherings were the nerve center of pro-life strategy. Most leading pro-life groups sent representatives to Life Forum strategy sessions. Held in Washington, DC, or at one of an ever-changing set of airport hotels, the meetings attracted some of the biggest names on the religious right. In 1996, NRLC lobbied Life Forum attendees to embrace partial-birth abortion bans as a practical strategy that would win widespread support and make the pro-life movement look like a political powerhouse. The group's executive director, David O'Steen, promised that with the focus on partial-birth abortion, "pro-life groups will get to do the hammering." O'Steen dedicated as much time to the issue of campaign finance. Insisting that opposing spending limits was smart politics, he circulated NRLC's internal polling data suggesting that most voters wanted

PACs and interest groups to be able to spend money however they wished. Those present at the Hyatt Regency Irvine that October day thought about what O'Steen had to say, but few socially conservative organizations joined NRLC on the front lines of the campaign finance struggle. They thought that fights about money in politics consumed already limited resources needed to defend the rights of the unborn—and seemed more likely to empower wealthy donors and business groups than Christian conservatives.[38]

Bopp and O'Steen also argued that all campaign finance limits were unconstitutional, especially after the Supreme Court's 1996 decision in *Colorado Republican*. The justices voted 7-2 that the Colorado Republican Federal Campaign Committee had not violated FECA by running its 1986 ad against Senate candidate Timothy Wirth. Beyond that, the case fragmented the Court. In a plurality opinion, Justices Stephen Breyer, Sandra Day O'Connor, and David Souter admitted that the committee's ad probably hurt Wirth's campaign, but the Colorado Committee had not coordinated with Wirth's opponent or given him any money directly. That made its spending an independent, rather than coordinated, expenditure. Only coordinated expenditures were treated the same as contributions, whereas *Buckley* had held that independent expenditures could not be capped. Breyer, O'Connor, and Souter saw *Colorado Republican* as an easy case. *Buckley* was the beginning and end of the conversation.[39]

Anthony Kennedy, joined by William Rehnquist and Antonin Scalia, agreed that the committee's ads were an independent expenditure, but he also renounced part of *Buckley*. There, the Court had signed off on strict limits on coordinated expenditures since candidates would have significant control over how funds were spent, much as they did with direct contributions. In Kennedy's view, *Buckley*'s treatment of coordinated expenditures was incoherent, at least when it came to political parties. He reasoned that because parties existed largely to help candidates, their coordinated expenditures should be exempt from regulation, just like candidates' independent expenditures on their own behalf. Clarence Thomas wrote a separate opinion, signed by two other justices, suggesting that all spending limits, whether they involved contributions or expenditures, violated the Constitution.[40]

The Court's opinion in *Colorado Republican* made future attacks on *Buckley* seem likely. For those who opposed any regulation of election spending,

Buckley was far from perfect. The 1976 decision made it much more complicated to give large amounts to candidates directly. *Colorado Republican* signaled for the first time that a plurality on the Supreme Court thought *Buckley* did not do enough to protect spending. Charles Bell, the vice chairman of the Federalist Society's Free Speech and Election Law Practice Group, believed that *Colorado Republican* had lit "the path toward reconsideration of *Buckley*."[41]

But in the short term, *Colorado Republican* seemed to benefit the GOP establishment. The decision freed up party organizations to raise and spend more independent expenditures. Establishment leaders had used soft money to shore up their control of the party, and *Colorado Republican* seemed to make that even easier.

Selling Pragmatism

Money certainly seemed to be flowing when the 1996 election season began. On the Republican side, Senator Bob Dole entered the season with a clear advantage in both name recognition and fundraising. In 1996, Dole asked voters whom they would ask to babysit their children: the flashy, scandal-prone Clinton or the wholesome Republican senator? But Dole was famously difficult. He could be brooding, and he held grudges. As one Senate supporter put it, "Bob Dole never forgives and never forgets."[42]

Dole was also a gifted politician. He could move voters with stories about his struggles as a wounded war veteran and the joys of his small-town youth. He could make sharp partisan attacks wrapped in a message of unity. Dole's competitors included centrist senator Arlen Specter of Pennsylvania, his more conservative Senate colleague Phil Gramm of Texas, magazine publisher Steve Forbes, and populist Pat Buchanan. Dole's candidacy tested whether anti-abortion voters and other social conservatives would pick candidates who best reflected their principles or those with the best chance of success.[43]

NRLC leaders again worked with the GOP establishment to focus anti-abortion voters on picking a winner. Dole was not perfect, but he had a better chance of crossing the finish line than the candidates who were preferable ideologically.[44] The head of NRLC's PAC, Carol Long (later Carol Long Tobias), had her hands full defusing grassroots anger about Dole.

Long had grown up in the pro-life movement. Her parents had helped to organize a chapter of NRLC in North Dakota, and she had been involved with the group her entire adult life. In 1991 she became the group's political director, part of a wave of new female leaders in the group. Long was hardly in love with Dole's candidacy. The Kansas senator emphasized his support for rape and incest exceptions to abortion bans, and even played with the idea of picking a pro-choice running mate. When the Christian Coalition circulated a pledge to primary candidates to maintain strong abortion language in the GOP platform, Dole refused to sign. Instead, after locking up the nomination, he called for a "declaration of tolerance" that would welcome both pro-life and pro-choice voters.[45]

Phyllis Schlafly's Republican Coalition for Life put out a press release warning Dole to change his tune or lose the support of anti-abortion activists. Operation Rescue announced that it would launch blockades in San Diego during the Republican National Convention to push the GOP to take a more uncompromising stand. Long, meanwhile, worked to rally pro-life support behind Dole, arguing that he had not proposed changing the platform's existing endorsement of a ban—a change pro-choice Republicans had requested, without success—but only wanted to *add* a statement of tolerance. Long pitched Dole's move as a way to advance pro-life principles while increasing the odds of success at the polls. Ever since *Casey*, NRLC leaders had emphasized the importance of winning elections, even if that meant choosing a less principled candidate. Dole was being baldly strategic, but to pro-lifers intent on controlling the Supreme Court, the candidate's strategy seemed smart, not weak. He might not have said exactly what pro-lifers wanted, but it was for a good cause. He was doing it to win.[46]

Dole, for his part, sought to borrow heavily from NRLC's strategic playbook. One of his campaign staffers, Brandt Pasco, contacted Doug Johnson for more information on partial-birth abortion. NRLC used partial-birth abortion to establish that "being pro-life gives a candidate an advantage among voters," and Dole wanted to emphasize partial-birth abortion as a way to establish his pro-life bona fides without alienating pro-choice Republicans and independents.[47]

Pro-life groups also helped to make the 1996 election the most expensive to that point in U.S. history. The GOP establishment used its financial edge—and soft money—to help Dole's campaign for the nomination. In a flurry of $1,000-a-plate shrimp dinners and black-tie events, he took the lead in the money race in the summer of 1995, raising $100,000 a day. The donors who got behind Dole were not especially impressed by his policies. Instead, as the *New York Times* reported, his donors wanted "a stake, not a statement." Dole's name recognition and establishment connections made him look like a winner.[48]

Money also helped Dole fend off populist Pat Buchanan, who believed a lack of campaign spending had crippled him in 1992 and was not about to make the same mistake again. In early 1993, Buchanan's campaign founded a nonprofit, American Cause, led by the candidate's sister and campaign manager, Angela "Bay" Buchanan. In 1995, with American Cause ready to spend, Pat Buchanan called on his "brigaders" to return to the political battlefield. By March 1996, his campaign had raised roughly $10 million. While Dole courted donors who expected him to win, wealthy donors like South Carolina textile magnate Richard Milliken gave Buchanan money because they liked his populism. Asked to explain a $1.8 million donation to American Cause, a lobbyist for Milliken & Company explained simply that his boss "agrees with Pat's policies."[49]

Plenty of Republican voters liked what Buchanan had to say. He tapped into the same rage at the legacy media and blue-collar anxiety that gave Rush Limbaugh such impressive ratings. Plus, to the right kind of audience, he was good television. He loved mocking the Kansas senator, remarking that anyone going to a Dole rally "felt like they were walking into a funeral parlor."[50] He was fond of waving a pitchfork (literally) and vowing to fight until hell froze over. Whatever Buchanan was doing, it seemed to be working. In February, he won the then first-in-the-nation Louisiana Caucus and finished second to Dole in Iowa. Then he edged out Dole in New Hampshire. After his New Hampshire win, an elated Buchanan promised a "fight for the heart and soul of the Republican Party."[51]

Buchanan believed that if the most conservative voters rallied around him, the race was his. Although he did outlast other social conservatives, he still lost. Dole beat him in South Carolina and Georgia, damaging Buchanan's prospects. Then, when Dole neared his primary spending limit under the federal matching system, party leaders, most of whom saw Buchanan as unelectable, stepped up to help Dole raise soft money. David Koch, the vice chairman of Dole's campaign, stood ready to pump money into Dole's campaign (the Koch family was Dole's third-largest donor). The Kansas senator could rely on big-dollar donations from agribusiness, real estate brokerages, and investment banks, with the Gallo Winery leading the way. Although Buchanan raised impressive amounts of money following his New Hampshire win, he never came close to catching Dole, whose fundraising advantage probably saved his campaign.[52]

As Dole's survival story suggests, soft money defined the 1996 race, particularly dollars spent on attack ads. The parties raised eye-popping amounts of soft money, ostensibly to strengthen state or local parties—but often to bankroll ads for federal candidates. Researchers at the Annenberg Center at the University of Pennsylvania reported that interest groups had spent between $135 and $150 million on issue ads, political spots that often targeted specific candidates but did not directly tell anyone whom to vote for. The two parties raised more than $262 million in soft money in 1996—roughly three times the total in 1992, the last presidential election year.[53]

But Dole did not have enough money to come close to beating Bill Clinton. He carried nineteen states and lost the popular vote by 8.5 percent. Within the GOP, moderates suggested that abortion had felled Dole, much as it had taken down Bush four years earlier. Carol Long answered with talking points suggesting that Dole had failed not because of abortion but because of issues like education and the economy. Nevertheless, he had lost, and pro-choice Republicans were convinced that abortion was the reason. Absolutists like Judie Brown and Phyllis Schlafly blamed Dole's defeat on his drift to the center. Pat Buchanan had given Dole a scare with a shoestring budget, and Buchanan refused to compromise on abortion (or any other issue). Looking at the Buchanan campaign, Brown questioned NRLC's entire strategy.[54]

Absolutists made a bid to redirect the politics of partial-birth abortion, using the issue to drive away Republicans with different views on *Roe*. In 1997, Tim Lambert, a GOP committeeman from Texas, proposed a resolution for the next big gathering of the Republican National Committee that would deny funding to any Republican candidate who did not oppose partial-birth abortion. Many interpreted the move as a thinly veiled attack on pro-choice Republicans like New Jersey governor Christine Todd Whitman and New York mayor Rudy Giuliani. NRLC stayed mostly mum about the proposal, for obvious reasons. The partial-birth abortion issue was meant to popularize the pro-life movement, not divide the GOP.[55]

The cracks in the anti-abortion movement grew wider after 1996 when NRLC and its leaders put even more emphasis on attacking campaign finance laws. Many abortion foes thought campaign finance battles had nothing to do with abortion. Some grassroots activists could imagine a world in which Congress had banned intact dilation and extraction, the GOP uniformly opposed campaign finance reform, and the Supreme Court invalidated any campaign finance limit it saw. How would that bring the nation any closer to recognizing a right to life?

Creating a Majority for Money in Politics

Dismay about the orgy of spending during the 1996 election season kick-started moribund reform efforts in Congress. Led by Fred Thompson of Tennessee, Senate Republicans announced a probe of 1996 campaign finance violations, originally focused on the president. Pro-BCRA groups like Public Citizen and Common Cause announced a signature drive to renew interest in McCain and Feingold's proposal. Clinton responded by again proposing a soft money ban.[56]

NRLC leaders found it worrisome that the GOP was willing to use the issue to score political points. Bopp, Richard Coleson, and Douglas Johnson went to the 1997 Conservative Political Action Conference (CPAC) in Washington to persuade social conservatives and GOP leaders to lobby against campaign finance reform. Since its founding in 1984, CPAC had grown from a small group of two hundred hardcore activists to a gathering of thousands crammed into ballrooms full of American flags. Bopp felt at home with the CPAC crowd—he had first attended as a young lawyer twenty years before—but he was not sure how his message about campaign finance would be received. Rather than just repeat his usual points about freedom of speech, he now argued that strengthening campaign finance rules would "bring more regulation and more government into citizens' lives, just what liberals want."[57]

In many states, no one seemed to be listening. California followed Minnesota in passing a ballot initiative on campaign finance, and reformers targeted more states. As Congress investigated abuses in the 1996 election, House and Senate Republicans forced party leaders to agree to a broader inquiry that included congressional as well as presidential fundraising. NRLC and other advocacy groups found themselves on the subpoena list.[58]

Panic within NRLC was palpable. Carol Long stressed that neither pro-lifers nor ordinary voters were well enough informed "concerning the threat to free speech" posed by BCRA. In April, Bopp discussed with the NRLC Board the idea of setting up a "legal fund to challenge state election laws." But NRLC leaders struggled to get any guarantee from Republican leaders or pro-life allies that they would join in opposing campaign finance laws. At Life Forum meetings in 1997, Paul Weyrich complained that GOP leaders had downplayed, defunded, and marginalized anti-abortion goals while taking money and credit for casting token votes on the right to life. "I must now say," he bluntly told other right-to-lifers attending the October 1997 Life Forum meeting, "that it was a mistake to facilitate the marriage of the pro-life movement and the Republican Party." The criticism of groups like NRLC was obvious.[59]

But Bopp was hard at work on a new litigation strategy to challenge campaign finance limits and help Republican candidates. Regulators continued going after anti-abortion political ads, voter guides, and PACs by taking advantage of the slippery distinction between contributions, coordinated expenditures, and independent expenditures. To solve that problem, Bopp sought to deregulate contributions too. He consulted with John R. Lott Jr., an economist then visiting as a professor at the University of Chicago. Lott was on his way to becoming a conservative star, an iconoclast famous for articles claiming that allowing adults to carry concealed firearms had significantly cut crime in America. Lott had something to say about campaign finance too. He drew on arguments made by veteran opponents of reform from Yale law professor Ralph Winter to Bradley Smith, but Lott argued that he had the data to back up his points. He asserted that it was impossible to stop the flow of money into politics. If the government limited contributions, donors would just find another way to spend. Lott blamed the cost of campaigns on the size of government. Big government invited people to spend to gain influence, and so campaign finance limits were made to fail. Besides, whatever *Buckley* said, contributions did not lead to corruption. Bopp and Lott argued that voters gave to candidates because of the issues they embraced, not because they expected any quid pro quo. Campaign finance reform rewarded party machines, incumbents, and media conglomerates that could crush small issue-based groups. Spending on political speech was not the problem. It was campaign finance regulation that created "greater corruption," harmed democracy, and ensured that "voters learn less about candidates per dollar spent" than they had before.[60]

In drawing on the work of Lott and others writing before him, Bopp forged a vision of campaign spending meant to draw in a variety of conservatives. Of course, right-leaning activists at places like the American Enterprise Institute had opposed campaign finance limits from the beginning, but Bopp was approaching a more complex conservative movement and a less reliable Republican Party. He framed the shocking price tag of national elections as a symptom of big government and suggested that more regulation meant more corruption. The cases he brought helped convince some politicians and activists that campaign finance limits were unconstitutional. But he also presented them as something no sensible conservative should support.

A More Institutionalized Attack

To institutionalize a plan of attack on campaign finance bills, Bopp cofounded the James Madison Center for Free Speech, a national organization with its headquarters in Terre Haute, in 1997. The town still claimed to have the nation's biggest homecoming parade, but the aluminum and steel plants were gone. The Pfizer drug factory was a shadow of itself. The best news was the expansion of the town's federal prison. If the prison was the most important business in Terre Haute, James Bopp's law firm might have come a close second. Two years earlier, he had purchased the elegant Merchants Savings and Loan building. Now it housed his law firm and the Madison Center, Bopp's home base for an effort to revolutionize campaign finance laws across the country.[61]

While full of NRLC leaders, the Madison Center's original board of directors also had some GOP heavyweights. Mitch McConnell was the group's honorary chairman. Don Hodel, a former secretary of the interior and president of the Christian Coalition, sat on the board. So did Betsy DeVos, a major GOP donor from Michigan. Betsy and her husband, Dick, both came from money and then made plenty of their own. Betsy was the daughter of a billionaire auto parts supplier, while Dick's father ran the marketing company Amway. Betsy had fallen into Republican politics as a college student volunteering for Gerald Ford's 1976 campaign. While educating her four children in Christian schools, she got involved again. She took a special interest in the issue of school choice but was offended by campaign finance limits. "My family is the largest single contributor of soft money to the national Republican Party," she wrote in 1997. "I have decided to stop taking offense at the suggestion that we are buying influence. Now I simply concede the point. They are right."[62]

The Madison Center proposed a multi-pronged attack on election spending rules. Bopp, whose firm did most of the center's work, proposed press releases and articles to change public attitudes, media coverage, and scholarly studies that might sway elite opinion. But litigation remained the centerpiece of the group's work. Bopp explained that the cases brought by the center had four purposes: "(1) restore lost free speech rights . . .; (2) educate the public on the issues; (3) discourage further unconstitutional campaign finance reform efforts; and (4) provide court precedent to attack other laws that limit free political speech."[63]

The center's $1 million 1998 budget allowed it to bring four new cases in addition to the more than a dozen that Bopp was already litigating (over time, the Madison Center would receive financial support not only from the Republican Party but also from leading right-wing donors, including the John William Pope Foundation, the Mercer Family Foundation, the Lynde and Harry Bradley Foundation, and the Dick and Betsy DeVos Family Foundation). The scope of Bopp's early cases revealed the ambition of his campaign. Many of the cases, including *Right to Life of Dutchess County v. Federal Election Commission* and *Klepper v. Christian Coalition of New York*, involved familiar issues: express advocacy and spending by nonprofit corporations. Despite having done fairly well in the First Circuit, Bopp also planned an appeal in *Clifton v. Federal Election Commission*, where the court had held that the FEC's new regulations on voter guides were unconstitutional, but not on the basis Bopp had urged. The FEC had prohibited any interest group creating a voter guide from coordinating with candidates. To avoid coordination, advocacy groups had to either have no direct communication with a candidate or limit candidates to written questions and answers. Bopp had relied partly on the Supreme Court's 1986 decision in *Massachusetts Right to Life*, which carved out protections for the independent expenditures of some ideological nonprofits. But it was tricky to determine whether Maine Right to Life was the right kind of corporation. In 1990, in *Austin v. Michigan Chamber of Commerce*, the Court upheld a ban on direct corporate independent expenditures for nonprofits funded exclusively by for-profit businesses. Maine Right to Life fell somewhere between the Massachusetts pro-life group in *MCFL* and the Michigan Chamber of Commerce; the group accepted token amounts of money from for-profit businesses. The First Circuit Court of Appeals decided that it would not have to resolve whether Maine Right to Life's independent expenditures were protected because the FEC's regulations violated the First Amendment for other reasons—the Constitution barred the FEC from compelling those preparing voter guides to speak a message that they did not believe. But the court said nothing about regulators' theory that it was constitutional to stop corporations from coordinating with candidates in the creation of voter guides. The Madison Center wanted to stop that FEC theory in its tracks.[64]

But the Madison Center's work went further. In part, this reflected Bopp's growing conviction that there was no firm line between contributions and expenditures—and that pro-life spending on political speech would not be protected unless courts struck down contribution limits too. Bopp represented affiliates of Ralph Reed's Christian Coalition and took on contribution limits in Arkansas.[65]

The Madison Center also fought for donor anonymity. In 1996, Vermont had commissioned veteran Democratic pollster Celinda Lake to survey voters about their attitudes about campaign spending and laws limiting it. Lake found that voters worried about outside spending and wanted to learn more about who was behind the ads that had flooded the airways. Vermont passed a law requiring disclosure of who paid for any political ad and the identity of the person on whose behalf the ad ran. The state also required reporting of any "mass media activities," including dollars spent on literature drops, commercials, and mass mailings. NRLC had previously not focused on disclosure rules, but in 1998, Bopp framed the issue as pivotal. "Faced with such speech-chilling statutes and regulations," he wrote, "not-for-profit ideological organizations, such as the Vermont Right to Life Committee, are especially hampered in the exercise of their free speech rights." Bopp saw donor disclosure as an issue that particularly harmed pro-life groups. Because the abortion issue was controversial, some donors would refuse to open their wallets if their identities would be made public. Ensuring donor privacy was important to keep the money flowing.[66]

California offered Bopp his first chance to test his ideas about campaign spending and big government. In 1996, voters had approved Proposition 208. When it went into effect, the law contained fifty or so campaign finance provisions that dictated "who may contribute to political campaigns, how much may be contributed, when contributions can be made, what purposes the contributions may be put to, the contents of various political advertisements and, indirectly, the extent of expenditures." The California measure imposed very low contribution limits, and Bopp's strategy in challenging them hinged on what corruption meant. *Buckley* seemed to assume that corruption was a likely (even inevitable) consequence of a large contribution.[67]

Bopp did not begin by arguing that contributions and expenditures were hard to tell apart—or that campaign finance restrictions did not prevent corruption. Instead, he demanded empirical proof that the government had a corruption problem. The Eighth Circuit Court of Appeals had adopted that approach, and he wanted to see how far it would spread. In January, a district court agreed that Proposition 208's contribution limits were unconstitutional, but not because there was inadequate evidence of corruption. Instead, the court invalidated the contribution limits because they were "set at a level precluding an opportunity to conduct a meaningful campaign." For Bopp, it did not matter too much that the court had not adopted his theory. He had won. And the more Bopp won, the more credibly NRLC could claim that courts, not politicians, would decide what happened to campaign spending limits.[68]

Building an Alliance against Campaign Finance Limits

John McCain, an avowed opponent of abortion, waged a war with Bopp for the loyalty of anti-abortion voters. In the spring of 1998, McCain wrote an open letter to the National Conference of Catholic Bishops asking the organization to endorse reform. He argued that NRLC's focus on campaign finance was not only distracting but destructive. He accused NRLC of being "increasingly less interested in the abortion cause than they were . . . in the pursuit of political power for its own sake." Doug Johnson responded that campaign finance limits would cripple the anti-abortion movement. "To effectively influence public policy," he wrote, "it is essential that we continue to enjoy the right to speak to the public directly." While the bishops did not take a position on the issue, the dispute exposed how deeply the issue still divided both abortion foes and Republicans.[69]

In the spring of 1998, House Republican leaders managed to block a vote on Shays-Meehan, the House version of the McCain-Feingold bill, but reform proponents circulated a discharge petition. If 218 members of Congress signed on, the bill would go to the floor, where enough GOP defectors might vote either for BCRA or for a compromise proposed by Arkansas representative Asa Hutchinson. To defeat both proposals, NRLC put special emphasis on the votes of wavering Republicans. "All pro-life House members," Doug Johnson wrote in an internal memo, "need to hear clearly from NRLC affiliates and other issue-oriented citizen groups . . . that . . . votes for or against [campaign finance] restrictions will be given heavy weight in evaluating the records of incumbent lawmakers."[70]

But the more headway NRLC made on campaign finance, the more some activists protested. Phyllis Schlafly's Republican National Coalition for Life condemned NRLC's decision not to help Linda Smith's Senate bid because of her support for campaign finance reform. Schlafly's group insisted that Smith's pro-reform stand on campaign finance was irrelevant. In voting for BCRA "against strong and often hostile opposition from friend and foe alike because she believes it is right," RNC-Life contended, "Linda Smith has shown the kind of steadfast commitment she will bring to the defense of life in the U.S. Senate." Schlafly had seen enough of NRLC's crusade, and she was not afraid to say so.[71]

Everyone agreed that a Senate filibuster would eventually doom BCRA. "You're more likely to see Elvis again than you are to see this bill pass the Senate," Mitch McConnell proclaimed with glee. Behind the scenes, NRLC invited groups like the Christian Coalition to lobby the RNC to oppose any reform. That effort paid off handsomely. In a months-long study of the issue, the RNC's Task Force on Campaign Finance heard extensive testimony (including Bopp's) and then voted unanimously to reject "the flawed premise that Americans engage in too much political advocacy and the perverse notion that government can be trusted to decide and enforce the correct amount thereof."[72]

Although Bopp hoped that political victories would fuel interest in his court challenges, results in the courts were mixed. While he fared well in an Arkansas contribution case, he lost the first round of the Vermont disclosure challenge. The state required disclosure of the identities of anyone paying for or benefiting from political ads, as well as any communication that "expressly or implicitly advocates the success or defeat of a candidate." A district court interpreted the law narrowly, applying it only to commercials that expressly endorsed a candidate. Bopp believed it could not plausibly be interpreted that way and launched an appeal.[73]

NRLC's strategy, centered on both partial-birth abortion and opposition to campaign finance limits, seemed poised for a reckoning before the Supreme Court. The justices agreed to hear one case, *Stenberg v. Carhart*, involving a Nebraska ban on partial-birth abortion. A second case, *Nixon v. Shrink Missouri Government PAC*, took on one of the many state laws putting low caps on direct campaign contributions. The coming presidential election also put both issues center stage.

The Path to *Shrink PAC* and *Stenburg*

As the Republican primaries heated up, partial-birth abortion and campaign finance topped the national agenda. George W. Bush held the early lead. Fast-moving and constantly upbeat, he came from Republican royalty. He saw most political issues at least partly as moral ones, and yet he came across as easygoing, the opposite of sourpuss Bob Dole. Businessman Steve Forbes, former Tennessee governor Lamar Alexander, former vice president Dan Quayle, and McCain all contested the primaries, but McCain soon emerged as Bush's primary rival. On the campaign trail, McCain trumpeted his record on campaign finance and tried to turn Bush's prodigious fundraising into a liability. By the summer of 1999, Bush had responded by going on record to demand a soft money ban for unions and corporations. Regardless of who won the nomination, McCain threatened to unsettle the GOP's opposition to spending limits, making it doubtful that either party would consistently oppose campaign finance reform.[74]

Bopp felt more optimistic about a major campaign finance case, *Nixon v. Shrink Missouri Government PAC* (*Shrink PAC*). In 1997, Missouri had set a formula that capped contributions to any candidate for state office. Zev Fredman, a candidate for state auditor, joined a right-leaning Missouri PAC in challenging the law. A district court upheld the limit, but the Eighth Circuit Court of Appeals reversed.[75]

Shrink PAC offered Bopp and other lawyers their first shot since *Colorado Republican* at persuading the Court to reevaluate contribution limits. At the end of March 1999, the Madison Center hosted a strategy session for groups planning to submit briefs in *Shrink PAC*. The mood was heady. The American Conservative Union sent its veteran leader David Keene, who had hated spending limits since his days working for Ronald Reagan's 1976 primary campaign. Since then, he had made himself into one of the GOP's most powerful men. He had run ACU since 1984 and advised Dole's 1996 presidential campaign. His power in conservative circles earned him the nickname Baby Doc David Keene, after the iron-fisted former dictator of Haiti. Keene brought John Bolton, who had left ACU to work at the American Enterprise Institute, where he still argued against campaign spending rules. Bill Olson and a colleague represented the Free Speech Coalition. The RNC sent Tom Josefiak, the former chairman of the FEC under Ronald Reagan.[76]

Representatives from the National Republican Congressional Committee (NRCC) and National Republican Senatorial Committee also participated. Craig Engle of the National Republican Senatorial Committee (NRSC) had helped launch one of the first super PACs, the $90-million-per-cycle Republican National Political Action Committee. Allison Hayward, who was working as the NRCC's counsel, had become one of the best-known members of the Federalist Society's Free Speech and Election Law Practice Group. Hayward's husband, Steven, was a conservative author then affiliated with Georgetown University and the American Enterprise Institute. Allison was the star when it came to money in politics. Steven would later joke that he would not even discuss the subject because he had a wife for that.[77]

The lead counsel for Shrink Missouri Government PAC, Bruce La Pierre, a veteran constitutional litigator and professor of law at Washington University in St. Louis, symbolized the extent to which opposition to campaign finance was still neither partisan nor conservative. La Pierre had deep ties to the ACLU and had received an award from its Eastern Missouri chapter. In addition to campaign finance, he took an interest in school desegregation and had served as a special master in litigation to desegregate St. Louis's schools. Another attendee, Steve Shapiro, the ACLU's legal director, shared La Pierre's point of view. The son of civil servants, Shapiro was a dedicated liberal whose first political memory was the election of John F. Kennedy. By the late 1990s, he had established himself as "the Mick Jagger of civil liberties," leading the ACLU's work on everything from immigration to gay rights.[78]

La Pierre presented the *Shrink PAC* amici with several options. If attorneys wished to be cautious, they could simply shine a light on the deficiencies of Missouri's law. More ambitiously, they could follow the Eighth Circuit's approach and demand actual proof of corruption. La Pierre also floated the possibility of asking the Court to reverse *Buckley*. One attendee worried that the Court would not move so fast, raising "the danger of making the Supreme Court recoil as it did [on abortion] in *Casey*." Others responded that opponents of spending limits "should keep in mind that we do not get to pick our shots very often." La Pierre ultimately opted for a middle-ground approach, insisting that an interest in corruption had to be more than "merely conjectural." Shrink PAC would contend that to regulate contributions, a state had to develop substantial, objectively reasonable evidence of corruption—and proof that a spending limit mitigated that harm in a "direct and material way."[79]

Bopp was intrigued by the possibility of eliminating *Buckley*. He believed there was no coherent difference between contributions (defined as money given directly to candidates) and any other campaign expenditure. A "contribution will very likely result in the very same message as an independent expenditure, and indeed, one that is more favorably placed in the political marketplace," he wrote in a strategy memo. What mattered was "the quantity and diversity of speech in the political marketplace." It made no difference where that speech came from or whether the money that enabled it went directly into a candidate's coffers.[80]

In support of this argument, Bopp wrote that the framers of the First Amendment would have abhorred contribution limits. But he believed those limits had become more damaging than ever. "Efforts to regulate have been likened to stopping the flow of a river," he wrote. "One way or another, water diverts to a different course. The low contribution limits have channeled unspent money into independent expenditures, . . . money laundering, and family bundling." To make matters worse, contribution limits undercut the most effective method of political involvement. "Individuals are working more, and thus have far less free time to devote to activities such as working for a campaign," he stated. "Thus, sometimes, the only meaningful way an individual may participate in, and associate with, a campaign is through his or her campaign contribution." Ultimately, Bopp, like La Pierre, did not think the time was right for a direct hit on *Buckley*. Nevertheless, *Shrink PAC* inspired a vision of post-*Buckley* law that would carry forward in the years to come.[81]

While *Shrink PAC* was pending, the Court agreed to hear *Stenberg v. Carhart*, a challenge to a state partial-birth abortion ban. Dr. LeRoy Carhart, a physician who performed the procedure, sought a declaration that the law violated the Constitution. In a 1998 ruling, Nebraska judge Richard Kopf sided with Carhart. A three-judge panel of the Eighth Circuit Court of Appeals struck down the law in its entirety.[82]

Focusing on partial-birth abortion made sense to NRLC leaders no matter what the Court did. Just a decade earlier, the organization had struggled with massive debt and political irrelevance. Partial-birth abortion had fueled its rise to the point that *Fortune* magazine ranked NRLC as one of the ten most influential DC lobbies for several years running. Doug Johnson, who had become one of the most significant voices on Capitol Hill, argued that "focus groups and polls show that the knowledge of partial-birth abortion has turned many Americans away from support for abortion in general." Perhaps most important, partial-birth abortion helped Republicans win elections. "Whatever the Court does," Johnson stressed, "the most important single point to get across in our response is the fact that Al Gore opposes state and federal bans on partial birth abortion."[83]

Bopp's campaign finance strategy wove together constitutional and political arguments. He built conservative groups' support for his position on campaign finance by defending them when they got in trouble with the FEC. The most prominent case of this kind involved Ralph Reed and the Christian Coalition. The FEC had sued the Christian Coalition in 1996, arguing that it had violated federal campaign finance laws in 1990, 1992, and 1994. Taking on such a high-profile case helped Bopp convince social conservatives that campaign finance rules were not in their best interest. The case also gave him his first crack at persuading the DC Circuit Court of Appeals—the circuit that oversaw most advocacy organizations and party committees—to reject the FEC's new approach to express advocacy, which the FEC defined to include any speech with "the intended effect" of endorsing or condemning a candidate. The FEC similarly argued that voter guides prepared in consultation with a candidate counted as illegal corporate in-kind contributions.[84]

The district court rejected the FEC's definition of express advocacy and concluded that only one of the Christian Coalition's mailings, a letter sent by the Georgia Christian Coalition about the 1994 Georgia primary, met the stricter definition used in *Buckley.* When it came to coordinated expenditures, Bopp had wanted the court to hold that the FEC could limit the Christian Coalition's independent expenditures only when there was express advocacy, no matter how much coordination went on behind the scenes. The court declined this invitation, reasoning that an opposite holding would "open the door to unrestricted corporate or union underwriting of numerous campaign-related communications that do not expressly advocate a candidate's election or defeat." But the court also rejected the FEC's definition of coordination, which applied to any consultation between potential spenders and campaigns. Instead, the court held that an expenditure would be coordinated only if there was "substantial discussion or negotiation" about the content, timing, or intended audience of a communication. *Christian Coalition* was not a complete victory, but Bopp argued that after the ruling, "all corporations [could] rest a little more securely." This framing was no accident. Taking cases like the Christian Coalition's made it easier to suggest that campaign finance laws hurt all GOP constituencies, from for-profit corporations to religious right groups.[85]

Bopp also worked to strengthen the bond between his movement and the GOP by helping congressional Republicans outraise and outspend the opposition. In advance of the 2000 election, he helped to popularize so-called 527 committees. The tax-exempt committees, which got their name from the part of the federal tax code that created them, were formed to influence federal, state, or local races. The legal basis for 527s had existed for decades, but Bopp had considerable success in convincing Republicans to take advantage of them. He argued that if these groups did not explicitly advocate for the election or defeat of specific candidates, they would have the right to raise unlimited amounts of money from individuals, corporations, and unions without disclosing their donors' identities. Bopp represented the Republican Majority Issues Committee (RMIC), one of the first 527s, started by Texas representative Tom DeLay to help vulnerable House Republicans. DeLay was a savvy dealmaker who represented suburbs from Houston to Sugar Land, a landscape of megachurches, McMansions, and malls. The son of a Texas wildcatter, he had made his money exterminating fire ants and scorpions. He entered politics because he hated the regulations that limited the kind of chemicals he could spray. He hated campaign finance limits too. He hosted top-dollar fundraisers in vintage railroad cars. Oil companies, tobacco corporations, guns rights advocates, pharmaceutical executives, and bankers happily paid the price to enter the most exclusive railroad car, "the Cloakroom," where they could hobnob with DeLay. In addition to the $3.5 million for his leadership PAC, he pledged to raise another $25 million for GOP candidates for Congress through RMIC and other 527s. RMIC helped make Bopp the go-to legal advisor for conservatives seeking to start their own 527s. The ties between NRLC and the Republican Party were as close as they had ever been.[86]

But the fight against campaign finance limits took a hit when the *Shrink PAC* decision upheld Missouri's law. Shrink PAC had emphasized a lack of empirical evidence that Missouri had a real problem with corruption. In rejecting this argument, the Court defined corruption more broadly than *Buckley* seemed to. *Buckley* had focused on quid pro quos. But David Souter's majority opinion maintained that corruption is "not confined to bribery of public officials but extends to the broader threat from politicians too compliant with the wishes of large contributors." If this counted as corruption, then Missouri could identify plenty of it.[87]

Nor did the Court distinguish Missouri's caps from the ones upheld in *Buckley*. Shrink PAC suggested that inflation had made *Buckley*-era contribution limits a joke. The majority framed this as irrelevant. What counted was not "the power of the dollar but the power to mount a campaign with all the dollars likely to be forthcoming."[88] Only three dissenters questioned the wisdom of *Buckley*. Opponents of spending limits were devastated. Russ Feingold, one of the prime sponsors of BCRA, argued that *Shrink PAC* "greatly advanced our efforts to reform our elections."[89]

In the summer of 2000, the Court dealt NRLC another blow, striking down Nebraska's ban on partial-birth abortion. Those on opposing sides of the abortion issue had contested the need for a health exception in Nebraska's bill. Dr. Carhart argued that in some circumstances, dilation and extraction would best protect the health and fertility of certain patients because it required fewer passes with a sharp instrument. Nebraska responded that the benefits and even safety of dilation and extraction were uncertain. The majority concluded that the Constitution required such an exception to protect women from "an unnecessary risk of tragic health consequences." Even if proponents of a health exception were wrong, requiring an exception would "simply turn out to have been unnecessary." *Stenberg* also concluded that Nebraska had outlawed not just dilation and extraction, the procedure most often labeled "partial-birth abortion," but also dilation and evacuation, the most common second-trimester procedure. As a result, Nebraska had unduly burdened women's right to choose.[90]

For NRLC, the bad news did not stop there. That summer, Bill Clinton signed into law an amendment to the Internal Revenue Code requiring 527s to disclose their donors and expenditures. Bopp's 527 clients mulled a constitutional challenge. But another Vermont case put NRLC and its allies on the defensive. It turned out that reformers too believed they could do better than *Buckley*.[91]

Several years earlier, Vermont had introduced what was arguably the nation's most comprehensive campaign finance bill, and a group of plaintiffs, Bopp among them, challenged its constitutionality. The National Voting Rights Institute, a Boston-based group focused on election law, intervened on behalf of several state advocacy groups defending the Vermont law. In their case, *Landell v. Sorrell*, reformers took their shot at *Buckley*. But whereas Bopp and his allies argued against Vermont's low contribution limits, the *Sorrell* defendants contended that the government should have even more power to restrict expenditures. Vermont first insisted that if the Court wanted to curb big money in politics, then expenditure limits should be fair game. But the state and the intervenors also identified new compelling interests: allowing officeholders to spend more time doing their jobs rather than raising money, preserving faith in democracy, allowing those without vast sums of money to access politicians, and diminishing the importance of political ads. The district court struck down Vermont's expenditure restrictions, upheld its low contribution limits, and invited the Supreme Court to take up the case. For the time being, it seemed, the constitutional campaign finance wars had been fought to a draw. Both sides detested *Buckley*, but unless the Court stepped in, everyone was stuck with it.[92]

5
Corporate Free Speech

THE FALL OF 2000 WAS SLEEPY IN Terre Haute, with little on the horizon beyond the annual Wabash Valley Classic, a high school basketball tournament that brought in carloads of parents from across the state. James Bopp was too busy to think about basketball. He was hoping to break down the difference between contributions and expenditures—and let nonprofits use both to fund more political speech. That October, he was working with North Carolina attorney Paul "Skip" Stam to challenge a federal law that barred corporations from donating directly to candidates. In 1986, in *Federal Election Commission v. Massachusetts Citizens for Life*, the Court had concluded that the free speech clause of the First Amendment protected independent expenditures by certain ideological nonprofits. In *Federal Election Commission v. Beaumont*, Bopp and Stam insisted that the FEC also could not constitutionally limit nonprofits' *contributions*—money given directly to candidates or campaigns. If nonprofits did not distort elections, then why could the government limit their spending at all?[1]

But the Court had long treated contributions differently from expenditures. Expenditures included any money, including for ads, party building, or bumper stickers, not given directly to a campaign. By contrast, if someone gave money directly to a candidate or a campaign, the justices assumed that the risk of corruption ran much higher. In the past, however, the Court had created broad First Amendment protections for nonprofits. By focusing on "contributions by . . . not-for-profit ideological corporations," Bopp hoped to erode the justifications for all contribution limits.[2]

He also planned to whittle away at the government's corruption-based justification for any campaign finance law. The Court had recently flirted with a broader idea of corruption: one that included efforts to buy influence. *Beaumont* gave Bopp the chance to fight for a narrower definition.[3]

Bopp won in the district court, and less than a week before Halloween, Judge Terrence William Boyle blocked the FEC from enforcing its contribution limits against North Carolina Right to Life. Stam told the press he and Bopp would keep up the fight against incumbents, big-money interests, and the party machines that benefited from campaign finance regulations. "Politicians," he noted, "just can't keep their hands off people who want to talk about politicians."[4]

From a Bush Win to *Colorado Republican II*

While *Beaumont* was pending, George Bush, the former governor of Texas, was on a campaign spending spree. Bush became famous for discussing his Christian faith. He could speak in the vernacular of evangelical Protestants and often described his own conversion experience on the campaign trail. Many absolutist abortion opponents still did not trust him. He refused to commit to nominating justices who opposed *Roe v. Wade*, reiterated his support for abortion access in cases of rape and incest, and repeatedly acknowledged that good people could disagree about abortion. He did not stumble on this framing by accident. Karl Rove, his chief campaign strategist, helped him with it.[5]

In some ways, Rove owed his political life to Lee Atwater. If Atwater wanted to be a rock star, Karl Rove wanted to be a policy guru. The two had gotten close in the summer of 1973, when Rove ran to lead the College Republican National Committee, touring the country in a Ford Pinto. Atwater was his campaign manager. But Rove had rough edges: at nineteen, he had broken into the office of Alan Dixon, a candidate for Illinois state treasurer, stolen a thousand sheets of campaign stationary, and printed fake rally flyers promising "free beer, free food, girls, and a good time for nothing." The incident resurfaced in 1973 during Rove's campaign to lead the

College Republicans. Atwater pleaded with the RNC chairman, George H. W. Bush, to overlook the Dixon incident. He also begged Bush to pick Rove over his competitor, Terry Dolan, after both won different votes to lead the College Republicans. Atwater brought Rove into Bush's circle, a development that would define Rove's career.[6]

Rove fell in love with direct-mail marketing in the 1970s. A good direct-mail marketer had to know his numbers, know his customer, understand the fault lines of American politics, and know how to work them. Rove, who was very good, helped Republicans engineer a takeover of Texas and put George W. Bush in the governor's mansion. Now, he wanted to apply those principles to the GOP presidential primary. He worked with pollsters like Fred Steeper to inch Bush past his main competitor, John McCain. Steeper recognized that McCain's emphasis on campaign finance had boosted his poll numbers. "McCain's claim is basically that I'm going to challenge money/special interest influence and then do all the other things [Republicans] do," wrote one of Steeper's staffers. "This 'me, too' positioning makes it tough for us to get any issue traction against him." Playing down the abortion issue made sense when Bush could rely on his faith to signal sympathy with the movement. Rove and his allies pursued a similar plan for campaign finance. If the public supported changes to the law, Bush would not oppose them, at least not openly. Instead, the campaign would position McCain as a hypocrite. "The fix is going to have to include casting some doubt on McCain's sincerity," wrote one staffer.[7]

Bush also tried to fend off McCain's challenge by burnishing his own credentials as a pragmatist. Focusing too much on abortion would risk portraying McCain as the sensible one. As one of Rove's team members wrote, the plan was to emphasize that "we have a track record for bipartisanship and effective leadership while McCain has a record of recalcitrant opposition."[8]

NRLC endorsed Bush early because he looked like a winner, and he raised money like one too. Over four months in 1999, Bush raised $36.3 million, smashing records set for entire primary seasons. Despite that war chest, populists still tried to test the establishment's hold on the party. Pat Buchanan launched another presidential campaign, this time seeking the nomination of Ross Perot's Reform Party. So did Gary Bauer, who had been the head of the Family Research Council. Both men's sputtering campaigns soon made it seem that the GOP had turned its back on the brand of populism that had seemed so popular in 1996. If anyone remembered Bauer's campaign, it was for a pancake-flipping contest hosted by Bisquick for all GOP primary candidates. When it was Bauer's turn, he tossed his pancake too high, and in his efforts to retrieve it, fell backward off the stage and disappeared behind a curtain. Buchanan hardly covered himself in glory either. In the Reform Party nomination contest, he competed against real estate mogul Donald Trump and John Hagelin, a physicist associated with the U.S. transcendental meditation movement. Hagelin, who served as chair of the physics department at Maharishi University of Management in Iowa, had run in 1992 and 1996 for president as a fringe candidate for the Natural Law Party, which was affiliated with Maharishi Mahesh Yogi and transcendental meditation. Trump dropped out after violent confrontations between Hagelin and Buchanan supporters dissolved into chaos. The two sides sent opposing delegate slates to the Reform Party convention, forcing a court to decide who would represent the party. Buchanan, the eventual nominee, ended up with fewer than 450,000 votes, a far cry from his 1996 showing. Bush's strength made the GOP establishment look untouchable, especially after Buchanan flamed out.[9]

But concerns about campaign finance did not fade away. The soft money flooding the election gave parties even more financial pull. That year, for the first time, national party organizations spent more than candidates on television advertising: $79.9 million to $67.1 million. Together, Republican and Democratic national fundraising committees raised over $392 million in soft money—nearly twice the amount raised in 1996—with Republicans beating the Democrats' soft money haul by nearly $36 million.[10]

Bush needed every dollar to beat Al Gore. The GOP nominee's margin of victory was razor thin—so close that a recount was begun in the deciding state of Florida. James Bopp, his law firm, and Bush's counsel developed an argument that the recount procedures violated the equal protection clause of the Constitution, and Bush's attorney presented that argument to the Supreme Court. The justices agreed that the recount violated the equal protection clause but, more controversially, a majority concluded that no constitutional solution to the problems with the recount could be found in time. Although NRLC's favored candidate won, McCain's unsuccessful run for the GOP nomination had increased the visibility of campaign finance reform proposals. Democrats, many of whom favored reform, picked up several House seats and four Senate seats, creating a fifty-fifty split in the upper chamber.[11]

In April 2001, despite intense resistance from NRLC and its allies, the Senate passed a new version of the McCain-Feingold bill. Doug Johnson pumped out letters to Congress criticizing the bill as preventing ordinary citizens from participating in the political process. It seemed likely that BCRA would become law if the House could vote on it, but Senate Majority Leader Trent Lott refused to send the bill to the House.[12]

Lott's decision seemed even more consequential after the Supreme Court threw cold water on plans for a quick strike on campaign finance reform. Years earlier, the Colorado Republican Federal Campaign Committee had run a negative ad against Democratic Senate candidate Tim Wirth. In *Colorado Republican I*, the Court held that the committee had not coordinated with Wirth's opponents and therefore had not violated any federal law. But in 2001, the committee was back with a star team of lawyers that included Jan Baran, Carol Laham, a veteran of both *MCFL* and *Colorado Republican I*, and Tom Kirby, a Louisiana State University graduate who litigated cases on copyright and campaign finance. Baran and his colleagues asserted that even if a party coordinated its spending with a candidate, the First Amendment should protect it. Political parties existed to get candidates elected, and therefore any limit on coordination with candidates imposed a serious burden on parties' freedom of expression. Besides, because parties' and candidates' interests were so closely aligned, coordination between the two was not a source of corruption.[13]

The government responded that coordinated expenditures made a mockery of efforts to limit corruption. If donors could not give massive sums to candidates for federal office, they should not be able to circumvent the rules simply by giving an equal sum to a political party for it to funnel to a campaign. The district court and the Tenth Circuit had sided with the committee, but the Supreme Court reversed.[14]

In a 5-4 decision, the justices upheld restrictions on political parties' coordinated expenditures. The majority rejected the claim that parties would be ineffective if they could not coordinate with candidates. Parties had done fine influencing elections for decades while coordinated spending was prohibited. The Court reaffirmed that lawmakers could treat coordinated spending as a contribution and impose strict limits on it.[15]

For opponents of campaign finance reform, *Colorado Republican II* sent a chilling message. The Court not only allowed limits on coordinated spending by parties but also seemed to embrace one of the reformers' justifications for campaign finance limits. McCain and his allies often called for tough new rules to stop donors from circumventing existing caps. The Supreme Court also seemed to be looking for similar loopholes. If Congress ever passed the McCain-Feingold bill, it seemed possible that the Court would give it a warm reception.[16]

An Alternative to Bans on Partial-Birth Abortion

NRLC and its allies soldiered on, while also remaining committed to bans on partial-birth abortion. In 2001, it seemed hard to imagine the justices upholding a ban identical to the one they had just struck down in *Stenberg v. Carhart*. Nevertheless, when lawyers for NRLC, the Christian Coalition, and the National Conference of Catholic Bishops held a strategy discussion immediately after that decision, everyone favored passing a retooled federal ban on partial-birth abortion.[17]

But establishment anti-abortion groups' dual focus on campaign finance and partial-birth abortion remained intensely controversial. In the late 1990s, attorney Harold Cassidy launched the National Foundation for Life, a new legal initiative to establish a right to life. Cassidy had spent most of his life in New Jersey's horse country and hated media attention. He had no desire to appear in any history book. The irony was that he fully believed that he was changing the fate of legal abortion in America. His parents, both Democrats, had nurtured his commitment to protecting "the little guy," and he had a talent for putting himself at the heart of big cases: first the criminal defense of boxer Rubin "Hurricane" Carter, then Mary Beth Whitehead, a working-class surrogate mother locked in a vicious custody fight. Whitehead's case stayed with Cassidy longer than most. Something about motherhood gripped him.[18]

Cassidy later made motherhood the core of his work. He represented surrogates and birth mothers seeking relationships with children adopted by other people. By 1990, his ideas about motherhood had converted him from a supporter of abortion rights into one of the pro-life movement's most dogged defenders. He came to believe that abortion cheated women of their most precious constitutional right—the liberty to be mothers. But the more Cassidy got into abortion work, the more NRLC's strategy struck him as stupid. Focusing on campaign finance, working so closely with the GOP, and favoring incremental restrictions that played well at the polls got the anti-abortion movement almost nothing, and yet NRLC did not change course.[19]

Cassidy worked with a group of Catholic and evangelical Protestant pro-lifers who did not invest at all in the campaign finance battle. He did not take cues from focus groups or polls. He proposed, instead, to highlight what he saw as scientific evidence of fetal personhood and to stress that abortion violated a woman's fundamental right to enjoy a relationship with her unborn children. This strategy won the support of leading pro-life academics like Robert George at Princeton.[20]

Jay Sekulow, the lawyer leading Pat Robertson's American Center for Law and Justice (ACLJ), supported Cassidy too. Sekulow had worked for the Internal Revenue Service after graduating from law school and then gone into business flipping historic properties on behalf of wealthy investors. After tax regulations changed and his real estate interests collapsed, he filed for bankruptcy but then quickly reinvented himself in the 1990s as a defender of clinic blockaders like Randall Terry. His work caught the attention of televangelist Pat Robertson, who asked him to head a new legal project, ACLJ. There, Sekulow made himself into a conservative media personality and notched several wins in the Supreme Court. The National Institute of Family and Life Advocates, a group that provided legal advice to crisis pregnancy centers, also threw its support to Cassidy.[21]

Cassidy planned to use expert testimony and the availability of DNA technology to "compel the Court to decide whether the child possesses his or her own rights, an issue the Court has never directly decided." National Foundation for Life leaders also stressed that the existence of "a mother-child bond . . . was never challenged in *Roe* or *Casey*." The support of groups like ACLJ and NIFLA showed that many conservatives still doubted the wisdom of relying on the GOP to control the Supreme Court.[22]

NRLC lawyers remained committed to partial-birth abortion bans. When Betsy DeVos received a funding request from Cassidy, she asked James Bopp to review it. Bopp did not mince words. "It is not that they [the Court] don't know about the humanity of the unborn," he wrote. "It's that they just don't care." DeVos declined the funding request, but Cassidy's proposal attracted broad support. Many abortion foes had never believed in NRLC's incremental approach, or in tying the pro-life cause to the battle over money in politics.[23]

Those who championed so-called natural law strategies harbored similar doubts about the leadership of the anti-abortion movement. Natural law posited the existence of a body of unchanging moral principles, not of human invention, governing all human conduct. Pro-life champions of natural law often referred at least partly to religious understandings of natural law, including those developed by St. Thomas Aquinas. More recently, pro-life scholars like Germain Grisez, John Finnis, and Robert George had tried to develop a comprehensive approach to natural law. These analyses did not stop with abortion. George, for example, dealt with gay rights, religious liberty, the separation of church and state, and complementarity—the idea that each sex served a unique but equally important and respected role in the family and in society.[24]

As frustration with larger anti-abortion groups mounted, some abortion foes wove natural law into alternative political strategies. Hadley Arkes, a natural law scholar at Amherst College, proposed a federal law banning the killing of a child who survived abortion. He had been working since 1992 on creating a grand theory of conservative constitutional interpretation and had built a deep relationship with Richard John Neuhaus, the Catholic priest who founded and oversaw the conservative, ecumenical religious journal *First Things.* A brilliant preacher's son, Neuhaus had begun his public life as a Lutheran pastor and passionate supporter of the civil rights movement. Over time, he came to believe that the Christian left had traded in civil rights for an agenda of cultural revolution, including support for abortion rights. He began writing against the abandonment of what he called "first things," the basic ingredients of any society that recognized the gospel. That writing brought Neuhaus into both the Catholic Church and the political right. Arkes, who had been raised Jewish, perceived the *First*

Things crew as a family, and his place in it as "magnificently right." He spent most of his life far from the tumult of Washington, DC, teaching political science in the green hills of Amherst, Massachusetts. But by 2000, hungering for something more practical, he founded the James Wilson Institute on Natural Rights and the American Founding. The Wilson Institute held events for law students, appellate lawyers, and federal judges, all in an effort to change how conservatives approached the Constitution.[25]

With the Born-Alive Act, Arkes wanted to try changing the law. In theory, if a doctor killed a living child after an attempted abortion, virtually every state already treated that act as murder—and in any case, there were almost no reports of infanticide of this kind. Still, Arkes believed such a born-alive bill would be the best first step toward securing fetal rights. He first outlined his proposal in a 1999 article in the conservative magazine *Weekly Standard*, where he contended that a ban on partial-birth abortion was not enough. "The most decisive thing that Congress could do," he wrote, "is erect that simple bar to infanticide by insisting that the child who survives abortion be protected."[26]

Arkes soon reached out to Representative Charles Canady of Florida and Senator Rick Santorum of Pennsylvania, the lawmakers leading the charge on a federal partial-birth abortion ban. "The people who are trying to advance the pro-life cause," Arkes wrote Neuhaus, "simply cannot be passive in this case without our seriousness being questioned."[27] Doug Johnson of NRLC considered Arkes's proposal both unnecessary and distracting. But Arkes managed to convince Canady and Santorum despite NRLC's skepticism. After George W. Bush's election, a push for the born-alive bill resumed. Arkes contended that the bill would have a better chance of success than NRLC's proposal while doing more to protect fetal rights. It would establish that "there is, in the child marked for abortion, a real entity that the law may protect."[28]

President Bush signed Arkes's Born-Alive Infants Protection Act in 2002. His signing message stressed the kinds of personhood claims that Arkes and his allies prioritized. The Born-Alive Act proved that other abortion foes could compete with NRLC in Congress—and suggested that the choice between political influence and absolutism had always been a false one.[29]

In any case, NRLC leaders did not seem to have the upper hand on campaign finance. Since 2001, BCRA had remained on the shelf as Senate Republicans found creative ways to avoid a vote. But by 2002, the Enron scandal had made further delay untenable. Enron, a large energy company, was not only a major seller of natural gas but also operated pipelines, pulp mills, power plants, and broadband hubs. In 2001, reporters questioned the stunning discrepancy between its high stock price and its relatively low earnings. The opacity of Enron's accounting triggered an investigation by the Securities and Exchange Commission. Shares plummeted. By the fall of 2001, credit agencies had downgraded the company to junk status, and Enron had filed for bankruptcy. Arthur Andersen, the accounting firm that had winked at Enron's fraudulent accounting practices, also went into freefall. Enron shareholders lost roughly $74 billion, and the company's employees saw their retirement savings wiped out. Subsequent reporting disclosed that Enron had donated $10.2 million in support of candidates in federal races between 1997 and 2000. It seemed everyone was cozy with the former energy giant. In a supreme irony, virtually every member of the House and Senate charged with investigating Enron had received money from it.[30]

That revelation jump-started efforts to pass BCRA. At the time, the conservative media did not generally take a stand against the idea. Fox News Channel, which became the nation's top-rated cable news program that year, carried arguments on both sides. Bush signed BCRA into law in March 2002, but in his signing statement, he noted the common constitutional arguments against the bill and suggested that the courts would work out its legality.[31]

Lawyers opposed to campaign finance regulation lined up to challenge the law. Senator Mitch McConnell, the lead plaintiff in one case, introduced a team of star lawyers before the law even passed. The National Rifle Association filed suit before McConnell did. The plaintiff list quickly grew, with libertarian congressman Ron Paul, the Republican National Committee, the Chamber of Commerce, and the National Right to Life Committee all filing suit. But progressives also took issue with the statute. Some unions and advocacy groups worried that it would limit their election spending or put them at an unfair disadvantage. Civil libertarians sometimes contended political spending deserved First Amendment protection. The ACLU, the

California Democratic Party, and the AFL-CIO also joined as plaintiffs. Both Bopp and Kathleen Sullivan, the liberal dean of Stanford Law School, served on McConnell's team of lawyers. Beyond NRLC, right-to-life groups did not contribute to the *McConnell* litigation.[32]

The *McConnell* plaintiffs presented a grab bag of claims regarding the law's impact on everyone from minors to politicians of color. But they focused on two main provisions: the soft money ban and the limits on political advertising. Before BCRA, congressional committees as well as state, local, and national parties could receive unlimited soft money—donations "made solely for the purpose of influencing state or local elections." For the law's framers, these cash infusions created a gaping loophole. Soft money almost inevitably helped candidates for federal office, but so long as there was a middleman between a candidate and the cash, the law had not intervened. BCRA prohibited national parties and their agents from receiving, soliciting, directing, or spending any soft money. State and local parties and party committees could not raise or spend soft money to influence federal elections.[33]

BCRA's second central provision addressed so-called electioneering communications, meaning any broadcast or ad that referred to a specific candidate broadcast within thirty days of a primary or sixty days of a general election. The law did not allow corporations or unions to directly bankroll electioneering communications (although they could create a PAC to do so). Finally, BCRA required anyone spending more than $10,000 on electioneering communications to make certain disclosures.[34]

McConnell and his allies contended that BCRA violated the right to freedom of speech. In some ways, this argument faced an uphill battle. In *Buckley*, the Court had upheld limits on contributions to party committees that then gave money directly to candidates or campaigns. The government argued that the soft money ban was essentially the same. Just as important, recent decisions, including *Colorado Republican II*, seemed to focus on the circumvention of contribution limits.[35]

McConnell responded that the soft money provision was unconstitutional under any standard of scrutiny. Soft money, he argued, posed little danger of quid pro quo corruption because it involved "only donations to and disbursements by political parties, rather than federal officeholders or candidates."

McCain and Feingold had tried to define corruption more broadly—by looking at "the 'possibility of the appearance of corruption,' or 'circumvention' of existing limits." But this definition would "allow the regulation of virtually *any* activity in the realm of campaign financing." Besides, McConnell argued, the soft money regulation was unfair to parties—interest groups could still spend unlimited amounts on party building, while federal parties themselves could not.[36]

McConnell also targeted the electioneering communication provision. He argued that "the government may constitutionally regulate only independent expenditures for speech expressly advocating the election or defeat of a candidate." Corporations likewise enjoyed protection unless they engaged in express advocacy. NRLC agreed that Congress could not stop corporations, especially nonprofits, from spending their own money on issue advertising.[37]

McCain, Feingold, and other pro-reform lawmakers intervened to defend the law. McCain and his colleagues planned to create an impressive trial record to show how soft money and issue ads had become "a conduit for corruption."[38] As for electioneering communications, the intervenors insisted that *Buckley* had never formally adopted the express advocacy test. And regardless of what the Court had said about the test before, McCain described it as a failure that had unleashed a "tidal wave of circumvention."[39]

The stakes seemed high. In 2002, with no one running for the White House, political parties raised well over $1 billion in soft money, roughly the same amount collected two years before in a competitive presidential election season. BCRA did not go into effect until November, and politicians rushed to spend before it kicked in.[40]

Republicans picked up two Senate seats in the midterm and took control of both chambers. To no one's surprise, less than three months into 2003, the new Senate majority passed a federal ban on partial-birth abortion, and Bush signed it into law (the statute included extensive congressional findings on the dangers of dilation and extraction, together with a clearer definition of the procedure, designed to distinguish the federal ban from the state law struck down by the Supreme Court in 2000). For NRLC, the partial-birth abortion campaign had more than proven its worth. The ban enjoyed public support and seemed to nudge voters toward identifying as pro-life.[41]

The passage of the federal Partial-Birth Abortion Ban Act did not win over Harold Cassidy and other pro-lifers who saw no reason to focus on campaign finance and believed that doing so had distracted Bopp and his colleagues from finding an abortion strategy that worked. Religious conservative leaders were listening. In 2003, Cassidy helped launch a new group, the Culture of Life Leadership Coalition. The anti-abortion movement lacked a master plan, he argued, so he proposed one.[42]

Cassidy's take resonated with important religious right groups, including the Alliance Defense Fund (later the Alliance Defending Freedom). By backing the idea of a new coalition, the Alliance Defense Fund and other organizations, such as the Family Research Council, signaled that the center of power in the anti-abortion movement might be shifting. Cassidy plotted out a strategy to show that "abortion hurt . . . women" and violated women's rights to a relationship with their unborn children. This tactic very much reflected Cassidy's plan to litigate tort and constitutional cases to "demonstrat[e] the humanity of the unborn in the context of showing harm to the mother."[43]

The Culture of Life Leadership Coalition took no position on campaign finance and said little about partial-birth abortion. Some of those who joined the coalition wanted to try for a more sweeping win. By the fall of 2003, groups from the United States Conference of Catholic Bishops (a new group formed in 2001 through the merger of the National Conference of Catholic Bishops and a sister organization) to Priests for Life had signed on. The coalition soon flamed out, partly over tactical disagreements. Nevertheless, its rise and fall reflected continuing anxiety about the strategy that had defined the pro-life movement for years. Cassidy and his allies thought that under NRLC's stewardship, the rights of the unborn had at times seemed like an afterthought, second to the needs of the GOP and the fight against campaign finance regulations.[44]

From *Beaumont* to *McConnell*

For those worried about the flow of big money into politics, the greatest concern had often been corporate money. The Supreme Court certainly seemed to think so. In *Federal Election Commission v. Beaumont* (2003), the

Court rejected North Carolina Right to Life's challenge to limits on nonprofits' political contributions. Writing for a six-justice majority, David Souter began by revisiting the history of corporate spending. In his telling, corporations raised massive sums but had limited legal liability. For this reason, he wrote, even nonprofit corporations had "an unfair advantage in the political marketplace." In some ways, *Beaumont* might not have been an earth-shattering ruling since the Court had long approved tougher limits on contributions. But for those opposed to campaign finance regulations, *Beaumont* held ominous signs. The Court recognized the government's interest in preventing "circumvention of contribution limits." This embrace of the circumvention theory did not bode well for a challenge to BCRA.[45]

And the Court seemed skeptical that nonprofit corporations were really so different. Nonprofits, Souter wrote, were "no less susceptible than traditional business companies to misuse as conduits for circumventing the contribution limits imposed on individuals."[46]

The Supreme Court's decision in *McConnell* did not make NRLC leaders feel any better. By a 5-4 vote, the Court upheld the core provisions of BCRA: the soft money, disclosure, and electioneering communications provisions. The majority conceded that BCRA's soft money ban affected both contributions and expenditures. But the Court reasoned that the provision did not burden speech any more or any differently than a contribution limit would—for example, the measure did not limit how much parties could spend in total. Because the provision "prevents circumvention" of contribution limits, the Court did not scrutinize the ban very closely.[47]

Was the soft money provision justified? The *McConnell* decision answered yes, suggesting that Congress had legitimate concerns about corruption for reasons well beyond "cash for votes exchanges." McCain and Feingold rightly worried about the risk of "undue influence on an officeholder's judgment, and the appearance of such influence." The Court also suggested that Congress could reasonably try to put a stop to circumvention of contribution limits.[48]

Further, *McConnell* validated BCRA's restrictions on electioneering communications. Those challenging the law complained that it regulated corporate expenditures protected by *Buckley*—which, they argued, allowed for strict regulation of express advocacy and nothing more. But for the *McConnell*

Court, the express advocacy test had never been "a first principle of constitutional law." Nor, the majority reasoned, did the express advocacy test make much sense. It had not "aided the legislative effort to combat real or apparent corruption," and Congress could reasonably "correct the flaws it found in the existing system." *McConnell* easily upheld BCRA's disclosure limits. *Buckley* had upheld a similar requirement, and BCRA simply extended it to electioneering communications. The Court saw no problem with that.[49]

After *Beaumont* and *McConnell*, arguing that nonprofits deserved special protection might no longer work. Besides, for right-to-lifers, there were obvious reasons to defend all corporate spending. Bopp began looking for a way around *McConnell*—one that would help many conservative movements, not just his own.

McConnell also emboldened those who were convinced that pro-lifers should never have been involved with campaign finance. But within a year, NRLC leaders found themselves in a much stronger position. Judicial nominations topped the national agenda, with Democrats filibustering judges they considered too conservative and the president frequently invoking his power to make recess appointments. Equally important, the Supreme Court was back in the news. It seemed that whoever was elected president in 2004 would name several new justices.

The Next War over the Court

Conflict about judicial nominations had never gone away, but it seemed fiercer after George W. Bush took office. Tensions grew after the media leaked 2003 documents appearing to show that leading Democratic senators had long planned to filibuster any Bush nominee they found too conservative. In January 2004, on the advice of the Federalist Society, Bush nominated Charles Pickering Sr. to the Fifth Circuit Court of Appeals during a congressional recess (the Senate Judiciary Committee had declined to advance Pickering in 2001). That recess appointment, and several that followed it, ratcheted up interest in the courts. In any case, there was a presidential election coming.[50]

Bush used the prospect of controlling the courts—and the fear of the Democrats controlling them—to raise a staggering amount of money. The previous year, Congress had increased the individual contribution limit to $2,000, and Bush raised more than $130 million before 2004 even began. This mind-boggling haul drove home that despite years of back and forth, the GOP had established an edge in fundraising.[51]

Bopp helped the GOP build on its advantage. Earlier in the decade, he had helped advocacy groups popularize so-called 527 groups, tax-exempt organizations committed to influencing federal, state, and local elections. Before the 2004 election, he insisted that under *McConnell*, 527s were not covered by the BCRA soft money ban because they did not coordinate with candidates and would not create the same unseemly appearance. Reformers violently disagreed. The FEC ultimately decided to postpone a decision on 527s and soft money until after the 2004 election. To no one's surprise, prominent 527s like Swift Boat Veterans for Truth rocked the campaign. That group released spots featuring Vietnam veterans who claimed to have served with John Kerry, the Democratic nominee, accusing him of filing distorted reports about his and other soldiers' actions in Vietnam. 527s like Swift Boat shelled out $550.6 million in 2004, nearly twice the amount spent in 2002. In 2006, the FEC fined Swift Boat and two other 527s, the progressive MoveOn.org and the League of Conservation Voters, for acting as PACs without meeting registration or reporting requirements. The FEC also concluded that Swift Boat had accepted contributions well beyond the PAC limit. Swift Boat was ordered to disband, but it was too little too late. 527 spending had already reshaped the 2004 election.[52]

Bopp also launched a new attack on BCRA's ban on electioneering communications. For decades, the Supreme Court had allowed corporations more freedom to make independent expenditures when it came to issue ads. Bopp planned to argue that *McConnell* had not changed that; the Court had simply recognized that advocacy groups occasionally abused the idea of issue ads to endorse candidates. Endorsements of candidates *should* be treated differently than ads discussing the issues. The trick was to separate real issue ads from the rest.

He began refining this argument in a 2004 case involving Wisconsin Right to Life. The pro-life group planned to run ads opposing Russ Feingold's threat to filibuster some of Bush's judicial nominees. Bopp asked a court to allow Wisconsin Right to Life to air the commercials right before the election, even though *McConnell* had upheld BCRA's provision on electioneering communications. To get around that decision, Bopp argued that *McConnell* applied only to "sham ads" that all but endorsed a candidate. The Court, he insisted, had never considered "genuine issue ads," which were an important form of "grassroots lobbying." And what exactly was grassroots lobbying? Bopp's answer was simple: "asking citizens to tell lawmakers how to vote on a matter." He suggested that Wisconsin Right to Life had designed just such an ad.[53] In August 2004, a district court denied his request for an injunction that would have allowed the ads to go ahead, but the suit continued.[54]

Leaders of groups like NRLC felt relief when George W. Bush won a second term, carrying thirty-one states and winning a little less than 51 percent of the popular vote. With no need to face another campaign, Bush might be freer to prioritize abortion. But his success did not convince dissenters in the anti-abortion movement that NRLC had found an effective strategy. A new rebellion was brewing in South Dakota. Against the advice of leading pro-life groups, both houses of the state legislature passed a ban on abortion. Tom Monaghan, the founder of Domino's Pizza and Ave Maria University, a conservative Catholic institution, asked Harold Cassidy to defend the state provision. Cassidy did not think the nation was ready for an abortion ban, but he saw South Dakota as the perfect laboratory for new strategies.[55]

The state's ban did not pass, but working with Cassidy, state lawmakers created a task force to study abortion. The effort produced a new kind of informed consent statute. The government mandated disclosures for abortion providers to recite to their patients, including the statements that abortion "terminates the life of a whole, separate, unique living human being" and creates an increased risk of "suicide and suicide ideation." This strategy appealed to many grassroots pro-lifers who felt that their movement's leadership had focused so much on campaign finance that it had lost its way. As one activist said of Cassidy's approach, these sweeping attempts might fail or even hurt the GOP, but they would "remind state and federal elected officials that they are duty bound to protect the inalienable rights of unborn humans."[56]

The outcome of the partial-birth abortion litigation seemed less predictable following new openings on the Supreme Court. In 2005, Sandra Day O'Connor announced her retirement to care for her husband as he battled

Alzheimer's disease. The following September, William Rehnquist lost his battle with cancer. O'Connor's departure was particularly consequential. She had often served as a swing vote on contentious subjects, including abortion and campaign finance. The battle to replace her demonstrated again how the idea of controlling the courts could unite a divided conservative movement.[57]

New cracks in the GOP coalition had emerged over same-sex marriage. Between 1999 and 2003, state high courts in Vermont and Massachusetts had recognized a right of same-sex couples to marry. Whereas the Vermont Supreme Court required access only to the benefits tied to marriage, the Massachusetts Supreme Judicial Court in *Goodridge v. Department of Health* held that even a separate but equal institution for same-sex couples, such as domestic partnership, would be unconstitutional.[58]

Goodridge caused panic among conservative Christians. Some scholars across the ideological spectrum argued that the Constitution's full faith and credit clause (which addressed the states' relationship to one another) would compel every state to recognize same-sex marriages performed in another state. In the late 1990s, the backlash against same-sex marriage had prompted a wave of defense-of-marriage acts, statutes defining marriage as between a man and a woman. In February 2005, James Dobson of Focus on the Family wrote to the White House on behalf of a variety of Christian conservative groups, demanding that Bush fight for a constitutional ban. If not, Dobson threatened, pro-lifers and Christian conservatives would withhold support for the Bush administration's proposed changes to the federal Social Security program. By spring, the demand was widespread among Christian conservatives.[59]

Conservative media had also begun to tip the scales in favor of grassroots conservatives like those supporting Dobson. Over the decade, new conservative hosts built massive audiences. A former building contractor from Santa Barbara, California, Sean Hannity, built a loyal following as the co-host of a popular Fox News segment. Commentators from attorney Laura Ingraham to self-proclaimed conservative nationalist Michael Savage had nationally syndicated shows. As competition increased, hosts tacked further to the right to win over listeners. The base that listened to Hannity and Ingraham wanted pure adherence to conservative principles. To these listeners, Bush's lackluster efforts on abortion looked like a betrayal.[60]

The fight to replace O'Connor once again proved that the prospect of controlling the Court could (at least temporarily) heal almost any fracture in the Republican Party. For the first time in history, business conservatives, led by the National Association of Manufacturers and the U.S. Chamber of Commerce, prepared to campaign officially for the confirmation of a Supreme Court nominee. Another conservative group, Progress for America, pledged $18 million to support Bush's nominee before even knowing who it was.[61] The Family Research Council hosted "Justice Sunday," a series of religious conferences suggesting that anyone opposed to Bush's nominees was launching an "attack on people of faith."[62]

Most in the GOP coalition felt satisfied with Bush's eventual selection, John G. Roberts, a judge on the DC Court of Appeals. A product of an exclusive Indiana suburb and elite Catholic schools, Roberts had the perfect résumé for the Supreme Court: Harvard, a clerkship with William Rehnquist, a distinguished legal career. Detractors pointed out that he had fought to lift public school desegregation orders and weaken the federal Voting Rights Act. But Roberts had an earnest, boyish quality that made him hard to dislike. During his confirmation hearing, he presented himself as above the political fray, comparing his role on the Court to that of an umpire calling balls and strikes. Most Christian conservatives did not believe a word of it. Some pointed to a brief Roberts had helped prepare during his tenure as principal deputy solicitor general in the George H. W. Bush Administration, in which he stated that *Roe* was wrongly decided. But Roberts's charm counted for more than his track record, even with some Democratic senators. The Senate voted to make him the new chief justice by a vote of 78 to 22.[63]

The next confirmation battle made NRLC leaders think that pro-lifers might finally have gained more control over the selection of Supreme Court justices. To fill the second vacancy on the Court, Bush selected his attorney and longtime ally Harriet Miers. Miers lacked the judicial experience and Ivy League background the American Bar Association liked to see, but she had a career of firsts: first woman to lead a major Texas law firm, first woman to head the Texas Bar Association. She was hard working, careful, and very tight lipped. Those who had known her for years had no idea what her politics were. In some ways, she seemed ideal. But within a month, she had withdrawn from consideration.[64]

Opposition by the conservative legal elite was a big factor. Miers had not appeared on any Federalist Society list of prospective nominees—and with good reason. She was not a federal judge or the dean of a prestigious law school.[65] On October 19, Robert Bork, the society's co-chairman, published a scathing letter to the editor about Miers in the *Wall Street Journal*. Her nomination, he wrote, dealt "a blow in particular to the Federalist Society" and "damaged the prospects for reform of a left-leaning and imperialistic Supreme Court."[66]

Pro-lifers felt that they too had helped to destroy Miers's chances. Leonard Leo, also (ironically) a prominent member of the Federalist Society assisting with the administration's judicial nominees, had tried to preempt anti-abortion objections with a memo highlighting her leadership of the Texas State Bar Association. Miers, Leo wrote, had "led a campaign to have the American Bar Association end its practice of supporting abortion-on-demand and taxpayer-funded abortions."[67] NRLC supported her, citing its trust in Bush's record of nominating judges who would "abide by the text and history of the Constitution."[68] Jay Sekulow and the American Center for Law and Justice described Miers as "an excellent choice who represents the conservative mainstream."[69]

Many social conservatives were unconvinced.[70] Questions about a windfall Miers and her family received as part of a land deal in Texas further emboldened her opponents. Phyllis Schlafly's Eagle Forum joined two other groups in backing a website opposing Miers. Many groups that had stayed neutral made their opposition public. By the end of October, Bush had withdrawn her from consideration.[71]

Many had compared Miers to David Souter, another candidate who had drawn fire from both sides of the aisle. But much had changed since Souter's confirmation hearings. When selecting Miers's replacement, Samuel Alito, a Federalist Society darling, Bush consulted with many of the anti-abortion groups that had ultimately opposed Miers. Alito narrowly won confirmation, by a vote of 58-42. Except for Clarence Thomas, most of Alito's predecessors had won far more support, but anti-abortion leaders had no problem with the narrow margin. The point was to get the right person on the Court, even if many in the Congress or the country didn't like it. The era of consensus nominees seemed to have yielded to a new way of doing business.[72]

Resurrecting *Buckley*

It did not take long to see how a reconfigured Court could change the law on campaign finance. In January 2006, with Roberts and Alito on the bench, the Court reversed the district court's dismissal of *Wisconsin Right to Life*, holding that the *McConnell* ruling had not blocked all challenges to BCRA's provisions on electioneering communications. The lower courts would determine whether Wisconsin Right to Life's ad could still air, BCRA notwithstanding, after which the case was possibly headed back to the Supreme Court. Meanwhile, Bopp had another case, *Randall v. Sorrell*, already before the justices. *Randall* gave the Court its first look at Vermont's sweeping 1997 campaign finance bill. The state capped expenditures on campaigns for various state offices and set strict limits on the amount anyone could give to a candidate, political party, or political committee. In a suit joined by voters and some political organizations, state lawmaker Neil Randall argued that the law violated his right to freedom of speech. Originally, many had expected *Randall* to be reformers' chance to undo *Buckley* and open the door to expenditure limits. But in upholding Vermont's law, the Second Circuit had ruled more narrowly, claiming only that the statute could survive under *Buckley*.[73]

In theory, everyone agreed that *Buckley* should decide the case. But James Bopp knew that the meaning of a blockbuster judicial decision could change, both inside and outside the Court. *Roe v. Wade* could stand for a woman's right to choose, a physician's right to practice medicine, or an overreaching Court. The meaning of *Buckley*, too, could change over time. *McConnell* had not purported to gut *Buckley*, but the Court had defined corruption more narrowly. *Randall* represented a chance to revive a more muscular interpretation of *Buckley*.[74]

Because the Court planned to hear two of Bopp's cases, *Randall* and *Wisconsin Right to Life*, in the same term, he hosted a session in Washington, DC, to map out an overarching strategy for both cases. As ever, there was a large and diverse group of lawyers taking aim at BCRA. The ACLU and Citizens United, a conservative advocacy group that specialized in political ads and movies, wanted to help Bopp with *Wisconsin Right to Life*. The Chamber of Commerce planned to argue that corporations had "the right to speak on public issues," especially when it came to "ads that address active legislative issues."[75]

McConnell had muddied the difference between expenditures and contributions while making it easier to regulate both. Vermont wanted to push this argument further. The state insisted that the *Buckley* Court would have upheld expenditure limits if the justices had considered the state's reasons for acting: a desire to protect candidates' time and to ensure all citizens equal access to the political process. Bopp responded that *Buckley* had struck down expenditure limits even after considering the government's interest in preventing corruption, a goal much more important than any Vermont had identified. Besides, Bopp argued, the government could advance its goals in less restrictive ways, including contribution limits.[76] Moreover, Vermont's limits were unique, lower than any other in the nation. Yet there was no evidence that corruption was worse in Vermont than anywhere else.[77]

In June, the newly configured Court handed down a 6-3 decision in *Randall*. While six justices agreed that Vermont's law was unconstitutional, only two joined Justice Breyer's relatively narrow opinion invalidating the statute. Breyer concluded that *Buckley*'s distinction between expenditures and contributions remained rock solid. And he believed there was nothing new about Vermont's justifications for its law. The *Buckley* Court was "fully aware" that fundraising would consume candidates' time.[78]

Further, *Randall* suggested that some on the Court had grown more skeptical of contribution limits. The Court held that Vermont's contribution limits were so low that they created "danger signs." "Contribution limits that are too low," Breyer wrote, "also can harm the electoral process by preventing challengers from mounting effective campaigns against incumbent officeholders."[79]

Vermont and the reformers siding with it had asked the Court to reverse *Buckley*, no matter how remote that possibility seemed. The state had argued that *Buckley* had proven to be untenable. But for the *Randall* Court, the matter was not so simple. Breyer found no proof of either a "dramatic increase in corruption or its appearance in Vermont." And he believed that lawmakers had relied on *Buckley* in drafting their own campaign finance laws, increasing the costs of overruling it. Three other justices concurred only in the result of the opinion because they believed the First Amendment protected more spending than *Buckley* acknowledged.[80]

Randall brought back a version of *Buckley* that campaign finance opponents could make something of. State expenditure limits once again seemed to face a hard look from the Supreme Court. Even contribution limits, if low enough, might raise eyebrows. But *Randall* also suggested that the Court's conservative majority was restless. At least three of its members saw *Buckley* as only the beginning of First Amendment protections for election spending.

From *Gonzales* to *Wisconsin Right to Life II*

Randall hinted that the Court would once again welcome challenges to campaign finance laws. Bopp prepared to return to the Supreme Court for a second round in *Wisconsin Right to Life.*[81] The lawyers in the *Wisconsin Right to Life II* meeting reflected the cross-partisan appeal of free speech arguments against campaign finance reform. Bradley Smith had traveled to the meeting from Ohio. He was fresh off a six-year term on the Federal Election Commission, during which he never hid his opposition to campaign finance regulations. Shortly after leaving the FEC, he co-founded the Center for Competitive Politics in 2005 to champion the deregulation of campaign finance. Steve Hoersting, one of Smith's former students, had left a position as general counsel for the National Republican Senatorial Committee to help his former professor fight campaign spending limits. Steve Simpson had a shorter commute from the Institute for Justice, a libertarian public interest law firm founded in 1991 with seed funding from Charles Koch. By 2005, the institute had made the fight against campaign finance limits a priority. Mitch McConnell sent a policy advisor. The Chamber of Commerce had a lawyer present, as did the ACLU, the AFL-CIO, the Home School Legal Defense Association, and the RNC. Bill Olson brought several lawyers from his firm on behalf of Citizens United.[82]

By February, the attorneys had divvied up arguments on behalf of Wisconsin Right to Life. Bopp planned to stick to the argument that "*McConnell* left open the question of protecting genuine issue ads"—and that those ads could be distinguished from sham ads by "a carefully worded test based on content, not context." Amici would sow the seeds of much bigger changes. Joel Gora of the ACLU and Bill Olson's Citizens United team would stress that forming a PAC would not work for many organizations, including churches, business corporations, and nonprofits. Jim Henderson, an attorney at Pat Robertson's ACLJ, would highlight the danger that politicians would "plan unpopular activity for blackout periods"—and that "vital events" that would otherwise change an election could occur during those periods.[83]

The primary goal, as Bopp summarized it, was still to gain "recognized constitutional protection for grassroots lobbying with a holding stating a test broad enough to permit effective grassroots lobbying and protect all corporations and unions." Those litigating the case agreed that there was no longer any reason to focus on nonprofits. "All corporations," Bopp concluded, "are constitutionally entitled to engage in robust issue advocacy."[84]

Perhaps the biggest obstacle facing those at the meeting was *Austin v. Michigan Chamber of Commerce* (1990). *Austin* had upheld a Michigan law that prevented corporations that received all their money from for-profit businesses from spending their own funds on independent expenditures. Attorneys from Kathleen Sullivan's Stanford Law Constitutional Center planned to argue for a narrower interpretation of *Austin*—one that would establish that "nonprofits pose little risk of corporate-form corruption," even if they got their money from businesses. But Bopp and his allies also hoped to convince the Court that "*Austin* was wrongly decided and should be overturned."[85]

One way to go after *Austin* was to redefine the government's interest in corruption. Steve Simpson's Institute for Justice would frame circumvention as a bogus problem, a dragnet intended to catch innocent donors who just wanted to support their favored causes. Simpson would also chip away at the idea that Congress even had an interest in preventing corruption. Bopp summarized this argument: "There is no compelling interest in avoiding corruption because 'apparent' public perception of corruption was generated by special interests." Reformers had manufactured evidence of corruption, he asserted, to justify new regulations.[86]

Regulators, of course, could rely on *McConnell*. As the FEC saw it, *McConnell* created a new rule, focused on the purpose and effect of an ad. If a corporation intended an ad to help or hurt a candidate, *McConnell* stripped that ad of protection. And if an ad would have the same effect as one expressly endorsing a politician, the First Amendment would not shield it.[87]

Bopp and his allies sought to beat back this interpretation of *McConnell*. Pointing to examples of genuine issue ads given by the *McConnell* Court, he argued that surely the decision had not stripped protection from all ads. The question became how to identify genuine grassroots lobbying. Bopp proposed a definition: an ad that "focuses on a current legislative branch matter, takes a position on the matter, and urges the public to ask a legislator to take a particular position or action with respect to the matter in his or her official capacity." If the Court accepted this definition, many corporations could find a way to run their ads.[88]

While *Wisconsin Right to Life II* was pending, the Court also heard a challenge to the federal Partial-Birth Abortion Ban Act in *Gonzales v. Carhart*. Bopp hosted another strategy meeting at NRLC headquarters for groups preparing for the case. Jay Sekulow's American Center for Law and Justice, which had grown into a massive organization with a $30 million budget, sent a representative. Another group represented at the meeting, Liberty Counsel, had entered into a profitable partnership with Jerry Falwell's Liberty University. Even attorneys who had specialized in defending clinic blockaders and Operation Rescue leaders seemed to agree not to focus on fetal rights. As Clarke Forsythe of Americans United for Life explained, the plan was to convince the Court that "no significant medical authority demonstrates that . . . D&X [dilation and extraction] would be the safest procedure."[89]

Groups that were skeptical of NRLC's strategy continued to carve out alternative plans. After the collapse of the Culture of Life Leadership Coalition, Harold Cassidy had received requests for representation from the plaintiffs in both *Roe v. Wade* and its companion case, *Doe v. Bolton*. Norma McCorvey, the mercurial Jane Roe, had been a reluctant activist, brought along at times by pro-choice leaders' promises of money and fame. In 1995, low on cash and feeling ignored, she met minister Flip Benham, accepted Jesus as her savior, and joined the pro-life cause. Sandra Cano, the Doe of *Doe v. Bolton*, was also an anti-abortion convert. McCorvey and Cano both wanted to help get rid of *Roe*, and Cassidy passed their requests on to Allan Parker, the head of a conservative public interest law firm, the Justice Foundation. Parker, in response, launched Operation Outcry, an effort to collect affidavits from women who regretted their abortions.[90]

But in *Gonzales,* everyone in the anti-abortion movement was on the same page. The outcome of the case seemed to turn on whether the Court found that Congress needed to add a health exception to the ban on partial-birth abortion. Groups like NRLC thought there was no scientific certainty that an exception was needed. Operation Outcry argued instead that a health exception was a contradiction because abortion itself hurt women.[91]

While right-to-lifers unified around a strategy in *Gonzales*, the win-first strategy that had helped their movement so much in the political arena seemed to come up short in the 2008 presidential election. Republicans had suffered serious losses in the 2006 midterms, and conservatives disagreed passionately over what had gone wrong. In 2007, perhaps the most common view was that the GOP had done too much to cater to social conservatives. Several candidates who jumped into the presidential race certainly held this belief. The early frontrunner, Rudy Giuliani, a tough-talking former prosecutor, had become a household name as mayor of New York City during the 9/11 terrorist attack. A moderate supporter of abortion rights, he sought to be the candidate of the GOP establishment. So did former Massachusetts governor Mitt Romney, a milkshake-loving Utah native who had renounced his previous support for abortion rights. John McCain, who had run in 2000, decided to give it another go. A handful of social conservatives also decided to run, including Mike Huckabee. Huckabee began his career as a staffer for televangelist James Robison and later served as the head of the Arkansas Baptist Convention. As the governor of Arkansas, he was a coalition-building pragmatist. Huckabee the presidential candidate, on the other hand, was a hardcore pro-life Christian. Abortion opponents struggled to pick a favorite among these choices. Huckabee, who did his best to court conservative Christians, did not have an obvious path to the White House. Giuliani favored abortion rights, and Romney's conversion had not convinced everyone. NRLC had long opposed McCain because of his role on campaign finance reform. It seemed quite possible that the GOP nominee might support legal abortion.[92]

In the spring of 2007, the Court handed down two key decisions. First, in *Gonzales,* the justices voted 5-4 to uphold the federal Partial-Birth

Abortion Ban Act. The emphasis on facts proposed by NRLC and AUL seemed to have worked: Justice Anthony Kennedy opened his majority opinion with a graphic description of the outlawed procedure.[93]

Citing the Operation Outcry brief, Kennedy next concluded that the government had a valid interest in protecting women from regret they might suffer after having an abortion. "It is self-evident," he wrote, "that a mother who comes to regret her choice to abort must struggle with grief more anguished and sorrow more profound when she learns, only after the event, what she once did not know: that she allowed a doctor to pierce the skull and vacuum the fast-developing brain of her unborn child, a child assuming the human form."[94]

But what of the law's effect? Major medical organizations had stressed evidence that the outlawed procedure would sometimes do more to safeguard a woman's health and fertility than any other alternative. But because other experts disagreed, and because Congress had made findings to the contrary, the Court found that there was "scientific uncertainty" about the need for a health exception. "The Court has given state and federal legislatures wide discretion," Kennedy wrote, "to pass legislation in areas where there is medical and scientific uncertainty." *Gonzales* seemingly vindicated NRLC's focus on controlling the Court. For years, NRLC had promised that bans on partial-birth abortion would win over voters and increase opposition to any legal abortion. Now, this strategy appeared to be paying dividends.[95]

The Court's opinion in *Wisconsin Right to Life II* was just as heartening for NRLC. Chief Justice John Roberts, one of the Court's newest members, wrote the majority opinion invalidating the BCRA blackout period, at least as it applied to Wisconsin Right to Life's lobby ads. The government had insisted that after *McConnell*, Congress could apply the blackout to any ad that had the purpose or effect of influencing an election. *Wisconsin Right to Life II* concluded that *McConnell* had done no such thing.[96] Instead, Roberts proposed what he called an "objective" test: the Court would treat an ad as "the functional equivalent of express advocacy only if the ad is susceptible of no reasonable interpretation other than as an appeal to vote for or against a specific candidate." Roberts concluded that Wisconsin Right to Life's three ads had other possible interpretations.[97]

The Court then applied strict scrutiny to the blackout of the group's ads and found the government's justifications to be wanting. In blocking the ads, the FEC had identified a compelling interest in preventing corruption and stopping donors from circumventing contribution limits. Neither of these interests struck the Court's new majority as compelling, at least in the instant case. Roberts suggested that issue ads posed little or no threat of a quid pro quo. True, the Court had expressed concern about the corrupting potential of corporate wealth. But this concern applied only to corporate "campaign speech." Corporations remained free to advocate for issues, *Austin* notwithstanding.[98]

The four dissenters realized that *Wisconsin Right to Life II* marked a significant departure from *McConnell*. As Justice Souter wrote, much of *McConnell* had turned on the dangers the Court saw in corporate election spending. The *McConnell* Court had also worried considerably about the circumvention of contribution limits. Neither concern carried much weight with the Court's new majority. *McConnell* and *Beaumont* had suggested that if pro-life groups truly wanted to influence elections, the Court would have to protect all corporate spending. After *Wisconsin Right to Life*, it appeared the new conservative majority might do just that.[99]

The Making of *Citizens United*

The case that would transform corporate election spending began when Citizens United, a conservative advocacy group founded in 1988, wanted to broadcast a film, *Hillary: The Movie*, before the 2008 presidential election. The group claimed that Senator Hillary Clinton of New York, the presumed frontrunner in the Democratic primary, had a dark side. *Hillary* reflected a change in direction made by Citizens United since the passage of BCRA. The organization had moved away from traditional political ads and now portrayed itself as a documentary filmmaker. This shift had everything to do with BCRA. Documentary filmmakers were one of the types of media organizations exempted from its provisions on electioneering communication.[100]

By 2007, Citizens United was ready to see if its strategy worked. It planned to air *Hillary* right before Americans went to the polls in 2008. In January 2007, Michael Boos, the group's vice president and general counsel, asserted that Citizens United would qualify as an exempt media organization under federal law. Boos had taken a job with Roger Stone's National Conservative PAC right out of college. Later, while working for Young Americans for Freedom, he concluded that the Washington police selectively enforced a law against carrying signs or placards outside foreign embassies—conservatives protesting outside the Soviet embassy, he thought, found themselves in trouble much more than anyone else. He decided to hire a lawyer. The case, *Boos v. Barry*, went all the way to the Supreme Court. Boos won, and not long after, he decided to become a lawyer himself. He started at Citizens United in 1995.[101]

Hillary struck David Bossie, the head of Citizens United, as his masterpiece. There was nothing he hated more than the Clintons. He had volunteered for Ronald Reagan's campaign before he was old enough to drink alcohol and later dropped out of college to pursue politics full-time. In the early 1990s, after he got a job as a congressional staffer for several Republicans investigating the Clintons' financial dealings, exposing them became a lifetime pursuit. When he leaked heavily edited prison phone calls from Webster Hubbell, the former associate attorney general, Bossie lost his job in Congress and landed at Citizens United. The group's issue ads were fine, Bossie thought, but he wanted a venue that would permit more time to make his point. Citizens United started producing full-length films on everything Bossie disliked about the American left, from the ACLU to immigration policy.[102]

Bopp and his colleague Richard Coleson thought that Boos's strategy in *Hillary* would fail. The media exemption applied to organizations "devoted to the collection of information and its dissemination to the public" and "in the regular business of imparting news to the public." While Citizens United had directed considerable resources to making movies, its primary purpose remained political advocacy. And the statute's exemption for media broadcasts applied only to a "news story, commentary, or editorial"—a definition that seemed to exclude *Hillary*. In any case, Bopp wanted to use the case to fight for something bigger—anonymity for all political donors—and using the media exemption would give the Court a way to avoid a broader ruling. As he explained to Bossie: "A victory on the primary argument [about BCRA] would provide broad relief to numerous advocacy groups, not just [Citizens United], so it would provide the greater service to liberty."[103]

Citizens United released *Hillary: The Movie* in January 2008, and Bopp sought a preliminary injunction to air the film during the blackout period. The district court denied the request. The litigation continued amid growing anxiety among NRLC leaders about the 2008 election. Social conservatives had not united behind a candidate. Romney racked up endorsements from several social conservatives, including Bopp, Paul Weyrich, and Jay Sekulow of the American Center for Law and Justice; but NRLC backed Fred Thompson, a late entrant into the race, because of his Senate record on abortion. John McCain ultimately emerged as the nominee.[104]

What NRLC had long seen as a winning formula seemed to fail McCain. He struggled to raise money at anything near George W. Bush's pace. To reassure Christian conservatives, McCain selected Alaska governor Sarah Palin as his running mate. A former sports reporter for Anchorage station KTUU, she presented herself as an irreverent hockey mom, a rebel who loved big-game hunting and hated big media. Palin energized social conservatives, but she alienated many swing voters. Her few TV interviews came across as blooper reels to her detractors. Bopp thought McCain was just as big a problem. Rather than settling on one winner, social conservatives had divided their votes, opening the door to a maverick who could neither raise enough money nor excite many constituents.[105]

At least for the moment, the Court's conservative majority seemed to welcome challenges to campaign finance rules. In the summer of 2008, five justices voted to strike down another part of BCRA, the so-called Millionaire's Amendment, which lifted contribution limits for anyone running against a self-funded candidate. The attorney whose firm led the litigation in *Davis v. Federal Election Commission*, Stanley Brand, first made a name for himself at twenty-seven years old when he sold Speaker Tip O'Neill on the idea of hiring him to be the first general counsel for the House of Representatives. With a client list drawing on every DC scandal from the Savings and Loan crisis to the Whitewater investigation, Brand made a career out of helping defendants under the microscope for violating ethics rules and campaign finance regulations. Another attorney at Brand's firm, Andrew Herman, handled oral argument at the Supreme Court. Their client, Jack Davis, never seemed to stop running for office. He despised the GOP's free trade policies, which he believed shipped most manufacturing jobs overseas. A former marine who had gotten rich in manufacturing himself, Davis owned a company that made heating elements; he boasted that he had never outsourced a job. He had worshipped Barry Goldwater but quit the Republican Party in 2003 after getting kicked out of a fundraiser for Vice President Dick Cheney (Davis pushed too hard for a conversation with Cheney about trade). He then became a Democrat but quit a year later to found his own party. By 2008, he was a Republican again. He had already lost two races for Congress by the time the Court was ready to issue a decision in *Davis*.[106]

In litigating *Davis*, Brand and Herman insisted that *Buckley v. Valeo* had recognized a distinction between expenditures and contributions because contributions raised the odds of a corrupt quid pro quo. If contributions to candidates were so bad, Davis asked, why did the law punish people financing their own campaigns more than those relying on other people's money? The Court saw his point. In *Davis*, the majority emphasized that *Buckley* had already struck down limits on self-financing, especially when the law treated candidates differently on that basis. In *Davis v. Federal Election Commission*, the Court reasoned that the Millionaire's Amendment could not stand either.[107]

The 2008 Debacle

For conservatives opposed to campaign spending limits, the exhilaration of *Davis* did not last long. In November, John McCain got shellacked in the race for the White House; his opponent, Barack Obama, won over 52 percent of the popular vote and 365 of 538 electoral votes. Obama's star power helped candidates all the way down the ballot. So did the fact that Americans struggled with a deep recession and an endless war in Iraq. The Democrats also fared well in congressional races, picking up eight Senate seats and twenty-one House seats.[108]

Obama had won the post-BCRA money race too. He was the first presidential candidate from a major party to refuse public funding for the general election, but even without public money, he managed to raise over $745 million, much of it in small online donations. Bradley Smith, one of the leading voices against campaign finance limits, wrote in the *Washington Post* that Obama's success raising money should "put to rest all the shibboleths about campaign reform—that it's needed to prevent corruption, that it equalizes the playing field, or that tax subsidies are needed." Party organizations remained dominant despite BCRA: five of the top six outside spenders were party committees.[109]

Reporting from Levittown, Pennsylvania, a place at the heart of Ronald Reagan's America, *New York Times* journalist Michael Sokolove argued that Obama's triumph marked a broader shift in U.S. politics. A mass-produced hamlet for veterans returning from the Second World War, Levittown had become a symbol of a certain kind of down-on-its-luck American suburb, overwhelmingly white, with older residents outnumbering younger ones. And yet Levittown had voted for Obama. Sokolove's message was clear: 2008 might have been a nightmare for Republicans like Bopp, but things would not get better anytime soon.[110]

The RNC looked at Levittown and thought that not much had changed at all. George W. Bush had bequeathed John McCain an unpopular war, a failed response to Hurricane Katrina, and a historic economic collapse. It might have been that voters were not progressive at all. They were angry, and John McCain paid the price.[111]

Those running to lead the RNC out of the 2008 debacle included two Black candidates, Michael Steele, the former lieutenant governor of Maryland, and John Kenneth Blackwell, the treasurer of Ohio. Steele, the ultimate winner, had fundraising experience in leading Newt Gingrich's GOPAC. He argued that redistricting, the process by which legislative districts' boundaries are drawn, would be "the foundation that will determine which party controls power at both the state and national level for years to come."[112] Under Steele's guidance, the Republican Party launched the Redistricting Majority Project, known as Project REDMAP, to give their party the power to create an unassailable majority.[113]

Bopp thought that changing the rules on campaign finance would help the GOP bounce back. He focused on donor disclosure, an issue that motivated GOP donors and NRLC leaders alike. Ongoing fights over same-sex marriage illuminated the stakes of anonymity for conservative donors. Social conservatives, many of them connected to the National Organization for Marriage (NOM), a group co-founded by Robert George and conservative activist Maggie Gallagher, had fought to reverse laws in progressive states that gave same-sex couples the right to marry. In 2007, Washington passed a law allowing same-sex couples to enter civil unions, and Protect Marriage Washington, an ally of NOM's, hoped to use the state's referendum process to eliminate the civil union provision. After Protect Marriage obtained the requisite signatures for a referendum, the Washington Coalition for Open Government filed a public records request, seeking the names and addresses of everyone who had signed Protect Marriage's petition. Two other groups, WhoSigned.org and KnowThyNeighbor.org, announced plans to release a searchable list of signers online. Representing Protect Marriage, Bopp sued to block release of the names. He argued that Washington's public records law was unconstitutional, at least as applied to his client. He pointed out that online blacklists, graffitied walls, and boycotts had greeted NOM supporters in California after they reestablished bans on marriage for same-sex couples. Unless the Supreme Court protected the anonymity of Protect Marriage's supporters, most would remain silent rather than deal with similar fallout.[114]

Bopp planned to make donor secrecy the centerpiece of *Citizens United* too. BCRA required a disclaimer identifying the organization or individual responsible for any ad that referred to a candidate by name. Anyone who spent more than $10,000 in a calendar year running that kind of ad also had to tell the government her name, the amount spent, and certain contributors' identities.[115]

Bopp planned to argue that the Court should read *Wisconsin Right to Life* to apply to corporate disclosure. He had long focused on express advocacy—the idea that the Constitution protected certain corporate attack ads and other forms of campaign speech that stopped short of telling voters whom to choose. He hoped that *Wisconsin Right to Life* could resurrect a related idea. No one, he argued, should have to disclose anything about an ad unless there was a "clear plea for action that may reasonably be considered an 'appeal to vote.'" *Citizens United* could establish that "disclosure requirements are a serious per se burden on 'political speech' requiring strict scrutiny." Bopp especially cautioned his allies not to push Chief Justice Roberts "to the other side." A decision that eliminated disclosure requirements would be the best of both worlds: it would delight conservative organizations and donors without asking the chief justice to move outside his comfort zone.[116]

But Bopp was not going to stop with donor disclosure. He wanted to argue that *Wisconsin Right to Life* applied to every campaign finance case—that is, the government could not limit any spending or require any disclosure unless it was "unambiguously related to a candidate's campaign." All other forms of soft money (which meant *most* soft money) could not be capped. He and the RNC also challenged the constitutionality of BCRA's soft money ban. A separate case, filed by Bopp in Louisiana, centered on the RNC's ability to coordinate with candidates. Bopp was especially excited about the prospect of unraveling disclosure requirements. "Any soft money not required to be reported by some state . . . would be totally unreported and the donors' identity would be protected from disclosure," he wrote. "That would be quite a result."[117]

In November 2008, after the Supreme Court announced that it would hear *Citizens United,* Bossie and Boos decided to replace Bopp as counsel with Ted Olson. Olson had been solicitor general in George W. Bush's first term, representing the government (and winning) in *McConnell.* Olson's about-face was not much of a surprise. It had been his job as solicitor general to defend BCRA, and while he considered himself socially liberal and supported same-sex marriage, Olson was a lifelong Republican, and the GOP had come increasingly to oppose BCRA.[118]

Olson broke with Bopp's strategy, shifting the focus away from disclosure. While still challenging the disclosure requirements, his brief primarily suggested that full-length films, available through video on demand, did not pose any danger of corruption unless they contained express advocacy. Viewers had no choice about the ads that flooded the airways, which might "persuade viewers or listeners to vote for a candidate for whom they otherwise would not." But viewers had to "opt in" before they could watch *Hillary,* which made the risk of corruption much lower. *Hillary* was not express advocacy but a "critical biography," no different than the ones found on the shelves of many bookstores. Nor, Olson argued, did it make sense to apply the ruling of *Austin* to *Hillary.* In that case, the Michigan Chamber of Commerce had been funded entirely by for-profit businesses. *Hillary* depended almost exclusively on funding from conservative individual donors who shared the ideological mission of Citizens United. But Olson also invited the Court to overrule *Austin* altogether.[119]

Austin took on even more importance in June 2009, when the Court scheduled *Citizens United* for reargument. Reporter Jeffrey Toobin suggested that the justices had planned to issue a 5-4 opinion siding with Citizens United and overruling *Austin*, but Justice Souter, furious about what he viewed as a breach of the Court's own procedure, planned to write an opinion publicly airing his grievances. To avoid this fight becoming public, the Court scheduled another argument, this time asking the parties to address the validity of *Austin*.[120]

Prior to reargument, Bopp's Madison Center for Free Speech submitted an amicus brief (which Bopp wrote) on behalf of several former FEC members, stressing that the First Amendment made no exceptions based on the speaker's identity.[121] He next detailed why *Austin* had become unworkable. Over time, he wrote, the rules governing corporate spending had become hopelessly complex, adding to the considerable burden already carried by corporate speakers. BCRA did allow corporations and unions to create PACs to carry on political spending, but managing or setting up a PAC was so expensive that most small companies were shut out. After adding in the cost of experts needed to navigate the maze of campaign finance laws, some corporate speakers chose to stay silent.[122]

But the arguments in *Citizens United* went well beyond those made by right-to-lifers. The ACLU submitted an amicus brief arguing that BCRA's rules on corporate "electioneering" were impossibly vague and chilled protected political speech. Ed Meese's brief on behalf of the Center for Constitutional Jurisprudence, an arm of the conservative Claremont Institute, argued that the Constitution's framers would not blink an eye at the concentration of wealth in the contemporary United States—or the vast sums spent on election ads. Charles Cooper, the long-serving outside counsel for the NRA, stressed that the electioneering provision had to be unconstitutional, at least as applied to issue-based nonprofits, because "nonprofit advocacy organizations funded by individuals, have always been constitutionally distinct from business corporations." The Alliance Defending Freedom maintained that *Wisconsin Right to Life* had become unworkable—and that *Austin* had to give way to protections for speech "at the core of the First Amendment." The Center for Competitive Politics, the Institute for Justice, and the Cato Institute also worked on the case.[123]

When the Court announced its decision in *Citizens United* in January 2010, eight of the justices (all but Clarence Thomas) voted to uphold requirements governing donor disclosure. As Justice Kennedy explained for the majority, those measures did not "prevent anyone from speaking." Bopp's plans for *Citizens United*—centered on donor disclosure—ended in failure, but it hardly mattered. Foes of campaign finance won a far more significant victory on corporate spending on political speech.[124]

The Court saw BCRA's prohibition of corporate speech—and its own previous decision in *Austin*—as deeply problematic. Olson's original strategy did not fare well, however. Citizens United had argued that *Hillary* was different because it was funded by individuals and available only on demand—but the Court thought it would be untenable to anchor the First Amendment to that kind of detail. Doing so might mean one rule for video on demand, another for social media, another for broadcast television—an unworkable approach. And Kennedy reasoned that Citizens United received too much of its money from corporations to be any different from the corporation in *Austin*.[125]

What about *Wisconsin Right to Life II*? Bopp's original plan had been to extend that ruling. Olson had tried a variation of this argument, insisting that only corporate express advocacy created a real risk of corruption, at least when it came to feature-length films. But the *Citizens United* Court seemed to define genuine issue ads more narrowly. Kennedy described *Hillary* as little more than "a feature-length negative advertisement."[126]

For Citizens United to win, it seemed, it had to win big, and that was exactly what happened. The Court began by concluding that BCRA had functionally banned speech, and that its prohibitions counted as "classic examples of censorship." The availability of a PAC did nothing to change this analysis. PACs were "expensive to administer and subject to extensive regulations." The point remained that Congress had banned speech, as the Court saw it, and this was something the Constitution prohibited.[127]

Reformers had contended—and past Courts had agreed—that corporate speech was different, but the current Court no longer saw things that way. Instead, Kennedy's majority opinion stressed that the First Amendment did not permit restrictions based on the identity of the speaker. "By taking the right to speak from some and giving it to others," he wrote, "the Government deprives the disadvantaged person or class of the right to use speech to strive to establish worth, standing, and respect for the speaker's voice."[128]

Next, the Court overturned *Austin.* That decision had emphasized that corporate wealth could distort the results of elections, but the Court now found this rationale at odds with the very idea of free speech. The rationale could easily apply to media corporations—organizations that amass considerable wealth and spread views that have little correlation with public support for any given position. As Kennedy saw it, the First Amendment would not tolerate such a result.[129]

In ditching *Austin,* the Court also overhauled its understanding of corruption in elections. In recent decisions, the justices had expressed concern about the purchase of many kinds of influence and access. But in *Citizens United,* the Court recognized no corruption beyond direct quid pro quos. "The fact that speakers may have influence over or access to elected officials does not mean that these officials are corrupt," Kennedy wrote. Money in politics would do nothing to damage democracy, and the public's faith in the system would not decline simply because corporations were spending to ingratiate themselves with the nation's leaders.[130]

Bopp had planned and failed to rewrite the rules on donor disclosure, but *Citizens United* did something much more significant from the standpoint of the anti-abortion movement. Everyone knew that *Citizens United* would mean more money in politics, but few foresaw how completely it would upend the Republican hierarchy. For decades, NRLC had argued that politicians should be mere vehicles for the agenda of conservative social movements. Now the country was about to see firsthand exactly what that meant.

6

The Rise of Trump

JAMES BOPP WAS RIGHT TO THINK THAT *Citizens United* was just the beginning. In March 2010, in *SpeechNow.org v. Federal Election Commission*, the DC Circuit Court of Appeals gave a green light to a new spending vehicle, super PACs. Steve Simpson of the Institute for Justice and Steve Hoersting of the Center for Competitive Politics represented David Keating, a man as committed to overthrowing campaign finance rules as his attorneys. Keating acquired his hatred of machine politics as a high schooler, when he learned that only Republicans could get jobs as lifeguards in his hometown. The episode persuaded him to be an independent, and he remained one for the rest of his career. He nevertheless had a clear political vision, which involved as few regulations and taxes as possible. In 2010, he worked as the executive director of the Club for Growth, a conservative nonprofit corporation that helped fund insurgent candidates. He also wanted to start a super PAC, SpeechNow.org, to pay for political ads in the 2010 elections.[1]

Citizens United overturned restrictions on independent expenditures from corporations and unions. Keating wanted to extend the decision further, arguing that super PACs like his 527 should be able to accept unlimited *contributions* from individuals as long they used the money exclusively for independent expenditures, such as paying for attack ads. The Federal Election Commission advised Keating that contributions made to SpeechNow would fall under federal contribution limits—and that SpeechNow would have to register as a political committee once it spent a certain amount to influence an election. Keating argued that federal disclosure requirements, contribution limits, and political committee registration requirements imposed on SpeechNow were unconstitutional. The DC Circuit Court of Appeals agreed. After *Citizens United*, the government's only interest in the campaign finance setting was in preventing quid pro quo corruption, and *Citizens United* had held "that independent expenditures do not corrupt or create the appearance of *quid pro quo* corruption." Since super PACs like SpeechNow made only independent expenditures, the government could have no anticorruption interest in limiting contributions to those organizations. Keating's arguments about organization and reporting requirements were not as successful. The DC Circuit easily rejected them.[2]

Bopp's disclosure case on behalf of opponents of same-sex marriage, *John Doe Number One v. Reed*, also did not fare well. The majority in *John Doe Number One* applied the test for disclosure rules set out in *Citizens United*—there had to be a substantial relation between the disclosure requirement and a sufficiently important governmental interest. Chief Justice Roberts's majority opinion held that Washington State had legitimately acted to protect the integrity of elections. The state's law could help to ferret out duplicate signatures, bait and switches, and other forms of fraud. Bopp argued that even if the government had a crucial interest in election integrity, *Buckley v. Valeo* and *Citizens United* made an exception for donors when there was "a reasonable probability that the compelled disclosure will subject them to threats, harassment, or reprisals." Because the Court understood Bopp to be challenging Washington's public records law on its face, however, the majority found little evidence that most such laws would heavily burden donors as a general rule. Justice Samuel Alito, in a concurring opinion, hinted that Protect Marriage could try again later to show that the harassment it expected had come to pass. But *John Doe Number One* hardly felt like a victory. A majority had yet again rejected a challenge involving anonymity. Worse, Justice Antonin Scalia suggested that the First Amendment had nothing to say about disclosure rules.[3]

SpeechNow and *John Doe Number One* sent the same message: outside money could flow into national elections, but donors did not have any guarantee of secrecy. On any controversial issue, donors were increasingly demanding anonymity as a precondition of opening their wallets. James Bopp made it his mission to find ways to ensure that money in American politics would be private as well as unlimited.

The Rise of the Tea Party

The Republican hierarchy had long worked to weed out candidates who appeared too far to the right to be electable. For decades, the party establishment had a near-monopoly on seasoned campaign staff, the best access to major donors, and connections to reporters who could make a candidate a public name. Denying insurgent candidates these resources could starve their campaigns. In 1992 and 1996, insurgent Pat Buchanan had a devoted following, but the GOP hierarchy stopped him in his tracks.[4]

In 2010, when the Tea Party tested the party hierarchy, the pillars of control—especially media access and campaign dollars—had begun to fall away. In 1992 and 1996, when Buchanan ran his most effective campaigns, conservative media began and ended with Rush Limbaugh, and Fox News was just getting started. By 2010, Fox News had been the nation's top cable news network for nine years running. New conservative radio hosts and online news sites seemed to appear every day. Breitbart, founded in 2007 as an online news aggregator by conservative activist Andrew Breitbart, had seen strong gains since Barack Obama took office. Tucker Carlson, a conservative journalist who had just become a Fox News commentator, cofounded another conservative site, the Daily Caller, in 2010. The former journalist Christopher Ruddy had started Newsmax, another online news site, with seed money from the Scaife Foundation. In 2010, he launched the online broadcaster Newsmax TV. While the legacy media struggled, conservative outlets thrived: Newsmax reported a $10 million increase in revenue between 2008 and 2009 alone.[5]

The party establishment's stranglehold on election spending was also starting to weaken. *Citizens United* and *SpeechNow* had opened the door to more spending by super PACs, unions, and corporations. After *SpeechNow*, super PACs became the fastest growing form of election spending. Whereas individuals could contribute only $5,000 to a regular PAC (which could not accept any money from corporations or unions), super PACs could accept unlimited (and uncapped) contributions from individuals, corporations, and labor unions so long as they made only independent expenditures. That made them extremely attractive to both conservative donors and issue-based organizations.

Some of the first groups to take advantage were those that formed the backbone of the Tea Party. The movement got its start in February 2009 with an outburst from CNBC reporter Rick Santelli. Furious about the emerging details of President Obama's foreclosure-relief plan, Santelli invited those who shared his outrage to a "Chicago Tea Party." The first rally was small, but conservative bloggers and radio jocks saw potential in Santelli's rant. Soon, self-described Tea Partiers could be found everywhere on social media. Protestors' demands were inchoate but centered on the idea that the government had betrayed its existing commitments to Social Security and Medicare by expanding programs for those who were less deserving, especially immigrants, the poor, and the young.[6]

The daughter of a Methodist minister, Jenny Beth Martin was a mother of twins whose husband ran a successful temp agency. But the recession, together with a dishonest business partner, forced the business to shut its doors, and the Martins lost their home in the 2008 financial crisis. Martin heard Santelli on the radio while driving to clean houses, and his call for a tea party triggered something in her. She organized her first rally in Atlanta not long after that.

California native Mark Meckler had fared better during the recession. He had tried everything from running a coffee shop to selling ski equipment before earning a law degree and setting up a practice specializing in the law of online marketing. Meckler was well off by 2009, but Santelli struck a nerve with him too. A hundred and fifty people with homemade signs attended his first rally. Meckler and Martin later organized Tea Party Patriots, a group that tried to connect local Tea Party chapters.[7]

Other Tea Partiers were veteran political operators. Sal Russo, a longtime political activist who ran a Republican consulting firm in Sacramento, was once the youngest staffer in the Reagan administration and now saw himself as a lifelong enemy of the establishment. He founded the Tea Party Express to support sympathetic candidates nationwide.[8]

Established groups also tried to ride the Tea Party wave. FreedomWorks, launched in 2004 with the aid of conservative megadonors David and

Charles Koch, tried to supercharge the Tea Party's growth. Led by former Texas representative Dick Armey, FreedomWorks spent $10 million in 2010 backing Tea Party candidates and initiatives. Its sister organization, Americans for Prosperity (the two groups had emerged from an internal rift that divided the Koch-founded Citizens for a Sound Economy in 2004), shelled out $30 million on issue ads, bus tours, phone banks, and organized protests at town halls on Obama's proposed health-care reform. By 2010, a wide range of groups, some lavishly funded and with deep roots in Republican politics, were combining to give the Tea Party movement coherence and force.[9]

Pro-life activists initially viewed the Tea Party with ambivalence. Tea Partiers rarely focused on social issues. Some prioritized what they saw as rampant voter fraud that helped Democrats win. In the Houston suburbs, Catherine Engelbrecht had focused on raising her family and supporting her husband's business, which specialized in manufacturing machine components. But in 2009, she caught the Tea Party fever and founded an aligned group, King Street Patriots, in Houston's Harris County. In August 2010, Engelbrecht announced that her group had found thousands of incomplete, inaccurate, or false voter registrations in the county. King Street Patriots launched an organization called True the Vote. While Engelbrecht described True the Vote as a campaign to fight voter fraud, her critics argued that it was a voter suppression tool aimed at voters of color. Many Tea Partiers also looked to slash government spending. The movement's cornerstone proposal, the Contract from America, originated with Houston attorney Ryan Hecker, who launched a website to crowdsource ideas for a possible Tea Party platform. FreedomWorks worked with Hecker to cull the submissions, and attendees of the 2010 Conservative Political Action Conference narrowed the list to ten. The final Contract from America focused almost exclusively on economic issues, including a commitment to a balanced federal budget and a plan to dump Obama's cap-and-trade proposal to curb carbon emissions. Social issues barely seemed to register. Some abortion foes worried that the Tea Party might be pro-choice or might ignore the abortion issue altogether. Writing about the Tea Party in the *Human Life Review*, pro-life commentator George McKenna cautioned that "the enemy is not 'big government,' it is this big government."[10]

His own misgivings notwithstanding, Bopp pushed the GOP establishment to bring the Tea Party into the fold. He had become the Republican National Committee's vice chairman in 2008, two years before the Tea Party wave. Earlier in his career, Bopp had led the county-level campaigns of Indiana Republicans running for governor or senator, served on the Indiana team working on George W. Bush's reelection, and worked as treasurer and general counsel of the Indiana Republican Party. In 2008 he was an advisor to Mitt Romney's presidential campaign. Two years later, he thought that establishment candidates like Romney were doomed unless they won over the Tea Party. He urged his colleagues to learn from the disastrous 2009 special congressional election in upstate New York, where Tea Partiers had rejected the GOP nominee, Assemblywoman Dede Scozzafava, as a liberal pretender and backed a third-party candidate. Scozzafava eventually withdrew from the race and threw her support behind her Democratic challenger, Bill Owens, whose victory put the seat into Democratic hands for the first time in a century. Any Republican, Bopp warned, could be the next Dede Scozzafava if the GOP did not woo Tea Partiers. Unless the Tea Party was part of the GOP, more third-party candidates would emerge, split the vote, and toss races to Democrats.[11]

In January 2010, Bopp sponsored a resolution requiring Republican candidates to agree to at least eight of ten conservative positions to win support from the RNC. He framed the "purity test" as a way of restoring the party's credibility with grassroots conservatives. "The problem is that many conservatives have lost trust in the conservative credentials of the Republican Party," Bopp explained in defending his resolution.[12] The RNC passed a compromise that "urged," but did not require, the group to consider withholding support for candidates who did not support the party's platform. Publicly, Bopp declared the resolution even better than his own. Behind the scenes, Tea Party conservatives did not conceal their disgust. RNC chairman Michael Steele made overtures to Tea Partiers at the party's 2010 gathering in Honolulu, but many viewed Steele himself as part of the problem. Linda Lingle, the Republican governor of Hawaii, had to plead with a visibly unhappy audience not to boo him. Many believed that the RNC would never capture Tea Party support with Steele at the helm. He was part of the establishment, and *establishment* had become a dirty word.[13]

Bopp himself was at least as conservative as many Tea Partiers and did not mind the rise of candidates who ran further to the right. Over time, the Tea Party would open his eyes to broader possibilities. Republicans had proclaimed theirs to be the party of life since 1980, and yet abortion remained legal. It seemed that any popular, successful candidate would inevitably prioritize his own agenda (and reelection) over promises about abortion. The Tea Party, however, was a kind of proof of concept that under certain circumstances, conservative, issue-based movements could control candidates rather than depend on them. The question was what that control required.

A Post–*Citizens United* Roadmap

Bopp thought the answer probably involved money. *Citizens United* had given opponents of campaign finance laws a tremendous boost. As vice chairman of the RNC, Bopp encouraged his party to fight even harder against these laws, and he, the RNC, and other organizations opposed to campaign finance limits began outlining a litigation strategy for the post–*Citizens United* world. Recognizing that *Citizens United* and *SpeechNow* had made outside spending far more attractive to many donors, Bopp highlighted ways for the party to gain an advantage over super PACs and nonprofits.[14]

In the golden age of soft money, the two major parties' revenues had risen dramatically, from a total of $425 million in 1988 to over $1 billion in 2000. Soft money revenues alone had jumped from $45 million to $495 million in the same period. With soft money flowing, political parties reigned as the kings of campaign finance. BCRA had changed this to a degree. Although the law raised the contribution limits, all money raised, spent, received, or transferred by any entity controlled by the national parties still fell under strict contribution limits, and the parties had no access to soft money. Equally important, corporations could not donate directly to political parties, candidates, or campaigns. Parties had hardly given up on spending: the Democratic and Republican leadership solicited small donors and broadened their donor base while establishment operatives formed and staffed nonprofit corporations and super PACs. Nevertheless,

Republican leaders recognized that the establishment had less control over outside spending than it once had over soft money, and some outside spending organizations had more interest in replacing or transforming the establishment than in empowering it. Recognizing that the GOP had been able to raise more soft money than the Democrats, the RNC wanted Bopp to take on soft money limits as well as the ban on direct corporate donations to parties. Bopp also imagined challenging virtually every disclosure requirement, from those involving state and local elections to those governing political ads.[15]

But how could anyone challenge disclosure requirements after *Citizens United* and *SpeechNow*? Bopp hinted at a new argument: since being introduced years earlier, disclosure rules had never been adjusted and were thus overbroad. *Buckley*, along with more recent decisions, had suggested that "the real point behind disclosure laws is to inform the public who has a financial stake in the outcome of an election or ballot measure contest." But in Bopp's view, those who donated just $200 in 2010 had no stake in anything. Inflation had altered the landscape since *Buckley*. Forcing so much disclosure burdened " 'substantially' more associational and speech rights than is justified."[16]

Neither Bopp nor the RNC had a hand in the Supreme Court's next campaign finance suit. In *Arizona Free Enterprise Club's Freedom Club PAC v. Bennett*, two separate suits took aim at Arizona's public financing scheme; the libertarian Institute for Justice filed one suit (with attorneys Steve Simpson, Chip Mellor, William Maurer, Jeanette Peterson, Timothy Keller, and Paul Avelar working on the case), while the Goldwater Institute, another libertarian group organized by Institute co-founder Clint Bolick, filed the other (Bolick and Nicholas Dranias litigated the case on behalf of Goldwater). A New Jersey native, Bolick had reconsidered his politics when studying school desegregation. He found inspiration in *Brown v. Board of Education*, the Court's renowned 1954 desegregation decision, but he saw affirmative action as a subversion of its intent. He became a libertarian litigator, working with the Mountain States Legal Foundation for two years before taking a job under Clarence Thomas at the Equal Employment Opportunity Commission. In 1991, Bolick co-founded the Institute for Justice with Mellor, a colleague from his Mountain States days who had helped litigate *SpeechNow.* The two took a passionate interest in property rights, gun rights, civil rights, and free speech. Bolick and Mellor despised limits on campaign finance, and the Arizona law struck them as one of the worst. Under that system, candidates could choose to participate or opt out of public financing. Participating candidates—who had to receive a certain number of $5 donations to qualify—received grants from the government. But those who opted out suffered a key disadvantage: for every dollar in independent expenditures received by the independently funded candidate or spent against his publicly funded opponent, his rival would receive close to a dollar in public funding (no one received matching funds if someone spent money against an independently funded candidate). The Institute for Justice and the Goldwater Institute compared Arizona's scheme to the Millionaire's Amendment that the Supreme Court had struck down in *Davis v. Federal Election Commission.* Just as in *Davis,* Arizona candidates had to choose between raising as much money as they wanted and seeing dollars pour into their opponents' coffers.[17]

In 2010, a district court struck down the law, but four months later, the Ninth Circuit Court of Appeals reversed. The court agreed with Bolick that the public financing scheme should be subject to strict scrutiny, but it did not believe Arizona had created a burden nearly as heavy as the one in *Davis. Davis,* like *Citizens United,* involved a law that discriminated against a speaker based on her identity (being very wealthy in one case, being a corporation in the other). The Ninth Circuit saw no such discrimination at work in Arizona. The public financing scheme applied equally to all candidates regardless of their personal wealth. Besides, *Buckley* had upheld a federal public financing scheme decades ago, so there was nothing wrong with Arizona doing the same.[18]

The New Outside Spending

The Supreme Court decided to hear *Arizona Free Enterprise,* and while the case was pending, the 2010 election season began to take shape. The race represented campaign finance attorneys' first chance to experiment in the aftermath of *Citizens United.* Crossroads Grassroots Policy Strategies (Crossroads GPS), a group set up by former George W. Bush advisor Karl Rove, represented one alluring option. Crossroads was a 501(c)(4) corporation, a kind of nonprofit. Another kind of nonprofit, 501(c)(3) corporations, focused on charitable, educational, or religious aims. Donations to 501(c)(3) nonprofits were tax deductible. While these organizations could engage in limited amounts of lobbying, they were prohibited from participating in campaigns for political office. A 501(c)(4) like Crossroads GPS, on the other hand, could spend up to 50 percent of its money on political activity, but donations to it were not tax deductible. Both (c)(3) and (c)(4) nonprofits had to report their independent expenditures and spending on certain kinds of political ads to the IRS, but neither kind had to disclose their donors to the public. James Bopp recognized the appeal of 501s and argued that the limits placed on their political activity violated the Constitution. In the short term, however, such arguments were hardly worth the trouble. If these nonprofit corporations violated the law, no federal agency had much incentive to do anything about it. The Internal Revenue Service, the agency most closely charged with monitoring 501 organizations, focused on revenue collection, not election integrity, and often knew little about the political activity of 501s until an election was long over—if ever. In 2010, 139,000 501(c)(4)s registered with the IRS but only 65 reported their spending. *Citizens United* had opened the door to corporate spending on political ads, and ideological 501s stepped up to take advantage.[19]

Unnamed donors became a defining feature of the 2010 race. Direct contributions to parties and candidates still accounted for the majority of all campaign spending, but outside spending made up more of the total than ever before. More than 90 percent of 501s did not reveal where their money was coming from, and conservative groups outspent liberal ones by nearly a 5-1 margin. The spread of anonymous donors helped to shatter spending records for a midterm race, beating the previous record for spending on all federal races, set in 2006, by roughly $1 billion.[20]

The results of the race were just as eye-catching. In the House of Representatives, Republicans recorded their best gains since the 1930s, picking up more than sixty seats. But state legislatures proved to be the real story. Going into 2010, Democrats held majorities in fifty-two of the eighty-eight state legislative houses up for election, while Republicans held only thirty-three. By the end of the election, the GOP controlled fifty-three of the nation's ninety-nine chambers, while Democrats held thirty-two.[21]

For NRLC leaders, the wave of 2010 was a revelation. Tea Partiers had defied conventional wisdom in more ways than one. Often running without the blessing of the party establishment, they had found their own sources of support. James Bopp saw the Tea Party's victory as the start of a roadmap for reshaping the GOP. He had not originally focused on outside spending in *Citizens United*, but when the case presented his movement with new opportunities, he was ready to take advantage. Issue-based movements no longer had to waste their time looking for a perfect candidate—or convincing imperfect candidates to change. Anti-abortion groups could engineer their own takeover.

Resistance to Incrementalism

At first, however, the Tea Party's success forced a difficult debate about what the anti-abortion movement should expect from GOP-controlled state legislatures. Abortion foes had long divided into different camps, with absolutists questioning the wisdom of relying on victory in the Supreme Court. Pragmatists like those leading NRLC and Americans United for Life had consistently had the upper hand in these struggles. NRLC and AUL far outraised and outspent the absolutist groups, routinely supplied staffers to GOP presidential administrations, and maintained close ties with Republican state legislatures. After the Tea Party wave, NRLC and AUL planned to make the best possible use of these connections. AUL had been putting out model anti-abortion legislation since the late 1980s. NRLC had begun even earlier. With the Tea Party's success, leaders like Bopp expected more of these bills to start passing.[22]

NRLC harkened back to an argument made during the fight for a federal ban on partial-birth abortion. In lobbying for that law, the group had asserted that as early as twenty weeks into a pregnancy, abortion caused unborn children tremendous pain. The American College of Obstetricians and Gynecologists rejected this claim, but some studies indicated that fetal pain at that stage was possible. In 2010, NRLC lobbyist Doug Johnson pushed a model law banning all abortions at twenty weeks, the point when NRLC said a fetus could feel pain. By April 2010, Nebraska had passed the "pain-capable" ban. Johnson hoped the bills would give the Supreme Court a chance to extend *Gonzales v. Carhart* while allowing states to outlaw abortions before viability.[23]

AUL renewed its campaign to defund Planned Parenthood. Long one of the nation's leading advocates for abortion rights, Planned Parenthood had by 2011 become one of the nation's largest abortion providers. That year, it received about $330 million in federal money, both through Medicaid and family planning grants. The group's abortion services, offered at 40 percent of centers, relied on private funding. But in state legislatures and Congress, AUL insisted that money was fungible: any federal money received by Planned Parenthood freed up cash to be spent on abortions.[24]

Anti-abortion leaders blitzed state legislatures, offering dozens of model laws for Tea Party lawmakers to choose from—a process that journalist Emily Bazelon called "incrementalism on steroids." But resistance to a court-centered strategy continued to build. Activist Les Riley, one of the rebels, was a devout evangelical Protestant living in Horn Lake, Mississippi, a town kept alive by a factory that made seasonings and the Circle G Ranch, purchased by Elvis Presley on a horse-buying spree in 1967. Riley and his wife, learning that an abortion clinic was operating in the nearby town of Southaven, began going there to protest in 1991. In time they found a community of like-minded Christians through Operation Rescue. Their collective efforts eventually contributed to the closure of the Southaven clinic—which, to Riley's delight, was bought by a church.[25]

Then the two drifted away from pro-life work. Riley's wife, Christy, became a mother of ten. Riley himself tried a run for public office. On the campaign trail, he ran into New Right veteran Howard Phillips, who told him that lawmakers had the power to ban abortion immediately through recognizing fetal personhood. Riley wanted to give it a try. In 2004, he co-founded Personhood Mississippi and began working to put personhood measures on the ballot. In 2011, the group's efforts paid off: Mississippians would have the chance to vote on personhood.[26]

NRLC and a local Catholic diocese declined to endorse Mississippi's personhood amendment. Bopp argued that even if it passed, such an amendment would inevitably fail at the U.S. Supreme Court. Worse, the Court could use the Mississippi case to strengthen abortion rights, perhaps by relying on the idea that abortion restrictions constituted sex discrimination under the equal protection clause. But personhood proponents saw the Tea Party rewriting the rules of American politics. With Mississippi set to vote, they hoped to prove that they could win too.[27]

A Redefined RNC

Personhood proponents were not the only ones reimagining the partnership between the GOP and grassroots activists. Bopp had planned to use *Citizens United* to open the door to anonymous campaign spending. But later in 2010, especially in light of the Tea Party insurgency, he understood the decision differently. He joined Solomon Yue and Dick Armey to create the RNC Conservative Caucus. Yue had grown up in China idolizing his grandfather, John, who had fled from Mao Zedong's regime to Hong Kong while Yue and his family remained in China. Yue admired his grandfather's entrepreneurialism (he ran a successful tailoring business) and rebellious streak (he practiced Methodism, a taboo under Communism). When his teachers denounced Western music, Yue learned the violin. In school, he argued with his teachers and eventually was sent away to do forced labor in the fields. His fortunes changed when his grandfather helped arrange a student visa for him at Alaska Pacific University. Learning English from scratch, he waited tables at a Chinese restaurant and worked night shifts as a janitor to make his way through school. After graduating from business school, Yue fell in love with another immigrant, Dr. Ourania Otey, whom he met during the physical he needed to get his green card. They were a perfect match: both hated Communism and loved the Second Amendment and classical music. After marrying, moving to Oregon, and starting a business, Yue also deepened his involvement in GOP politics. He served on Bob Dole's Asian-American Steering Committee in 1996 and afterward remained deeply involved with the party.[28]

Armey was an economist who had bounced from faculty to faculty. In 1984, he entered Congress as one of the "Texas Six Pack," a group of conservative representatives from that state. He started out as a classic Reagan Republican, left Congress in 2003, and became a lobbyist who charged $20,000 and up to give a speech, in which he came across as a plain-speaking lover of country music whose heart had never left Texas. He established himself early on as a leader of the Tea Party movement.

The Conservative Caucus spoke the Tea Party's language. It asserted that Obama would "redistribute wealth," "engineer a government takeover of the healthcare industry," "engage in out-of-control deficit spending," and "create entitlements that lead to government dependency," which in turn would damage the "moral fabric" of the country. The Tea Party had threatened to break away from the Republican Party, but Bopp, Armey, and Yue hoped to show that it could take over the GOP instead.[29]

The three men were in a stronger position to put their ideas into action when Michael Steele's chairmanship of the Republican National Committee fell into disarray. In 2011, the RNC was roughly $23 million in debt and seemed to be slipping into irrelevance. Most of the money spent on the 2010 election came not from the RNC but from 501 groups like Crossroads GPS or 527s like the Republican Governors' Association. The heads of these groups often served as the party's de facto strategists. The RNC had no more pull at the local level.[30]

Steele's former backers lined up to run against him. Reince Priebus, the chairman of the Wisconsin Republican Party and Steele's former chief liaison, threw his hat in the ring. The son of a union electrician, Priebus moved to Green Bay, Wisconsin, at age seven and became equally obsessed with politics and the Green Bay Packers. His NFL prospects were dim, but he volunteered for his first campaign in high school. As a law student at the University of Miami, he finished fifth in a student presidential poll. His sole campaign promise was to make the Packers, rather than the Dallas Cowboys, "America's team."[31]

But Priebus's interest in politics was not a joke. In 2004, he ran and lost his only race. The truth was that Priebus lacked star power. Those who knew him unfailingly described him as nice, even normal, but never as charismatic. He was very good, however, at the rest of politics, the strategy and fundraising, the mastery of delegate counting and arcane party rules. In 2007, at thirty-five, he became the youngest person ever to lead the Wisconsin Republican Party. His rise in the RNC was just as fast. James Bopp endorsed him, noting that in Wisconsin, Priebus had helped bridge the divide between the GOP and the Tea Party. Besides, Priebus seemed to understand that the GOP could no longer be defined by specific candidates. Outside spending had weakened the traditional party, and issue-based groups wanted to take advantage. "Years ago," Bopp wrote in December 2010, "we elected Politicians as our 'Leaders,' who told the People what government policies they should support. This paradigm has been destroyed. The most prominent manifestation of this is the tea party movement, but it is universal." In *Citizens United*, Bopp had not focused on expanding outside spending or empowering super PACs and nonprofits. But now he saw that the decision could upend the Republican hierarchy. He hoped that specific candidates would become irrelevant—mere vehicles for the social movements (and outside organizations) that drove the GOP. He voted for Priebus because Priebus seemed to understand this vision.[32]

Personhood and Its Fallout

Much seemed bright for Bopp and NRLC in 2011. A five-justice majority sided with the Institute for Justice and the Goldwater Institute in *Arizona Free Enterprise* and invalidated Arizona's public funding scheme. Writing for the majority, Chief Justice Roberts saw the Arizona law as strikingly similar to the Millionaire's Amendment just struck down in *Davis v. Federal Election Commission*. In Roberts's view, Arizona gave publicly financed candidates a strong boost without a real justification for doing so. "We have repeatedly rejected the argument that the government has a compelling state interest in 'leveling the playing field' that can justify undue burdens on political speech," he wrote. Nor did Arizona have a compelling interest in checking corruption, at least when it came to public funding. The state's contribution limit and disclosure rules took care of that. Writing in dissent, Justice Elena Kagan took issue with the idea that Arizona had burdened anyone. "What the law does—all the law does," she wrote, "is fund more speech." Kagan's view aside, the Court seemed to have a solid majority deeply skeptical of many campaign finance limitations. NRLC attorneys hoped to take advantage.[33]

Bopp also looked for ways to bring more money into the GOP's coffers. His latest organization, Republican Super PAC, solicited corporations and individuals for donations. Critics, including election law specialist Rick Hasen, argued that Republican Super PAC functionally coordinated with GOP candidates—or donated directly to their campaigns—and therefore fell under contribution limits. The FEC soon weighed in on the rules that applied to super PACs. The public paid the most attention to a stunt pulled by late-night TV host Stephen Colbert, who portrayed a mock-conservative pundit on his show, *The Colbert Report.* He informed federal regulators of his desire to form a super PAC to fund attack ads and cover "normal administrative expenses, including, but not limited to, luxury hotel stays, private jet travel, and PAC mementos from Saks Fifth Avenue and Neiman Marcus." The FEC, apparently lacking a sense of irony, granted him a limited media exemption and approved his bid to form a super PAC in June 2011.[34]

The retired navy admiral James Carey and his National Defense PAC posed more serious questions. Carey wanted to create a super PAC while opening a separate bank account that would make direct contributions to candidates and their campaigns. He filed suit against the FEC, arguing that it would be unconstitutional for regulators to stop him from doing so. In June 2011, a district court entered an injunction on behalf of Carey and National Defense PAC. Two months later, the FEC entered into a consent judgment that allowed hybrid PACs to operate as long as they maintained a separate bank account for contributions. These so-called Carey committees, or hybrid PACs, became a major source of outside spending, chipping in nearly $47 million in 2016 alone. Super PAC spending continued to rise.[35]

It was less clear if pragmatists like Bopp had the upper hand in abortion politics too. Leaders of both the Republican and Democratic parties in Mississippi, including both parties' candidates for governor, had backed a personhood proposal. National personhood organizations worked behind the scenes to promote Mississippi's initiative. Personhood USA, founded in 2008, quickly became one of the personhood movement's powerhouses, attracting many activists who had broken away from groups like NRLC. Brian Rohrbough, one of Personhood USA's leaders, got into abortion politics after his son was one of the thirteen high school students murdered in the Columbine massacre of 1999. Rohrbough blamed the shooting on the nation's fraying cultural fabric. A nation that legalized abortion and turned its back on religion, he thought, nurtured a culture of death that made mass shootings inevitable. He became the leader of NRLC's Colorado affiliate. But he opposed NRLC's fight for a partial-birth abortion ban, reasoning that by disallowing only some abortions it implicitly condoned others. In 1999, he wrote a scathing letter denouncing all pro-lifers who, by supporting the ban, had "joined together to call evil good." He quit NRLC to help start Personhood USA.[36]

Disgust with the partial-birth abortion campaign also won over Dan Becker, the head of a Georgia NRLC affiliate. Becker had studied with evangelical Protestant luminary Francis Schaeffer and developed an abiding sense that abortion was the greatest sin of his time. He was the pastor of Little River Church in Woodstock, Georgia, and ran a small woodworking business to make ends meet. Pro-life advocacy was his calling. He became president of Georgia Right to Life (GRL) in 2007 and immediately pushed for a state personhood amendment. He further announced that GRL would endorse candidates for office only if they backed no-exception bans. He took an explicitly faith-based position in defending personhood. All that was too much for NRLC, and GRL ultimately broke away. Becker became a board member of Personhood USA and a leading strategist for the personhood movement. "A Personhood approach produces outstanding political and legislative gains," he argued, "while accomplishing a dramatic shift in public opinion."[37]

He certainly seemed right when it came to Mississippi. Leading evangelical groups, such as James Dobson's Family Research Council, endorsed the proposal. Four of the candidates for the GOP presidential nomination, including frontrunner Mitt Romney, declared their support. Incrementalists had managed to hold back the personhood movement for a time, Becker observed, but after Mississippi, "all bets are off."[38]

The state's voters proved him wrong. Mississippi rejected the personhood amendment by a vote of 58 to 41. Becker had believed that after winning Mississippi, Personhood USA could put its cause on the ballot in states from Florida to Montana. After the proposal failed in one of the most pro-life states in the nation, those plans seemed unrealistic.[39]

But if Bopp and his colleagues thought the Mississippi debacle would create more support for NRLC's strategy, they would have to think again. With the personhood amendment still in the headlines, Janet Folger Porter, a former lobbyist for Ohio's NRLC affiliate, proposed an alternative. She had become strongly opposed to abortion after seeing a slideshow in high school. In her thirties, she moved to Florida to take a position with D. James Kennedy Ministries in Fort Lauderdale. Kennedy was a star in evangelical circles, with a nationally broadcast radio program and TV show. Within the ministry, Porter launched a campaign, Truth in Love, that promoted "ex-gay ministries." In 2003, she founded her own pro-life organization, Faith2Action.[40]

Porter had her own ideas about what the pro-life movement should do. When other people in the movement told her that it was impossible to ban abortions immediately, she responded that her God knew nothing impossible. She also tried to make her life relatable to reach a broader audience. She thought that if she put out a romantic comedy about her search for love, she could help end abortion in America. To no one's surprise, she tried to make it happen. She had already written a group of successful Christian self-help books, and she planned to turn one of them into a tale of a single woman's quest for romance while fighting to ban partial-birth abortion. Porter even filmed a trailer for the movie. Actor Stephen Baldwin would have a starring role, and former presidential candidate Mike Huckabee would make a cameo. Porter would play herself.[41]

While the film never happened, Porter took more concrete steps to criminalize abortion. Starting in Ohio, she launched a campaign to ban abortion when a doctor could detect a heartbeat or fetal cardiac activity, usually around the sixth week of pregnancy (or roughly two weeks after many women would have missed a menstrual period). She loved red roses and sent bunches of them to legislators, asking them to pass her bill before the roses and the babies died. Bopp and Johnson saw her as a loose cannon. "There has always been a division between those who want to concentrate on what will make a difference," Bopp said, "and those who are more interested in making a statement that makes them feel better."[42]

The pragmatists certainly had reasons for confidence. Holding majorities in many state houses, Tea Party Republicans passed a record number of abortion restrictions in 2011—135 compared to 89 just a year earlier. Many lawmakers copied their statutes directly from the AUL or NRLC playbook. But Porter was just the latest activist to reject the overarching framework that had bound the GOP to the pro-life movement. "If the choice is between unity and life," said one activist who had quit Ohio Right to Life to side with Porter, "we choose life."[43]

Funding the 2012 Campaign

The leaders of groups like NRLC wanted to ban abortion as much as Janet Folger Porter did. But they believed that as a matter of strategy, Porter was wasting her time. NRLC leaders felt that focusing on incremental restrictions—and helping to change the rules of campaign finance—would make a much bigger difference. As the 2012 election season began, however, Bopp and his allies had to defend *Citizens United* against a renewed attack. Montana's attorney general, Steve Bullock, had made the fight against *Citizens United* his political launching pad. Montana had a 1912 law that prevented corporations from directly spending money on state elections. The law clearly contradicted *Citizens United*, but Bullock argued in *American Tradition Partnership v. Bullock* that Montana's statute differed from the one the justices had invalidated. After a federal district court invalidated the statute, the Montana Supreme Court reversed, relying on an extensive record suggesting that corporate corruption had been a problem in the state. Bopp, arguing before the U.S. Supreme Court to strike down Montana's law, maintained that Bullock had simply ignored what the justices had said just two years before.[44]

In April 2012, before *American Tradition Partnership* was decided, another case appeared on Bopp's radar. RNC chairman Reince Priebus asked his advice about a possible challenge to FECA's aggregate contribution limits. Congress had created inflation-adjustable aggregate contribution limits for candidates and political committees. In 2013–14, donors giving to both candidate and noncandidate committees could not exceed $123,200. Priebus explained that aggregate limits severely hindered the RNC's fundraising because the GOP's largest donors were willing to spend far more than FECA allowed. Although *Buckley* had rejected a challenge to the aggregate contribution limits, Bopp thought it was worthwhile to try again, but he wanted to find an individual to challenge the individual aggregate limits while the RNC focused on the aggregate limits for parties. Priebus agreed, and as Bopp was preparing the RNC's suit, he was contacted by Steve Hoersting and Brad Smith, who suggested that Bopp's firm take on the case of Shaun McCutcheon, an Alabama man who wanted to contribute more money to Republican candidates than the current law seemed to allow. Hoersting believed McCutcheon's lawsuit could serve a larger purpose. "For years," he wrote to Bopp in April 2012, "four justices have been hinting they would overrule *Buckley v. Valeo*'s contribution limits if presented with the question squarely. The best way to find out is to challenge a federal contribution limit that can be invalidated without disturbing *Buckley*."[45]

The *Buckley* decision made the job harder than Hoersting suggested. In less than four sentences, the Court had upheld an aggregate contribution limit. Congress had worried that contributions could trigger corrupt exchanges of votes for cash. But if donors could spend large amounts of money annually, spreading their contributions among many candidates, that spending might have a similarly corrupting effect. In *McCutcheon*, Congress could justify its aggregate contribution limit as a way to stop donors from circumventing the rules on contributions.[46]

Hoersting did not find this argument to be much of a hurdle. He stressed that the Supreme Court had rejected a similar circumvention argument in both *Arizona Free Enterprise* and *Citizens United*. If donors rerouted their money to super PACs or 501 nonprofits—which was perfectly legal—the Supreme Court's new conservative majority might not worry much. On Bopp's advice, the RNC agreed to add McCutcheon to its suit. Bopp would represent both, and the RNC would cover the costs.[47]

While Bopp prepared his challenge in *McCutcheon*, the RNC was close to deciding on the best candidate to challenge Barack Obama. True the Vote was ready for the general election. The previous year, Catherine Engelbrecht had rolled out a program to train Tea Party volunteers in thirty states to monitor for voter fraud, hosted events at the Heritage Center, sided with Republicans in voter registration disputes in Florida and Wisconsin, and advocated for legislation that required voters to show ID before casting a ballot. Prominent Republicans, from Ed Meese to Wisconsin governor Scott Walker, embraced the organization. Conservatives found less to agree on when it came to the GOP primary. Mitt Romney, the former Republican governor of Massachusetts, was mounting a second presidential run after his disappointing 2008 bid. Romney seemed made to run for president.

He had graduated from Harvard Law School and Harvard Business School at the same time. He had made a fortune at Bain Capital, saved the 2002 Olympics, and done a decent job governing Massachusetts. He looked like a movie star and adored his family. But movement conservatives questioned his past support for abortion rights and a state health-care plan that had provided much of the basis for Obama's Affordable Care Act. On the campaign trail he could be awkward. He unconvincingly described himself as "severely conservative." Three other major candidates vied to be the alternative to Romney: former House Speaker Newt Gingrich of Georgia, Senator Rick Santorum of Pennsylvania, and Representative Ron Paul of Texas. Paul, a self-proclaimed libertarian, had a strong anti-abortion record, and Santorum, who boasted sterling socially conservative credentials, had led the fight for a ban on partial-birth abortion. Nevertheless, by February, Bopp had already endorsed Romney. His reasons were simple: Romney had "the broadest support among all elements of the Republican party electorate, . . . the most appeal to independents and swing voters and was, therefore, the most electable."[48]

Romney stumbled early in the campaign, finishing in a virtual tie with Santorum in Iowa and losing South Carolina to Gingrich, but in April, Santorum and then Gingrich suspended their campaigns, in large part because Romney simply outspent them. Romney's campaign and super PAC finished January with $24 million in the bank—more than the campaigns and super PACs of Ron Paul, Santorum, and Gingrich combined. His spending on political ads—$5.7 million by March—was roughly the same as Santorum's, Gingrich's, and Rick Perry's put together. His strategy throughout the primaries aligned closely with the goals of NRLC and AUL.[49] Some grassroots anti-abortion activists were no more sold on him than they had been on a court-centered strategy. Even after he clinched the nomination, some refused to endorse him.[50]

With the news that came in June, the super PACs and nonprofits supporting Romney's campaign could rest easy: the Supreme Court's decision in *American Tradition Partnership*, a short per curiam ("by the Court") opinion, held that Montana had failed to distinguish its law from the one struck down in 2010 in *Citizens United*. This result was no surprise, but *Citizens United* was still not winning any popularity contests. In 2012, a *New York*

Times poll showed that just 17 percent of Americans approved of the decision. The leaders of NRLC, however, cared only about its consequences: the vast majority of outside spending in 2012—78 percent of the $465 million spent through September—would have been impermissible without *Citizens United.* By Election Day, super PACs, nonprofits, and unions reported $1.28 billion in outside spending. The Koch-backed Americans for Prosperity alone spent $122 million. Large donors found the new 501s and super PACs attractive: 132 donors, each chipping in at least $1 million, accounted for over 60 percent of the money raised by super PACs. The cost of elections would almost certainly have continued to spiral even if *Citizens United* had come down the other way. The decision nevertheless opened the door to ideological PACs and 501s seeking more influence on the GOP. Many outside spenders supported profoundly conservative candidates. After *Citizens United,* those candidates more often had enough money to win.[51]

The Fight for the RNC

The 2012 election season was a moment of reckoning for the relationship between the GOP and conservative movements. *Citizens United* had created opportunities for issue-based organizations that seemed even more important than Bopp had originally envisaged. The Tea Party insurgency, together with changes to the campaign finance landscape produced by *Citizens United,* had encouraged advocates like Bopp to imagine a Republican Party controlled by activist movements that could tell candidates what to do. But Mitt Romney's success in gaining the GOP nomination contradicted that narrative. Romney won Bopp's support—and outlasted his primary opponents—because he had the broadest appeal, not because he was the favored candidate of movement conservatives. The 2012 race tested how a candidate like Romney could proceed in the *Citizens United* era—and whether the relationship between popular candidates, the RNC, and conservative movements had to change fundamentally.[52]

In 2012, Bopp lost his seat on the RNC. He had supported the primary bid of Richard Mourdock, a Tea Party favorite, when he tried to unseat veteran Republican senator Richard Lugar of Indiana. Bopp blamed his ouster on bitter Lugar supporters. Whatever the reason, he retained significant influence within the RNC. He took on a new role as its special counsel, which gave him a front-row seat to the 2012 showdown between the Romney campaign and movement conservatives. The week before the Republican National Convention, a group of establishment lawyers worked with Romney staffer Ben Ginsberg to change the rules governing delegate selection.[53]

Ginsberg was worried about the RNC's delegate selection procedures because of one man, Ron Paul. A representative of Texas's Fourteenth Congressional District, Paul favored conventional Republican policies on abortion, taxes, health care, and guns, but he denounced the criminalization of marijuana and wanted to shrink the security state. He had not won a single primary, but he had a cult libertarian following, and his supporters worked the rules to stage a takeover of the Maine delegation. Romney desperately wanted to present a united front heading into the general election, and Ginsberg led efforts to change the rules to allow candidates to pick delegates in states they won. Ginsberg also proposed rule changes that would bind delegates to the primary result in a state, let the RNC change other rules between Republican National Conventions, and limit the candidates who could appear on the national convention ballot.[54]

The move sparked outrage from Paul delegates, Tea Partiers, grassroots conservatives, and pro-lifers. Movement conservatives had a well-established plan to influence delegate selection, perfected by groups like NRLC and Phyllis Schlafly's Republican National Coalition for Life. If candidates could pick their own delegates, there was little to stop the party from backing away from conservative positions. Bopp angrily wrote erstwhile GOP chairman Haley Barbour that Ginsberg's proposal represented "an unprecedented power grab." The Paul rebellion, together with the anger of the RNC Conservative Caucus, convinced the Convention Rules Committee to withdraw Ginsberg's rule change allowing candidates to pick delegates before anyone could vote on it. The remaining rule changes that Ginsberg proposed, designed to give establishment candidates like Romney an edge, passed on the convention floor in a voice vote.[55]

As the dust settled from that fight, Bopp wrote Solomon Yue that a new GOP was emerging: "conservative, ideological, activist, grass roots, and bottom up." Ginsberg represented the old party: "moderate, elitist, east coast, culturally liberal, and top down." Bopp saw the anti-abortion movement—and himself—as the vanguard of the new party. *Citizens United* had given outside groups more influence on elections. Bopp and Yue hoped to transform the RNC too. The real powerbrokers, they hoped, would be issue-based activists, with the pro-life movement at the forefront.[56]

Setbacks

While Bopp thought nearly all campaign finance restrictions were unconstitutional, the *McCutcheon* case struck him as especially important. Biennial contribution limits were not new, and outside spending groups had ways of working around them. Some had formed joint fundraising committees (JFCs), which allowed multiple candidates, PACs, and political committees to share the costs of fundraising. Donors to JFCs could cut one large check to more than one candidate or political organization, but because wealthy donors could not give to that many groups before hitting the biennial cap, the totals run up by JFCs remained relatively low. *McCutcheon* would change that.[57]

Mitt Romney's 2012 presidential campaign weighed in on how the challenge in *McCutcheon* would be framed. Romney's staff wanted Bopp to try to invalidate aggregate limits across the board, a solution that the campaign called "a lot cleaner and harder to circumvent." Ultimately, two sets of plaintiffs challenged the various aggregate limits written into federal law, with the RNC focusing on the limits on political committees and McCutcheon taking the rest.[58]

The Federal Election Commission responded that McCutcheon did not shoulder much of a burden at all. If he wanted to help a dozen candidates, he had plenty of options, including volunteering his time and energy. Bopp responded that Shaun McCutcheon was not superhuman. A donor who wanted to give to a dozen campaigns could hardly volunteer for all of them. This was a heavy burden indeed—so heavy, Bopp argued, that the aggregate limit would be unconstitutional no matter what standard the Court applied to it.[59]

For Bopp, it was important to suggest that the aggregate limits functioned as an expenditure limit—and not just for the purpose of the *McCutcheon* case. He wanted the Supreme Court to define corruption narrowly, as a quid pro quo. Any other definition, he believed, would reach far beyond *Mc-*

Cutcheon. It would effectively transform many independent expenditures into contributions—and cast doubt on the legality of 501s, super PACs, and much more.[60]

In the district court, a three-judge panel unanimously granted the FEC's motion to dismiss. Bopp and Hoersting, who had designed *McCutcheon* for the Supreme Court, viewed this setback as temporary. Besides, Bopp had no shortage of cases in the pipeline, including a challenge to new FEC regulations defining express advocacy, a lawsuit challenging Montana's contribution limits, an attack on Vermont's caps on PAC contributions, and a challenge to a West Virginia disclosure law. Shaun McCutcheon did not accept the loss so easily. He believed Bopp had shot too high by demanding that the court rethink the distinction between expenditures and contributions—and had done too little to convince the judges that the limits would fail even if the court treated them as contributions. This rift would deepen until McCutcheon replaced Bopp as his counsel in the Supreme Court (Bopp would continue to represent the RNC).[61]

If the news in *McCutcheon* seemed bad for groups like NRLC, the 2012 election was a disaster. Barack Obama won a second term. While Romney improved on John McCain's 2008 performance, losing the popular vote by less than 4 percent, Obama racked up over 330 Electoral College votes. For decades, groups like NRLC had relied on the GOP establishment to move closer to controlling the Supreme Court. But after 2010, more pro-lifers felt they had to repudiate the establishment. Bopp explained this logic in detailing the steps Reince Priebus could take to save his job as RNC chairman after Romney's defeat. "Reince needs to be attacked by the [GOP] liberals in order to not be thought of by conservatives as part of the Rep. establishment," he wrote. Only by repudiating the establishment could Priebus "galvanize support among the conservatives . . . to ensure his election."[62]

Other Republicans thought differently. According to the RNC's official autopsy, the euphemistically named *Growth and Opportunity Project Report*, the party had "marginalized itself" with its positions on racial issues, immigration, gay rights, and job creation. In appealing to the Tea Party, the report argued, Republicans had alienated young, nonwhite, and working-class voters, many of whom found the GOP a "scary," "out of touch" party for "stuffy old men."[63]

Establishment leaders thought the damage done by the Tea Party was reversible: the GOP establishment simply needed to regain its old dominance in campaign spending. Karl Rove's American Crossroads, a super PAC, launched the Conservative Victory Project to help establishment candidates fending off Tea Party challenges. Lacking an in with party leaders, Tea Party groups had gained power through financially powerful 501s and super PACs. Rove and his allies argued that the flood of outside spending had produced "suboptimal candidates" and that to keep up, the establishment needed to create more formidable 501s and super PACs.[64]

But there were hints that even traditional GOP leaders recognized that the party's establishment might be beyond repair. Jonathan Collegio, the spokesman for three Rove-aligned PACs, argued that in the *Citizens United* era, outside groups, including issue-based organizations not easily controlled by the conventional hierarchy, had far more pull. "We are in an era where power is not centralized in the parties," he admitted. Besides, some Tea Party candidates had done just fine, especially in GOP primaries. Nineteen conservatives, including David Bossie of Citizens United, wrote a letter to American Crossroads donors arguing that in 2012, "not one moderate Republican challenger won." In Bossie's view, there was no longer any trade-off between pragmatism and purity: for the new Republican Party, purity *was* pragmatism. Even those closest to Rove were skeptical about the establishment's future. "If I was in a Republican primary and Karl Rove came out against me," one Rove ally quipped, "it would be the single best thing that could happen to my campaign."[65]

While pro-lifers' views on party politics were in flux, larger anti-abortion groups had not changed their strategies for unraveling abortion rights. In 2013, AUL unveiled its Women's Protection Project, a vehicle for arguments that restrictions protected "women and girls from the profit-driven abortion industry that consistently ignores the deadly consequences of abortion." NRLC continued promoting twenty-week abortion bans. These strategies, however, faced growing skepticism from rank-and-file activists. When Janet Folger Porter first proposed a fetal heartbeat bill, many politicians had treated her as a fringe player—some also knew that she had taken to the airwaves to claim that the Obama administration would use swine flu to put Americans in internment camps. By 2013, 501s and 527s were helping the Tea Party take control of the GOP, and no one was dismissing Janet Porter anymore. If radical change was possible, maybe her impatience was warranted. Perhaps the rules of conservative politics had changed.[66]

A Post-*McCutcheon* Election

Bopp still saw no logic in Porter's willingness to ignore the Supreme Court, especially when the justices seemed hostile to campaign finance regulations. His brief for the RNC in *McCutcheon* focused on the idea that there was no principled way to tell expenditures and contributions apart, in general or in McCutcheon's case. As a result, Bopp reasoned, the Court should strictly scrutinize every campaign finance limit.[67] McCutcheon's brief made the narrower argument he had favored from the beginning. Congress had never worried about corruption when contributions were less than $2,600. How risky could multiple small contributions really be? McCutcheon also argued that the aggregate limits were unnecessary: the system was already "chock-full of much more direct anti-corruption and anti-circumvention measures," and the aggregate limit added no value.[68]

In a 5-4 decision, the Court struck down the aggregate contribution limit. Chief Justice John Roberts's majority opinion took note of the parties' vigorous debate about the line between contributions and expenditures. But Roberts saw no need to grapple with that difficult question, because aggregate limits failed either way. BCRA had eliminated the justification the *Buckley* Court found so compelling. "With more targeted anticircumvention measures in place today," Roberts wrote, "the indiscriminate aggregate limits under BCRA appear particularly heavy-handed."[69]

He then turned to the burden the aggregate limits created. "A donor must limit the number of candidates he supports and may have to choose which of several policy concerns he will advance—clear First Amendment harms," Roberts reasoned. True, he wrote, eliminating the aggregate caps would allow the super-wealthy to dump vast sums into the campaigns of dozens of candidates. But political influence as such created no real problem. Unless there was an explicit exchange of promises, there was no corruption.[70]

What about the tailoring of the aggregate limits? Roberts picked up on the argument that Congress had already decided what size of donation would create corruption. If Congress thought that an individual contribution of $2,600 was not corrupting, why would anyone worry about multiple donations of that size? And if circumvention was the concern, BCRA already had in place any number of safeguards to take care of that.[71]

The dissenters wondered what was left of the government's power to check corruption. "Where enough money calls the tune, the general public will not be heard," Justice Stephen Breyer chastised the majority. But he was on the losing side. *McCutcheon* meant that wealthy donors would be more pursued than ever.[72]

Bopp's role in cases like *McCutcheon* attracted attention from campaign finance reformers, who argued that he was breaking the rules. In July 2014, the Center for Responsibility and Ethics in Washington called on the IRS to investigate Bopp's James Madison Center, arguing that virtually all of the money paid to the center, a nonprofit, went to cover litigation brought by his law firm. While the center argued Bopp had engaged in "self-dealing transactions" and violated the rules on using charitable organizations for private benefit, Bopp argued that the complaint was part of a smear campaign led by progressives who did not like his politics (the IRS investigated but took no action against the Madison Center).[73]

The 2014 election proved the importance of both *McCutcheon* and *Citizens United*. Republicans picked up nine Senate seats—the most since 1980—and thirteen in the House. Although the number of donors dropped by 11 percent, the election cost more than any previous midterm. Nonparty outside spending exceeded $567 million. In the wake of *McCutcheon*, the average individual donation reached an all-time high of more than $2,600. The largest donors, who once had to stop at just over $123,000, now could open the floodgates.[74]

Spending also surged following passage of the Consolidated and Further Continuing Appropriations Act. Passed by a Democratic Congress in December 2014, the bill allowed national party committees to create up to three segregated accounts to fund their presidential nominating convention, build headquarters, and cover election-related legal expenses. The annual limits on contributions to these federal accounts were up to three times higher than the ceilings on other contributions to party committees. The act opened the door to more party fundraising, but outside spending still allowed the most conservative candidates to flourish.[75]

Conservative media, which had blossomed in the 2010s, further boosted right-wing candidates. Robert Herring Sr., the son of a white Louisiana sharecropper, made most of his money printing circuit boards before getting into the TV business. In 2004, he launched A Wealth of Entertainment (Wealth TV), a San Diego–based network that specialized in "vicarious living" programming, showing splashy trips to luxury destinations. A lifelong insomniac, Herring consumed more and more headlines as he aged. After retiring, he got into the news business, founding One America News Network (OAN) in 2013 as a partnership with the conservative *Washington Times*. At first, OAN proclaimed an intention to avoid punditry and "hit the news down the center and lean right." But OAN became more thoroughly conservative than Fox News. A variety of new online sites, including the Blaze (founded 2010), the Federalist (2013), and the Daily Wire (2015), competed with Breitbart and the Daily Caller for conservative viewers.[76]

Social conservatives watching Fox News or OAN felt that the nation had left them behind—and not just on abortion. In 2011, President Obama introduced a contraceptive mandate as part of the federal Affordable Care Act, making eighteen forms of female contraception available without a co-pay. Employers who failed to comply faced a penalty of $100 per individual per day. The mandate initially exempted churches but not religious businesses such as universities or hospitals; it amplified existing concern about religious liberty within conservative faith communities. In 2009, Robert George, a natural law scholar, and Chuck Colson, the former Nixon administration "hatchet man" turned evangelical leader, developed a set of principles to which all conservative Christians could agree. Their *Manhattan Declaration: A Call of Christian Conscience* (2009) asked believers to fight to protect "the sanctity of human life, the dignity of marriage as a union of husband and wife, and the freedom of religion." The contraceptive mandate deepened some conservative Christians' sense of persecution. In the face of protests, the Obama administration broadened the exemption to include religious nonprofits, which it said could opt out of providing direct coverage if they filled out a form stating their objections (the insurer would bypass the employer and directly cover the required contraceptive instead). But the new exemption did not diminish anxieties about religious liberty. At the same time, Christianity in the United States appeared to be in decline:

the number of Americans who identified as Christian began to decrease in the mid-2010s and continued to drop throughout the decade, increasing the belief of some Christian conservatives that they were being marginalized.[77]

The Supreme Court's 2014 decision in *Burwell v. Hobby Lobby Stores* exposed new fault lines over the meaning of religious liberty. A 5-4 majority held that the contraceptive mandate violated the federal Religious Freedom Restoration Act by forcing compliance on closely held, for-profit businesses run by religious believers. Litigation over the mandate continued: in *Zubik v. Burwell* (2016), believers argued that the mandate's opt-out mechanism itself put a serious burden on religious belief. The Supreme Court dodged the case, ordering the parties back to the table to resolve their issues. Increasing support for same-sex marriage further convinced conservative Christians that their voices were no longer welcome in mainstream American society. In 2015, in *Obergefell v. Hodges*, the Supreme Court held that state laws disallowing same-sex marriage violated the due process and equal protection clauses of the Constitution. Writing in *National Review*, Alexandra DeSanctis framed *Obergefell* as proof that "the nation's courts and commissions have placed a constantly evolving collection of gay rights above the free exercise of religion." The *Federalist* warned that "overnight, the sincerely-held opinions of a great many good, well-intentioned Americans became verboten."[78]

Trump's Primary Run

By the start of the 2016 election season, conservative Christians were looking for a political savior. A study put out that year by the Public Religion Research Institute and the Brookings Institute showed that three-quarters of Republicans—and nearly eight in ten evangelical Protestants—believed that discrimination against Christians was at least as big a problem as discrimination against racial minorities. Few of them would have predicted that a foul-mouthed real estate mogul would be the savior they were looking for.[79]

Little about Donald Trump's early campaign reassured pro-lifers. Earlier in his career, he had regularly donated money to Democratic candidates, including Hillary Clinton, the frontrunner for the Democratic nomination in 2016. He had opposed the federal ban on partial-birth abortion and made headlines for his extramarital affairs. He had helped to popularize the "birther" theory that Obama had been born abroad, was not a citizen, and had never been qualified to be president. In announcing his candidacy, Trump eagerly embraced controversy, focusing on Islamic terrorism, the loss of U.S. manufacturing jobs, and illegal immigration, famously stating that Mexico sent rapists and drug pushers to the United States. Abortion (or any other social issue) played no part in his announcement.[80]

Anti-abortion leaders were not impressed. When NRLC held its national convention in January 2016, the group invited every Republican primary candidate except Trump. Pro-life women found Trump particularly dismaying. Marjorie Dannenfelser, the head of the Susan B. Anthony List, a GOP powerhouse that spent $18 million in 2016, joined other pro-life women in an open letter to GOP voters in Iowa, urging them to vote for "anyone but Trump."[81]

True the Vote was already focused on defeating Hillary Clinton. In February, the group sent a fundraising email raising the possibility that Clinton "was capable of stealing the election" and warning that the Republican Party could not and would not stop her unless True the Vote stepped in. But as the primary season went on, some right-to-lifers were still focused on making sure that Trump was not the GOP nominee. At an MSNBC town hall, he answered a question from host Chris Matthews by stating that women should be punished for having abortions. For decades, anti-abortion groups had worked to show that abortion hurt women and that their movement sought to protect women rather than punish them. After Trump's principal rival, Ted Cruz, won the Wisconsin primary, anti-abortion leaders endorsed Cruz.[82]

For a time, abortion foes thought their party was heading toward a contested convention. Bopp wanted to address this possibility in a way that would "enhance the overall influence of the conservative movement by increasing the overall number of conservatives as delegates and on important committees." Working with Solomon Yue and Russ Walker, a veteran political consultant who had helped lead the Tea Party giant FreedomWorks, Bopp had written the Club for Growth in June 2015 asking for $5 million to ensure that the GOP maintained its conservative DNA no matter who was nominated. The proposal identified a range of potential partners in this effort, including the Tea Party and guns rights and pro-life groups, who would wage a floor fight at the GOP Convention to keep the party from shifting to the center. "We have an opportunity to institutionalize the conservative influence in the Republican Party so as to make it a more powerful vehicle for the conservative cause," the proposal argued. "The key to accomplish our mission successfully is to focus on ideology, not an individual Presidential candidate."[83]

By April 2016, Bopp and Yue had expanded the Club for Growth plan to cover efforts to "mobilize conservatives to elect a conservative nominee." They asked the Club for Growth for another $298,000 to ensure that conservatives served as delegates for Trump or his two remaining competitors, Ted Cruz and John Kasich. Those delegates, in turn, would guarantee that the platform stayed conservative and the rules remained the same. If no candidate had a majority of delegates by the time of the Republican National Convention in July, Bopp and Yue laid out a simple but explosive plan for delegate poaching "if any . . . matter of conservative interest is at stake, including the nomination for President." They received contributions from several sources, with the Club for Growth's being the most substantial.[84]

The RNC's rules allowed for delegate poaching if no candidate arrived at the convention with a majority of delegates. But Trump sailed to victory in Indiana, depriving Cruz of a much-needed win and convincing him to suspend his campaign. Together with Trump's delegate haul, a new Supreme Court decision on abortion suppressed most of the remaining anti-abortion resistance to Trump. The case, *Whole Woman's Health v. Hellerstedt*, dealt with two provisions of a Texas law known as HB2 that had become cornerstones of Americans United for Life's strategy to reverse *Roe*. One of the provisions required doctors working in abortion clinics to have admitting privileges at a hospital within thirty miles of the clinic. The second mandated that all abortion clinics meet the standards set for other ambulatory surgical centers in the state. A district court had found that the laws would cut the number of abortion clinics in Texas down to eight. HB2 would certainly lower the abortion rate, but it mattered to groups like AUL and NRLC for other reasons. Since *Gonzales*, the meaning of the Court's undue burden standard was far from clear. AUL wanted the justices to equate the standard with "rational basis," the least protective form of judicial review, which required only that the government have some rational basis for enacting a law. This would open the door for almost any abortion restriction.[85]

The Court that decided *Whole Woman's Health* had just eight members because of the sudden passing of Justice Antonin Scalia, but a 5-3 majority had no trouble striking down both parts of HB2. The Court first gave new bite to the undue burden test, ruling that it called for balancing the benefits and burdens of a law rather than deferring to the legislature. This was a tighter standard than the one in *Gonzales v. Carhart*, which seemed to require almost complete deference in cases of scientific uncertainty. Now, laws that created relatively minor obstacles could still be unconstitutional if they served no purpose.[86]

Whole Woman's Health spurred anti-abortion leaders to focus more intensely on the 2016 presidential election. The next president would have the opportunity to nominate at least one justice—the one who would replace conservative stalwart Antonin Scalia. Mitch McConnell had blocked a vote on Obama's choice, Merrick Garland, leaving the decision to the next president. And several other justices were elderly, including feminist icon Ruth Bader Ginsburg, who had major health issues. Hillary Clinton was likely to nominate justices who were more pro-choice than most currently on the bench. She was running on what was arguably the most pro-choice platform in history, one that prioritized repeal of the Hyde Amendment, which banned Medicaid funding for abortion. After *Whole Woman's Health*, Anthony Lauinger, an NRLC veteran, described a prospective Clinton presidency as "catastrophic."[87]

If some national pro-life leaders came around to backing Trump, many in the GOP leadership did not. On conservative Hugh Hewitt's talk radio show, Bush administration veteran Karl Rove floated the idea of choosing a "fresh face" at the 2016 convention. Some speculated that Romney's 2012 running mate, Paul Ryan, might parachute in to displace Trump. For Never Trump Republicans searching for an alternative, Ryan, Nebraska senator Ben Sasse, and former presidential candidate Mitt Romney topped the list.[88]

As early as March, Solomon Yue and Jim Bopp concluded that kicking Trump off the ticket would "blow up the party for good" because the base would think the "establishment is stealing the nomination." To head off the arrival of a "white knight," Yue proposed a change to the Republican National Convention's rulebook. The GOP generally followed the rules used by the House of Representatives, which gave the RNC chairman considerable power. Under those rules, Reince Priebus would have the power to reopen the nomination in a bid to replace Trump. Yue proposed instead that the convention adopt Robert's Rules of Order, which would require a majority vote to reopen the nomination. Priebus asked Yue to withdraw the rule change, and when he refused, John Ryder, a Priebus ally and RNC general counsel, named a team to lobby against it. While Ryder managed to defeat Yue's proposal, he promised that Priebus would require a two-thirds majority vote before he would reopen nominations. Behind the scenes, the efforts to replace Trump continued.[89]

Movement conservatives hoped to benefit from the palace intrigue. If the establishment was plotting against Trump, perhaps his campaign would try to weaken the establishment by putting more power in the hands of issue-based organizations and grassroots conservatives. Bopp and Yue worked on the rules fight with Bruce Ash, the chair of the Republican National Convention Standing Committee on Rules and an Arizona committeeman. The Jewish son of an Olympic weightlifter, Ash had led the RNC's Rules Committee since 2010, and he thought that dislodging Trump would hand the election to Clinton. In strategizing about how to change the rules, Bopp, Yue, and Ash broke down the party into six factions: establishment leaders, RNC loyalists "committed to the leadership of the current RNC chairman," Cruz proponents, Trump devotees, grassroots conservatives, and Never Trumpers, who wanted to permit—and then persuade—convention delegates to "vote their conscience." Bopp, Yue, and Ash hoped that their faction could prevail on Cruz and Trump supporters to push for rules changes that would undercut the RNC establishment, such as reducing the number of committee appointments made by the RNC chairman or preventing the RNC from changing the rules between conventions. "The common thread uniting these three groups," Bopp later explained, was "their anti-establishment grassroots focus."[90]

The RNC continued flirting with options to eliminate Trump. Priebus named anti-Trump Republicans, including Romney allies Enid Greene Mickelsen and Ron Kaufman, to head the Rules Committee. Before Mickelsen took charge, the convention rules prevented "a bound delegate from nominating or casting a vote for a different presidential candidate than the one to whom the delegate was legally bound by state law or state party rule."[91] Mickelsen proposed jettisoning the rule, a change that, at least in theory, would allow party leaders to remove Trump from the ticket. Yue, Ash, and Bopp recall that Priebus schemed to remove Trump until two weeks before the convention. According to Ash, Priebus insisted that the entire GOP leadership felt they had to get rid of Trump because he could not win.[92]

But on the eve of the convention, the Trump campaign and the GOP brokered a ceasefire. Trump had long been wary of working with Cruz loyalists on anything, particularly since some of them favored allowing delegates to vote their consciences. By contrast, the RNC leadership had something to offer Trump: clear opposition to the effort to unbind delegates, plus staffers and a get-out-the-vote operation that Trump lacked. Voting in lockstep, Trump and RNC loyalists managed to defeat any rules change that would place more power in the hands of issue-based organizations like NRLC.[93]

The Free the Delegates movement also failed. Launched by Kendal Unruh, a teacher at a Christian high school (and an eight-time former delegate), Free the Delegates independently proposed a rule change that would allow delegates to vote for the candidate of their choice rather than the one who had won that state's primary. The RNC's Rules Committee rejected Unruh's proposal by voice vote. Joined by the leaders of nine other delegations, Unruh's Colorado delegation pressed for a roll call vote on the floor. When that effort failed, the Colorado delegation staged a walkout.[94]

Backroom plotting at the Republican National Convention deepened Trump's sense that the powers that be were out to get him. He warned supporters that the election might be rigged in Clinton's favor and urged them to become election monitors. The Republican National Lawyers Association planned what one member called a "Navy-SEAL-type operation" to prevent voter fraud, with Don McGahn, the Trump campaign's attorney, offering suggestions.[95]

Even without friendly fire from the RNC, Trump's success was far from assured. He and his opponent, Hillary Clinton, were more disliked than any presidential candidates in the history of polling. Election spending reflected that reality: both candidates spent less than their counterparts had in 2012. Nevertheless, the *McCutcheon* decision made itself felt. In 2016, wealthy donors spent more than on the previous race: the average contribution total per donor went up by nearly $100,000. The GOP narrowly led the way with post-*McCutcheon* donors, some of whom, like Las Vegas casino magnate Sheldon Adelson, donated over $40 million.[96]

Many expected that Clinton would be the one to overcome the public's obvious antipathy, but Trump defied expectations, losing the popular vote while narrowly winning in the Electoral College. As a candidate, he thrived on the country's deepening polarization, and little changed once he assumed office. But if Trump was a different kind of president, Bopp and his colleagues increasingly embraced that difference.

Power in the Party

At first, Donald Trump struck Jim Bopp as an obstacle: a candidate with no interest in conservative policy, and one who could make the GOP pro-choice. After Trump won, conservative movements began to wonder if his liabilities could work in their favor. Trump knew no one in the nation's capital and had few political connections. He had no fundraising apparatus of his own. He was singularly unpopular for a newly elected president. His approval ratings would remain historically low throughout his term.

Despite having lost their fight to change the rules, Bopp and his allies hoped that the Trump presidency could still put more power in the hands of activist organizations. Trump's weakness, unpopularity, and isolation might make him far more dependent on conservative movements than his predecessors. If Bopp envisioned a GOP whose candidates answered to conservative movements, it seemed that Donald Trump might make that vision a reality.

Conclusion: Democracy in a Post-*Roe* America

FROM 2016 TO 2020, Donald Trump seemed to delight in the kind of controversy that limited his popularity. Some scandals cut deeper than others. Allegations that Russia had interfered in the 2016 election prompted an investigation and the indictment of top Trump aides. While his supporters dismissed the investigation as a witch hunt, Trump fired FBI director James Comey, energizing opponents who claimed the president had obstructed justice. As a candidate, Trump had often inveighed against Muslims and called for a "Muslim ban" on the campaign trail. In office, he introduced a policy prohibiting entry to people from certain Muslim-majority countries. After several organizations sued, the administration more than once modified the policy, first exempting visa and green card holders and taking Iraq off the list of prohibited countries, and later adding a few non-Muslim countries to the ban. The Supreme Court ultimately concluded that the travel ban was constitutional.[1]

In 2017, Trump's views on race again came to the fore after the Unite the Right rally in Charlottesville, Virginia. The city planned to remove a statue of Confederate general Robert E. Lee, and a group that included many white supremacists and neo-Nazis gathered to protest the move. One self-identified white supremacist, James Alex Fields Jr., drove his car into counter-protestors, killing one, Heather Heyer, in the process. Trump, while condemning violence, insisted that there were "very fine people on both sides," a comment many saw as sympathetic to white supremacists.[2]

Trump's reelection hopes rode on the United States' strong economic performance, but his willingness to stoke racial tensions ensured that Americans who disliked him would not change their minds. Starting in 2018, critics denounced Trump's "zero tolerance" immigration policy, which separated parents and children seeking to enter the country illegally at the border. In 2019, the Democratic majority in the House began investigating a whistleblower allegation that Trump was trying to undercut his likely opponent in the 2020 election, Joe Biden. Trump was accused of strong-arming the government of Ukraine into announcing an investigation into Biden's son Hunter and promoting the theory that Ukraine, not Russia, had meddled with the 2016 presidential race. The House inquiry culminated in Trump's impeachment for abuse of power and obstruction of Congress. Although the Senate acquitted him in February 2020, the spread of coronavirus disease (COVID-19) again damaged his standing. Trump closed U.S. borders to travelers from overseas belatedly and inconsistently, and only after the disease had already begun to spread. He downplayed the seriousness of the pandemic, insisted that the virus would disappear, and refused to wear the mask recommended by medical authorities. At one point, he even contended that top health officials should study the injection of bleach into the human body as a strategy for fighting the virus. At the time he left office, the United States had the highest official tally of COVID deaths—and one of the highest per capita mortality rates—in the world. Trump's handling of the virus deepened the distrust of independents who had never approved of his performance.[3]

As COVID spread across the country, Trump waded into growing conflict about racial justice. In the summer of 2020 in Minneapolis, police responded to a call from a convenience store clerk who claimed that George Floyd, a forty-six-year-old Black man, had tried to pass off a counterfeit $20 bill. While supposedly trying to arrest Floyd, Derek Chauvin, a white police officer, murdered him by kneeling on his neck for over eight minutes. The murder, caught on video, touched off protests across the United States and much of the world. Trump offered a pro forma condemnation of Floyd's death, but as protests continued, the president enthusiastically fanned the flames, blaming Democrats for property damage in major metro areas, calling on his supporters to launch counter-protests, advising law enforcement to use tear gas and unmarked vehicles against protestors, and threatening to call in the military to enforce his wishes. His supporters liked the law-and-order rhetoric, and the president seemed uninterested in appealing to anyone else.[4]

Trump's relative unpopularity gave him strong reason to address the demands of his pro-life supporters. He went beyond what would ordinarily be expected of a pro-life president. He not only reinstated but expanded what critics called the "global gag rule," barring any NGO receiving U.S. foreign health aid from providing or advocating for abortion-related services. His administration created a new Conscience and Religious Freedom Division within the Department of Health and Human Services and expanded the categories of employees who could refuse to participate in abortions, sterilizations, and other services. Other regulations, aimed at Planned Parenthood, mandated that any clinic receiving Title X family planning funding keep its abortion practice physically and financially separate and prohibited recipients from providing abortion referrals, even when requested to do so. Nearly fifty years after *Roe*, he became the first president to attend the March for Life in person.[5]

Many pro-lifers cared most about Trump's impact on the courts. The Senate confirmed more than 220 of his nominees to the federal bench, including 54 to the circuit courts of appeal. Three Trump nominees ultimately sat on the U.S. Supreme Court. After the Republican-controlled Senate refused to hold hearings on President Obama's nominee, Merrick Garland, to fill the seat vacated by Antonin Scalia in 2016, it confirmed Trump's choice, Neil Gorsuch, in 2017. A year later, Trump chose Brett Kavanaugh to succeed the Court's longtime swing justice on abortion, Anthony Kennedy. And shortly before the 2020 election, Amy Coney Barrett took the place of Ruth Bader Ginsburg, a hero to progressives.[6]

When Trump left office, the Supreme Court had not yet said a word about *Roe*, but few expected that silence to last. The Court began to retreat from protecting abortion rights after Kavanaugh joined the Court. In 2020, in *June Medical Services v. Russo*, a majority struck down a Louisiana law identical to one invalidated just four years earlier in *Whole Woman's Health v. Hellerstedt*. Chief Justice John Roberts joined his more liberal colleagues in voting that the Louisiana law was unconstitutional. But Roberts—whose opinion may well be the law of the case—set forth a much less protective version of the undue burden standard, allowing courts only to consider the burdens imposed by a law, not to weigh whether it delivers any benefit. Soon, Roberts's degree of willingness to reverse *Roe* was far less concerning to the anti-abortion movement. After the Senate confirmed Barrett, there were five potential votes to reverse *Roe* even without him. Then, in spring of 2021, the Supreme Court agreed to hear a major abortion challenge to *Roe v. Wade*. *Dobbs v. Jackson Women's Health Organization* involved a Mississippi law banning abortion at fifteen weeks, the point at which state lawmakers said fetal pain was possible. Although *Roe* and *Casey* protected a right to choose before viability, the prohibition went into effect a full nine weeks before most physicians believed a child could survive outside the womb. If the justices upheld Mississippi's law—as many expected they would—then the Court would either have to undo the viability limit or reverse *Roe* outright. Many pro-lifers were well aware of Trump's flaws. But for the right Supreme Court justices, almost no price was too high.[7]

James Bopp was an enthusiastic Trump supporter in 2020. He did not like the president's personality any more than he had four years ago, but Trump delivered the results the pro-life movement wanted. The rest, Bopp thought, was secondary. He had taken on the Trump campaign as a client, and in October 2019 he became Trump's special counsel for strategic and campaign finance law advice. He helped Trump win the money race: the president raised $1.96 billion in 2020, compared to only $1.69 billion for his opponent, Joe Biden. In 2020, outside spending surged again, jumping from roughly $1.7 billion in 2016 to $3.2 billion in 2020, with pro-Biden outside spending ($687.3 million) almost double the amount spent by pro-Trump groups ($369.6 million) (Trump made up the difference by raising far more through his campaign committee).[8]

After Election Day, as news networks called the race for Biden, Trump began a quest to undo the result. Conservative attorneys stood ready to help. James Bopp had become more deeply involved with True the Vote. In 2017, he joined the team suing the Internal Revenue Service for discriminating against True the Vote and other conservative groups seeking registration as nonprofits. The same year, he represented True the Vote in challenging the constitutionality of Texas's campaign finance limits. By 2019, he had become the group's general counsel. Well before voting began in 2020, Bopp and his allies claimed that voter fraud was already rife, particularly in states that moved to allow mail-in voting during the pandemic. As early as April 2020, he filed lawsuits in New Mexico and Virginia to stop those states from mailing ballots to all registered voters (rather than just those who requested them). Progressive groups filed suits of their own, arguing that the GOP was trying to disenfranchise voters and sideline communities of color, particularly when the pandemic made face-to-face contact risky. Bopp responded that he had evidence that over 20 million registered voters were ineligible: the voter lists were riddled with duplicate names, names of dead people, and names of felons or noncitizens who should never have been registered in the first place. He described universal mail-in voting as the "most massive fraud scheme in the history of America."[9]

In November 2020, after Trump's defeat, Bopp filed four lawsuits on behalf of True the Vote challenging polling practices in eighteen counties across the crucial states of Pennsylvania, Georgia, Michigan, and Wisconsin. He recalls several conversations with Mark Meadows, the White House chief of staff, about representing the Trump campaign in its own lawsuits. Bopp hoped to hold a trial, hire a company that would help him audit voter lists, and find evidence of fraud. While Trump seemed content to claim that the election must have been fraudulent, Bopp believed no court would overturn a result without a trial and extensive, concrete proof. But even after the campaign had theoretically hired Bopp, Trump's attorney and friend Rudy Giuliani began making public statements that contradicted Bopp's strategy. Bopp says he learned that the campaign had little interest in a hearing and instead planned to focus on appeals to the Supreme Court, reasoning that since the president had nominated three of the Court's members, they would want to repay him. Bopp believed that no court, including the Supreme Court, would do Trump's bidding without a court finding of fraud. Trump, however, despite having filed sixty-two lawsuits in state and federal court to overturn the result in key states he lost, had no interest in a trial: he apparently thought that if he rolled the dice enough times, one of his attempts would pay off.[10]

Disturbed by a strategy he was sure would fail, Bopp filed notices to dismiss each of the four suits in which he was involved. Other prominent attorneys also bowed out of Trump's campaign in the courts. Trump went on to lose sixty-one of the suits. Judges, including some nominated by the president, concluded either that he lacked standing or that he had no evidence of fraud. Fred Eshelman, a billionaire donor, sued for the return of $2.5 million he gave to True the Vote; he claimed that the group had broken its promise to use his money "to undertake sophisticated data modeling and statistical analysis to identify potential illegal or fraudulent balloting." (A Texas state court ultimately concluded that Eshelman lacked standing to bring the suit and dismissed it.)[11]

Trump did not stop with the courts. Some states did not have rules obliging lawmakers to choose electors who reflected the will of voters. Trump pressured Republican lawmakers to send alternative delegate slates that would unravel Biden's victory. When states certified their results, and when Congress seemed poised to do the same in January, Trump mounted a campaign to push his vice president, Mike Pence, to declare him the winner. Pence asserted—and legal experts agreed—that the vice president's role in certifying the election was merely ceremonial, and he had no authority to do as Trump requested. But as the vote loomed, Trump and other Republican officials urged his "patriots" to protest the congressional certification (thirteen senators and over a hundred members of the House had already vowed to object). At the so-called March to Save America, thousands gathered in Washington, DC, to hear Trump and other speakers, including Federalist Society leader John Eastman, urge attendees to march on the Capitol and prevent the certification. At one o'clock that afternoon, a mob overwhelmed the Capitol police and entered the halls of Congress. Some seemed intent on injuring or even assassinating those they blamed for Trump's removal from office, including Pence, who had arguably been more loyal to Trump than anyone.[12]

When the Capitol riots were over, five people were dead, and Joe Biden was still the president-elect. Within weeks, the Federal Bureau of Investigation had made over one hundred arrests and opened files on an additional one hundred suspects. The House again impeached Trump, this time for incitement of insurrection. Some abortion foes quickly distanced themselves from Trump, but other pro-lifers, like most Republicans, did not for a moment consider abandoning him. With the approach of the 2021 March for Life, many celebrated his record in office. When the Senate had the chance to convict Trump and forbid him from ever holding office again, only seven Republicans voted to do so.[13]

On the nights that followed, Bopp often could not sleep. It was not because he regretted working to overturn the election; he did not. Instead, he spent many hours playing out how Trump's attempt could have gone if he had used better strategy or tactics—or a better lawyer. Bopp felt equally gutted by what he saw happening to conservatives. He thought Trump supporters had been forced "into a ghetto" by the corporate world and the mainstream media. Twitter and Facebook had removed Trump from their platforms, and Amazon Web Services had stopped hosting Parler, a conservative alternative to Twitter, after users continued to threaten election-related violence. Major corporate donors suspended contributions to politicians who had objected to the election certification. If Bopp's critics saw him as a man who peddled lies to conservative voters, Bopp accused Democrats of making conservatives feel that they were no longer safe or welcome in America. As he saw it, the country was courting another civil war.[14]

If anything made Bopp feel better, it was the Supreme Court's decisions in a pair of cases on donor disclosure, *Americans for Prosperity Foundation v. Bonta* and *Thomas More Law Center v. Bonta*. The cases involved a California law requiring all charitable organizations operating in the state to disclose the names and addresses of their largest donors. The state claimed that the law prevented fraud, but two conservative charities, the Thomas More Law Center, an anti-abortion public interest litigator, and the Koch-affiliated nonprofit Americans for Prosperity, contended that the disclosure requirement violated their freedom of association. The Supreme Court agreed, applying "exacting scrutiny" to the statute and reasoning that California had chilled donors' giving without seriously considering less burdensome alternatives for uncovering fraud, such as a subpoena or audit letter. *Americans for Prosperity* and *Thomas More* were not campaign finance cases, but the Court's decision promised to make it easier to shield the identities of donors to conservative nonprofits. If Jim Bopp felt hopeless about the future of the country, he had to admit that *Americans for Prosperity* was good news. The fight for donor anonymity had certainly helped his cause before.[15]

Trump's shocking upending of U.S. politics was decades in the making. Some studies, seeking to explain his rise, focused on the GOP's commitment to courting southern white voters—a version of Richard Nixon's southern strategy. Others spotlighted the politics of white identity. Different research centers on the GOP's embrace of property rights and the interests of the nation's wealthiest citizens. Some scholars contend that since working-class whites may not benefit from slashing taxes and regulations, Republicans have relied on racial resentment to hold their political coalition together. Historians have grappled with the rise of Christian nationalism, a political vision defined by an identity-based strain of conservative Christianity. Others have chronicled the shifts in evangelical Christianity itself—the embrace of authoritarian, white Christian masculinity as a weapon to protect the faith, a response to the demographic decline of Christianity (and evangelicalism in particular), or a reflection of what Sarah Posner calls "white nationalist grievance." These scholars trace how the GOP's recent transformation contributes to the contemporary state of U.S. democracy.[16]

Populism, commitment to a particular vision of Christianity, white racial politics, a dedication to the interests of the wealthy—none of these are new in Republican politics. In past decades, however, Republicans had always tempered the impulses of the party's right flank. It is only recently that party leaders have lost the ability to sideline insurgents. The rise of Trump and candidates like him is not only the story of why many in the GOP embraced a populist. It is the story of the Republican establishment's demise.[17]

We tend to see the pro-life movement as a bit player in this story. GOP leaders made promises to pro-life organizers and sometimes passed legislation, but rarely changed their party's underlying priorities. The history I have recounted here suggests a more complex relationship. The anti-abortion movement helped to make control of the Supreme Court a central issue for rank-and-file Republican voters. After hoping for a constitutional amendment for much of the 1970s and early 1980s, right-to-lifers began to put national elections at the center of their work. Their goal was not primarily to pass federal legislation or implement pro-life executive orders. For the most part, they cared far more about control of the Court. The Reagan administration understood that the prospect of conservative judges could bring social conservatives to the polls. But right-to-lifers were not happy with just any judge a Republican president selected. Between 1991 and 2005, right-to-lifers increasingly demonstrated more passion for nominees like Clarence Thomas or Robert Bork than for the men who nominated them. The voices of social conservatives doomed putative consensus picks like Harriet Miers, elevated divisive choices like Samuel Alito and Amy Coney Barrett, and shaped what conservative voters thought mattered on Election Day.[18]

Right-to-lifers inspired the Republican Party to change its approach to judicial nominations—away from a model based on consensus toward one based on energizing base voters. The more social conservatives and right-to-lifers demanded of Supreme Court nominees, the more groups like NRLC urged other movement conservatives to see the Court as the most important issue on Election Day. The importance of the Court as an election issue should not be overstated. It was not until the 1960s that either party treated control of the Court as an election issue, and as recently as 2016, neither party's nominee made it a central topic. The same was not true for interest groups, particularly on the right. Republicans, particularly strong conservatives, choose primary candidates and vote partly based on their expected effect on the High Court.[19]

Trump understood the importance of the Court. In 2020, he broke with tradition and spoke frequently about the justices on the campaign trail, touting his conservative nominees, urging Joe Biden to release a list of prospective judges, and even predicting how "his" Supreme Court would rule on the validity of the election. Voters on the left as well as the right seemed to agree that the Court was a crucial issue. In 2020, at the height of the COVID-19 pandemic and a serious recession, Pew found that the percentage of voters ranking the Court as a "very important" election issue—64 percent—was behind only those mentioning the economy and health care. The prospect of Supreme Court picks could firm up the loyalty of voters who might have second thoughts about a candidate.[20]

The right-to-life movement's work on campaign finance also helped to weaken a GOP establishment that might otherwise have stood in Trump's way. Campaign finance rules alone are not to blame for the decline of the traditional party hierarchy. The American electorate itself seems to have changed in the decades since the passage of the Federal Election Campaign

Act. There is much evidence that over time, the relationship between voters' ideology and party affiliation has grown much closer. Scholars disagree about the extent to which they have become polarized as well—whether their positions on issues from guns to global warming have become more extreme, or whether party elites polarized and voters simply followed their lead. Scholars also debate how this partisan divide deepened—whether Americans moved to neighborhoods where a majority shared their views, or simply took their cues from party leaders.[21]

What is clear is that party polarization has coincided with a spike in negative partisanship: Americans increasingly scorn those in the opposing political party. Negative partisanship allows extremists to flourish. It increases straight-ticket voting, nationalizes local races, and strengthens party loyalty. The more entrenched negative partisanship became, the more easily a deeply flawed candidate like Trump could overcome voters' doubts simply by stoking hatred for Democrats. On both sides, negative partisanship made it much harder for the party establishment to keep insurgents on the sidelines.[22]

The ascendancy of conservative media also helped to weaken the GOP establishment. By 2004, talk radio had become an almost exclusively conservative medium. In the decade that followed, conservative outlets like Fox News, Breitbart, and Newsmax became many Americans' primary source of information. Establishment Republicans had long cultivated relationships with reporters and acted as gatekeepers for ambitious candidates. Conservative media bypassed these leaders and rewarded extreme candidates for their partisan purity. The conservative media also stoked distrust of the very idea of journalism. Radio personalities like Rush Limbaugh and Laura Ingraham framed the mainstream media as biased. Politicians like Trump could promote any narrative without any institution to check them effectively. To stay competitive, mainstream media outlets often covered Trump's tweets and theories as much as did their conservative competitors.[23]

But money had a key role in this new politics. The anti-abortion movement joined a broader effort to lift all restrictions on money in politics, and groups like the National Right to Life Committee made a significant contribution to the strategies, arguments, and focus of the fight to eliminate campaign finance laws. James Bopp hoped to convince the Supreme Court that any campaign finance regulation—any disclosure requirement or expenditure or contribution limit—was unconstitutional unless it was limited to clear pleas for action directed to voters. Bopp hoped to use *Citizens United* to revolutionize the rules on donor disclosure, but the decisions in both *Citizens United* and *SpeechNow* did something quite different: they opened the door to far more fundraising and campaign spending by nonprofits and super PACs.

Nevertheless, there would have been no *Citizens United* if right-to-lifers had not redirected the fight to undo campaign finance restrictions, litigating cases and reframing campaign finance limits both inside and outside of court. After *Citizens United*, the party establishment lost another tool to put down conservative insurgencies: an overwhelming advantage in campaign fundraising and spending.

Between 2000 and 2016, overall spending rose dramatically. Issue-based outside spending accounted for only some of this increase. Presidential candidate committees' spending increased exponentially between 1992 and 2016. More donors also joined in. Fewer than seventy thousand people gave candidates money in 1982, but 3.2 million did in 2016. Even as more people participated, megadonors represented a greater share of total spending: in 2016, fewer than sixteen thousand people accounted for half of all contributions. Parties have struggled to keep up. In 2016, for example, contributions to the GOP were 40 percent below what it received in 2004.[24]

After *Citizens United* and *SpeechNow*, more and more donors sent their money to nonprofits and super PACs instead of parties. There was little daylight between some of these organizations and the party itself. Veteran political operatives, some with party ties, ran potent "outside" groups. But however much these groups ran in lockstep with specific candidates, the establishment did not control them. Ideological groups had long had a seat at the table in Republican politics, but they lacked the sway that activists like Bopp had long wanted. As outside spending grew in importance, issue-based groups gained influence over GOP strategy, policy, and priorities. The center of power in conservative politics shifted.[25]

The party establishment had once used its edge in campaign fundraising and spending to eliminate fringe candidates like Pat Buchanan. After *Citizens United*, donors found ways to anonymously bankroll candidates with controversial positions. An insurgent like Trump would have struggled and failed to win the Republican nomination even a decade before 2016. In the world of campaign finance that abortion foes had helped to remake, he thrived.

Weakening the GOP establishment and helping Donald Trump may seem to the leaders of the right-to-life movement like a wise move. Trump nominated three Supreme Court justices to forge a conservative supermajority. Shortly after he left office, the Court agreed to hear a case that will open the door to some pre-viability abortion bans or overturn *Roe* altogether. But even if the Court does reverse *Roe*, the most likely outcome will be a decision allowing, but not requiring, the states to ban abortion. Half or more of the states would not immediately do so.[26]

In states that criminalize abortion, enforcement will be difficult. Even the harshest penalties are not likely to eliminate abortions, particularly in communities of color, which have disproportionately high abortion rates. While Trump made gains with voters of color in 2020, the fact that the anti-abortion movement relies on a Republican Party still defined by loyalty to Trump will likely make it harder for either the party or pro-life organizations to engage productively with communities of color—or to adopt policies that would help low-income people who wish to carry pregnancies to term.[27]

Like pro-lifers, Republicans once viewed their bargain with Trump as a smart one. He electrified the Republican base and brought many conservative voters to the polls for the first time. The campaign finance system from which Trump profited also seemed to strengthen the party. The success of the campaign that produced *Citizens United* led to a steady increase in outside spending, much of which benefited Republican candidates. But outside spending also created a financial base for insurgents. Partisan polarization and the spread of conservative media had already dealt populist candidates a stronger hand. Partly because of the anti-abortion movement's campaign finance work, populists now had the money to compete too. The changing rules of campaign finance helped to bring the GOP to its present moment of uncertainty and chaos.[28]

Anti-abortion leaders argued that allowing more spending on political speech would make our democracy more vibrant, participatory, and energetic. But the intertwined campaigns to reverse *Roe*, deregulate campaign finance, and pack the federal courts with conservatives not only wreaked havoc on our political parties but altered American politics.

U.S. politics in the early twenty-first century has been beset by gridlock, negative partisanship, and growing support for political violence. The pro-choice and pro-life movements are major characters in this drama—and not only because the abortion issue itself so bitterly divides Americans. Other developments contributed: the rise of Tea Party organizations and other purist political groups, the explosion of social media, and the ascendancy of conservative programming. The changes in campaign finance were not driven by the anti-abortion movement alone. A broad coalition of libertarians, champions of civil liberties, corporate leaders, and Republican veterans made significant contributions. But often, the anti-abortion movement was the link between social conservatives and big-money donors that made the coalition work.

Because of the movement's loyalty to the Republican Party and to Trump, it is easy to filter its effect on democracy through an ideological lens. Conservatives tend to see changes to campaign finance as giving voice to those ignored by the mainstream media and the party establishment. Progressives see cases like *Citizens United* as enabling plutocrats and racists to ignore the will of the people.

We should resist the impulse to adopt this partisan lens. Campaign finance rules have always had an ambiguous relationship to democracy. Opponents of campaign finance limits on both the right and the left took up the fight partly because they believed that public financing systems and spending limits gave an unfair advantage to incumbents and party hierarchies. There is evidence that more spending leads to better turnout and more political engagement. As the 2008 race suggested, looser spending rules do not necessarily preclude smaller donors from drowning out big-money interests. Even after *Citizens United*, small donors fueled the campaigns of candidates, like Bernie Sanders, who forced their party to debate ideas that might otherwise have been ignored. On the right and left, more money flowing to nonprofits fueled activism that might have otherwise remained under the surface. More campaign spending sometimes meant more political participation.[29]

But the changes wrought by pro-lifers looking to deregulate campaign finance also caused damage. As voter participation increased, so did polarization. The more power the issue-based groups gained within the Republican Party, the harder it became for the party to tack back to the center. A more ideologically pure party has rarely been willing to compromise to get anything done. Even something as illiberal as refusing to acknowledge the result of the 2020 election became a purity test for Republican officeholders.[30]

As it has grown increasingly conservative in recent decades, the GOP has struggled mightily to win the popular vote. The forces empowered by *Citizens United* do not reward the kind of pragmatism that might appeal to a wider range of voters. Rather than broaden the party's appeal, Republicans have often looked to shrink the electorate. A program of litigation and lobbying ostensibly meant to allow more expression has fed a process in which smaller and smaller groups of Americans dominate national politics.[31]

The downfall of the Republican establishment has also weakened U.S. democracy in other ways. Republican leaders had always spoken to voters who would gladly have embraced a populist in Trump's mold. But when Trump ran for office, the establishment no longer had either the money or the credibility to put him off course. And when Trump urged voters to distrust the system, reject democracy, and side with him, the establishment mostly stayed silent. The party's most significant response to the January 6 insurrection was to remove the politician who most vocally insisted on blaming Trump for the violence, Wyoming representative Liz Cheney, from her position as chair of the House Republican Conference. Most GOP officeholders sided with Trump out of fear that if they did not, his supporters' wrath would be expressed as a primary challenge. The former president succeeded in making the Republican Party a vehicle for his personal ambitions in part because the traditional establishment was too weak to stop him.

Many abortion foes struggled in the aftermath of the 2020 race. Janet Folger Porter pledged a campaign of "shock and awe," telling other pro-lifers that they had arrived at "our 1775"—the time for a new and potentially violent revolution. James Bopp, too, wondered if the country was slouching toward war. By the spring of 2021, the mood had changed: the overruling of

Roe seemed to be just a matter of time. The *Dobbs* case created almost unprecedented excitement within the anti-abortion movement.[32]

Democracy had long been a talking point for those seeking to reverse the *Roe* decision. *Roe*, they argued, took a hotly contested issue away from the people and resolved it nationally, through the will of an unelected judiciary. Far better to allow each state to make its own decisions about abortion, at least as far as democracy was concerned. But with a six-justice conservative majority in place, some right-to-lifers no longer talked as much about democracy when criticizing *Roe*. That was not an accident. Once the end of *Roe* seemed near, the movement returned to its original, abiding goal: the recognition of fetal personhood and the criminalization of abortion.[33]

In their quest to reverse *Roe*, some right-to-lifers have already transformed American politics, making the Supreme Court a more central election issue and upending the rules of campaign finance. But if the justices undo abortion rights, the anti-abortion movement will not stop trying to change the GOP. That is because in a deep sense, for those on both sides, the abortion wars have always been about fundamental human rights. The ultimate ambition of the pro-life movement is not a world in which states decide for themselves whether to legalize abortion, just as the pro-choice movement does not want the Supreme Court to leave states free to make their own choices. Abortion foes see unborn children as rights-holding persons and believe that abortion is immoral and unconstitutional. Anything short of a nationwide abortion ban will not satisfy them.

Public opinion on abortion has been remarkably stable. Most voters do not feel positively about abortion and favor some restrictions, but they strongly resist criminalizing the procedure or eliminating abortion rights.[34] As a result, popular majorities are not likely to deliver on the pro-life movement's goal—an absolute prohibition on abortion from coast to coast—now or in the foreseeable future. For this reason, in a post-*Roe* America, control of the Supreme Court—and influence over the Republicans who will nominate Supreme Court justices—will likely remain a central objective for the right-to-life movement. Already, some pro-life scholars have sketched arguments, aimed at the Court's conservative majority, that the Fourteenth Amendment recognizes fetal personhood and thus makes abortion unconstitutional. Pro-lifers will continue to focus on the Court precisely because the justices could render a decision that would be impossible to achieve through popular politics.[35]

It is hard to predict how the right-to-life movement will change the Republican Party or the rules of campaign finance. But for the time being, pro-lifers need the Court and the GOP to help them advance their vision of civil rights. And if the past is any example, as the movement fights for a right to life, neither campaign spending nor the rules of the democracy itself will likely be the same.

NOTES

Abbreviations

ACCL American Citizens Concerned for Life, Inc., Records, Gerald R. Ford Presidential Library and Museum, University of Michigan, Ann Arbor

ACF Arthur Culvahouse Jr. Files, Ronald Reagan Presidential Library and Museum, Simi Valley, California

AUL Americans United for Life Records, Executive File, Concordia Seminary, Lutheran Church-Missouri Synod, St. Louis, Missouri

AUS Americans United for the Separation of Church and State Subject Files, Rare Book and Manuscript Library, Columbia University, New York, New York

BFP Betty Friedan Papers, Schlesinger Library, Radcliffe Institute, Harvard University, Cambridge, Massachusetts

CCF Christopher Cox Files, Ronald Reagan Presidential Library and Museum, Simi Valley, California

CRP Charles Rice Papers, on file with the author

EMP Edwin Meese III Papers, Ronald Reagan Presidential Library and Museum, Simi Valley, California

FFF Fred Fielding Files, Ronald Reagan Presidential Library and Museum, Simi Valley, California

FSP Frederick T. Steeper Papers, Gerald R. Ford Presidential Library and Museum, University of Michigan, Ann Arbor

FWHC Feminist Women Health Center Records, David M. Rubenstein Rare Book and Manuscript Library, Duke University, Durham, North Carolina

GBP Gary Bauer Papers, Ronald Reagan Presidential Library and Museum, Simi Valley, California

GHW George Huntston Williams Papers, Andover-Harvard Theological Library, Harvard Divinity School, Cambridge, Massachusetts
JBP James Bopp Jr. Papers, Terre Haute, Indiana
JLF Jay Lefkowitz Files, George Herbert Walker Bush Presidential Library and Museum, College Station, Texas
JRS Dr. Joseph Stanton Human Life Issues Library and Resource Center, Our Lady of New York Convent, Bronx, New York
JSF John Sununu Files, George Herbert Walker Bush Presidential Library and Museum, College Station, Texas
KGF Kristen Gear Files, George Herbert Walker Bush Presidential Library and Museum, College Station, Texas
LLF Lee Liberman Files, George Herbert Walker Bush Presidential Library and Museum, College Station, Texas
MBF Morton Blackwell Files, Ronald Reagan Presidential Library and Museum, Simi Valley, California
MUR Matter under Review
PAW People for the American Way Collection of Conservative Political Ephemera, Bancroft Library, University of California, Berkeley
PMF Powell Moore Files, Ronald Reagan Presidential Library and Museum, Simi Valley, California
PPFA Planned Parenthood Federation of America Records, Sophia Smith Collection, Smith College, Northampton, Massachusetts
PWA Peter Wallison Files, Ronald Reagan Presidential Library and Museum, Simi Valley, California
PWP Paul Weyrich Papers, University of Wyoming, American Heritage Archive Center, Laramie
RJN Richard John Neuhaus Papers, American Catholic History Research Center and University Archives, Catholic University of America, Washington, DC
RLM Right to Life of Michigan Records, Bentley Historical Library, University of Michigan, Ann Arbor
RNCL Republican National Coalition for Life Collection, Phyllis Schlafly Center Archives, Clayton, Missouri
SBL Southern Baptists for Life Records, Southern Baptist Historical Library and Archives, Nashville, Tennessee
SYP Solomon Yue Papers, on file with the author
WCX Wilcox Collection of Contemporary Political Movements, Kenneth Spencer Research Library, University of Kansas, Lawrence

Preface

1. See Philip Bump, "What We Know about Trump's Efforts to Subvert the 2020 Election," *Washington Post*, January 25, 2021, https://www.washingtonpost.com/politics/2021/01/25/what-we-know-about-trumps-efforts-subvert-2020-election/,

accessed February 2, 2021; Jeremy Herb, Clare Foran, Manu Raju, and Phil Mattingly, "Congress Completes Electoral Count, Finalizing Biden's Win After Violent Delay from Pro-Trump Mob," *CNN*, January 7, 2021, https://www.cnn.com/2021/01/06/politics/2020-election-congress-electoral-college-vote-count/index.html, accessed February 2, 2021; Jim Rutenberg, Jo Becker, Eric Lipton, Maggie Haberman, Johnathan Martin, Matthew Rosenberg, and Michael S. Schmidt, "77 Days: Trump's Campaign to Subvert the Election," *New York Times*, January 31, 2021, https://www.nytimes.com/2021/01/31/us/trump-election-lie.html, accessed February 2, 2021. For Bopp's involvement, see Jacob Gershman, "Conservative Group Drops Election Lawsuits in Several States," *Wall Street Journal*, November 16, 2020, https://www.wsj.com/livecoverage/latest-updates-biden-trump-election-2020/card/I9ELmBDeCfKIxTzakywv, accessed February 9, 2021. The conclusion discusses Bopp's litigation with True the Vote at greater length. On Porter's reaction, see Janet Folger Porter, Mass Email, "4 Action Steps to Make Sure That Those Who Represent Us Don't Certify Fraud" (January 5, 2021), on file with the author; Janet Folger Porter, Mass Email, "Tell the Senate: Don't Certify the Fraud" (January 4, 2021), on file with the author; Janet Folger Porter, Mass Email, "Happy Thanksgiving! Election Update: Trump Won, We Won" (November 25, 2020), on file with the author.

2. On the rise of Christian nationalism and its relationship to Trump, see Andrew L. Whitehead and Samuel L. Perry, *Taking America Back for God: Christian Nationalism in the United States* (New York: Oxford University Press, 2020); Katherine Stewart, *The Power Worshippers: Inside the Dangerous Rise of Religious Nationalism* (London: Bloomsbury, 2020). For more on Trump's reliance on anti-abortion voters, see Danielle Kurtzleben, "The Complicated Importance of Abortion to Trump Voters," *NPR*, September 17, 2020, https://www.npr.org/2020/09/17/913589176/the-complicated-importance-of-abortion-to-trump-voters, accessed February 9, 2021.

3. For a sample of scholarship on the incorporation of the religious right into the GOP, see Daniel K. Williams, *God's Own Party: The Making of the Christian Right* (New York: Oxford University Press, 2010); Neil J. Young, *We Gather Together: The Religious Right and the Problem of Interfaith Politics* (New York: Oxford University Press, 2016); Angie Maxwell and Todd Shields, *The Long Southern Strategy: How Chasing White Voters in the South Changed American Politics* (New York: Oxford University Press, 2019); David Courtwright, *No Right Turn: Conservative Politics in a Liberal America* (Cambridge, MA: Harvard University Press, 2010); Clyde Wilcox and Carin Robinson, *Onward Christian Soldiers? The Religious Right in American Politics*, 4th ed. (New York: Taylor and Francis, 2011); Darren Dochuk, *From Bible Belt to Sunbelt: Plain-Folk Religion, Grassroots Politics, and the Rise of Evangelical Conservatism* (New York: Norton, 2010); Christopher Baylor, *First to the Party: The Group Origins of Party Transformation* (Philadelphia: University of Pennsylvania Press, 2017). For more on the GOP and its relationship with the anti-abortion movement, see Heather Cox Richardson, *To Make Men Free: A History of the Republican Party* (New York: Basic Books, 2014); Geoffrey Kabaservice, *Rule and Ruin: The Downfall of Moderation and the Destruction of the Republican Party, from*

Eisenhower to the Tea Party (New York: Oxford University Press, 2012); Andrew Lewis, *The Rights Turn in Conservative Christian Politics: How Abortion Transformed the Culture Wars* (New York: Cambridge University Press, 2017); Donald T. Critchlow, *The Conservative Ascendancy: How the Republican Right Rose to Power in Modern America* (Cambridge, MA: Harvard University Press, 2007).

4. See Maxwell and Shields, *The Long Southern Strategy*, 1–30; Kabaservice, *Rule and Ruin*, 1–25; Alan I. Abramowitz, *The Great Alignment: Race, Party Transformation, and the Rise of Donald Trump* (New Haven: Yale University Press, 2018), 3–16; Jacob S. Hacker and Paul Pierson, *Let Them Eat Tweets: How the Right Rules in an Age of Extreme Inequality* (New York: Liveright, 2020). On the influence of Christian nationalism and the transformation of evangelical Protestantism, see Kristin Kobes Du Mez, *Jesus and John Wayne: How White Evangelicals Corrupted a Faith and Fractured a Nation* (New York: Liveright, 2020); Whitehead and Perry, *Taking America Back for God*, 1–23.

5. On the relative polarization of the Democrats and Republicans, see Jacob S. Hacker and Paul Pierson, "Confronting Asymmetric Polarization," in *Solutions to Political Polarization in America*, ed. Nathaniel Persily (New York: Cambridge University Press, 2015), 59–67; Matt Grossman and David A. Hopkins, *Asymmetric Politics: Ideological Republicans and Group Interest Democrats* (New York: Oxford University Press, 2016), 1–12; Joseph Fishkin and David E. Pozen, "Asymmetric Constitutional Hardball," *Columbia Law Review* 118 (2018): 918–982. On negative partisanship within the Democratic Party, see Lilliana Mason, *Uncivil Agreement: How Politics Became Our Identity* (Chicago: University of Chicago Press, 2018), 28, 94; Matthew Levendusky, *The Partisan Sort: How Liberals Became Democrats and Conservatives Became Republicans* (Chicago: University of Chicago Press, 2009), 2–8. For an example of outside spending favoring liberals rather than conservatives, see Center for Responsive Politics, "2020 Outside Spending by Group," https://www.opensecrets.org/outsidespending/summ.php?cycle=2020&type=p&disp=O, accessed June 23, 2021.

6. On the spread of conservative media, see Nicole Hemmer, *Messengers of the Right: Conservative Media and the Transformation of American Politics* (Philadelphia: University of Pennsylvania Press, 2016); Brian Rosenwald, *Talk Radio's America: How an Industry Took over a Political Party That Took over the United States* (Cambridge, MA: Harvard University Press, 2019).

7. On the relative outside spending for Democrats and Republicans across election cycles, see Open Secrets, "Total Outside Spending by Election Cycle, Excluding Party Committees," 2021, https://www.opensecrets.org/outsidespending/cycle_tots.php, accessed June 17, 2021. There were exceptions to the Republicans' dominance in outside spending, including the 2020 presidential race. See ibid.

8. On the polarization of small donors, see Raymond La Raja and Brian Schaffner, *Campaign Finance and Political Polarization: When Purists Prevail* (Ann Arbor: University of Michigan Press, 2015), 138, 166; Richard Pildes, "Participation and Polarization," *University of Pennsylvania Journal of Constitutional Law* 22 (2019): 341–366. On the small donors to Greene and other members of Congress who

refused to certify the 2020 election, see Fredeka Schouten and Sergio Hernandez, "Marjorie Taylor and Other Trump Allies Ride Small-Donor Wave during 1st Quarter as Political Committee Donations Fall," *CNN*, April 17, 2021, https://www.opensecrets.org/outsidespending/summ.php?cycle=2020&type=p&disp=O, accessed June 23, 2021.

Chapter 1. The Fall of Personhood

1. James Bopp Jr., interview with Mary Ziegler, December 4, 2015; James Bopp Jr., interview with Mary Ziegler, January 15, 2021; see also "Field Narrowed," *Terre Haute Tribune*, August 6, 1959, 20; "Pairings Announced for Spring Handicap Golf Tournament," *Terre Haute Tribune*, May 30, 1956, 12; "Auxiliary Medical Society Picnic Planned," *Terre Haute Tribune*, September 13, 1950, 11; "Clubs," *Terre Haute Star*, February 10, 1950, 8; "Tri Kappa Style Show and Bridge Wednesday Night," *Terre Haute Tribune*, March 10, 1968, 10.
2. On Ruhl's case, see "Richmond Woman Is Arrested in Breakup of Abortion Racket," *Palladium Item*, May 21, 1950, 1; "Innocent Plea Is Entered in Abortion Case," *Palladium Item*, June 7, 1950, 1. On Stott's case, see "Woman Held for Death in Abortion Try," *Chicago Tribune*, January 19, 1960, 17; "Conclude Testimony in Abortion Trial," *Munster Times*, April 7, 1960, 2.
3. On Storer's campaign to criminalize abortion, see James C. Mohr, *Abortion in America: The Origins and Evolution of National Policy, 1800–1900* (New York: Oxford University Press, 1978), 144–200; Leslie J. Reagan, *When Abortion Was a Crime: Women, Medicine, and Law in the United States, 1867–1973* (Berkeley: University of California Press, 1997), 11–82; Mary Ziegler, *Abortion and the Law in America:* Roe v. Wade *to the Present* (New York: Cambridge University Press, 2020), 13–17.
4. For a sample of stories in the *Chicago Times* exposé, see "The Evil and the Remedy," *Chicago Times*, December 13, 1888, 4; "Doctors Who Advertise," *Chicago Times*, December 16, 1888, 4; "Infanticide," *Chicago Times*, December 1888, 1. On the rarity of criminal prosecutions, see Reagan, *When Abortion Was a Crime*, 131; Alicia Gutierrez-Romine, *From the Back Alley to the Border: Criminal Abortion in California, 1920–1969* (Lincoln: University of Nebraska Press, 2020), 137. Precise numbers on maternal mortality in the 1920s are hard to come by because relatively few states collected data on the subject. See Irvine Loudon, "Maternal Mortality in the Past and Its Relevance to Developing Countries Today," *American Journal of Clinical Nutrition* 72 (2000): 241–246. On declining rates of maternal mortality in the United States in the 1930s, see Christopher Tietze, "Abortion as a Cause of Death," *American Journal of Public Health* 38 (1948): 1437–1438; Irvine Loudon, "Puerperal Fever, the Streptococcus and the Sulfonamides, 1911–1945," *British Medical Journal* 2 (1987): 485–490.
5. See Reagan, *When Abortion Was a Crime*, 77; Patricia Miller, *Good Catholics: The Battle over Contraception in the Catholic Church* (Berkeley: University of California Press, 2014), 38.

6. See Reagan, *When Abortion Was a Crime*, 80–100; Kristin Luker, *Abortion and the Politics of Motherhood* (Berkeley: University of California Press, 1984), 46–52; Rickie Solinger, "A Complete Disaster: Abortion and the Politics of Hospital Committees, 1950–1970," *Feminist Studies* 19 (1993): 249–260.
7. Harry A. Pearse and Harold A. Ott, "Hospital Control of Sterilization and Therapeutic Abortion," *American Journal of Obstetrics and Gynecology* 60 (August 1950): 285; see also Herbert L. Packer and Ralph J. Gampell, "Therapeutic Abortion: A Problem in Law and Medicine," *Stanford Law Review* 11 (May 1959): 429.
8. Mary S. Calderone, ed., *Therapeutic Abortion in the United States* (New York: Harper and Bros., 1958), 84.
9. On the Stanford study, see Packer and Gampell, "Therapeutic Abortion," 417–455; C. Lee Buxton, "One Doctor's Opinion of Abortion Laws," *American Journal of Nursing* 68 (1968): 1026–1028. For Guttmacher's estimation, see Daniel K. Williams, *Defenders of the Unborn: The Pro-Life Movement Before* Roe v. Wade (New York: Oxford University Press, 2016), 33.
10. "Continuation of Discussion on the Model Penal Code," *Annual ALI Meeting Proceedings* 36 (1959): 255. On Guttmacher's life and background, see "Alan Guttmacher, Pioneer in Family Planning, Dies," *New York Times*, March 19, 1974, https://www.nytimes.com/1974/03/19/archives/alan-guttmacher-pioneer-in-family-planning-dies-planned.html, accessed December 8, 2020; David J. Garrow, *Liberty and Sexuality: The Right to Privacy and the Making of* Roe v. Wade (Berkeley: University of California Press, 1998), 270–275.
11. On Kimmey's life, see "About Jimmye Kimmey," Texas Portal to History, https://texashistory.unt.edu/explore/collections/JKPC/, accessed December 8, 2020. On Lader's background, see Elizabeth Mehren, "Champion of Choice: Larry Lader's 1966 Book Launched a Fight for Reproductive Rights. Now 76, He's Backing an Abortion Drug for the U.S. Market," *Los Angeles Times*, November 30, 1995, https://www.latimes.com/archives/la-xpm-1995-11-30-ls-8883-story.html, accessed December 8, 2020; Douglas Martin, "Larry Lader, Champion of Abortion Rights, Is Dead at 86," *New York Times*, May 10, 2006, https://www.nytimes.com/2006/05/10/nyregion/10lader.html, accessed December 8, 2020. For Lader's book, see Larry Lader, *Abortion* (New York: Bobbs-Merrill, 1966).
12. On the ASA, see Suzanne Staggenborg, *The Pro-Choice Movement: Organization and Activism in the Abortion Conflict* (New York: Oxford University Press, 1991), 16–18; Garrow, *Liberty and Sexuality*, 182–193. For the ALI proposal: American Law Institute, Model Penal Code: Abortion (1959).
13. On the founding of NRLC, see Mary Ziegler, *After* Roe: *The Lost History of the Abortion Debate* (Cambridge, MA: Harvard University Press, 2015), 23–42; Williams, *Defenders of the Unborn*, 166–180; Ziegler, *Abortion and the Law*, 12–15.
14. Fred C. Shapiro, " 'Right to Life' Has a Message for New York State Legislators," *New York Times*, August 20, 1972, https://www.nytimes.com/1972/08/20/archives/-right-to-life-has-a-message-for-new-york-state-legislators-the.html, accessed December 8, 2020; see also Ziegler, *After* Roe, 31. On Rice's involvement with the Conservative Party, see Kevin Phillips, *The Emerging Republican Majority*

(Princeton: Princeton University Press, 2015), 178–182; Patrick Allitt, *Catholic Intellectuals and Conservative Politics, 1950–1985* (Ithaca: Cornell University Press, 1993), 185.

15. On the Mecklenburgs and MCCL, see Ziegler, *After* Roe, 31–35; Williams, *Defenders of the Unborn*, 179–184. For Mecklenburg's clinic, see Michael Robinson, "House Defeats Abortion Bill," *Jacksonville Daily Journal*, May 19, 1971, 15; see also Jack Coffman, "Panel Approves Family Aid Bill," *Minneapolis Star Tribune*, February 19, 1975, 16.
16. On the rights arguments used by abortion foes in the period, see Jennifer L. Holland, *Tiny You: A Western History of the Anti-Abortion Movement* (Berkeley: University of California Press, 2020), 4–15; Ziegler, *After* Roe, 38–52; Williams, *Defenders of the Unborn*, 3–15.
17. See Williams, *Defenders of the Unborn*, 166–180; Ziegler, *After* Roe, 150–172.
18. On the events in Colorado, see Richard D. Lyons, "Colorado Abortion Law Assessed," *New York Times*, December 8, 1969, 1; William Droegemueller, E. Stewart Taylor, and Vera Drose, "The First Year of Experience in Colorado with the New Abortion Law," *American Journal of Obstetrics and Gynecology* 103 (1969): 694–702. On the California experience, see Keith D. Monroe, "How California's Abortion Law Isn't Working," *New York Times*, December 29, 1969, SM10; Keith P. Russell and Edwin Jackson, "Therapeutic Abortions in California: First Year's Experience under New Legislation," *American Journal of Obstetrics and Gynecology* 105 (1969): 757–765.
19. See Meeting Minutes of the National Organization for Women (November 18–19, 1967), 1–7, BFP, Carton 127, Folder 1553; see also *Before* Roe v. Wade*: Voices That Shaped Debate Before the Supreme Court's Ruling*, ed. Reva B. Siegel and Linda Greenhouse (New Haven: Yale University Press, 2010), 36; Staggenborg, *The Pro-Choice Movement*, 20–23. For Planned Parenthood's support of repeal, see Meeting Minutes, Planned Parenthood-World Population (May 8, 1969), PPFA 1, Box 49, Folder 19; Morris Kaplan, "Abortion, Sterilization Win Support of Planned Parenthood," *New York Times*, November 14, 1968, 50.
20. On Maginnis's story, see Ninia Baehr, *Abortion without Apology: A Radical History for the 1990s* (Boston: South End, 1990), 3–10; Laurence H. Tribe, *Abortion: The Clash of Absolutes* (New York: Norton, 1992), 39; Lili Loofbourow, "They Called Her 'the Che Gueverra of Abortion Reformers,'" *Slate*, December 4, 2018, https://slate.com/human-interest/2018/12/pat-maginnis-abortion-rights-pro-choice-activist.html, accessed December 9, 2020. On Phelan, see Baehr, *Abortion without Apology*, 3–7; Michelle Murphy, *Seizing the Means of Reproduction: Entanglements of Feminism, Health, and Technoscience* (Durham: Duke University Press, 2012), 190.
21. For Friedan's story, see Betty Friedan, *Life So Far: A Memoir* (New York: Simon and Schuster, 2000). On the founding of NARAL, see Myra MacPherson, "Abortion Laws: A Call for Repeal," *Washington Post*, February 17, 1969, D1; Lyle Lilliston, "National Group to Change Abortion Laws Formed," *Los Angeles Times*, February 18, 1969, E1.

22. On the population control movement and abortion, see Donald Critchlow, *Intended Consequences: Birth Control, Abortion, and the Federal Government in Modern America* (New York: Oxford University Press, 1999), 147, 177–178; Matthew Connelly, *Fatal Misconception: The Struggle to Control World Population* (Cambridge, MA: Harvard University Press, 2008); Simone M. Caron, *Who Chooses? American Reproductive History since 1850* (Gainesville: University of Florida Press, 2008), 150–163.
23. On bipartisan support for the ERA and women's rights in the 1960s, see Christina Wolbrecht, *The Politics of Women's Rights: Parties, Positions, and Change* (Princeton: Princeton University Press, 2000), 5, 34–50. On the broad appeal of population control arguments, see Critchlow, *Intended Consequences*, 3–21; Connelly, *Fatal Misconception*, 1–30; Ziegler, *After* Roe, 130–139.
24. See Gallup poll, November 1969, in Gallup Organization, *America's Opinion on Abortion* (Princeton, NJ: Gallup Organization) (unpaginated). On Goldwater and Reagan, see Williams, *Defenders of the Unborn*, 100–102. On the support for legal abortion within Young Americans for Freedom, see Bernard Weinraub, "Unrest Spurs Growth of Conservative Student Groups," *New York Times*, October 12, 1969, 70.
25. See Williams, *Defenders of the Unborn*, 100–105; Gene Burns, *The Moral Veto: Framing Abortion, Contraception, and Cultural Pluralism in the United States* (New York: Cambridge University Press, 2005), 13–18; Critchlow, *Intended Consequences*, 104–153.
26. On concerns about a specific state becoming an abortion mecca, see "Colorado's Abortion Law Signed," *Atlanta Journal Constitution*, April 26, 1967, 2; "Model Statute on Abortion Is Now North Carolina Law," *Atlanta Journal Constitution*, May 9, 1967, 12.
27. See *Griswold v. Connecticut*, 381 U.S. 479 (1965).
28. See ibid., 501–512.
29. For examples of decisions recognizing abortion rights, see *People v. Belous*, 458 P.2d 194 (Cal. 1969); *Abele v. Markle*, 342 F.Supp. 800 (D. Conn. 1972).
30. On conservatives' reaction to the Warren Court, see Ken Kersch, *Conservatives and the Constitution: Reimagining Constitutional Restoration in the Heyday of American Liberalism* (New York: Cambridge University Press, 2019), 88–100; Laura Kalman, *The Long Reach of the 1960s: LBJ, Nixon, and the Making of the Supreme Court* (New York: Oxford University Press, 2017), xi–xiii; Thomas M. Keck, *The Most Activist Supreme Court in History: The Road to Modern Judicial Conservatism* (Chicago: University of Chicago Press, 2004), 94–100.
31. "The Supreme Court Jumps the Track," *Chicago Tribune*, June 19, 1957, 18.
32. Arthur Edson, "Dissatisfaction with the Supreme Court Is No New Thing, Historians Recall," *Daily Press*, June 24, 1956, 47. For more on reaction to Red Monday and the impeachment campaign, see D. J. Mulloy, *The World of the John Birch Society: Conspiracy, Conservatism, and the Cold War* (Nashville: Vanderbilt University Press, 2014), 113; Arthur J. Sabin, *In Calmer Times: The Supreme Court and Red Monday* (Philadelphia: University of Pennsylvania Press, 1999), 113.

33. For the Court's decision in *Engel*, see *Engel v. Vitale*, 370 U.S. 421 (1962). For the Court's decision in *Schempp*, see *School District of Abington Township v. Schempp*, 374 U.S. 203 (1963). On mobilization around the school prayer decisions, see Michael W. Flamm, "The Liberal-Conservative Debates of the 1960s," in *Debating the 1960s: Liberal, Conservative, and Radical Perspectives*, ed. Michael W. Flamm and David Steigerwald (Lanham, MD: Rowman and Littlefield, 2008), 99–110; Natalie Mehlman Petrzela, *Classroom Wars: Language, Sex, and the Making of Modern Culture* (New York: Oxford University Press, 2015), 143. On religious response to the decisions, see Barry Friedman, *The Will of the People: How Public Opinion Has Influenced the Supreme Court and Shaped the Meaning of the Constitution* (New York: Farrar, Straus and Giroux, 2009), 264–266.
34. "Nixon Links Court to Rise in Crime," *New York Times*, May 31, 1968, 18. For more on reaction to the Warren Court's criminal procedure opinions, see Richard H. Fallon Jr., *Law and Legitimacy in the Supreme Court* (Cambridge, MA: Harvard University Press, 2018), 118.
35. See Martin McKernan, NRLC Legal Counsel, "Legal Report: Court Cases" (July 1970), 3–4, ACCL, Box 4, 1970 NRLC Folder. For the decision allowing lawsuits based on prenatal injuries, see *Bonbrest v. Kotz*, 65 F.Supp. 138, 143 (D.D.C. 1946). On the state of the law, see American Law Reports, *Liability for Prenatal Injuries* 40 (1971): 1222–1225. For more on Liley, see Sara Dubow, *Ourselves Unborn: A History of the Fetus in Modern America* (New York: Oxford University Press, 2010), 113–115.
36. For scholarship on abortion and equal protection from the period, see Robert M. Byrn, "Abortion in Perspective," *Duquesne Law Review* 5 (1966): 134–135; see also Robert M. Byrn, "Abortion on Demand: Whose Morality?" *Notre Dame Law Review* 46 (1970–1971): 26–27. For the Court's decision in *Brown*, see *Brown v. Board of Education*, 347 U.S. 483 (1954). For a sample of the Court's illegitimacy decisions, see *Levy v. Louisiana*, 391 U.S. 68 (1968); *Glona v. American Liability and Insurance Company*, 391 U.S. 73 (1968); *Labine v. Vincent*, 401 U.S. 532 (1971).
37. John T. Noonan and David Louisell, "Constitutional Balance," in *The Morality of Abortion: Legal and Historical Perspectives*, ed. John T. Noonan (Cambridge, MA: Harvard University Press, 1970), 229–235. For more on Louisell, see Christopher Mueller, "David B. Louisell: In Memoriam," *California Law Review* 66 (1978): 921–934.
38. On Horan's life, see "Dennis M. Horan, 56, a Lawyer and Author," *New York Times*, May 3, 1988, https://www.nytimes.com/1988/05/03/obituaries/dennis-m-horan-56-a-lawyer-and-author.html, accessed January 20, 2021; Eugene F. Diamond, "Eulogy Given at the Funeral of Dennis Horan," *Linacre Quarterly* 55 (1988): 55–60; Clarke D. Forsythe, "The Legal Legacy of Dennis Horan, Esq., for Protecting Human Life—Chairman of the Board of Americans United for Life—on the Occasion of the Twenty-Fifth Anniversary of His Death," *Americans United for Life*, May 2, 2013, https://aul.org/2013/05/02/the-legal-legacy-of-dennis-horan/, accessed January 20, 2021.
39. Glen Elsasser, "Guardian of Unborn Tells How He Attained Unique Court Role," *Chicago Tribune*, February 15, 1971, A4. On the suit, see "Jury Sought for Abortion

Law Test Case," *Chicago Tribune*, June 14, 1970, 22; Glen Elsasser, "Doctor Fights Abortion Ruling," *Chicago Tribune*, February 3, 1971, 4.

40. For more on pro-life efforts to establish guardianships for fetuses or unborn children, see *Steinberg v. Brown*, 321 F.Supp. 741, 743–748 (N.D. Ohio 1970); "Lawyer Denied 'Guardian of the Unborn' Plea," *Los Angeles Times*, June 3, 1971, D8; "Guardian for Fetus Named," *Los Angeles Times*, October 8, 1971, A20; "Guardian Is Named as Bar to Abortion," *Chicago Tribune*, December 4, 1971, 17.

41. "Guardian Is Named as Bar to Abortion," 17; see also Robert E. Tomasson, "A Lawyer Challenges the Abortion Law," *New York Times*, December 4, 1971, 29; Judy Klemesrud, "He's the Guardian for Fetuses about to Be Aborted," *New York Times*, December 17, 1971, 48.

42. Klemesrud, "He's the Guardian," 48.

43. Morris Kaplan, "State Abortion Law Upheld on Appeal," *New York Times*, February 26, 1972, 1. On the *Byrn* litigation, see *Byrn v. New York City Health and Hospitals Corporation*, 286 N.E.2d 887 (N.Y. 1972); *Byrn v. New York City Health and Hospitals Corporation*, 38 A.2d 316 (N.Y. App. Div. 1972).

44. For the Court's decision in *Vuitch*, see *United States v. Vuitch*, 402 U.S. 62 (1971). For decisions invalidating abortion laws, see *Babbitz v. McCann*, 310 F.Supp. 393 (E.D. 1970); *Doe v. Bolton*, 319 F.Supp. 1048 (N.D. 1970); *Doe v. Scott*, 321 F.Supp. 1385 (N.D. Ill. 1971); *State v. Barquet*, 262 So.2d 431 (Fl. 1972); *Young Women's Christian Association of Princeton, New Jersey v. Kugler*, 342 F.Supp. 1048 (N.J. 1972).

45. *Eisenstadt v. Baird*, 405 U.S. 438, 446–455 (1972). For a sample of scholarly reaction to the decision, see Gerald Gunther, "The Supreme Court 1971 Term—Foreword: In Search of Evolving Doctrine on a Changing Court: A Model for a Newer Equal Protection," *Harvard Law Review* 86 (1972): 1–48; Philip B. Kurland, "1971 Term: The Year of the Stewart-White Court," *Supreme Court Review* 1972 (1972): 181–329. On the connection between *Eisenstadt* and *Roe*, see Bob Woodward and Scott Armstrong, *The Brethren: Inside the Supreme Court* (New York: Simon and Schuster, 1979), 210–211.

46. See *State v. Shirley*, 237 So.2d 676 (La. 1970); *Corkey v. Edwards*, 322 F.Supp. 1248 (W.D.N.C. 1971); *Lashley v. State*, 268 A.2d 502 (Md. 1970); *State v. Bartlett*, 270 A.2d 168 (Vt. 1970).

47. On the Michigan referendum, see Walter Mossberg, "A Key Battle: Outcome of Next Tuesday's Referendum in Michigan Will Likely Have National Implications," *Wall Street Journal*, November 3, 1972, 30; Gillian Frank, "The Colour of the Unborn: Anti-Abortion and Anti-Bussing Politics in Michigan, United States, 1967–1973," *Gender and History* 26 (2014): 351–378. On the North Dakota referendum, see Williams, *Defenders of the Unborn*, 143–168. On Nixon and McGovern's abortion politics, see ibid., 173–190; see also Critchlow, *Intended Consequences*, 148; "Nixon Abortion Statement," *New York Times*, April 4, 1971, 28.

48. "Poll on Abortions Scored by Prelate," *New York Times*, September 1, 1972, https://www.nytimes.com/1972/09/01/archives/poll-on-abortions-scored-by-prelate.html, accessed January 20, 2021; see also "Gallup Poll Finds Public Divided on Abortions in First Three Months," *New York Times*, January 28, 1973, https://

www.nytimes.com/1973/01/28/archives/gallup-poll-finds-public-divided-on-abortions-in-first-3-months.html, accessed January 20, 2021.

49. On early drafts of *Roe*, see Garrow, *Liberty and Sexuality*, 549–576; Bernard Schwartz, *Decision: How the Supreme Court Decides Cases* (New York: Oxford University Press, 1996), 232; Michael J. Graetz and Linda Greenhouse, *The Burger Court and the Rise of the Judicial Right* (New York: Simon and Schuster, 2016), 140–141; see also Clarke Forsythe, *Abuse of Discretion: The Inside Story of* Roe v. Wade (New York: Encounter Books, 2013).

50. See Motion for Leave to File a Brief and Brief of Ferdinand Buckley as Amicus Curiae in Support of Appellees, 5, *Roe v. Wade*, 410 U.S. 113 (1973) (No. 70-40); Motion for Leave to File Brief and Brief of Amicus Curiae Robert Sassone in Support of Respondent, 4–17, *Roe v. Wade*, 410 U.S. 113 (1973) (No. 70-40).

51. See Brief of Americans United for Life, Amicus Curiae, 8, *Roe v. Wade*, 410 U.S. 113 (1973) (No. 70-40).

52. For examples of such arguments, see Motion and Brief of Certain Physicians, Professors, and Fellows of the American College of Obstetricians and Gynecologists in Support of Appellants, 62, *Roe v. Wade*, 410 U.S. 113 (1973) (No. 70-40).

53. See Garrow, *Liberty and Sexuality*, 412–415. On Nixon's transformation of the Court, see Kalman, *The Long Reach of the 1960s*, 200–260; John Anthony Maltese, *The Selling of Supreme Court Nominees* (Baltimore: Johns Hopkins University Press, 1998), 12–20.

54. See Rick Perlstein, *Nixonland: The Rise of a President and the Fracturing of America* (New York: Simon and Schuster, 2008), 728; Kevin Kruse and Julian Zelizer, *Fault Lines: A History of the United States since 1974* (New York: Simon and Schuster, 2019), 230–238.

55. See Anthony Corrado, "Money and Politics: A History of Campaign Finance Law," in *Campaign Finance Reform: A Sourcebook*, ed. Trevor Potter et al. (Washington, DC: Brookings Institute, 1997), 32; see also John Samples, *The Fallacy of Campaign Finance Reform* (Chicago: University of Chicago Press, 2008), 234–240; Conor Dowling and Michael Miller, *Super PACs! Money, Elections, and Voters After* Citizens United (New York: Taylor and Francis, 2014), 132.

56. Bopp, December 4, 2015 interview; Bopp, January 15, 2021 interview. For the Court's decision in *Roe*, see *Roe v. Wade*, 410 U.S. 113 (1973). For an overview of Bopp's later work, see David D. Kirkpatrick, "A Quest to End Spending Rules for Campaigns," *New York Times*, January 24, 2010, https://www.nytimes.com/2010/01/25/us/politics/25bopp.html, accessed December 8, 2020; Mary Beth Schneider, "Hoosier's Campaign-Finance Crusade Pays Off," *Indianapolis Star*, April 2, 2014, https://www.indystar.com/story/news/politics/2014/04/02/hoosiers-campaign-finance-crusade-pays/7228163/, accessed December 8, 2020; Viveca Novak, "Citizen Bopp," *American Prospect*, January 2, 2012, https://prospect.org/power/citizen-bopp/, accessed December 8, 2020.

57. On Terre Haute's reputation, see "Sin City Special Reports on Changing Terre Haute," *Indianapolis Star*, October 7, 1962, 1.

58. On Bopp's involvement with the Teenage Republicans, see Kirkpatrick, "A Quest"; Novak, "Citizen Bopp." On Bopp's involvement with Young Americans

for Freedom, see Jason S. Lantzer, "The Other Side of Campus: Indiana University's Student Right and the Rise of National Conservatism," *Indiana Magazine of History* 101 (2005): 153–178; see also Stephanie Mencimer, "The Man behind Citizens United Is Just Getting Started," *Mother Jones*, May/June 2011, https://www.motherjones.com/politics/2011/05/james-bopp-citizens-united/, accessed December 8, 2020; Bopp, January 15, 2021 interview.

59. Bopp, January 15, 2021 interview; Bopp, December 4, 2015 interview.
60. *Roe v. Wade*, 410 U.S. 113, 147–155 (1973).
61. Ibid., 156–162.
62. On Rockefeller and abortion, see Stacie Taranto, *Kitchen Table Politics: Conservative Women and Family Values in New York* (Philadelphia: University of Pennsylvania Press, 2017), 143–180; Richard Norton Smith, *On His Own Terms: A Life of Nelson Rockefeller* (New York: Random House, 2014), 132–176. Chapter 2 further discusses Reagan's position on abortion. On Eagleton, see Scott H. Ainsworth and Thad E. Hall, *Abortion Politics in Congress: Strategic Incrementalism and Policy Change* (New York: Cambridge University Press, 2010), 61, 109; Ziegler, *Abortion and the Law*, 71. On Chisholm, see Shirley Chisholm and Shola Lynch, *Unbought and Unbossed* (New York: Take Root Media, 2010), 129–150; Loretta J. Ross, "African-American Women and Abortion," in *Abortion Wars: A Half-Century of Struggle, 1950–2000* (Berkeley: University of California Press, 1998), 183–196.
63. A Bill to Provide That Human Life Shall Be Deemed to Exist from Conception, before the Senate Judiciary Committee, Subcommittee on Separation of Powers, 97th Congress, 1st Sess. (May 21, 1981), 308–311 (Statement of Prof. Robert Bork). For Ely's view, see John Hart Ely, "The Wages of Crying Wolf: A Comment on *Roe v. Wade*," *Yale Law Journal* 82 (1973): 920–938. For Byrn's article, see Robert M. Byrn, "An American Tragedy: The Supreme Court on Abortion," *Fordham Law Review* 41 (1973): 807–812.
64. On Evans, see Adam Clymer, "M. Stanton Evans, Who Helped Shape Conservative Movement, Is Dead at 80," *New York Times*, March 4, 2015, https://www.nytimes.com/2015/03/04/us/m-stanton-evans-pioneer-of-conservative-movement-dies-at-80.html, accessed January 22, 2021; Matt Schudel, "M. Stanton Evans, Guiding Force in Modern Conservatism, Dies at 80," *Washington Post*, March 5, 2015; Bopp, January 15, 2021 interview; Bopp, December 4, 2015 interview.
65. Bopp, January 15, 2021 interview; Bopp, December 4, 2015 interview.
66. See R. W. Apple Jr., "Dismay and Outrage over Nixon Erupt at Conservatives' Parley: Ronald Reagan Is Hailed," *New York Times*, January 27, 1974, 44; M. Stanton Evans, "The Ronald Reagan Story," *Human Events*, January 24, 1976, 17; "Can Reagan Win?" *Human Events*, April 17, 1976, 16.
67. On the ads that Stanton ran for Reagan, see Joseph Lelyveld, "Reagan Aided by Ads Conservative Group Paid For," *New York Times*, May 6, 1976, 43; James Coates, "FEC 'Dead,' Reagan Backers Make Hay," *Chicago Tribune*, May 9, 1976, 12. Chapter 2 studies *Buckley* and Stanton's involvement in the case.

Chapter 2. Controlling the Court

1. Meeting Minutes, NRLC Ad Hoc Strategy Meeting (February 11, 1973), ACCL, Box 4, 1973 NRLC Folder 1. On the Buckley and Hogan Amendments, see Mary Ziegler, *After* Roe: *The Lost History of the Abortion Debate* (Cambridge, MA: Harvard University Press, 2015), 38–45; National Committee for a Human Life Amendment, "Human Life Amendment: Major Texts," available at http://www.nchla.org/datasource/idocuments/HLAmajortexts.pdf, accessed February 13, 2013. For an analysis of the Hogan Amendment, see, e.g., Harriet Pilpel, "The Fetus as Person: Possible Legal Consequences of the Hogan-Helms Amendment," *Family Planning Perspectives* 6 (1974): 6–7; see also James Bopp Jr., *Restoring the Right to Life: The Human Life Amendment* (Provo: Brigham Young University Press, 1984). On the early pro-life movement, see Daniel K. Williams, *Defenders of the Unborn: The Pro-Life Movement Before* Roe v. Wade (New York: Oxford University Press, 2016), 3–10, 94–95; Ziegler, *After* Roe, 37–45; Donald T. Critchlow, *Intended Consequences: Birth Control, Abortion, and the Federal Government in Modern America* (New York: Oxford University Press, 1999), 138; Jennifer Holland, *Tiny You: A Western History of the Anti-Abortion Movement* (Berkeley: University of California Press, 2020). On Willke, see Holland, *Tiny You*, 68–73; Williams, *Defenders of the Unborn*, 138–145; Ziegler, *After* Roe, 38–42.
2. See AUL Fundraising Letter (September 20, 1972), 2, AUL, Executive File, Box 91; Ziegler, *After* Roe, 24–38.
3. See Dennis Horan to NRLC Policy Committee (September 5, 1973), 1–3, ACCL, Box 8, 1973 NRLC Folder; Joseph Witherspoon to NRLC Executive Committee (August 14, 1973), ACCL, Box 4, 1973 National Right to Life Committee Folder 3; Robert Sassone to Marjory Mecklenburg (November 8, 1973), ACCL, Box 4, National Right to Life Committee Folder 3; National Right to Life Committee Board of Directors Meeting Minutes (December 2, 1973), ACCL, Box 4, National Right to Life Committee Folder 3; Nellie Gray to the National Right to Life Board of Directors (December 8, 1973), ACCL, Box 4, National Right to Life Committee Folder 1; Joseph Witherspoon to Dr. Joseph Stanton (December 21, 1973), ACCL, Box 4, National Right to Life Committee Folder 1.
4. On efforts to craft a perfect constitutional amendment, see Dennis J. Horan, "The Constitutional Amendment and the NRLC," *National Right to Life News*, January 1974, 1, JRS, 1974 National Right to Life News; Dennis Horan to NRLC Board of Directors et al. (January 19, 1974), 1–5, ACCL, Box 8, 1974 NRLC Folder; Dennis Horan to NRLC Board of Directors et al. (January 19, 1974), 1–5, ACCL, Box 8, 1974 NRLC Folder.
5. On McFadden, see Patrick Allitt, *Catholic Intellectuals and Conservative Politics in America: 1950–1985* (Ithaca: Cornell University Press, 1993), 192; Ziegler, *After* Roe, 60–72.
6. Allitt, *Catholic Intellectuals*, 191; see also Carol Mason, *Killing for Life: The Apocalyptic Narrative of Pro-Life Politics* (Ithaca: Cornell University Press, 2002), 142–149.

7. See Nicole Hemmer, *Messengers of the Right: Conservative Media and the Transformation of American Politics* (Philadelphia: University of Pennsylvania Press, 2016), 248–251. On the political diversity of the anti-abortion movement in the period, see Ziegler, *After* Roe, 32–44; Williams, *Defenders of the Unborn*, 102–150.
8. For Agnew's statement: Wayne E. Green, "Broadcasters Uneasy After Agnew Attack and Praise for It by FCC's New Chairman," *Wall Street Journal*, November 19, 1969, 6. For more on the controversy about media balance in the period, see Hemmer, *Messengers of the Right*, 236–240. For more on Agnew, see Charles J. Holden, Zach Messitte, and Jerald Podair, *Republican Populist: Spiro Agnew and the Origins of Donald Trump's America* (Charlottesville: University of Virginia Press, 2019).
9. C. Gerald Fraser, "Last Senate Debate Marked by Harsh Charges," *New York Times*, November 2, 1970, https://www.nytimes.com/1970/11/02/archives/last-senate-race-debate-marked-by-harsh-charges-senate-candidates.html, accessed June 21, 2021; see also Maurice Carroll, "James Buckley Maps Strategy on Campaign for Senate Seat," *New York Times*, September 10, 1968, 32; "The Buckley Victory," *Wall Street Journal*, November 5, 1970, 14; see also Mark J. Green, *James L. Buckley: Conservative Senator from New York* (Charlottesville: University of Virginia Press, 1972).
10. On the impact of the Fairness Doctrine, see "Fairness Doctrine Hurts Ad Campaign," *National Right to Life News*, July 1975, 14, JRS, 1975 National Right to Life News Box. For Buckley's objection to the coverage of the pro-life movement, see *Freedom of Information Center Report* (Minneapolis: University of Minnesota Press, 1972), 3. The fairness doctrine was ultimately repealed in 1987. See Bruce Schulman and Julian Zelizer, *Media Nation: The Political History of News in Modern America* (Philadelphia: University of Pennsylvania Press, 2017), 142.
11. "New York State Convention Hears Candidate: Analyst," *National Right to Life News*, August 1974, 19, JRS, 1974 National Right to Life News Box. For more on Keating's work, see Stacie Taranto, *Kitchen Table Politics: Conservative Women and Family Values in New York* (Philadelphia: University of Pennsylvania Press, 2017), 139–142; Barbara Keating, "Right to Life Television Commercials," JRS, Ellen McCormack Papers. For Keating's description of Javits and Clark: Steven Weisman, "Javits and Clark Clash as Mrs. Keating Mocks Them," *New York Times*, October 26, 1974, 15. On Javits, see James F. Clarity, "Jacob Javits Dies in Florida at 81: Four-Time Senator from New York," *New York Times*, March 8, 1986, https://www.nytimes.com/1986/03/08/obituaries/jacob-javits-dies-in-florida-at-81–4-term-senator-from-new-york.html, accessed September 11, 2020. On Clark, see David Margolick, "The Long and Lonely Journey of Ramsey Clark," *New York Times*, June 14, 1991, https://www.nytimes.com/1991/06/14/washington/the-long-and-lonely-journey-of-ramsey-clark.html, accessed July 21, 2020.
12. See Dr. Willke and Mrs. J. C. Willke, "There Is a Pro-Life Vote," *National Right to Life News*, February 1975, 4, JRS, 1975 National Right to Life News Box. On Willke's significance to the movement, see Williams, *Defenders of the Unborn*, 138–142. For the Willkes' own account, see John C. Willke and Barbara Willke with Marie C. Willke Meyers, *Abortion and the Pro-Life Movement: An Inside Story* (West Conshohocken, PA: Infinity, 2014).

13. Willke and Willke, "There Is a Pro-Life Vote," 4.
14. On the early New Right PACs, see Laura Kalman, *Right Star Rising: A New Politics, 1974–1980* (New York: Norton, 2010), 145; "1980 Federal Elections: PACs Play a Larger Role," *American Bar Association Journal*, March 1981, 281; Larry Powell, "NCPAC and the Development of Third-Party Expenditures," in *Campaign Finance Reform: The Political Shell Game*, ed. Melissa M. Smith, Glenda C. Williams, and Larry Powell (Lanham, MD: Rowman and Littlefield, 2010), 28–49. On Weyrich, see Rick Perlstein, *Reaganland: America's Right Turn, 1976–1980* (New York: Simon and Schuster, 2020), 36–40; Daniel K. Williams, *God's Own Party: The Making of the Christian Right* (New York: Oxford University Press, 2010), 133–140.
15. On ALEC, see Alexander Hertel-Fernandez, *State Capture: How Conservative Activists, Big Businesses, and Wealthy Donors Reshaped the American States—and the Nation* (New York: Oxford University Press, 2019), 28–42; Christopher Leonard, *Kochland: The Secret History of Koch Industries and Corporate Power in America* (New York: Simon and Schuster, 2019), 328–340; Dan Kaufman, *The Fall of Wisconsin: The Conservative Conquest of a Progressive Bastion and the Future of American Politics* (New York: Norton, 2018), 134–145.
16. On Weyrich's PAC, see Daniel Schlozman, *Why Movements Anchor Parties: Electoral Alignments in American History* (Princeton: Princeton University Press, 2015), 82–87; Robert Biersack, Paul S. Herrnson, and Clyde Wilcox, *Risky Business: PAC Decision Making and Strategy* (Lanham, MD: Rowman and Littlefield, 2016), 100–104; Donald T. Critchlow, *Phyllis Schlafly and Grassroots Conservatism: A Woman's Crusade* (Princeton: Princeton University Press, 2005), 263–270.
17. See Robert E. Mutch, *Buying the Vote: A History of Campaign Finance Reform* (New York: Oxford University Press, 2014), 1–12, 130; Raymond La Raja, *Small Change: Money, Political Parties, and Campaign Finance Reform* (Ann Arbor: University of Michigan Press, 2008), 55–68. For more on the history of campaign finance laws, see Robert E. Mutch, *Campaign Finance: What Everyone Needs to Know* (New York: Oxford University Press, 2016); Adam Winkler, *We the Corporations: How American Business Won Their Civil Rights* (New York: Liveright, 2018), 324–376; Andrew R. Lewis, *The Rights Turn in Conservative Christian Politics: How Abortion Transformed the Culture Wars* (New York: Cambridge University Press, 2017), 49–52; Wayne Batchis, *The Right's First Amendment: The Politics of Free Speech & the Return of Conservative Libertarianism* (Stanford: Stanford University Press, 2016).
18. See Anthony Corrado, "Money and Politics: A History of Federal Campaign Finance Law," in *The New Campaign Finance Sourcebook*, ed. Anthony Corrado, Thomas Mann, Daniel Ortiz, and Trevor Potter (Washington, DC: Brookings Institute, 2005), 20; Anthony J. Gaughan, "The Influence of Technology on Presidential Primary Campaigns," in *The Best Candidate: Presidential Nomination in Polarized Times*, ed. Eugene D. Mazo and Michael Dimino (New York: Cambridge University Press, 2020), 319. On the Justice Department's underenforcement of disclosure rules, see Mutch, *Buying the Vote*, 130. For more on the New Right, see

Geoffrey Kabaservice, *Rule and Ruin: The Downfall of Moderation and the Destruction of the Republican Party, from Eisenhower to the Tea Party* (New York: Oxford University, 2012), 39–45. For the text of the 1971 FECA, 52 U.S.C. § 30101 et seq. On the federal Corrupt Practices Act, see 15 U.S.C. § 78 et seq.

19. See Stanley I. Kutler, *The Wars of Watergate: The Last Crisis of Richard Nixon* (New York: Norton, 1990), 371; Mark Feldstein, *Poisoning the Press: Richard Nixon, Jack Anderson, and the Rise of Washington's Scandal Culture* (New York: Farrar, Straus, and Giroux, 2010), 225–249.
20. For the text of FECA, see 52 U.S.C. § 30101 et seq. On the history and significance of FECA, see Frank Soroaf, *Inside Campaign Finance: Myths and Realities* (New Haven: Yale University Press, 1992), 2–20; Bruce Ackerman and Ian Ayres, *Voting with Dollars: A New Paradigm for Campaign Finance* (New Haven: Yale University Press, 2008); Mutch, *Buying the Vote*, 8.
21. For Stanton's statement: Mark Tapscott, "M. Stanton Evans: A Conservative Giant," *Washington Examiner*, March 4, 2015, https://www.washingtonexaminer.com/m-stanton-evans-a-conservative-giant, accessed January 6, 2021. For ACU's support of Reagan—and its relationship to *Buckley*—see James M. Naughton, "Reagan Will Seek to Seize Initiative in Race with Ford," *New York Times*, March 25, 1976, 1; Joseph Lelyveld, "Reagan Aided by Ads Conservative Group Paid For," *New York Times*, May 6, 1976, 43; "Vital Role of American Conservative Union," *Human Events*, December 6, 1975, 10.
22. "Court Asked to Uphold Campaign Act," *Los Angeles Times*, June 14, 1975, 9. For more on the early litigation of *Buckley*, see Linda Mathews, "Justices Will Rule on Campaign Laws," *Los Angeles Times*, October 7, 1975, A7; Albert R. Hunt, "Disillusion with Election Reform," *Wall Street Journal*, November 12, 1975, 4. On early opposition to campaign finance law, see Ann Southworth, "Speech: The Campaign to Unleash Big Money in American Politics," 27–33, on file with the author.
23. Steven A. Holmes, "Jesse Helms Dies at 86; Conservative Force in Senate," *New York Times*, July 5, 2008, https://www.nytimes.com/2008/07/05/us/politics/00helms.html, accessed June 9, 2021.
24. "Congressional Liaison Group Holds Initial Meeting," *National Right to Life News*, October 1975, 3, JRS, 1975 National Right to Life News Box; see also "Oberstar Tells Convention He Has Hope for House Hearing," *National Right to Life News*, April 1975, 3, JRS, 1975 National Right to Life News Box; "New Sponsors to Oberstar Bill," *National Right to Life News*, May 1975, 2, JRS, 1975 National Right to Life News Box. On the failure of the amendments, see Alice Hartle, "Senate Subcommittee Votes Down All Amendments Brought before It," *National Right to Life News*, October 1975, 1, JRS, National Right to Life News Box.
25. See *Buckley v. Valeo*, 424 U.S. 1, 14–19 (1976). On the lower-court litigation in *Buckley*, see *Buckley v. Valeo*, 519 F.2d 821 (D.C. Cir. 1975); *Buckley v. Valeo*, 401 F.Supp. 1235 (D.D.C. 1975). For the Court's earlier decisions on symbolic expression, see *United States v. O'Brien*, 391 U.S. 367 (1968); *Cox v. Louisiana*, 379 U.S. 559 (1965).
26. *Buckley v. Valeo*, 424 U.S. 1, 17 (1976).

27. Ibid., 19–21.
28. See ibid., 23–29.
29. Ibid., 39–59.
30. Ibid., 39–51. For more on the express advocacy distinction, see Miriam Galston, "Emerging Constitutional Paradigms and Justifications for Campaign Finance: The Case of 527 Groups," *Georgetown Law Journal* 95 (2007): 1200–1216; L. Paige Whitaker, Congressional Research Office, *Campaign Finance Reform: An Analysis of Issue and Express Advocacy* (Washington, DC: Congressional Research Office, 2002), 2.
31. *Buckley v. Valeo*, 424 U.S. 1, 41–49 (1976).
32. Ibid., 49–59.
33. See ibid., 59–70.
34. See ibid., 85–104. For more on *Buckley*, see Mutch, *Buying the Vote*, 5–10; Richard Hasen, "The Untold Drafting History of *Buckley v. Valeo*," *Election Law Journal* 2 (2003): 241–253; Melvin I. Urofsky, *The Campaign Finance Cases:* Buckley, McConnell, Citizens United, *and* McCutcheon (Lawrence: University Press of Kansas, 2020), 10–35; Winkler, *We the Corporations*, 35–60.
35. "Ellen McCormack's Campaign to Bring Up Pro-Life Issues," *National Right to Life News*, November 1975, 4, JRS, 1975 National Right to Life News Box; Keating, "Right to Life Television Commercials," 3.
36. On Reagan's position, see "Reagan Likes HLA, Gives Views on Abortion, Euthanasia," *National Right to Life News*, December 1975, 1, JRS, 1975 National Right to Life News Box. On Carter and Ford's positions on abortion, see Laurence H. Tribe, *Abortion: The Clash of Absolutes* (New York: Norton, 1992), 148; Raymond Tatalovich, *The Politics of Abortion in the United States and Canada* (New York: Routledge, 1997), 168; Rickie Solinger, *Pregnancy and Power: A Short History of Reproductive Politics in America* (New York: New York University Press, 2005), 20.
37. Robert F. Greene, "Nightmare for State Legislatures," *National Right to Life News*, May 1976, 11, JRS, 1976 National Right to Life News Box. On Nellie Gray's summit with Ford, see "White House Finally Agrees to See Pro-Life Delegation," *National Right to Life News*, March 1976, 6, JRS, 1976 National Right to Life News Box.
38. "NRLC Board Chairman Hits Politicians' Abortion Stand," *National Right to Life News*, August 1976, 8, JRS, 1976 National Right to Life News Box. On the tabling of the HLA proposed by Helms, see Alice Hartle, "Tabling Motion Prevails on Helms HLA in Senate," *National Right to Life News*, June 1976, 1, JRS, 1976 National Right to Life News Box. For more on Helms, see William Link, *Righteous Warrior: Jesse Helms and the Rise of Modern Conservatism* (New York: St. Martin's, 2008).
39. See Janet Grant, "Democratic Convention Blended Bitter and Sweet," *National Right to Life News*, August 1976, 1, JRS, 1976 National Right to Life News Box.
40. Ibid., 1, 6. For Ford's view on a constitutional amendment on abortion, see Richard Bergholz, "Ford Abortion View Encourages Bishops," *Los Angeles Times*, September 11, 1976, 26. For more on Gerald and Betty Ford's positions on abortion,

see Marjorie J. Spruill, *Divided We Stand: The Battle over Women's Rights and Family Values That Polarized American Politics* (London: Bloomsbury, 2017), 94; Tribe, *Clash of Absolutes*, 148.

41. On Duncan, see Ben A. Franklin, "Nixon Got a Quarter-Million from a Democratic Donor," *New York Times*, September 25, 1972, https://www.nytimes.com/1972/09/25/archives/nixon-got-quartermillion-from-a-democratic-donor-nixon-got.html, accessed January 6, 2020. On Palevsky and the Malibu Mafia, see Kenneth Reich, "Palevsky Drops Plan for Independent Carter Drive," *Los Angeles Times*, May 14, 1976, 11; Ronald Brownstein, *The Power and the Glitter: The Hollywood-Washington Connection* (New York: Vintage, 1990), 203–211.
42. Albert R. Hunt, "Campaign Spending Law Did Its Job," *Wall Street Journal*, December 6, 1976, 18; see also John B. Anderson, "The New Campaign Finance Law Appraised . . . as 'an Antidote to Influence of Money,' " *Los Angeles Times*, November 21, 1976, I2.
43. Lelyveld, "Reagan Aided," 43. On Reagan's financial situation, see Jon Nordheimer, "Reagan Campaign, in Debt in April, Now Reports $1.2 Million Surplus," *New York Times*, September 13, 1976, 14. On Koch's involvement in *Buckley* and early interest in campaign finance, see Edward Crane to Charles Koch, September 24, 1975, Koch Documents, https://kochdocs.org/2020/02/06/breaking-new-documents-show-charles-kochs-fortune-subsidizing-attacks-on-election-laws-since-more-than-40-years-ago/, accessed September 10, 2021.
44. See Jon Margolis, "GOP Faction Working to Unseat Party Liberals," *Chicago Tribune*, October 31, 1977, A6. For more on Keene's work for Reagan, see Patrick Buchanan, "The Reagan Gang's Game Plan," *Chicago Tribune*, September 16, 1975, A4.
45. See David Ignatius, "Reluctant Donors: Firms Get a Slow Start in Inducing Employees to Give to Politicians," *New York Times*, May 20, 1976, 1; Anderson, "New Campaign Finance Law Appraised," I2. On the chilling effect of new rules on political committees, see Andrew Mollison and Norman Gutharz, "Tiny Loophole: Edict Opens No Floodgate of Political Money," *Atlanta Journal-Constitution*, October 24, 1976, 14C.
46. On Stone, see Jeffrey Toobin, "The Dirty Trickster," *New Yorker*, June 2, 2008, https://www.newyorker.com/magazine/2008/06/02/the-dirty-trickster, accessed July 22, 2020; Stephanie Mansfield, "The Rise and Gall of Roger Stone," *Washington Post*, June 16, 1986, https://www.washingtonpost.com/archive/lifestyle/1986/06/16/the-rise-and-gall-of-roger-stone/d8ce308b-7055–4666–860e-378833f46e17/, accessed July 22, 2020. On Dolan, see "The New Right Takes Aim," *Time*, August 20, 1979, http://content.time.com/time/subscriber/article/0,33009,947346,00.html, accessed July 22, 2020.
47. Margolis, "GOP Faction," A6; see also "Conservatives Challenge Anderson in Primary," *Human Events*, March 4, 1978, 3; "Highlights of CPAC '78," *Human Events*, April 1, 1978, 8.
48. James Bopp Jr., interview with Mary Ziegler, June 14, 2015; James Bopp Jr., interview with Mary Ziegler, June 13, 2020. On Terre Haute in the 1970s, see

Howard Greninger, "Changes Continue for Honey Creek Mall," *Tribune Star*, September 28, 2019, https://www.tribstar.com/news/local_news/changes-continue-for-honey-creek-mall/article_f01edfac-2ebb-5116–9e3e-4371aab6ddea.html, accessed June 9, 2021.

49. Bopp, June 2015 interview. For more on Bopp's journey, see Mark Bennett, "Terre Haute's James Bopp Jr. a Conservative Titan," *Washington Times*, June 29, 2014, http://www.washingtontimes.com/news/2014/jun/29/terre-hautes-jim-bopp-jr-a-conservative-titan/, accessed June 27, 2017; Peter Overby, "The 'Country Lawyer' Shaping Campaign Finance Law," *NPR*, June 22, 2011, http://www.npr.org/2011/06/22/137318888/the-country-lawyer-shaping-campaign-finance-law, accessed June 12, 2017.

50. James Bopp Jr. and Eugene Fife to Mary Hunt (June 25, 1978), 1–4, JBP, Matter Boxes, File 177. For more on the cases brought by Bopp and the Legal Action Project, see James Bopp to Ed Moran (June 27, 1979), JBP, Matter Boxes, File 177; James Bopp to Richard Bradley (July 2, 1979), JBP, Matter Boxes, File 177.

51. See Bopp and Fife to Hunt, 1–6.

52. On early AUL litigation efforts, see Dennis Horan to NRLC Board of Directors et al. (January 19, 1974), 1–5, ACCL, Box 8, 1974 NRLC Folder; David Mall to AUL Board of Directors, First Quarterly Report (1975), GHW, Box 6, Folder 3. For AUL's briefs, see Brief Amicus Curiae for Dr. Eugene Diamond and Americans United for Life, 18–52, *Planned Parenthood of Central Missouri v. Danforth*, 428 U.S. 52 (1976) (No. 74-1151); Motion for Leave to File Brief and Brief Amicus Curiae, Americans United for Life, 1–6, *Poelker v. Doe*, 432 U.S. 519 (1977) (No. 75-442).

53. See *Planned Parenthood of Central Missouri v. Danforth*, 428 U.S. 52, 66–68 (1976). For the Court's decisions in *Maher, Poelker,* and *Beal*, see *Poelker v. Doe*, 432 U.S. 519 (1977); *Maher v. Roe*, 432 U.S. 464 (1977); *Beal v. Doe*, 432 U.S. 438 (1977).

54. On LAPAC, see Ziegler, *After* Roe, 81–83; Michele McKeegan, *Abortion Politics: Mutiny in the Ranks of the Right* (New York: Free Press, 1992), 25, 60. For more on right-to-life election efforts, see Richard Doak, Steven Walter, and Cornell Fowler, "Local Races Shape Up," *Des Moines Register*, June 7, 1978, 8. On Goeken's voter identification project, see "Illinois Federation Puts out Voter Guide," *National Right to Life News*, April 1976, 15, JRS, 1976 National Right to Life News Box.

55. Doak, Walter, and Fowler, "Local Races," 8; see also "Anti-Abortion Clout Shown," *Des Moines Register*, June 22, 1978, 2; Daniel Pederson, "Abortion—Most Agree It Was Factor in Senate Race," *Des Moines Register*, November 13, 1978, 7; "Abortion Foes Back Jepsen against Clark," *Des Moines Register*, October 1, 1978, 8. For more on Viguerie's work, see Perlstein, *Reaganland*, 35, 96–100.

56. On Moral Majority's budget, see Clyde Wilcox, *God's Warriors: The Christian Right in Twentieth Century America* (Baltimore: Johns Hopkins University Press, 1992), 95. For more on Christian Voice, see Williams, *God's Own Party*, 170–175; Ziegler, *After* Roe, 201. For more on the Moral Majority, see Michael Sean Winters, *God's Right Hand: How Jerry Falwell Made God a Republican and Baptized the American Right* (New York: Harper Collins, 2019); David Snowball, *Continuity and Change in the Rhetoric of the Moral Majority* (New York: Praeger, 1991).

57. See Dr. John Willke to Carolyn Gerster (December 19, 1978), JBP, Matter Boxes, File 141; Mary Reilly Hunt to Judie Brown (June 21, 1978), JBP, Matter Boxes, File 141; Robert Krebsbach to James Bopp Jr. (September 22, 1977), JBP, Matter Boxes, File 141. On Jefferson's conflict with NRLC before her ouster and after the founding of the Right to Life Crusade, see Mary Reilly Hunt to Mildred Jefferson (1977), JBP, Matter Boxes, File 487; Mary Reilly Hunt to NRLC Board of Directors (July 25, 1978), JBP, Matter Boxes, File 487; Carolyn Gerster to Chapter Presidents (January 15, 1979), JBP, Matter Boxes File 487; Carolyn Gerster to State Leader (January 15, 1979), JBP, Matter Boxes, File 487. On Gerster's story, see Helen Epstein, "Abortion: An Issue That Won't Go Away," *New York Times*, March 30, 1980, https://www.nytimes.com/1980/03/30/archives/abortion-an-issue-that-wont-go-away-abortion.html, accessed September 11, 2020.
58. Gerster to State Leader, 1. For more on the Bothell matter, see Mary Reilly Hunt to Board of Directors (June 25, 1978), JBP, Matter Boxes, File 478; Gerster to Chapter Presidents; James Bopp Jr. to Thomas Havey & Company (January 23, 1984), JBP, Matter Boxes, File 478.
59. On NARAL's new PAC, see Suzanne Staggenborg, *The Pro-Choice Movement: Organization and Activism in the Abortion Conflict* (New York: Oxford University Press, 1991), 106; Leslie Bennetts, "For Pro-Abortion Group, 'An Aggressive New Campaign,'" *New York Times*, May 1, 1979, C22.
60. See Sheila Mallon, "Yes, Abortion and Politics Do Mix," *Atlanta Constitution*, April 28, 1980, 5A; Anna Crittenden, "Pro-Abortion Group Sets a Major Political Drive," *New York Times*, June 24, 1982, B2; Richard Phillips, "The Shooting War over 'Choice' or 'Life' Is Beginning Again," *Chicago Tribune*, April 20, 1980, J3. On the FEC complaints filed by NARAL, see Anthony Lauinger to Felicia Goeken (October 27, 1979), JBP, Matter Boxes, File 141; NRLC Fundraising Letter (Fall 1979), JBP, Matter Boxes, File 141; "Gerster Charges NARAL with Intimidation of Pro-Lifers," *National Right to Life News*, October 1979, 13, JRS, 1979 National Right to Life News Box.
61. On the complaints, see James Bopp Jr. to John Willke (April 27, 1981), JBP, Matter Boxes, File 188; National Right to Life Committee, Inc., Life Amendment Political Action Committee, and National Right to Life Political Action Committee, MUR 961, (1981), JBP, Matter Boxes, File 188; Gail Harmon to Federal Election Commission (April 30, 1979), JBP, Matter Boxes, File 188. The FEC ultimately found reason to believe that LAPAC was a connected PAC of NRLC that had illegally solicited nonmembers—and that NRLC's Voter Identification Project was an illegal in-kind contribution. On the resolution of the complaints, see Charles Steele to Gail Harmon (May 4, 1981), MUR 996, 1981; Charles Steele to Gail Harmon (April 27, 1981), MUR 958, 1981; Charles Steele to Gail Harmon (May 4, 1981), MUR 961, 1981; In the Matter of Life Amendment PAC et al. (June 27, 1979), MUR 960; In the Matter of the Right to Life Committee of New Mexico (December 15, 1979), MUR 959.
62. "Gerster Charges NARAL with Intimidation of Pro-Lifers," 13; 1979 NRLC Fundraising Letter, 1–4.

63. Sandra Faucher, interview with Mary Ziegler, February 4, 2012.
64. Scott Sherry, "Political Action Committee Formed," *National Right to Life News*, October 1979, 4, JRS, 1979 National Right to Life News Box. On the emphasis put on a fetal-protective amendment, see Charles Donovan to Carol Gerster, Re: A Three-Year Plan for a Human Life Amendment (January 30, 1979), JBP, Matter Boxes, File 487.
65. On Carter's abortion position, see J. Brooks Flippen, *Jimmy Carter, the Politics of Family, and the Rise of the Religious Right* (Athens: University of Georgia Press, 2011), 182. On the 1980 candidates, see Steven V. Roberts, "Anderson Drive Appears to Be Slowing at Home," *New York Times*, March 17, 1980, A14; Neil J. Young, "How George H. W. Bush Enabled the Rise of the Religious Right," *Washington Post*, December 5, 2018, https://www.washingtonpost.com/outlook/2018/12/05/how-george-hw-bush-enabled-rise-religious-right/?utm_term=.5dec6144250d, accessed February 22, 2019.
66. "Reagan for President: 1980 Campaign Conditions for Victory," *Ronald Reagan Presidential Library and Museum*, 1980, https://www.reaganlibrary.gov/sites/default/files/documents/campaign1980.pdf, accessed February 22, 2019. On Devine's role, see John M. Barry, "Anti-Abortion Issue Is Severing Cords of the Roosevelt Coalition," *Atlanta Journal Constitution*, April 18, 1980, 42A.
67. See NRLC Board of Directors Meeting Minutes (June 26, 1980), 3, JBP, Matter Boxes, File 178; see also Williams, *Defenders of the Unborn*, 241; Right to Life of Michigan Board Meeting Minutes (April 2, 1980), RLM, Box 1, Administrative Board Minutes Folder; Jo Freeman, "Republicans: Feminists Avoid a Direct Confrontation," *In These Times*, July 30, 1980, 5.
68. National Right to Life PAC, Brochure (1980), JBP, Matter Boxes, File 487. On the platform vote, see James Perry and Albert Hunt, "GOP Retreats from Backing ERA, Approves Strong Antiabortion Support," *Wall Street Journal*, July 9, 1980, 7.
69. David Gaetano, "Pro-Life Gains: President, 10 Senators, and More," *National Right to Life News*, November 10, 1980, 7, JRS, 1980 National Right to Life News Box.
70. On Republicans' success in the election, see Richard Wirthlin, "The Republican Strategy and Its Electoral Consequences," in *Party Coalitions in the 1980s*, ed. Seymour Lipset (New York: Routledge, 1981), 240–248; Andrew Busch, *Reagan's Victory: The Presidential Election of 1980 and the Rise of the Right* (Lawrence: University of Kansas Press, 2008), 141; Jefferson Cowie, *Stayin' Alive: The 1970s and the Last Days of the Working Class* (New York: New Press, 2010), 310–311.
71. Jack Willke, "From the President's Desk: We Did It," *National Right to Life News*, November 10, 1980, 7, JRS, 1980 National Right to Life News Box.
72. See "PACs Pack Clout in Right Turn," *Chicago Tribune*, February 21, 1982, B16. On soft money in the 1980 election, see Mutch, *Campaign Finance*, 103–104; Thomas Edsall, "Reagan Campaign Gearing Up Its 'Soft Money' Machine for '84," *Washington Post*, November 27, 1983, https://www.washingtonpost.com/archive/politics/1983/11/27/reagan-campaign-gearing-up-its-soft-money-machine-for-84/6633d356-a5c6-4007-93c6-b3be8d9f7a45/, accessed September 10, 2021.

73. See James Bopp to Fred Hart (September 11, 1980), JBP, Matter Boxes, File 167. For activists' acknowledgment that there were not enough votes in Congress for a fetal-protective amendment, see John Willke, "We Have a Bill," *National Right to Life News*, February 23, 1981, 1, 4, JRS, 1981 National Right to Life News Box; James Bopp Jr., "The Abortion Funding Proscription Bill," *National Right to Life News*, February 23, 1981, JRS, 1981 National Right to Life News Box. On the proposed unity amendment, see John Willke, "Which Will It Be—HLB or HLA?" *National Right to Life News*, January 18, 1982, JRS, 1982 National Right to Life News Box; James Bopp Jr., "Proposals for a Human Life Amendment" (September 9, 1981), JRS, 1981 National Right to Life News Box.
74. On the push for the Human Life Bill, see Joan Beck, "The Pro-Life Groups Turn to Congress on Abortion," *Chicago Tribune*, January 30, 1981, B2; "Abortion Foes Offer Bill," *Chicago Tribune*, February 11, 1981, 8; Jon Margolis, "The Abortion Struggle on Capitol Hill," *Chicago Tribune*, March 22, 1981, A2; Bernard Weinraub, "Abortion Becoming a Top Priority Issue in Congress," *New York Times*, March 13, 1981, A18. On Galebach, see "Stephen Galebach," *Galebach Law*, http://galebachlaw.com/, accessed September 11, 2020. For Galebach's article, see Stephen H. Galebach, "A Human Life Statute," *Human Life Review* (Winter 1981): 5–33.
75. On absolutists' views, see Charles Rice to Judie Brown (June 1, 1981), CRP. On Brown's background, Judie Brown, interview with Mary Ziegler, August 9, 2011; see also Judie Brown, *It Is I Who Have Chosen You: An Autobiography of Judie Brown* (Stafford, VA: American Life League, 1997).
76. On the view that the Human Life Bill was not constitutional, see, e.g., Testimony on S. 158, A Bill to Provide That Human Life Shall Be Deemed to Exist from Conception, before the Senate Judiciary Committe, Subcommittee on Separation of Powers, 97th Congress, 1st Sess. (May 21, 1981), 242–256 (Statement of Prof. Laurence Tribe); Testimony on S. 158, A Bill to Provide That Human Life Shall Be Deemed to Exist from Conception, before the Senate Judiciary Subcommittee on Separation of Powers, 97th Congress, 1st Sess. (June 10, 1981), 515–576 (Statement of Prof. Norman Dorsen); Testimony on S. 158, A Bill to Provide That Human Life Shall Be Deemed to Exist from Conception, before the Senate Judiciary Subcommittee on Separation of Powers, 97th Congress, 1st Sess. (May 21, 1981), 308–317 (Statement of Prof. Robert Bork).
77. For Rhodes's recommendation: John Dressendorfer to Max Friedersdorf (June 22, 1981), FFF, Box 37F, Supreme Court Recommendations Folder. On opposition to the O'Connor nomination, see Carolyn Gerster to William French Smith (July 15, 1981), PMF, OA 3209, Sandra Day O'Connor File 1; NRLC Press Release, "Did President Reagan Know?" (July 22, 1981), PMF, OA 3209, Sandra Day O'Connor File 3.
78. For Willke's statement: Memorandum from Marilee Melvin to Ed Thomas (July 6, 1981), EMP, OA 2408, Box 7, Sandra Day O'Connor File 1. For Gerster's letter, see Gerster to Smith, 1.
79. For Reagan's letter, see Patrick Buchanan, "Reagan Letter Fuel for 'Pro-Lifers,' " *Chicago Tribune*, August 15, 1981, S7. On the pro-life rally against O'Connor, see

"Conservative Groups Oppose O'Connor," *Los Angeles Times*, August 29, 1981, B1; "Anti-Abortion Group Asks Nominee's Withdrawal," *Atlanta Journal-Constitution*, September 4, 1981, 3A; "Reagan Draws Criticism on Justice Choice," *Atlanta Journal-Constitution*, July 8, 1981, 1A.

80. "O'Connor Reiterates Abortion Opposition," *Los Angeles Times*, September 9, 1981, A2; see also Francis X. Clines, "Baker Vows Support for Nominee," *New York Times*, July 8, 1981, A1. On the testimony against O'Connor, see Linda Greenhouse, "Abortion Foes Assail Judge O'Connor," *New York Times*, September 12, 1981, 6; Jim Mann, "O'Connor Fails to Placate Her Abortion Critics," *Los Angeles Times*, September 12, 1981, A1.
81. John Willke, "So Now What?" *National Right to Life News*, September 28, 1981, 1, JRS, 1981 National Right to Life News Box.
82. Memorandum from Michael Uhlmann to Edwin Meese (July 6, 1981), EMP, OA 2408, Box 7, Sandra Day O'Connor Folder 1.
83. Perlstein, *Reaganland*, 34. On Hatch, see Doug Robinson, "The Two Lives of Orrin Hatch," *Deseret News*, July 6, 2003, https://www.deseret.com/2003/7/6/19781926/the-two-lives-of-orrin-hatch, accessed July 23, 2020; William Neikirk, "Orrin Hatch: A Penchant for Upsets," *Chicago Tribune*, December 21, 1999, https://www.chicagotribune.com/news/ct-xpm-1999-12-21-9912210239-story.html, accessed July 23, 2020. On Hatch's proposal, see "Hatch Introduces New Federalism Amendment," *National Right to Life News*, September 21, 1981, 1, JRS, 1981 National Right to Life News Box; Leslie Bennetts, "Antiabortion Forces in Disarray Less Than a Year After Victories in Election," *New York Times*, September 22, 1981, B5.
84. Willke, "Which Will It Be?" For Bopp's argument, see Bopp, "Proposals for a Human Life Amendment" (September 9, 1981), JRS, 1981 National Right to Life News Box.
85. See Judie Brown, "Senator Hatch, No!" *ALL about News*, January 1982, 1, WCX, ALL about News Box. For more on ALL's view of Hatch and the Human Life Bill, see Christopher Wolfe, "The Human Life Bill—Yes!" *ALL about News*, February 1982, 6, WCX, 1982 National Right to Life News Box. On the division about the Hatch Amendment within NRLC, see Anthony Lauinger to NRLC Board of Directors (February 13, 1982), JBP, Matter Boxes, File 300; John Willke, "The Healing Commences," *National Right to Life News*, April 11, 1981, 3, JRS, 1981 National Right to Life News; Helen Dewitt to Friend of Life (August 23, 1982), JBP, Matter Boxes, File 300; NRLC Board of Directors Meeting Minutes (January 30, 1982), JBP, Matter Boxes, File 300. On the December 1981 vote, see Ziegler, *After* Roe, 87.
86. Judie Brown to John Willke (February 19, 1982), JBP, Matter Boxes, File 300; see also Judie Brown, "Facing the Battle," *ALL about News*, February 1982, WCX, ALL about News Box.
87. See Dewitt to Friend of Life, 1–6.
88. On the panel vote, see Bernard Weinraub, "Abortion Curbs Endorsed, 10-7, by Senate Panel," *New York Times*, March 11, 1982, A1; John Herbers, "Abortion Battle Moving to States," *New York Times*, June 12, 1983, A27.

89. On the 1982 election, see John Herbers, "Democrats Made Widespread Gains in States' Control," *New York Times,* November 5, 1982, A1.
90. On the Hatch-Eagleton Amendment, see Steven V. Roberts, "Full Senate Gets Abortion Measure," *New York Times,* April 20, 1983, A12; Ellen Hume, "Anti-Abortion Amendment Killed in Senate," *Los Angeles Times,* June 29, 1983, B1; Dorothy Collin, "Abortion Amendment Defeated," *Chicago Tribune,* June 29, 1983, 3.
91. For Harper's statement: Edwin Harper to Gary Bauer (March 11, 1982), GBP, OA 9447, Box 16, Abortion (1). The chapter later discusses Bauer's strategy. For more on Gary Bauer, see William Saletan, "Gary Bauer's Moral Dilemma," *Mother Jones,* July/August 1998, https://www.motherjones.com/politics/1998/07/gary-bauers-moral-dilemma/, accessed July 23, 2020; Nina Easton, "The Power and the Glory," *American Prospect,* May 3, 2002, https://prospect.org/features/power-glory/, accessed July 23, 2020; Julie Johnson, "Working Profile: Gary Bauer—Fanning the Flames of Conservatives," *New York Times,* October 12, 1988, https://www.nytimes.com/1988/10/12/us/washington-talk-working-profile-gary-l-bauer-fanning-the-flames-of-conservatives.html, accessed September 10, 2020.
92. Edwin Harper and Gary Bauer to Edwin Meese (June 9, 1982), GBP, OA 9447, Box 16, Abortion (1). For Bauer's statement: Gary Bauer to Edwin Harper (June 2, 1982), GBP, OA 9447, Box 16, Abortion (1).
93. Bauer to Harper, 1–2.
94. On NRLC's debt, see Jean Doyle to National Right to Life Committee Members et al. (August 25, 1983), JBP, Matter Boxes, File 473. On the poll, see George Bishop to Ohio Right to Life (May 23, 1984), JBP, Matter Boxes, File 433. On NRLC's PAC in the 1980 race, see "NRL PAC Leads All Pro-Life PACs," *National Right to Life News,* March 11, 1982, 1, JRS, 1982 National Right to Life News Box; "Your PAC Dollars at Work," *National Right to Life News,* July 8, 1982, 3, JRS, 1982 National Right to Life News. On the expansion of voter identification projects, see "NRLC Voting ID Project Makes the Difference," *National Right to Life News,* January 11, 1982, 9, JRS, 1982 National Right to Life News Box; Felicia Goeken, "The Difference Is You," *National Right to Life News,* April 22, 1982, 7, JRS, 1982 National Right to Life News Folder.
95. See *City of Akron v. Akron Center for Reproductive Health,* 462 U.S. 416, 434, 444–445 (1983).
96. Ibid., 452–474 (O'Connor, J., dissenting).
97. Meeting with National Pro-Life Leaders, Talking Points (January 11, 1984), MBF, Box 16, American Life League Folder.
98. Fundraising Letter (n.d., ca. February 1984), JBP, Matter Boxes, File 433.
99. See Steven Teles, *The Rise of the Conservative Legal Movement: The Battle for Control of the Law* (Princeton: Princeton University Press, 2008); Amanda Hollis-Brusky, *Ideas with Consequences: The Federalist Society and the Conservative Counterrevolution* (New York: Oxford University Press, 2015). On the founding of the Federalist Society, see Michael Kruse, "The Weekend at Yale That Changed American Politics," *Politico,* September/October 2018, https://www.politico.

com/magazine/story/2018/08/27/federalist-society-yale-history-conservative-law-court-219608, accessed September 10, 2020; Martin Garbus, "A Hostile Takeover," *American Prospect*, February 20, 2003, https://prospect.org/features/hostile-takeover/, accessed September 10, 2020.

100. On LAPAC's struggles, see Thomas Gais, *Improper Influence: Campaign Finance, Political Interest Groups, and the Problem of Equality* (Ann Arbor: University of Michigan Press, 1996), 66. On NCPAC's troubles with the FCC, see "Federal Communications Commission Turns Down NCPAC," *National Right to Life News*, April 22, 1982, 4, JRS, 1982 National Right to Life News Box; Gregory Fossedal, "How Liberals Plan to Silence Conservative PACs," *Human Events*, May 1, 1982, 10.

101. See Gais, *Improper Influence*, 66–70. On the amount spent by PACs on House incumbents, see Adam Clymer, "PAC Money's Role in Congress Raises Suspicions," *New York Times*, January 19, 1983, A20. On outside spending in 1984, see National Institute for Money in Politics, "Non-party Independent Expenditures, 1976 to 2016," http://www.cfinst.org/pdf/federal/HistoricalTables/pdf/CFI_Federal-CF_18_Table4-02.pdf, accessed February 16, 2021.

102. On soft money in the 1984 election, see Peter Grier, " 'Soft Money' and '84 Campaign Financing," *Christian Science Monitor*, June 19, 1984, 4; Brooks Jackson, "Old Time Politics: Loopholes Allow Flood of Campaign Giving by Businesses, Fat Cats," *Wall Street Journal*, July 5, 1984, 1. On soft money spending in 1984, see Stephen Ansolabehere and James Snyder, "Soft Money, Hard Money, Strong Parties," *Columbia Law Review* 100 (2000): 606; Rebecca Carr, "As Soft Money Grows, So Does Controversy," *CNN*, 1996, https://www.cnn.com/ALLPOLITICS/1996/news/9611/21/campaign.finance/soft.money.html, accessed February 16, 2021.

103. National Right to Life PAC Script (July 2, 1985), JBP, Matter Boxes, File 497; see also National Right to Life Fundraising Letter (October 28, 1985), JBP, Matter Boxes, File 497.

104. See 2 U.S.C. 441(b).

105. Massachusetts Citizens for Life, "Special Election Edition, Everything You Need to Know to Vote Pro-Life" (1978), JBP, Matter Boxes, File 403.

106. James Bopp Jr. to Philip Moran (July 16, 1984), JBP, Matter Boxes, File 403. On the early litigation in *MCFL*, see *Federal Election Commission v. Massachusetts Citizens for Life*, 589 F.Supp. 646 (D. Mass. 1984); *Federal Election Commission v. Massachusetts Citizens for Life*, 769 F.2d 13 (1st Cir. 1985); Francis Fox to Phil Moran (June 2, 1984), JBP, Matter Boxes, File 403.

107. On the 1984 presidential election, see Jack W. Germond and Jules Witcover, *Wake Us When It's Over: Presidential Politics of 1984* (New York: Simon and Schuster, 1985). On GOP angst after the election, see Phil Gailey, "G.O.P. Gathering Considers Political Life After Reagan," *New York Times*, June 29, 1986, A22.

108. On the makeup of GOP voters, see Gailey, "GOP Gathering," A22; John Herbers, "New Politics Emerging out of Demographic Changes," *New York Times*, September 5, 1986, A21.

109. See *Federal Election Commission v. Massachusetts Citizens for Life*, 479 U.S. 238, 245–251 (1986). For the Court's decision, see *Federal Election Commission v. National Conservative PAC*, 470 U.S. 480 (1985). For more on the significance of *National Conservative PAC*, see Mutch, *Buying the Vote*, 285–287.
110. *Federal Election Commission v. Massachusetts Citizens for Life*, 479 U.S. 238, 249–250 (1986).
111. Ibid., 256.
112. Ibid., 259. For more on *MCFL*, see Mutch, *Buying the Vote*, 157–160; Robert Post, *Citizens Divided: Campaign Finance Reform and the Constitution* (Cambridge, MA: Harvard University Press, 2014), 69–70.

Chapter 3. The Price of a Nominee

1. See *Thornburgh v. American College of Obstetricians and Gynecologists*, 476 U.S. 747, 751–759 (1986). On the significance of the Court's decision, see David Garrow, *Liberty and Sexuality: The Right to Privacy and the Making of* Roe v. Wade (Berkeley: University of California Press, 1998), 652, 657, 662; Joseph Fiske Kobylka and Lee Epstein, *The Supreme Court and Legal Change: Abortion and the Death Penalty* (Chapel Hill: University of North Carolina Press, 1992), 255–257; James F. Simon, *The Center Holds: The Power Struggle within the Rehnquist Court* (New York: Simon and Schuster, 1995), 225–226.
2. On Meese's effort to make the judiciary a rallying point, see G. Edward White, *Law in American History*, vol. 3, *1930–2000* (New York: Oxford University Press, 2019), 380–391; Barry Friedman, *The Will of the People: How Public Opinion Has Influenced the Supreme Court and Shaped the Meaning of the Constitution* (New York: Farrar, Straus and Giroux, 2009), 308–310; Thomas M. Keck, *The Most Activist Court in History: The Road to Modern Judicial Conservatism* (Chicago: University of Chicago Press, 2014), 157–161. For more on Meese, see Nancy Blodgett, "The Ralph Nader of the Right," *American Bar Association Journal* (May 1984): 71–74; W. J. Rorabaugh, *Berkeley at War: The 1960s* (New York: Oxford University Press, 1989), 38–42.
3. See Jan Crawford Greenburg, *Supreme Conflict: The Inside Story of the Struggle for Control over the United States Supreme Court* (New York: Penguin, 2007), 41–43.
4. Patrick Buchanan, Memorandum to the Chief of Staff, July 10, 1985, on file with the author.
5. Memo on Supreme Court Nominees (n.d., ca. 1986), PWA, OA 14287, Scalia Folders.
6. Peter Wallison, Memo for the File (August 29, 1986), PWA, OA 14287, Scalia Folders. For more on Reagan's selection of Scalia, see Greenburg, *Supreme Conflict*, 40–45; Lou Cannon, *President Reagan: The Role of a Lifetime* (New York: Hachette, 2000), 724.
7. For LaHaye's and Smeal's statements: Stuart Taylor Jr., "Liberals Portray Scalia as Threat but Bar Group Sees Him as Open," *New York Times*, August 7, 1986, A19.

On the controversy surrounding Rehnquist, see Stephen Wermiel, "Hearings on Rehnquist's Confirmation End, but the Controversy Lingers On," *Wall Street Journal*, August 4, 1986, 1; "Voter-Challenging Issue Hinders Rehnquist's Climb to the Top," *Orlando Sentinel*, August 3, 1986, A7. For predictions of Scalia's limited influence, see David M. O'Brien, "Scalia and the Court: Pulling Consensus to Right," *Los Angeles Times*, June 29, 1986, F1. For Frank Neuborne's statements: "Chief Justice Burger Quits: Rehnquist to Succeed Him; DC Judge Picked for the Vacancy," *Los Angeles Times*, June 17, 1986, 1. On the confirmation totals for Rehnquist and Scalia, see Linda Greenhouse, "Senate, 65 to 33, Votes to Confirm Rehnquist as 16th Chief Justice," *New York Times*, September 18, 1986, A1.

8. On Powell's retirement, see Glen Elsasser and Janet Cawley, "Powell Quits Supreme Court," *Chicago Tribune*, June 27, 1987, 1; Stuart Taylor Jr., "Powell Leaves High Court," *New York Times*, June 27, 1987, 1.
9. See Laura Kalman, *The Long Reach of the Sixties: LBJ, Nixon, and the Making of the Contemporary Supreme Court* (New York: Oxford University Press, 2017). On the significance of Bork's nomination, see Steven M. Teles, *The Rise of the Conservative Legal Movement: The Battle for Control of the Law* (Princeton: Princeton University Press, 2008), 169–177; Mark Tushnet, *A Court Divided: The Rehnquist Court and the Future of Constitutional Law* (New York: Norton, 2005), 336.
10. Arthur B. Culvahouse, Memo to Jim Baker, William Ball III, and Kenneth B. Duberstein Re: Confirmation of Judge Bork (July 9, 1987), CCF, OA 15526, Robert Bork Nomination Folder 1. On the Block Bork Coalition, see Gwen Ifill and Ruth Marcus, "Lobbying Groups Gather Steam for Bork Confirmation Battle," *Washington Post*, July 7, 1987, A4; Ruth Marcus, "Abortion-Rights Groups Work to Block Bork's Confirmation," *Washington Post*, July 11, 1987, A2; David Lauter and Ronald Ostrow, "How Liberal Spectrum Fought to Block Bork," *Los Angeles Times*, October 8, 1987, 1.
11. Bork Candidate Notebook (n.d., ca. 1987), 2, 10–11, ACF, OA 15149, Bork Notebook File. On Bork's opposition to the *Roe* decision, see Jack M. Balkin, "Introduction: *Roe v. Wade:* Engine of Controversy," in *What* Roe v. Wade *Should Have Said: The Nation's Top Legal Experts Rewrite America's Most Controversial Decision*, ed. Jack M. Balkin (New York: New York University Press, 2005), 13–14; H. L. Pohlman, *Constitutional Debate in Action: Civil Rights and Liberties*, 2nd ed. (Lanham, MD: Rowman and Littlefield, 2005), 116; Andrew Hartman, *A War for the Soul of America: A History of the Culture Wars* (Chicago: University of Chicago Press, 2015), 153–155. For Bork's comments on the right to privacy and *Roe*, see Ruth Marcus, "Bork on 'Judicial Imperialism,'" *Washington Post*, July 2, 1987, https://www.washingtonpost.com/archive/politics/1987/07/02/bork-on-judicial-imperialism/60fb83a3-f529-4751-8066-7a9806883f0e/, accessed April 9, 2020.
12. Benedict Cohen to Arthur Culvahouse et al. (July 14, 1987), CCF, OA 15556, Robert Bork Internal Memos Folder 1; see also Peter Kessler to Arthur Culvahouse (July 23, 1987), CCF, OA 15556, Robert Bork Internal Memos Folder 1.

13. National Right to Life Committee, Fundraising Letter (September 21, 1987), JBP, Matter Boxes, File 692. For the NRLC editorials, see Dave Andrusko, "NARAL Vows All Out War to Defeat Nomination of Bork," *National Right to Life News,* July 30, 1987, 1, JRS, 1987 National Right to Life News Box.
14. Kenneth Noble, "Bork Backers Flood Senate with Mail," *New York Times,* September 3, 1987, A16; see also Ronald Brownstein, "Justice from Lobbies and Chambers: The Inside-Outside Battle about Seating Judge Bork," *Los Angeles Times,* October 4, 1987, 1. On the SBC's endorsement, see Dan Martin and Mark Kelly, "Public Affairs Committee Urges Bork Confirmation," *Baptist Messenger,* September 3, 1987, 5, JBP, Matter Boxes, File 692; "Bork Endorsement by PAC No Threat to SBC Tax Exempt Status" (September 14, 1987), JBP, Matter Boxes, File 692.
15. National Right to Life Committee Urgent Action Alert (Fall 1987), JBP, Matter Boxes, File 692.
16. Talking Points (September 1987), 1, 2–5, CCF, OA 15556, Robert Bork Internal Memos Folder; see Talking Points (July 4, 1987), 1–8, CCF, OA 15556, Robert Bork Internal Memos Folder 1. For more on the framing of Bork's nomination, see David T. Courtwright, *No Right Turn: Conservative Politics in a Liberal America* (Cambridge, MA: Harvard University Press, 2011), 173–182; Greenburg, *Supreme Conflict,* 51–60; Tushnet, *A Court Divided,* 335–338.
17. On the failure of Bork's nomination, see Al Kamen and Edward Walsh, "Senate Panel Votes 9-5 to Reject Bork," *Washington Post,* October 7, 1987, A1. On Bork's defeat in the Senate, see David Lauter, "Senate Rejects Bork, 58-42," *Los Angeles Times,* October 23, 1987, 1; Linda Greenhouse, "Judge Bork Is Stepping Down to Answer Critics and Reflect," *New York Times,* January 15, 1988, A1.
18. On the Ginsburg nomination, see "Ex-Meese Aide Nominated for Court," *Los Angeles Times,* October 29, 1987, 1; Stephen Wermiel, "Ginsburg's Sparse Record May Result in a Confirmation Process Unlike Bork's," *Wall Street Journal,* November 2, 1987, 1; David Lauter and Ronald Ostrow, "Bennett Calls on Ginsburg to Quit," *Los Angeles Times,* November 7, 1987, 1.
19. Steve A. Matthews to Special Project Committee Re: Judge Anthony M. Kennedy (May 23, 1986), 6, 9, PWA, OA 14287, Kennedy Memos File. For the decision in *Beller,* see *Beller v. Middendorf,* 632 F.2d 788 (9th Cir. 1980).
20. Don Feder, "The Kennedy Surrender" (November 16, 1987), 1–8, CCF, OA 15526, Kennedy Nomination Folder 1. On ALL's position, see Judie Brown, interview with Mary Ziegler, May 13, 2018.
21. "Judge Anthony Kennedy: Talking Points" (November 11, 1987), CCF, OA 15526, Kennedy Nomination Folder 1; see also Rebecca Range, Memorandum to Thomas Griscom (December 4, 1987), CCF, OA 15526, Kennedy Nomination Folder 1.
22. "Looking Ahead," *National Right to Life News,* January 22, 1988, 1, JRS, 1988 National Right to Life News Box. On AUL's expectations, see Mary Thornton, "Ruling on Illinois Abortion Curb Stands as Supreme Court Splits 4-4," *Washington Post,* December 15, 1987, A14. On the Kennedy confirmation vote, see Linda Greenhouse, "Senate, 97 to 0, Confirms Kennedy to the High Court," *New York Times,*

February 4, 1988, https://www.nytimes.com/1988/02/04/us/senate-97-to-0-confirms-kennedy-to-high-court.html, accessed June 19, 2021.

23. On Kemp, see Morton Kondracke and Fred Barnes, *Jack Kemp: The Bleeding Heart Conservative Who Changed America* (New York: Sentinel, 2015); David Frum, "Why Jack Kemp's Legacy Is More Important Than Ever," *Atlantic*, October 12, 2015, https://www.theatlantic.com/politics/archive/2015/10/jack-kemp-legacy/410152/, accessed July 25, 2020. For more on the 1988 race, see Ellen Hume and Rich Jaroslosky, "Republican Rift: Robertson's Candidacy Threatens a Deep Split in the GOP," *Wall Street Journal*, March 4, 1988, 1.

24. Ellen Hume, "Pat Robertson Hopes to Translate Evangelical Fervor into Political Constituency for Presidential Bid," *Wall Street Journal*, July 18, 1986, 1. For more on the divisions exposed by the GOP primary, see Phil Gailey, "GOP Gathering Considers Political Life After Reagan," *New York Times*, June 29, 1986, A22; Thomas B. Edsall, "The GOP's Right-Wing Center," *Washington Post*, November 22, 1987, C5. For more on Robertson's career, see Daniel K. Williams, *God's Own Party: The Making of the Christian Right* (New York: Oxford University Press, 2010), 159, 187–200; David Domke and Kevin Coe, *The God Strategy: How Religion Became a Political Weapon in America* (New York: Oxford University Press, 2003), 125–136; Frances Fitzgerald, *The Evangelicals: The Struggle to Shape America* (New York: Simon and Schuster, 2017), 113–140.

25. David N. O'Steen, "Facing the Challenge of 1988: An NRLC Special Report on the 1988 Presidential Campaign" (March 20, 1988), JBP, Matter Boxes, File 491. For Ailes's comment, see Jacob V. Lamar Jr., "George Bush: The Man Who Would Be President," *Time*, March 21, 1988, http://content.time.com/time/subscriber/article/0,33009,967052–3,00.html, accessed September 14, 2021.

26. O'Steen, "Facing the Challenge of 1988." For more on the reasons for NRLC's endorsement of Bush, see Dave Andrusko, "NRL-PAC Endorses Bush," *National Right to Life News*, August 1988, 1, JRS, 1988 National Right to Life News Box; James Bopp Jr., "Fate of *Roe v. Wade* May Hinge on Presidential Contest," *National Right to Life News*, October 30, 1988, 1, JRS, 1988 National Right to Life News Box.

27. On the fathers' rights campaign, see Richard Coleson to Paul Lewis Re: Fathers' Rights Case (July 28, 1988), JBP, Matter Boxes, File 1185; Petition for Writ of Certiorari, 8, 16, *Smith v. Doe* (No. 88-1837), on file with the author; see also Tamar Lewin, "Woman Has Abortion, Violating Court's Order on Paternal Rights," *New York Times*, April 14, 1988, A26; "Abortion Dispute Sent to Indiana Lower Court," *Chicago Tribune*, April 15, 1988, 3; "Father's Rights at Issue in Abortion Cases," *Chicago Tribune*, April 15, 1988, 3.

28. David Shribman, "Campaign '88—Holy War: Rift Widens in GOP between Traditionalist and Evangelical Wings," *Wall Street Journal*, August 16, 1988, 1. On the chaos surrounding the Michigan process, see James Risen, "Bush Wins in Michigan Chaos," *Los Angeles Times*, January 30, 1988, https://www.latimes.com/archives/la-xpm-1988–01–30-mn-10154-story.html, accessed April 10, 2020; "Bush Gets Most Michigan Delegates," *Los Angeles Times*, January 31, 1988,

https://www.latimes.com/archives/la-xpm-1988-01-31-mn-39686-story.html, accessed April 10, 2020. On the Georgia conflict, see Shribman, "Campaign '88," 1.

29. On the Common Cause litigation, see *Common Cause v. Federal Election Commission*, 692 F.Supp. 1391 (D.D.C. 1987); see also Federal Election Commission, "Rulemaking Petition: Notice of Disposition," *Federal Register* 51 (1986): 15915. On Kroc's donation, see Steve Goldberg, "Loophole Begets Infusion of 'Soft Money,' " *Richmond Times-Dispatch*, June 7, 1988, C5. On the spread of soft money, see Charles Babcock, "Big Donations Again a Campaign Staple," *Washington Post*, November 17, 1988, A20; Thomas Edsall, "Soft Money Competition," *Washington Post*, August 16, 1988, A1; Paul Houston, "Bush, Dukakis Got Record Big Gifts," *Los Angeles Times*, December 10, 1988, P2. On Bush's soft money advantage, see Lloyd Grove, "Bush to Spend at Least $32 Million on TV Ads," *Washington Post*, September 22, 1987, A27. On Bush's fundraising prowess, see Richard L. Berke, "National Fund-raising Base Eludes All but Bush," *New York Times*, September 1, 1987, A12. On the Trump fundraiser, see Georgia Dullea, "Reception for Bush Puts Money on Ice," *New York Times*, April 13, 1988, A25. On Bush's soft money donors, see Rita Beamish, "Republicans Raked in $20 Million in 'Soft Money' for Election," *AP*, November 21, 1988, https://apnews.com/article/45df8b373148310 4fb75bccc5470736c, accessed February 17, 2021. On the Koch brothers' growing influence, see Jane Mayer, *Dark Money: The Hidden History of the Billionaires behind the Rise of the Radical Right* (New York: Anchor Books, 2016), 199–200.

30. Operation Rescue, Brochure, "Repent and Rescue 1989: Atlanta" (n.d., ca. 1988), FWHC, Box 51, Operation Rescue Folder; see also Randall Terry, "Higher Laws," *Rutherford Institute Magazine*, March/April 1987, 4. For Terry's statement on the political-legal strategy: Pamphlet, "Operation Rescue Atlanta: July 18–22, 1988, FWHC, Box 51, Operation Rescue Newsletter Folder. For more on these criticisms, see Pamphlet: Repentance and Rescue Atlanta (n.d., ca. 1988), FWHC, Box 51, Operation Rescue Folder; Randall Terry, Letter to Operation Members, *Rescue News Brief* (n.d., ca. 1988), FWHC, Box 51, Operation Rescue Newsletter Folder.

31. On Bush's fundraising total, see Beamish, "Republicans Raked In"; Houston, "Bush, Dukakis," P2. On the outcome of the 1988 election, see John J. Pitney Jr., *After Reagan: Bush, Dukakis, and the 1988 Election* (Lawrence: University Press of Kansas, 2019); Larry M. Bartels, *Presidential Primaries and the Dynamics of Public Choice* (Princeton: Princeton University Press, 2020), 276–280.

32. For Bopp and Balch's statement: James Bopp Jr. and Burke Balch to NRLC State Affiliates, "Re: Six Possible *Webster* Scenarios" (June 16, 1989), LLF, OA/ID 45272, *Webster* File; see also Clarke Forsythe to James Bopp Jr. (April 12, 1989), JBP, Matter Boxes, File 837. For more on NRLC's views on the *Webster* case in the lead-up to a decision, see National Right to Life Committee, "Abortion: Questions and Answers" (1989), LLF, OA/ID 45272, *Webster* File. On the growing political and legal involvement of Focus on the Family and the Family Research Council, see Dan Gilgoff, *The Jesus Machine: How James Dobson, Focus on the Family, and Evangelical America Are Winning the Culture War* (New York: Macmillan, 2008),

151–176. On the founding of Christian Advocates and its work with Free Speech Advocates, see Sara Diamond, *Not by Politics Alone: The Enduring Influence of the Christian Right* (New York: Guilford, 1998), 86; Hans J. Hacker, *The Culture of Conservative Christian Litigation* (Lanham, MD: Rowman and Littlefield, 2005), 22; Amanda Hollis-Brusky and Joshua C. Wilson, "Playing for the Rules: How and Why New Christian Right Public Interest Law Firms Invest in Secular Litigation," *Law and Policy* 39 (2017): 121–141. On the rise of conservative Christian law schools, see Amanda Hollis-Brusky and Joshua C. Wilson, *Separate but Faithful: The Christian Right's Radical Struggle to Transform Law and Culture* (New York: Oxford University Press, 2020).

33. "From Randall's Desk," *Rescue News Brief*, January 31, 1989, 1, FWHC, Box 51, Operation Rescue Folder 1.
34. See Howard Kurtz, "Operation Rescue: Aggressively Antiabortion," *Washington Post*, March 6, 1989, A3. On the number of arrests recorded, see "16 Rescues during *Roe v. Wade* Weekend, over 1000 Arrested," *Rescue News Brief*, January 1989, 4, FWHC, Box 51, Operation News Folder 1. On Republican support for Operation Rescue, see "Republican Committee Task Force Sets Agenda to Help Operation Rescue," *Rescue News Brief*, March 23, 1989, 1, FWHC, Box 51, Operation News Folder 1.
35. For the challenged statute in *Webster*, see Mo. Rev. Stat. §§ 1.205.1(1), (2); § 188.029 (1986).
36. See *Webster v. Reproductive Health Services*, 492 U.S. 490, 514–518, 525–528, 532–536 (1989). For analysis of the *Webster* decision, see Garrow, *Liberty and Sexuality*, 680–699; David L. Faigman, *Laboratory of Justice: The Supreme Court's 200 Year Struggle to Integrate Science and the Law* (New York: Henry Holt, 2004), 223–226, 228; Laurence Tribe, *Abortion: The Clash of Absolutes* (New York: Norton, 1992), 109, 123, 141–142.
37. For Coleson's statement: Richard Coleson to Mike Aloi (August 8, 1989), JBP, Matter Boxes, File 768; see also Richard Coleson to Mike Aloi (August 14, 1988), JBP, Matter Boxes, File 1185.
38. On the aggressive strategies pursued by NRLC in the immediate aftermath of *Webster*, see "Idaho's Strict Abortion Bill Advances," *Los Angeles Times*, March 17, 1990, A22; Tamar Lewin, "States Testing the Limits on Abortion," *New York Times*, April 2, 1990, A14. For more on AUL's strategy in the period, see "Restoring Parents' Rights," *AUL Insights*, November 1990, 1, SBL, Box 1, AUL Folder 2; "3 Steps toward Protecting the Unborn," *AUL Forum*, September 1992, 2–3, SBL, Box 1, AUL Folder 1.
39. For discussion of the internal polling, see Richard John Neuhaus, Memo on August 22, 1991 Roundtable Convened by the Secretariat of Pro-Life Activities (Fall 1991), RJN, Box 3, Folder 22; Guy Condon to Richard John Neuhaus (February 11, 1991), RJN, Box 3, Folder 23.
40. E. J. Dionne Jr., "Abortion Ruling Shakes Up Races for Legislatures," *New York Times*, July 10, 1989, B8; see also Robin Toner, "GOP Women Raise Voices for the Right to an Abortion," *New York Times*, October 31, 1989, A1.

41. For Atwater's statement: Andrew Rosenthal, "GOP Leaders Urge Softer Line," *New York Times*, November 10, 1989, A1; see also R. W. Apple Jr., "The 1989 Election: The Abortion Backlash at the Polls," *New York Times*, November 9, 1989, B14. On the 1989 races and the role of abortion, see Dan Balz, "Republicans Weigh Lessons on Abortion," *Washington Post*, November 9, 1989, A37; John Ellis, " 'Wedge Issue' That Pierces GOP's Heart," *Los Angeles Times*, November 19, 1989, M3. On Atwater's background, see John Brady, *Bad Boy: The Life and Politics of Lee Atwater* (New York: Da Capo, 1997); Ed Rollins and Thomas DeFrank, *Bare Knuckles and Back Rooms: My Life in American Politics* (New York: Broadway, 1997); Michael Oreskes, "Lee Atwater, Master of Tactics for Bush and the GOP, Dies at 40," *New York Times*, March 30, 1991, https://www.nytimes.com/1991/03/30/obituaries/lee-atwater-master-of-tactics-for-bush-and-gop-dies-at-40.html, accessed July 13, 2020.
42. On the decline of Operation Rescue and the early years of Operation Rescue National, see Mary Ziegler, *Beyond Abortion:* Roe v. Wade *and the Fight for Privacy* (Cambridge, MA: Harvard University Press, 2018), 224–230.
43. Chapter 2 traces in greater depth the early campaign finance troubles of antiabortion groups.
44. James Bopp Jr. and Richard Coleson, "The First Amendment Needs No Reform: Protecting Liberty from Campaign Finance 'Reformers,' " *Catholic University Law Review* 51 (2002): 786.
45. For the disputed regulation in *Faucher*, see 11 C.F.R. § 114.4(b)(5). For early litigation in the case, see *Faucher v. Federal Election Commission*, 743 F.Supp. 64 (D. Me. 1990). For Bopp's arguments, see Brief for Sandra Faucher and Maine Right to Life Committee, 4–28, *Faucher v. Federal Election Commission*, 928 F.2d 468 (1st Cir. 1991) (No. 90-1382).
46. On the savings and loan crisis, see Kitty Kalavita, Henry N. Pontell, and Robert Tillman, *Big Money Crime: Fraud and Politics in the Savings and Loan Crisis* (Berkeley: University of California Press, 1997); Kathleen Reagan, *Broken Bargain: Bankers, Bailouts, and the Struggle to Tame Wall Street* (New Haven: Yale University Press, 2019), 120–138; Richard Vague, *A Brief History of Doom: Two Hundred Years of Financial Crises* (Philadelphia: University of Pennsylvania Press, 2019), 50–68.
47. On the support for campaign finance reform in the wake of the S&L scandal, see Jill Abramson and David Rodgers, "Keating Hearings Pressure Congress to Reform Campaign-Finance System," *Wall Street Journal*, January 10, 1991, A6; Jill Abramson, "Defenses of 'Keating Five' Senators Try to Focus on the Campaign-Finance System," *Wall Street Journal*, November 19, 1990, A16. On the Keating Five, see Vague, *A Brief History of Doom*, 64; William K. Black, *The Best Way to Rob a Bank Is to Own One: How Corporate Executives and Politicians Looted the S&L Industry* (Austin: University of Texas Press, 2005), 150–167.
48. Jason Zengerle, "Get Mitch," *Politico*, November 2013, https://www.politico.com/magazine/story/2013/11/get-mitch-mcconnell-099376, accessed July 25, 2020; see also "Mitch McConnell's Mastery," *The Week*, September 29, 2019, https://

theweek.com/articles/867934/mitch-mcconnells-mastery, accessed July 13, 2020; Bob Moser, "Mitch McConnell: The Man Who Sold America," *Rolling Stone*, September 17, 2019, https://www.rollingstone.com/politics/politics-features/mitch-mcconnell-man-who-sold-america-880799/, accessed July 13, 2020. For McConnell's claim that he had always opposed campaign finance laws, see John David Dyche, *Republican Leader: Political Biography of Senator Mitch McConnell* (Wilmington, DE: ISI Books, 2009), 28.

49. Zengerle, "Get Mitch;" Moser, "Mitch McConnell."
50. See *Faucher v. Federal Election Commission*, 743 F.Supp. 64, 65–81 (D. Me. 1990).
51. For Dole's statement: Brian Hecht, "Is Bush Courting Disaster?" *Harvard Crimson*, July 24, 1990, https://www.thecrimson.com/article/1990/7/24/is-bush-courting-disaster-pbfbor-george/, accessed April 10, 2020. On Bush's selection of Souter, see C. Boyden Gray to George H. W. Bush (January 22, 1991), LLF, OA/ID 45254, David Souter—Analysis Folder. For more on Souter, see Tinsley Yarbrough, *David Hackett Souter: Traditional Republican on the Rehnquist Court* (New York: Oxford University Press, 2005).
52. Talking Points: David Souter (n.d., ca. 1991), KGF, OA/ID 03161, Talking Points Folder. For staffers' assessment of Souter, see Steven Schmidt, Notes on David Souter (n.d., ca. 1991), KGF, OA/ID 03161, Talking Points Folder.
53. See David G. Savage, "Souter Supports 'Right to Privacy' as Hearings Open," *Los Angeles Times*, September 14, 1990, A1; Neil A. Lewis, "Souter Deflects Senators' Queries on Abortion Views," *New York Times*, September 14, 1990, A1; Neil A. Lewis, "Souter Seems Sure to Win Approval, Key Senators Say," *New York Times*, September 15, 1990, 1.
54. On abortion rights groups' opposition to Souter, see Richard L. Berke, "Souter Nomination Stirs Abortion-Rights Groups," *New York Times*, August 1, 1990, A12; Lyle Dennison, "Souter Confirmation Expected Despite Lingering Feminist Opposition," *Baltimore Sun*, September 25, 1990, 17A. On pro-life opposition to Souter, see "Both Sides of Abortion Issue Attack Souter," *Los Angeles Times*, September 18, 1990, P18; Tony Mauro, "Souter Hearing Heats Up," *USA Today*, September 19, 1990, 3A.
55. For Bauer's statement: Robin Toner, "GOP Blurs Focus on Abortion, to Dismay of Some Party Faithful," *New York Times*, January 18, 1990, A1. On Bauer's work at the Family Research Council, see Michele McKeegan, *Abortion Politics: Mutiny in the Ranks of the Right* (New York: Free Press, 1992); Jean V. Hardisty, *Mobilizing Resentment: Conservative Resurgence from the John Birch Society to the Promise Keepers* (Boston: Beacon, 1999).
56. On the founding of Republicans for Choice, see Robin Toner, "G.O.P. Group Formed to Support Abortion Rights," *New York Times*, April 24, 1990, A21; Maralee Schwartz and Dan Balz, "Republican PAC Created to Back Abortion Rights," *Washington Post*, April 29, 1990, A16. On the history of the organization, see Republicans for Choice, "Whatever Happened to the Big Tent?" 1–8 (July 1996), RNCL, Box 1, Folder 3. On Ann Stone, see Martha Sherrill, "The GOP's Abortion-Rights Upstart," *Washington Post*, April 4, 1992, https://www.washingtonpost.

com/archive/lifestyle/1992/04/04/the-gops-abortion-rights-upstart/a697aee6–7d6a-47bf-88a2-d3582a8f78df/, accessed July 25, 2020.

57. *Hodgson v. Minnesota*, 497 U.S. 417, 440–458 (1990); see also *Ohio v. Akron Center for Reproductive Health*, 497 U.S. 502, 512–520 (1990).
58. Phyllis Schlafly, Letter to Penny (September 5, 1990), RNCL, Box 10, Folder 8. For more on the founding of the group, see Washington Court Meeting Minutes (September 20, 1990), 1, 3, 6–8, RNCL, Box 10, Folder 8; RNC Life: Organization (September 1990), RNCL, Box 10, Folder 8.
59. See Washington Court Meeting Minutes, 1, 3, 6–8.
60. See *Faucher v. Federal Election Commission*, 928 F.2d 468, 470–472 (1st Cir. 1991).
61. Sam Fulwood III and William J. Eaton, "Thomas Invited to Meet with Board of NAACP," *Los Angeles Times*, July 9, 1991, https://www.latimes.com/archives/la-xpm-1991-07-09-mn-2062-story.html, accessed April 13, 2020. For the media strategy used to define Thomas in the summer of 1991, see "Clarence Thomas Media Points" (July 9, 1991), JSF, OA/ID CF00473, Talking Points Folder; Clarence Thomas Talking Points (July 10, 1991), JSF, OA/ID CF00473, Talking Points Folder. For Bopp's effort to publicize the result in *Faucher*, see James Bopp Jr. and Richard Coleson, "Supreme Court Lets FEC Defeat over Voter Guides Stand" (n.d., ca. 1991), JBP, Matter Boxes, File 971; James Bopp Jr. to NRLC Board of Directors (October 10, 1991), JBP, Matter Boxes, File 971.
62. Neil A. Lewis, "Court Candidate Linked to Anti-Abortion Stand," *New York Times*, July 3, 1991, https://www.nytimes.com/1991/07/03/us/court-nominee-is-linked-to-anti-abortion-stand.html, accessed April 13, 2020. On Thomas's background and beliefs, "Excerpts from the Senate Hearings on the Thomas Nomination," *New York Times*, September 11, 1991, A22; Linda Campbell, "Despite Murky Responses, Thomas's Conservative Bent Shows," *Chicago Tribune*, September 15, 1991, C1; Elizabeth Wright, "Black America and the Thomas Nomination," *Wall Street Journal*, July 24, 1991, A10.
63. See Lewis, "Court Candidate"; David G. Savage, "Thomas Backs off Abortion, Natural Law Statements," *Los Angeles Times*, September 11, 1991, 1; Terry Atlas, "Bush Chooses Conservative for Supreme Court: Judge's Views on Abortion May Hold Key," *Chicago Tribune*, July 2, 1991, NW1.
64. Andrew Rosenthal, "Bush Acts to Quiet Storm over TV Ad on Thomas," *New York Times*, September 6, 1991, A1. For NRLC's fundraising letter: National Right to Life Committee, Fundraising Letter (August 4, 1991), JBP, Matter Boxes, File 971. For more on conservative organizations' strong support of Thomas, see Steven A. Holmes, "Thomas Backers' Ad Faults Senators," *New York Times*, September 4, 1991, A18; "Endorsements of and Opposition to Thomas," *Chicago Tribune*, September 15, 1991, 4.
65. For Hatch's statement: Paul M. Barrett and Jill Abramson, "The Thomas Hearings: Unsolved Mysteries," *Wall Street Journal*, October 14, 1991, A1. For more on Hill and the effort to bury her accusations, see Linda Hirshman, *Reckoning: The Epic Battle against Sexual Abuse and Sexual Harassment* (New York: Houghton Mifflin, 2019), 76–84; Corey Robin, *The Enigma of Clarence Thomas* (New York: Henry Holt, 2019), 4, 6, 163–170.

66. National Right to Life Committee Draft Fundraising Letter (October 14, 1991), JBP, Matter Boxes, File 971. On NRLC's call for an FBI investigation, see NRLC Fundraising Letter (October 16, 1991), JBP, Matter Boxes, File 971. On the confirmation vote, see "The Thomas Confirmation: How the Senate Voted on Thomas," *New York Times*, October 16, 1991, https://www.nytimes.com/1991/10/16/us/the-thomas-confirmation-how-the-senators-voted-on-thomas.html, accessed April 13, 2020.
67. For NRLC's prediction: National Right to Life Committee Fundraising Letter (June 5, 1992), JBP, Matter Boxes, File 1067; see also Guy Condon to Richard John Neuhaus (October 1, 1991), RJN, Box 3, Folder 22; Guy Condon to Richard John Neuhaus (October 1, 1991), RJN, Box 3, Folder 23; "Agenda: Amici Conference" (January 23, 1992), JBP, Matter Boxes, File 1013; List of Issues for Amici Conference (January 1992), JBP, Matter Boxes, File 1013.
68. On the administration's anxiety about *Casey*, see Jay Lefkowitz to the Chief of Staff et al. (June 25, 1992), LLF, OA 45270, *Casey* File; Memorandum, "Will *Roe v. Wade* Be Overruled?" (n.d., ca. 1992), JLF, OA 07867, *Casey* File; Lee Liberman, Memorandum, "Some Thoughts on Abortion Decision Scenarios," 2–4 (July 4, 1992), LLF, OA 45272, *Casey* File.
69. On the NARAL gathering and Clinton's statement: Judy Keen and Mimi Hall, "Abortion Rekindled as '92 Issue," *USA Today*, January 23, 1992, 3A; see also "Governor Clinton's Litmus Test," *Washington Post*, July 9, 1992, A22; Joan Beck, "Another Salvo in the Endless War over Abortion," *Chicago Tribune*, July 2, 1992, 19.
70. On Buchanan's background, see Patrick J. Buchanan, *Nixon's White House Wars: The Battles That Made and Broke a President and Divided America Forever* (New York: Crown Forum, 2017); Joe Klein, "Patrick Buchanan Reveals Himself to Be the First Trumpist," *New York Times*, May 8, 2017, https://www.nytimes.com/2017/05/08/books/review/nixons-white-house-wars-patrick-j-buchanan.html, accessed July 13, 2020. For Buchanan's statement: Buchanan, *Nixon's White House Wars*, 128–147.
71. On the threat posed by Buchanan to Bush, see Andrew Rosenthal, "Bush Considering a Shift in Tactics to Fight Buchanan," *New York Times*, February 20, 1992, A1; E. J. Dionne Jr., "New Hampshire GOP Split on Impact of Buchanan Run," *Washington Post*, November 21, 1991, A14. On Nickles and the 1992 platform, see Andrew Rosenthal, "Militant Foe of 1973 Ruling Gets Platform Post," *New York Times*, January 23, 1992, A1; David E. Rosenbaum, "Abortion Issue Rips Away Veil of GOP Unity," *New York Times*, May 23, 1992, A1. On efforts to ensure that the platform strongly condemned abortion, see Phyllis Schlafly to Pro-Life Member of the Platform Committee (July 31, 1992), RNCL, Box 3, Folder 9; Pat Robertson to Phyllis Schlafly (July 7, 1992), RNCL, Box 3, Folder 9.
72. On Bush's February fundraising advantage, see David Lauter, "$9 Million Bush Election Fund Much Bigger Than Buchanan's," *Los Angeles Times*, February 21, 1992, https://www.latimes.com/archives/la-xpm-1992-02-21-mn-2733-story.html, accessed February 10, 2021. On Buchanan's fundraising totals, see Monte Paulsen, "Buchanan, Inc.," *Nation*, November 4, 1999, https://www.thenation.com/article/archive/buchanan-inc/, accessed February 10, 2021; Federal Election

Commission, *1992 Annual Report* (Washington, DC: Federal Election Commission, 1993), 16. On bundling and its influence, see Mark Stencel, " 'Bundling' Skirts Campaign Gift Curbs," *Washington Post*, April 20, 1992, A1; Ann Devroy and Mark Stencel, "Bush Dinner Raises Funds and Eyebrows," *Washington Post*, April 16, 1992, A1; Ann Devroy, Mark Stencel, Lucy Schackelford, and Charles Babcock, "GOP Dinner Criticized as Symptom of System," *Washington Post*, April 24, 1992, A1.

73. On Team 100 and Bush's soft money, see Jeffrey Denny, Vicki Kemper, and Viveca Novak, "A $100,000 Understanding? Do Big-time GOP Donors Get an Inside Whitehouse Track?" *Washington Post*, May 10, 1992, C1; Jill Abramson and Thomas Petzinger Jr., "Déjà Vu: Big Political Donors Find Ways around Watergate Reforms," *Wall Street Journal*, June 11, 1992, A1. On the total soft money haul, see Linda Feldman, "Give Money, and They Call Back," *Christian Science Monitor*, November 3, 1992, https://www.csmonitor.com/1992/1103/03031.html, accessed February 10, 2021.
74. See *Planned Parenthood of Southeastern Pennsylvania v. Casey*, 505 U.S. 833, 855–857 (1992) (plurality decision).
75. Ibid., 855–857.
76. Ibid., 856.
77. Ibid., 857–864, 872–888. For more on the significance of *Casey*, see Ziegler, *Abortion and the Law*, 112–130, 134–156; Garrow, *Liberty and Sexuality*, 700–720; Carol Sanger, *About Abortion: Terminating Pregnancy in Twenty-First Century America* (Cambridge, MA: Harvard University Press, 2017), 15–35.
78. National Right to Life Committee, Fundraising Letter (July 21, 1992), JBP, Matter Boxes 1067. On Condon's departure and new views, see "Guy Condon Takes the Helm at CAC," *Action Line*, January/February 1993, 1, PAW, Box 15, Folder 11.
79. See David Lauter and Douglas Jehl, "Parties Seeking Middle Ground on Abortions," *Los Angeles Times*, July 26, 1992, OCA1; Jean Latz Griffin, "Abortion Remains Most Divisive Issue," *Chicago Tribune*, October 19, 1992, NW5; E. J. Dionne Jr., "Bush Appears in Danger of Losing Much Conservative Support to Perot," *Washington Post*, June 8, 1992, A10.
80. Sara Fritz, "The Abortion Decision: Ruling Pleases Neither Side," *Los Angeles Times*, June 30, 1992, A10; see also Steven Daley, "Ruling Weakens Abortion Rights," *Chicago Tribune*, June 30, 1992, N1. For Bush's statement: Ruth Marcus, "At Issue: Abortion," *Washington Post*, August 16, 1992, A21.
81. On RNC-Life's efforts, see Schlafly to Pro-Life Member of the Platform Committee, 1; Robertson to Schlafly, 1. On Buchanan's role at the convention, see Sara Fritz, "Despite a Tightly Controlled Script, Watch for Surprises," *Los Angeles Times*, August 16, 1992, A7; E. J. Dionne Jr., "Buchanan Defends Focus on 'Values,' " *Washington Post*, September 12, 1992, A10; Andrew Rosenthal, "Bush Tries to Recoup from Harsh Tone on 'Values,' " *New York Times*, September 21, 1992, A1.
82. Steve Daley, "GOP Platform Veers Right," *Chicago Tribune*, August 13, 1992, NW1. On the 1992 platform dispute, see Thomas Hardey, "Schlafly Is a VIP Again in GOP Due to 2 Disputes," *Chicago Tribune*, June 9, 1992, 1; Elaine S.

Povich, "GOP Likely to Cling to Abortion Plank," *Chicago Tribune*, August 10, 1992, 1; James M. Perry, "Republican Abortion Plank Makes Clear that No Big Tent Is Going to Rise in Houston," *Wall Street Journal*, August 14, 1992, A12.

83. Barbara Jordan, 1992 Democratic National Convention Keynote Address, *C-SPAN*, July 13, 1992, https://www.c-span.org/video/?27052–1/barbara-jordan-1992-convention-keynote-address, accessed April 15, 2020. On the visibility of the abortion issue in Clinton's campaign, see Karen De Witt, "Huge Crowd Backs Right to Abortion in Capitol March," *New York Times*, April 6, 1992, A1; Mitchell Locin, "Clinton Rises from the Dead," *Chicago Tribune*, July 1, 1992, NW5; B. Drummond Ayres Jr., "The 1992 Campaign: Democrats—Buoyed Clinton Goes on the Offensive," *New York Times*, July 1, 1992, A15.
84. "A Pivotal Choice: Who Will Pick the Next Justice?" *USA Today*, October 5, 1992, A14. For NARAL's statement: Ann Devroy and Howard Kurtz, "NARAL Ads Ask Voters to Consider Candidates' Abortion Rights Stance," *Washington Post*, October 27, 1992, A13. For more on NARAL's advocacy from the period, see Harrison Hickman to Loretta Ucelli and Kate Michelman, "Re: Parental Consent/Notification Update" (February 12, 1991), FWHC, Box 63, Parental Notification Talking Points Folder.
85. On Perot's result, see Thomas Edsall and E. J. Dionne Jr., "White, Younger, Low-Income Voters Turn against the GOP," *Washington Post*, November 4, 1992, A21; Laurie Goering, "GOP Sees Suburban Strength Eroding," *Chicago Tribune*, November 5, 1992, A1; Robin Toner, "The 1992 Elections: The World—At Dawn of New Politics, Challenges for Both Parties," *New York Times*, November 5, 1992, B1. On the significance of abortion in the 1992 race, see Allan I. Abramowitz, "It's Abortion, Stupid: Policy Voting in the 1992 Presidential Election," *Journal of Politics* 57 (1996): 176–186.

Chapter 4. The Big-Money Party

1. Max Boot, "New GOP Leader Looks to Restore 'Party of Ideas,' " *Christian Science Monitor*, May 4, 1993, 3; see also Robert Shogan, "Republicans Show Signs of Bouncing Back," *Los Angeles Times*, May 23, 1993, A1; David S. Broder, "Republicans Launch Grass-roots Policy Forum," *Washington Post*, June 22, 1993, A9.
2. Market Strategies, "1992 Post-Election Report for RNC," 2–10 (January 10, 1993), FSP, Box 36, Post-election Folder 1; see also Post-election Survey Result (1992), 1, 17, 36, FSP, Box 36, Post-election Folder 1.
3. Hansen Post-election Report 1992 (1992), 3, FSP, Box 36, Post-election Folder 2.
4. For McCain's view, see Shogan, "Republicans Show Signs," A1. On the National Policy Forum, see Broder, "Republicans Launch," A9; Richard L. Berke, "GOP Hopes New Group Can Attract Support from Outsiders," *New York Times*, November 15, 1993, https://www.nytimes.com/1993/11/15/us/gop-hopes-new-group-can-attract-support-from-outsiders.html, accessed June 12, 2021. For more on the Republicans' effort to win over voters in the center, see James R. Kelly, "Truth,

Not Truce: 'Common Ground' on Abortion, a Movement within Both Movements," in *The American Culture Wars: Current Contests and Future Prospects*, ed. James L. Nolan Jr. (Charlottesville: University of Virginia Press, 1996), 231.

5. Russell Chandler, "Echo of '88: Robertson Moves to Fill Christian Right Vacuum," *Los Angeles Times*, May 15, 1990, https://www.latimes.com/archives/la-xpm-1990-05-15-mn-174-story.html, accessed March 2, 2020. For more on the founding and early years of the Christian Coalition, see Neil J. Young, *We Gather Together: The Religious Right and the Problem of Interfaith Politics* (New York: Oxford University Press, 2016), 244–248; Robert P. Jones, *The End of White Christian America* (New York: Simon and Schuster, 2017), 89–93; Sara Diamond, *Not by Politics Alone: The Enduring Influence of the Christian Right* (New York: Guilford, 2000), 95–98. On Reed, see Sean Flynn, "The Sins of Ralph Reed," *GQ*, July 11, 2006, https://www.gq.com/story/ralph-reed-gop-lobbyist-jack-abramoff, accessed July 26, 2020; Laurence I. Barrett, "Fighting for God and the Right Wing: Ralph Reed," *Time*, September 13, 1993, 14.
6. Steve Schwalm, "Conservative Spotlight: The National Institute of Family and Life Advocates," *Human Events*, August 30, 1996, 9. On Heartbeat International, see Margaret Hartshorn, *Foot Soldiers Armed with Love: Heartbeat International's First Forty Years* (Virginia Beach, VA: Donning, 2011), 33. For more on CPCs, see Karissa Haugeberg, *Women against Abortion: Inside the Largest Reform Movement of the Twentieth Century* (Champaign: University of Illinois Press, 2017), 39–55; Daniel K. Williams, *Defenders of the Unborn: The Pro-Life Movement Before* Roe v. Wade (New York: Oxford University Press, 2016), 244.
7. On the founding and early work of the Alliance Defense Fund, see "Pro-Life Speech at Risk," *ADF Quarterly Briefing*, Spring 1994, 1, AUS, Carton 1, Folder 14; Alliance Defense Fund Brochure (n.d., ca. 2001), AUS, Carton 1, Folder 14; "Victory! ADF Funded Cases Set Historic Precedents for America," *ADF Quarterly Briefing*, August 1995, 1, AUS, Carton 1, Folder 14.
8. James Bopp Jr. to Burke Balch (July 9, 1992), JBP, Matter Boxes, File 1067; see also James Bopp Jr. and Richard Coleson, Memo to Whom It May Concern (July 8, 1992), JBP, Matter Boxes, File 1067. For the *Casey* decision, see *Planned Parenthood of Southeastern Pennsylvania v. Casey*, 505 U.S. 833, 857–863 (1992). For Balch's argument, see Burke Balch to State Lobbyists for State Affiliates (July 8, 1992), JBP, Matter Boxes, File 1067.
9. On the earlier goals of pro-life incrementalism, see Mary Ziegler, *After* Roe*: The Lost History of the Abortion Debate* (Cambridge, MA: Harvard University Press, 2015), 62–72; Williams, *Defenders of the Unborn*, 134–157.
10. On Schlafly, see Donald T. Critchlow, *Phyllis Schlafly and Grassroots Conservatism: A Woman's Crusade* (Princeton: Princeton University Press, 2004); Marjorie J. Spruill, *Divided We Stand: The Battle over Women's Rights and Family Values That Polarized American Politics* (New York: Bloomsbury, 2017).
11. On the Triad controversy, see Wayne Leslie, "A Back Door for the Conservative Donor," *New York Times*, May 22, 1997, A10; Rebecca Carr, "Questions Arise about Tax Exempt Groups in '96," *Congressional Quarterly Weekly Report*, October

4, 1997, 2370–2371; "DC Consultant Engineered Last-Minute GOP Ad Blitz," *Sun*, May 22, 1997, 4A.

12. See Republican National Coalition for Life, Press Release (August 11, 1998), JBP, Matter Boxes, File 1931; Colleen Parro to Phyllis Schlafly et al. (July 2, 1995), RNCL, Box 1, Folder 2.
13. On Clinton's proposal, see Charles Babcock and Kenneth Cooper, "Clinton Campaign Finance Plan Would Eliminate 'Soft Money,' " *Washington Post*, March 26, 1993, A11. On the congressional reform plan, see Richard J. Berke, "Talk of Campaign Finance Laws Sets Off Scramble for Donations," *New York Times*, August 13, 1993, A18.
14. See Mark Weinberg to Members of Free Speech Coalition (October 1993), JBP, Matter Boxes, File 1310. For more on the Free Speech Coalition, see Bill McAllister, "From Left to Right: Lobbyists Unite," *Washington Post*, October 5, 1993, A12. For more on Olson, see "About Us: William J. Olson," William J. Olson, PC, Attorneys at Law, http://www.lawandfreedom.com/wordpress/william-j-olson/, accessed July 13, 2020. On the opposition of Koch and other wealthy donors to campaign finance rules in the period, see Ann Southworth, "Speech: The Campaign to Unleash Big Money in American Politics," 29–32, on file with the author; Jane Mayer, *Dark Money: The Hidden History of the Billionaires behind the Rise of the Radical Right* (New York: Anchor Books, 2016), 198–203.
15. See Beth Donovan, "Black Caucus Leads Defense of PAC Funds," *Pittsburgh New Courier*, October 2, 1993, A7; Helen Dewar and Kenneth J. Cooper, "Campaign Finance Faces PAC Impasse," *Washington Post*, May 25, 1993, A4; "PACs and the Black Caucus," *Washington Post*, July 14, 1994, A22. On the GOP's historic fundraising advantage and opposition to campaign finance limits, see Robert Mutch, *Buying the Vote: A History of Campaign Finance* (New York: Oxford University Press, 2014), 1–180. On the spread of business PACs and the favor they showed to Democratic incumbents, see ibid., 155–180.
16. For the disputed statute: see Minn. Stat. § 10A.25 subd. 13 (Supp. 1993). On the early litigation in the case, *Day v. Holahan*, see *Day v. Hayes*, 863 F.Supp. 940 (D. Minn. 1994).
17. For Sayon's statement: Karen Sayon to James Bopp Jr. (September 14, 1993), JBP, Matter Boxes, File 1314. On Minnesota activists' original ambitions, see James Bopp Jr. to David N. O'Steen and Jackie Schweitz (October 11, 1993), JBP, Matter Box 1314. For the decision in *Massachusetts Citizens Concerned for Life*, see *Federal Election Commission v. Massachusetts Citizens Concerned for Life*, 479 U.S. 238 (1986).
18. For the district court's decision, see *Day v. Hayes*, 863 F.Supp. 940 (D. Minn. 1994). For the Eighth Circuit's decision, see *Day v. Holahan*, 34 F.3d 1356 (8th Cir. 1994).
19. *Day v. Holahan*, 34 F.3d 1356, 1366 (8th Cir. 1994). For Bopp's statement: James Bopp Jr., "Federal Appeals Court Protects Pro-Life Independent Expenditures by Striking Minnesota Election Law" (n.d., ca. 1994), JBP, Matter Boxes, File 1203; see also James Bopp Jr. and Richard Coleson, "IRS Backs Down: Pro-Life Voter Guides Not Political" (n.d., ca. 1994), JBP, Matter Boxes, File 1203.

20. On the GOP's soft money success, see "Corporations' 'Soft Money' Boosts GOP," *Chicago Tribune*, November 23, 1994, 17. On spending in the 1994 election, see "GOP Raises $7.3 Million in 'Soft Money' Donations," *Los Angeles Times*, June 7, 1995, A19; Kurt Shillinger, "PAC Money Fills GOP Pockets on Capitol Hill," *Washington Post*, June 16, 1995, 1. On Gingrich, see McKay Coppins, "The Man Who Broke Politics," *Atlantic*, November 2018, https://www.theatlantic.com/magazine/archive/2018/11/newt-gingrich-says-youre-welcome/570832/, accessed July 13, 2020; James B. Stewart, *Blood Sport: The Truth behind the Scandals in the Clinton White House* (New York: Simon and Schuster, 2012). For GOPAC's description of its work: GOPAC, "History," https://www.gopac.org/history/, accessed September 10, 2021. On both parties' soft money haul, see "GOP 'Soft Money' Topped $16 Million in Two Months," *Wall Street Journal*, January 11, 1995, A6.
21. On the GOP fundraising advantage, see "GOP Raises," A18; Shillinger, "PAC Money," 1.
22. Kurt Shillinger, "Drive to Change Campaign Finance Gains in Congress," *Christian Science Monitor*, November 2, 1995, 1. Chapter 5 discusses BCRA at greater length. On McCain, see Robert Timberg, *John McCain: An American Odyssey* (New York: Simon and Schuster, 2007).
23. NRLC, Model Letter to Senator, (November 1995), JBP, Matter Boxes, File 1275.
24. On Barbour's concern about inaction on campaign finance, see Andrew Mollison, "Focus on Campaign Finance," *Atlanta Journal-Constitution*, April 18, 1996, A10; John E. Yang, "House Coalition Presses Campaign Reform Vote," *Washington Post*, September 20, 1995, A2.
25. On Linda Smith, see "Linda Smith," *History, Art, and Archives of the House of Representatives*, https://history.house.gov/People/Listing/S/SMITH,-Linda-(S000587)/, accessed July 26, 2020; Kathryn Robinson, "The Beltway's Worst Nightmare," *Seattle Weekly*, October 9, 2006, https://www.seattleweekly.com/news/the-beltways-worst-nightmare/, accessed July 26, 2020. On Graham, see Mark Binelli, "How Lindsey Graham Lost His Way," *Rolling Stone*, January 6, 2020, https://www.rollingstone.com/politics/politics-features/lindsey-graham-senate-trump-928948/, accessed July 26, 2020; Kirk Brown, "The Different Faces of Lindsey Graham," *Independent*, August 25, 2017, https://www.independentmail.com/story/news/local/2017/08/25/different-faces-sen-lindsey-graham/594369001/, accessed July 26, 2020. On Brownback, see Jason Beaubien, "How Brownback Learned to Be a Vocal Conservative," *NPR*, October 15, 2007, https://www.npr.org/templates/story/story.php?storyId=14961398, accessed July 25, 2020.
26. For more on conservative efforts to shape interpretation of the First Amendment, see Wayne Batchis, *The Right's First Amendment: The Politics of Free Speech and the Return of Conservative Libertarianism* (Palo Alto: Stanford University Press, 2016), 205–218.
27. On the early litigation in *Colorado Republican*, see *Federal Election Commission v. Colorado Republican Federal Campaign Committee*, 839 F.Supp. 1448 (D. Colo. 1993); *Federal Election Commission v. Colorado Republican Federal Campaign Com-*

mittee, 59 F.3d 1015 (10th Cir. 1995). On Baran's background, see "Jan Witold Baran," *Vanderbilt News*, https://law.vanderbilt.edu/news/jan-witold-baran-73/, accessed July 13, 2020.

28. See *Federal Election Commission v. Colorado Republican Federal Campaign Committee*, 839 F.Supp. 1448, 1443–1451 (D. Colo. 1993).

29. See Amanda Hollis-Brusky, *Ideas with Consequences: The Federalist Society and the Conservative Counterrevolution* (New York: Oxford University Press, 2015), 64–81; James Bopp Jr., interview with Mary Ziegler, June 13, 2020. For more on the growth of the Federalist Society in the mid-1990s, see Steve Rubin, "Conservative Spotlight: The Federalist Society," *Human Events*, July 19, 1996, 15. On the Federalist Society's donor base, see Michael Avery and Danielle McLaughlin, *The Federalist Society: How Conservatives Took the Law Back from Liberals* (Nashville: Vanderbilt University Press, 2013), 12–16. On the Federalist Society's budget, see Steve Teles, *The Rise of the Conservative Legal Movement: The Battle for Control of the Law* (Princeton: Princeton University Press, 2012), 145. For Smith's early writings on campaign finance, see Bradley Smith, "Should 'Committing Politics' Be a Crime? The Case for Deregulating Campaign Finance," *Free Speech and Election Law Practice Newsletter* 1 (Spring 1997); Bradley A. Smith, "Faulty Assumptions and Undemocratic Consequences of Campaign Finance Reform," *Yale Law Journal* 105 (1996); 1049–1091; Bradley A. Smith, "Soft Money, Hard Realities: The Constitutional Prohibition on a Soft Money Ban," *Notre Dame Journal of Legislation* 24 (1998): 179–200. For an example of Hayward's early writings, see Allison Hayward, "Election Law Observer," *Free Speech and Election Law Practice Newsletter* 1 (Fall 1997).

30. On the spread of talk radio, see Brian Rosenwald, *Talk Radio's America: How an Industry Took over a Political Party That Took over the United States* (Cambridge, MA: Harvard University Press, 2019), 47, 80. On the founding and early days of Fox News, see ibid., 102; Nicole Hemmer, *Messengers of the Right: Conservative Media and the Transformation of American Politics* (Philadelphia: University of Pennsylvania Press, 2016), 265–272. For examples of Fox News' coverage of campaign finance in the period, see John Carmody, "The TV Column," *Washington Post*, November 29, 1996, C4; "Democrats Offer Fund-raising Changes; GOP Urges Probe," *Florida Times Union*, November 3, 1996, A16. For Limbaugh's take on lobbying reform, see Susan Estrich, "Rush Isn't the Real Problem," *USA Today*, October 3, 1994, A13; Christopher Drew, "Religious Right Phone Banks Put Lobby Reform on Hold," *Chicago Tribune*, October 7, 1994, D1.

31. Douglas Johnson, "Partial-Birth Abortions: A Closer Look," *National Right to Life*, September 11, 1996, https://www.nrlc.org/abortion/pba/pbafact/m, accessed June 14, 2021. On the rise of the federal partial-birth abortion campaign, see Ziegler, *Abortion and the Law*, 156–174; Sara Dubow, *Ourselves Unborn: A History of the Fetus in Modern America* (New York: Oxford University Press, 2010), 153–174; Johanna Schoen, *Abortion after* Roe (Chapel Hill: University of North Carolina Press, 2015), 299–302.

32. National Right to Life Committee, Board of Directors Meeting Minutes (January 25, 1995), JBP, Matter Boxes, File 1275; see also National Right to Life Committee

Executive Committee Meeting Minutes (October 21, 1995), JBP, Matter Boxes, File 1275.

33. See *Maine Right to Life, Inc. v. Federal Election Commission*, 914 F.Supp. 8 (D. Me. 1996). On NRLC's response to *Maine Right to Life*, James Bopp Jr. to NRLC Board of Directors (November 19, 1996), JBP, Matter Boxes, File 1327. For the New Hampshire case, see *New Hampshire Right to Life Political Action Committee v. Gardner*, 99 F.3d 8 (1st Cir. 1996). For the first round in the West Virginia case, see *West Virginians for Life v. Smith*, 960 F.Supp. 1036 (S.D.W. Va. 1996).
34. On NRLC's partial-birth abortion campaign in 1996, see Talking Points, Doug Johnson to State Officers (April 4, 1996), JBP, Matter Boxes, File 1325; NRLC Board of Directors Meeting Minutes (April 13–14, 1996), JBP, Matter Boxes, File 1325; Douglas Johnson, Post-election Press Conference (November 7, 1996), 1–2, JBP, Matter Boxes, File 1327; NRLC Fundraising Letter (December 6, 1996), JBP, Matter Boxes, File 1327; Doug Johnson, Press Release (November 5, 1998), JBP, Matter Boxes, File 1931; Press Release, "National Right to Life Committee Responds to Senator Daschle's Phony Ban" (November 26, 1996), PWP, Box 80, Folder 2.
35. On Randall Terry's activities after 1994, see Joe Maxwell, "Sizing Up a New Target: Randall Terry Steps Down from Operation Rescue to Go on the Attack against Bill Clinton," *Chicago Tribune*, August 15, 1994, G1; Janny Scott, "Radical Anti-Abortion Alliance Described," *New York Times*, August 18, 1994, B11. On the murder of abortion providers, see Eyal Press, *Absolute Convictions: My Father, a City, and the Conflict That Divided America* (New York: Henry Holt, 2006), 220–223; Rickie Solinger, *Pregnancy and Power: A Short History of Reproductive Politics in America* (New York: New York University Press, 2005), 225.
36. On the unity pledge, see Mary Ellen to James Dobson (September 16, 1996), PWP, Box 81, Folder 3; Judie Brown to J. Thomas Smith (September 6, 1996), PWP, Box 81, Folder 3; Judie Brown, interview with Mary Ziegler, September 18, 2017.
37. For more on the American Life League, see Mary Ziegler, *After* Roe, 42–67; Michael W. Cuneo, "Life Battles: The Rise of Catholic Militancy within the American Pro-Life Movement," in *Being Right: Conservative Catholics in America*, ed. Mary Jo Weaver and R. Scott Appleby (Bloomington: Indiana University Press, 1995), 270–299; Michael W. Cuneo, *The Smoke of Satan: Conservative and Traditionalist Dissent in Contemporary American Catholicism* (Baltimore: Johns Hopkins University Press, 1999), 62–66. For Schlafly's statement: Phyllis Schlafly to Doug Johnson (June 2, 1995), RNCL, Box 1, Folder 2. For Parro's statement: Parro to Schlafly, 1–2.
38. Life Forum Meeting Minutes (September 26, 1996), PWP, Box 81, Folder 3. For O'Steen's campaign within Life Forum, see Life Forum Meeting Minutes (October 4, 1996), PWP, Box 81, Folder 4; David N. O'Steen, Model Letter to Senator (July 22, 1996), PWP, Box 81, Folder 4.
39. See *Colorado Republican Federal Campaign Committee v. Federal Election Commission*, 518 U.S. 604, 609–627 (1996). For more on *Colorado Republican*, see David G. Savage, "It's Party Time," *American Bar Association Journal*, February 2001, 34; Brian J. Brox, *Back in the Game: Political Party Campaigning in an Era of Reform* (Buffalo: State University of New York, 2013), 157; Henrik M. Schatzinger and

Steven E. Martin, *Game Changers: How Dark Money and Super PACs Are Changing U.S. Campaigns* (Lanham, MD: Rowman and Littlefield, 2020), 37.

40. For Kennedy's opinion, see *Colorado Republican Federal Campaign Committee v. Federal Election Commission*, 518 U.S. 604, 627–631 (1999) (Kennedy, J., concurring in part). For Thomas's opinion, see *Colorado Republican Federal Campaign Committee v. Federal Election Commission*, 518 U.S. 604, 648 (1996) (Thomas, J., concurring in part).
41. Charles Bell, "A Practitioner's View of *Colorado Republican Federal Campaign Committee v. Federal Election Commission*," *Free Speech and Election Law Practice Group Newsletter*, December 1, 1996, https://fedsoc.org/commentary/publications/a-practitioner-s-view-of-colorado-republican-federal-campaign-committee-v-federal-election-commission, accessed January 8, 2021.
42. Bernard Weinraub, "Politics: The Anger in Bob Dole Is One Key to His Power," *New York Times*, February 8, 1988, A15.
43. On the 1996 GOP field, see Thomas B. Edsall and Mario Brassario, "A Wide Divide in Constituencies," *Washington Post*, February 13, 1996, A1; David S. Broder and Kevin S. Merida, "Buchanan Urges Foes of Abortion to Rally Support," *Washington Post*, February 11, 1996, A24; Richard L. Berke, "Fight for Religious Right's Vote Turns Bitter," *New York Times*, February 10, 1996, A1.
44. On NRLC's effort to rally social conservatives, see National Right to Life Committee, Press Release, "Clean Sweep: National Right to Life Hails Pro-Life Republican Platform, Pro-Life Republican Primary Victories" (August 6, 1996), JBP, Matter Boxes, File 1327; NRLC Fundraising Script for Dole/Kemp (Fall 1996), JBP, Matter Boxes, File 1327; NRLC Fundraising Letter (September 22, 1996), JBP, Matter Boxes, File 1327; Karen Huggard to David N. O'Steen and Darla St. Martin (September 4, 1996), JBP, Matter Boxes, File 1327; Michelle Arocha Allen to Reporters and Journalists (October 22, 1996), JBP, Matter Boxes, File 1327.
45. On Dole's effort to move to the middle on abortion, see Adam Nagourney, "Dole Declares That His Running Mate Could Support Abortion Rights," *New York Times*, July 2, 1996, A1; Linda Feldmann, "Dole Shifts to the Center—Will His Party Follow?" *Christian Science Monitor*, June 14, 1996, 3; Richard L. Berke, "Dole Sends Message of Inclusion to Abortion-Rights Republicans," *New York Times*, July 22, 1996, 1. For Dole's position on the platform, see Richard L. Berke, "Filling in Blanks on Abortion Issue, Dole Creates Stir," *New York Times*, June 11, 1996, A1; Katherine Q. Seelye, "Under Pressure, Dole Reconsiders Abortion Plank," *New York Times*, July 13, 1996, 1. On Long Tobias, see Kathryn Jean Lopez, "I Am Woman, Waging War on Women?" *National Review*, April 25, 2011, https://www.nationalreview.com/2011/04/i-am-woman-waging-war-women-kathryn-jean-lopez/, accessed September 15, 2020; "Carol Long Tobias Elected National Right to Life President," *National Right to Life News Today*, April 11, 2011, https://www.nationalrighttolifenews.org/2011/04/carol-tobias-elected-national-right-to-life-president/, accessed September 15, 2020.
46. For the Republican National Coalition for Life's press release, see Republican National Coalition for Life, *Fax Notes* (June 1996), RNCL, Box 1, Folder 7; see also

Republican National Coalition for Life, *Fax Notes* (July 1996), RNCL, Box 1, Folder 7. On the Operation Rescue protest, see Maria La Ganga and Edwin Chen, "Abortion Controversy Continues to Dog Dole," *Los Angeles Times*, June 15, 1996, A19; "Abortion Foes Denounce 'Tolerance' Plank," *Baltimore Sun*, June 12, 1996, 10A. For NRLC's response to the plank, see Katharine Q. Seelye, "Dole Seeks Words to Broaden Plank on Abortion Issue," *New York Times*, June 07, 1996, A1.

47. On the interaction between the Dole campaign and NRLC, see Huggard to O'Steen and St. Martin, 1. For NRLC's statement: Talking Points (July 19, 1996), 1, JBP, Matter Boxes, File 1327; see also Michele Arocha Miller to Reporters and Editors Re: Abortion Coverage in Election (October 22, 1996), JBP, Matter Boxes, File 1327.
48. John M. Broder, "Dole Campaign Cashes in on Its Frontrunner Image," *Los Angeles Times*, July 28, 1995, https://www.latimes.com/archives/la-xpm-1995-07-28-mn-28933-story.html, accessed January 8, 2021. On Dole's lavish fundraisers, see Ron Scherer, "At the Waldorf, It's Beef, Shrimp, and a Lot of Campaign Cash," *Christian Science Monitor*, April 17, 1995, 2; David Samuels, "Presidential Shrimp," *Harper's*, March 1, 1996, 45. On Kemp's decision not to run, see "Citing Fundraising Grind, Kemp Says He Won't Run in '96," *Chicago Tribune*, January 31, 1995, D3. On Quayle's withdrawal, see Michael Tackett, "Quayle Withdrawal Catches GOP by Surprise," *Chicago Tribune*, February 10, 1995, N3.
49. Douglas Frantz, "Patrick Buchanan: Populist Candidate Has Sophisticated and Lucrative Political Apparatus," *New York Times*, March 4, 1996, https://www.nytimes.com/1996/03/04/us/politics-patrick-j-buchanan-populist-candidate-has-sophisticated-lucrative.html, accessed January 8, 2021. On American Cause, see ibid.
50. James Bennet, "Still Loud and Unbowed: Buchanan Emerges from 8-Way Failure Unbowed and Pledging to Remain Vocal," *New York Times*, March 7, 1996, A1.
51. Linda Anderson, "Dole Wounded in Cliffhanger," *Chicago Tribune*, February 21, 1996, SW1. For more on Buchanan's primary results, see Dan Balz and Edward Walsh, "Dole Edges Buchanan in Iowa GOP Vote," *Washington Post*, February 13, 1996, A1.
52. Robert Shogan, "Buchanan Edges Dole to Win N.H.," *Los Angeles Times*, February 21, 1996, 1. For Dole's fundraising, see Stephen Barr, "Top 50 Donors to Clinton and Dole Campaigns," *Washington Post*, August 27, 1996, A9. On Koch's involvement in Dole's 1996 campaign, see "Magazine Report Questions Dole's Ties to Koch Oil Company," *AP*, March 22, 1996, https://apnews.com/article/e1593ae7f1146d5bd7e04b209d5049b6, accessed September 16, 2021; Charles Babcock and Ruth Marcus, "Dole, Inc.: The Rise of a Money Machine," *Washington Post*, August 20, 1996, https://www.washingtonpost.com/archive/politics/1996/08/20/dole-inc-the-rise-of-a-money-machine/e0b6fa5d-b95d-4ebb-b82c-73ade72f6306/, accessed September 16, 2021.
53. For the Annenberg Center report, see Deborah Beck, Paul Taylor, Jeffrey Stranger, and Douglas Rivlin, "Issue Advocacy Advertising during the 1996 Election," Annenberg Public Policy Center, 1996, https://cdn.annenbergpublicpolicycenter.org/wp-content/uploads/REP161.pdf, accessed March 3, 2020. On the total

amount of soft money spending in 1996, see "Soft Money: A Look at the Loopholes," *Washington Post*, 1998, https://www.washingtonpost.com/wp-srv/politics/special/campfin/intro4.htm, accessed September 12, 2021. On the surge in soft money, see Charles Babcock and Ruth Marcus, "A Hard-Charging Flood of 'Soft Money,' " *Washington Post*, October 24, 1996, A1; Paul West, "Flood of Money Drowns Election Finance Reform," *Baltimore Sun*, October 31, 1996, 1A; Leslie Wayne, "Loopholes Allow Presidential Race to Set a Record," *New York Times*, September 1, 1996, 1. For scholarship on the potential impact of primary spending on candidate success, see Audrey Haynes, Paul-Henri Gurian, and Stephen M. Nichols, "The Role of Candidate Spending in Presidential Nomination Contests," *Journal of Politics* 59 (1997); Michael J. Goff, *The Money Primary: The New Politics of the Early Presidential Nomination Process* (Lanham, MD: Rowman and Littlefield, 2004), 3–15; Randall Adkins and Andrew Dowdle, "Continuity and Change in the Presidential Money Primary," *American Review of Politics* 28 (2008).

54. For NRLC's spin on the 1996 election results, see Carol Long to State Officers et al. (November 7, 1996), JBP, Matter Boxes, File 1327. For RNC-Life's position, see Phyllis Schlafly to Republican National Coalition for Life (December 1996), RNCL, Box 1, Folder 7.

55. See Thomas B. Edsall, "GOP Faces New Abortion Debate," *Washington Post*, December 30, 1997, A3; Richard L. Berke, "Chairman of Republican National Committee Fights 'Litmus Test' on Abortion," *New York Times*, January 7, 1998, A4.

56. On congressional probes of the 1996 election, see Janet Hook and Mark Lacey, "GOP Presses for Outside Counsel in Donor Probe," *Los Angeles Times*, March 5, 1997, A13; Helen Dewar, "Chairman Wants $6.5 Million for Campaign Finance Probe," *Washington Post*, January 30, 1996, A1; David Savage and Richard Serrano, "Clinton Not Told of China Donation Plan, Aides Insist," *Los Angeles Times*, March 10, 1997, A1.

57. "The Twenty-Fourth Conservative Political Action Conference," *Human Events*, March 21, 1997, 12.

58. On the California proposition, see "California and the West: Campaign Funding Limits Go on Trial," *Los Angeles Times*, November 3, 1997, A3. On the spread of campaign finance laws in the states, see Dana Milbank, "Campaign-Finance Reformers Pin Hopes on the States," *Wall Street Journal*, December 26, 1997, A10. On the subpoenas sent to advocacy groups, see Neil A. Lewis, "Nonprofit Groups to Defy Subpoenas in Senate Inquiry," *New York Times*, September 4, 1997, A16; Eliza Newlin Carney, "Abortion Foes Fight the 'Speech Police,' " *National Journal*, November 22, 1997, 2378–2379.

59. For Bopp's statement about a legal fund: National Right to Life Committee Board Meeting Minutes (April 11, 1997), JBP, Matter Boxes, File 1395. For Weyrich's statement about a partnership with the GOP: Life Forum Meeting Minutes (October 24, 1997), JBP, Matter Boxes, File 1395; see also Life Forum Meeting Minutes (July 25, 1997), PWP, Box 80, Folder 12. For Long's statement: National Right to Life Committee, Board of Directors Meeting Minutes (January 18–19, 1997), JBP, Matter Boxes, File 1395.

60. James Bopp Jr., *Colorado Right to Life Committee v. Buckley* Notes (Summer 1997), JBP, Matter Boxes, File 2538. For Lott's view, see John R. Lott Jr., Report to Robert Niemeyer on Colorado's Amendment 15, (June 13, 1997), JBP, Matter Boxes, File 2538. For more on this strategy during the California case, see Trial Transcript, *California Pro-Life Action Council v. Scully*, Civ. S. 96-96-1965 (E.D. Cal. 1997), 24–30, JBP, Matter Boxes, File 2538. For other arguments on which Lott drew, see Southworth, "Speech," 7–36.
61. See Michael Grunewald, "Campaign Finance Issue Divides Abortion Foes," *Washington Post*, September 14, 1999, A1; Terry Cooper, "The Big Bopper," *American Bar Association Journal*, November 24, 2006, https://www.abajournal.com/magazine/article/the_big_bopper, accessed July 13, 2020.
62. Jane Mayer, "Betsy DeVos, Trump's Big-Donor Education Secretary," *New Yorker*, November 23, 2016, https://www.newyorker.com/news/news-desk/betsy-devos-trumps-big-donor-education-secretary, accessed July 13, 2020. On DeVos, see Sarah Pulliam Bailey, "Betsy DeVos, Trump's Education Secretary, Is a Billionaire with Deep Ties to the Christian Reformed Community," *Washington Post*, November 23, 2016, https://www.washingtonpost.com/news/acts-of-faith/wp/2016/11/23/betsy-devos-trumps-education-pick-is-a-billionaire-philanthropist-with-deep-ties-to-the-reformed-christian-community/, accessed July 13, 2020; Katherine Stewart, "Betsy DeVos and God's Plan for Schools," *New York Times*, December 13, 2020, https://www.nytimes.com/2016/12/13/opinion/betsy-devos-and-gods-plan-for-schools.html, accessed July 13, 2020.
63. James Bopp to Trustees of the James Madison Center for Free Speech (December 8, 1997), JBP, Digital Records, Madison Center File. On the Madison Center leadership, see James Madison Center, Inc., "Board of Directors/Officers/Trustees," (n.d., ca. 1997), JBP, Digital Records, Madison Center File. On the group's original budget, see James Madison Center, Inc., Proposed Budget 1998 (December 1997), JBP, Digital Records, Madison Center File.
64. See Bopp to Trustees, 1–8. For the decision in *Right to Life of Dutchess County*, see *Right to Life of Dutchess County, Inc. v. Federal Election Commission*, 6 F.Supp. 2d 248 (S.D.N.Y. 1998). For the decision in *Klepper*, see *Klepper v. Christian Coalition of New York*, 259 A.D.2d 926 (N.Y. App. Div. 1999). For the decision in *Clifton*, see *Clifton v. Federal Election Commission*, 114 F.3d 1309 (1st Cir. 1997). On the sources of the Madison Center's funding, see Southworth, "Speech," 56.
65. See Bopp to Trustees, 7–8. For the decision in the Arkansas contribution case, see *Russell v. Burris*, 146 F.3d 563 (8th Cir. 1998).
66. Bopp to Trustees, 7–8. On the early litigation in *Sorrell*, see *Vermont Right to Life v. Sorrell*, 875 F.Supp. 2d 376 (D. Vt. 1998). On Lake's research, see Declaration of Celinda Lake, 10–15, *Randall v. Sorrell* and *Landell v. Sorrell* (Civ. Actions 2:99-CV-146, 2:99-CV-234) (2000), JBP, Matter Boxes, File 2538. Bopp and his colleagues believed that Lake's survey had slanted voters' responses by highlighting the influence of "special interests" and downplaying the role played by the media and other entities. See Deposition of Celinda Lake, April 5, 2000, *Randall v. Sor-*

rell and *Landell v. Sorrell* (Civ. Actions 2:99-CV-146, 2:99-CV-234) (2000), JBP, Matter Boxes, File 2538.

67. For the early litigation in the California case, see *California Pro-Life Council Political Action Committee v. Scully*, 989 F.Supp. 1282, 1299 (E.D. Ca. 1998).

68. Ibid. On the Eighth Circuit's jurisprudence on contributions, see *Russell v. Burris*, 146 F.3d 563 (8th Cir. 1998); *Shrink Missouri Government PAC v. Adams*, 161 F.3d 519 (8th Cir. 1998); *Minnesota Citizens Concerned for Life v. Federal Election Commission*, 113 F.3d 129 (8th Cir. 1997).

69. On support for campaign finance reform, see "USA Today/CNN/Gallup Poll Results," *USA Today*, February 11, 2002, 14, http://www.usatoday/com/news/2002–02–11-poll.html, accessed October 13, 2004. For McCain's letter and the dispute that it produced, see Allison Mitchell, "Foes of Abortion Split Sharply over Campaign Finance Bill," *New York Times*, March 26, 1998, A21. For more examples of this dispute, see John McCain, Dear Colleague Letter (February 11, 1998), JBP, Matter Boxes, File 1395; Letters from Senator John McCain and Letter of Response from National Right to Life Committee, February 25, 1998, https://www.nrlc.org/federal/freespeech/mccainbishop/, accessed March 3, 2020. For Johnson's response: Letter of Response from National Right to Life Committee, 1.

70. NRLC Legislative Alert (April 4, 1998), 4, JBP, Matter Boxes, File 1931. On the discharge petition, see Lizette Alvarez, "Novel Petition Drive May Save House Campaign Finance Bill," *New York Times*, April 18, 1998, https://www.nytimes.com/1998/04/18/us/novel-petition-drive-may-save-house-campaign-finance-bill.html, accessed March 3, 2020; Edwin Chen, "House Backs Bill to Reform Election Funding," *Los Angeles Times*, August 4, 1998, https://www.latimes.com/archives/la-xpm-1998-aug-04-mn-10020-story.html, accessed March 3, 2020.

71. Republican National Coalition for Life, Press Release (August 11, 1998), JBP, Matter Boxes, File 1931.

72. John Gizzi, "RNC Smacks McCain Campaign Bill, Calls for No Limit to Contributions," *Human Events*, August 7, 1998, 4. For McConnell's statement: Allison Mitchell, "Bill to Overhaul Campaign Finance Survives in the House," *New York Times*, August 1, 1998, 1.

73. For the decision in *Vermont Right to Life*, see *Vermont Right to Life v. Sorrell*, 875 F.Supp. 2d 376 (D. Vt. 1998). For the decision in *Arkansas Right to Life PAC*, see *Arkansas Right to Life State Political Action Committee v. Butler*, 29 F.Supp. 2d 540 (W.D. Ark. 1998).

74. On the Republican primary field, see George Will, "Early Aspirants," *Washington Post*, January 6, 1999, A25; Peter A. Brown, "Who Will Emerge from the GOP Field?" *Orlando Sentinel*, February 21, 1999, G1; Richard L. Berke, "Bush Announces a Record Haul, and Foes Make Money an Issue," *New York Times*, July 1, 1999, A1.

75. For the early litigation in *Shrink PAC*, see *Shrink Missouri Government PAC v. Adams*, 5 F.Supp. 2d 734 (E.D. Mo. 1998); *Shrink Missouri Government PAC v. Adams*, 161 F.3d 519 (5th Cir. 1998).

76. *Shrink PAC* Amici Meeting (March 30, 1999), JBP, Matter Boxes, File 1602; Notes from *Shrink PAC* Amici Meeting (March 30, 1999), JBP, Matter Boxes, File 1602. On Keene, see Andy Barr, "The Complex Legacy of David Keene," *Politico*, February 13, 2011, https://www.politico.com/story/2011/02/the-complex-legacy-of-david-keene-049445, accessed July 13, 2020; "David Keene," *NRA on the Record*, http://nraontherecord.org/david-keene/, accessed July 13, 2020.
77. See *Shrink PAC* Amici Meeting (March 30, 1999), 1–6. For more on Allison Hayward, see "Allison R. Hayward," *The Federalist Society*, https://fedsoc.org/contributors/allison-hayward, accessed July 13, 2020. On the *Shrink PAC* meeting, see Revised List (4/19/99) of Attendees of *Shrink PAC* Amici Meeting and Potential Amici (1999), JBP, Matter Box 1602.
78. On Shapiro: Marcia Coyle, "Steven Shapiro, 'Jagger' of Civil Liberties, Reflects on ACLU Career, Challenges," *Supreme Court Brief*, July 13, 2016, https://www.law.com/supremecourtbrief/almID/1202762459860/steven-shapiro-jagger-of-civil-liberties-reflects-on-aclu-career-challenges/, accessed July 13, 2020; Natalie Singer, "Freedom Fighter," *Harvard Law Today*, October 1, 2012, https://today.law.harvard.edu/qa-a-conversation-with-steven-r-shapiro-75/, accessed July 13, 2020. On La Pierre, see Nathaniel Sheppard Jr., "Problems Seen for St. Louis School," *New York Times*, March 10, 1983, A20.
79. Notes from *Shrink PAC* Meeting, 2–5.
80. "Possible Arguments against Contribution Limits for *Shrink PAC* Amicus Briefs," 1–7 (n.d., ca. 1999), JBP, Matter Boxes, File 1602.
81. Ibid., 2–6.
82. For the disputed statute: Neb. Rev. Stat. Ann. § 28-328(1) (Supp. 1999). On the litigation of dilation and extraction bans in the leadup to *Stenberg*, see *Hope Clinic v. Ryan*, 195 F.3d 857 (7th Cir. 1999); *Planned Parenthood of Greater Iowa v. Miller*, 195 F.3d 386 (8th Cir. 1999); *Eubanks v. Stengel*, 224 F.3d 576 (6th Cir. 2000); *Planned Parenthood of Central New Jersey v. Farmer*, 220 F.3d 127 (3d Cir. 2000); *Summit Medical Associates, Inc. v. Pryor*, 180 F.3d 1326 (11th Cir. 1999). On the early litigation of *Stenberg*, see *Carhart v. Stenberg*, 11 F.Supp. 2d 1099 (D. Neb. 1998); *Carhart v. Stenberg*, 11 F.Supp. 2d 1134 (D. Neb. 1998); *Carhart v. Stenberg*, 192 F.3d 1142 (8th Cir. 1999).
83. Doug Johnson to NRLC Board and State Offices et al. Re: Impending Supreme Court Ruling in *Stenberg v. Carhart* (June 19, 2000), JBP, Matter Boxes, File 1942. On NRLC's rise in power in DC, see National Right to Life Committee White Paper (November 29, 1999), JBP, Matter Boxes, File 1934.
84. On the controversy surrounding the case, see Richard L. Berke, "Lawsuit Says Christian Coalition Gave Illegal Help to Candidates," *New York Times*, July 31, 1996, A1; Ruth Marcus, "FEC Files Suit over Christian Coalition Role," *Washington Post*, https://www.washingtonpost.com/archive/politics/1996/07/31/fec-files-suit-over-christian-coalition-role/38535dd6-b355–4872-b828–309cb50c480b/, accessed September 16, 2020; Bill Miller and Susan Glasser, "A Victory for the Christian Coalition," *Washington Post*, August 3, 1999, A1.

85. For the district court's decision in *Christian Coalition*, see *Federal Election Commission v. Christian Coalition*, 52 F.Supp. 2d 45, 82–93, 94–99 (D.D.C. 1999). For Bopp's framing of the issue: James Bopp Jr., "Free Speech and the Christian Coalition Case," *The Federalist*, Summer 1999, 1, https://fedsoc.org/commentary/publications/free-speech-and-the-christian-coalition-case, accessed March 3, 2020.
86. On RMIC, see Karl Gallant, RMIC Fundraising Letter (November 8, 2000), JBP, Matter Boxes, File 2453; RMIC Advertising Scripts (November 6, 2000), JBP, Matter Box 2453; RMIC Fundraising Appeal (December 30, 2000), JBP, Matter Boxes, File 2453; Karl Gallant to Curt Anderson and Tom Smith (January 12, 2001), JBP, Matter Boxes, File 2453; see also Susan Glasser, "DeLay Advisers' Fundraising Goal: An Unfettered $25 Million," *Washington Post*, May 27, 1999, A14; Frank Greve, "Group May Be Big Boon to Right's Coffers," *Charleston Gazette*, August 7, 1999, 1. For more on Bopp's involvement with 527s, see "527 Menace," *Roll Call*, September 23, 1999, 1; Jim Van DeHei and Damon Chappie, "Veiled Groups Draw Scrutiny," *Roll Call*, September 20, 1999, 1. RMIC would later propose a variety of projects, including "a national effort to isolate the political operations of the National Education Association teachers' union" and a push to ensure the confirmation of John Ashcroft as attorney general. Republican Majority Issues Coalition, Project Prospectus (n.d., ca. 2001), JBP, Matter Boxes, File 2453; Gallant to Anderson and Smith, 1.
87. *Nixon v. Shrink Missouri Government PAC*, 528 U.S. 327, 386–398 (2000).
88. Ibid., 397. For more on the significance of *Shrink PAC*, see Martin Redish, *Money Talks: Speech, Economic Power, and the Values of Democracy* (New York: New York University Press, 2001), 115–121. For coverage of the decision, see Jan Crawford Greenburg, "Top Court Boosts Campaign Reform," *Chicago Tribune*, January 25, 2000, 1; David G. Savage, "Supreme Court Backs Political Donor Limits," *Los Angeles Times*, January 25, 2000, A1; Adam Clymer, "Court's Ruling Heartens Soft Money's Opponents," *New York Times*, January 25, 2000, A1.
89. Greenburg, "Top Court," 1. For the dissenting opinions: *Nixon v. Shrink Missouri Government PAC*, 528 U.S. 327, 404–410 (2000) (Kennedy, J., dissenting); ibid., 410–430 (Thomas, J., dissenting). For more on the political fallout from *Shrink PAC*, see Lyle Denniston, "Campaign Gift Limits Affirmed," *Baltimore Sun*, January 25, 2000, 1.
90. For the Court's decision in *Stenberg*, see *Stenberg v. Carhart*, 530 U.S. 914, 936–937 (2000). For contemporary discussion of the *Stenberg* decision, see Edward Walsh and Amy Goldstein, "Supreme Court Upholds Two Key Abortion Rights," *Washington Post*, June 29, 2000, A1; Edward Lazarus, "Court Crackup," *Washington Post*, July 25, 2000, A23; George F. Will, "An Act of Judicial Infamy," *Washington Post*, June 29, 2000, A31; Philip J. Hilts, "The Reaction: Doctors Express Relief over Decision: Foes of Abortion Vow to Continue Their Fight," *New York Times*, June 30, 2000, A20.
91. On the spread of 527s, see Ruth Marcus, "Hidden Assets," *Washington Post*, May 15, 2000, A1; Greg Hitt, " '527 Groups' Use Tax Loopholes to Promote Politicians,"

Wall Street Journal, May 25, 2000, A28. On the new regulation of 527s, see William Neikirk, "Senate Joins House to Close Campaign Finance Loophole," *Chicago Tribune*, June 30, 2000, 1; Mike Allen, "Campaign Secrecy Law's Impact Doubted," *Washington Post*, July 1, 2000, A6.

92. For the district court's decision, see *Landell v. Sorrell*, 118 F.Supp. 2d 459 (D. Vt. 2000). For Bopp's take on the decision, see Carey Goldberg, "Vermont Ruling Redefines Campaign Finance Law," *New York Times*, August 11, 2000, A10.

Chapter 5. Corporate Free Speech

1. For the district court's decision in *Beaumont*, see *Beaumont v. Federal Election Commission*, 137 F.Supp. 2d 648 (E.D. N.C. 2000). For the Court's decision in *Massachusetts Citizens for Life*, see *Federal Election Commission v. Massachusetts Citizens for Life*, 479 U.S. 238 (1986). For more on the suit, see "Right to Life Group Challenges Federal and State Campaign Laws," *Greensboro News Record*, January 13, 2000, B5; "The Right Ear," *Human Events*, October 13, 2000, 24. On the Wabash Valley Classic, see "Nobles Have High Hopes in 2000," *Noblesville Ledger*, November 24, 2000, 11; "Red Hill among 12 to Play in Wabash Classic," *Vincennes Sun-Commercial*, April 16, 2000, C8.
2. "Chief Justice Rehnquist on Stare Decisis" (n.d., ca. 2000), 2–6, JBP, Matter Boxes, File 2274.
3. See ibid.; see also Respondent's Brief, 13–39, *Federal Election Commission v. Beaumont*, 539 U.S. 146 (2003) (No. 02-403).
4. "The Region: N.C. Right to Life Cites Free Speech," *Wilmington Morning Star*, January 13, 2000, 2B. For the district court's decision in *Beaumont*, see *Beaumont v. Federal Election Commission*, 137 F.Supp. 2d 648 (E.D. N.C. 2000).
5. On NRLC's efforts to help Bush, see National Right to Life Committee, "Compare the Candidates" (n.d., ca. 2000), JBP, Matter Boxes, File 2264; National Right to Life Committee Board of Directors Meeting Minutes (February 2–4, 2000), JBP, Matter Boxes, File 2264; National Right to Life Committee, "Where Do the Candidates Stand on Abortion?" (n.d., ca. November 2000), JBP, Matter Boxes, File 2264. For an example of anti-abortion opposition to Bush, see American Life League, Press Release, "Bush's Pro-Life Honeymoon to End in Divorce" (December 21, 2000), on file with the author.
6. On Rove, see Craig Unger, *Boss Rove: Inside Karl Rove's Secret Kingdom of Power* (New York: Scribner, 2012); Karl Rove, *Courage and Conviction: My Life as a Conservative in the Fight* (New York: Simon and Schuster, 2010); Dan Balz, "Karl Rove: The Strategist," *Washington Post*, July 23, 1999, https://www.washingtonpost.com/wp-srv/politics/campaigns/wh2000/stories/rove072399.htm, accessed July 19, 2020.
7. For the statements made by Bush's campaign: Daron Shaw to Karl Rove et al. (December 8, 1999), FSP, Box 44, Email and Memos Folder 2; Jan Van Lohuizen to Karl Rove et al. (n.d., ca. 1999), FSP, Box 44, Email and Memos Folder 2; see

also Mark MacKinnon to Karl Rove et al. (June 28, 1999), FSP, Box 44, Email and Memos Folder 2. On Bush's shifting position on campaign finance during the 2000 presidential primaries, see Frank Bruni, "The Ad Campaign: Bush Attacks McCain on Finance Plan," *New York Times*, February 09, 2000, A26. For more on Rove's view of politics, see Todd Purdum, "Karl Rove's Split Personality," *Vanity Fair*, December 2006, https://www.vanityfair.com/news/2006/12/rove200612, accessed July 19, 2020.

8. Shaw to Rove et al., 2.
9. On Bush's record fundraising numbers, see Richard L. Berke, "Bush Announces a Record Haul, and Foes Make Money an Issue," *New York Times*, July 1, 1999, A1; Susan B. Glasser, "Bush to Set Record for Campaign Donations," *Washington Post*, June 30, 1999, A1. On Bauer's race, see Steve Johnson, "New Hampshire, Footwear, Presidential Politics—and Madonna," *Chicago Tribune*, February 4, 2000, 5. On Buchanan's campaign, see Katherine Q. Seelye, "In New Hampshire, Buchanan Rides Again," *New York Times*, March 3, 1999, https://www.nytimes.com/1999/03/03/us/in-new-hampshire-buchanan-rides-again.html, accessed February 12, 2021; B. Drummond Ayres Jr. and Michael Janofsky, "Rift on Buchanan Leads to a Split in the Reform Party," *New York Times*, August 11, 2000, A1; "Buchanan Wins Reform Party's Nomination," *Orlando Sentinel*, August 12, 2000, A4; Ruth Marcus, "Costliest Race Nears End," *Washington Post*, November 6, 2000, A1. On Hagelin, see Massie Ritsch, "Campaign 2000: For Dark Horses, the Race Can Be Lonely," *Los Angeles Times*, February 27, 2000, A3; "Campaign 2000: Trail Mix," *Los Angeles Times*, April 2, 2000, 6.
10. On television spending by parties, see Brennan Center for Justice, Press Release, "2000 Presidential Race First in Modern History Where Political Parties Spend More on TV Ads Than Candidates," December 11, 2000, https://www.brennancenter.org/our-work/analysis-opinion/2000-presidential-race-first-modern-history-where-political-parties-spend, accessed February 12, 2021; Peter Marks, "Parties Playing a Larger Role in Election Ads," *New York Times*, September 28, 2000, A1. On soft money in the 2000 race, see Don Van Natta Jr. and John M. Broder, "The 2000 Campaign: Fundraising—With Finish Line in Sight, an All-Out Race for Money," *New York Times*, November 3, 2000, https://www.nytimes.com/2000/11/03/us/2000-campaign-fund-raising-with-finish-line-sight-all-race-for-money.html, accessed February 12, 2021.
11. On the strategy used by Bush's attorneys to challenge the recount, see Bopp Complaint, *Bush v. Smith, Jones* (n.d., ca. 2000), JBP, Digital Records, Bush v. Gore File. For more on Bopp's role in *Bush v. Gore*, see Adam Winkler, *We the Corporations: How American Businesses Won Their Civil Rights* (New York: Liveright, 2018), 338–340; James Bopp Jr. and Richard Coleson, "Vote Dilution Analysis in *Bush v. Gore*," *St. Thomas Law Review* 23 (2011): 461–465. For more on *Bush v. Gore*, see Jeffrey Toobin, *Too Close to Call: The Thirty-Six-Day Battle to Decide the 2000 Election* (New York: Simon and Schuster, 2001); James T. Patterson, *Restless Giant: The United States from Watergate to* Bush v. Gore (New York: Oxford University Press, 2007), 262–300. On the soft money splurge in 2000, see Richard L. Berke, "Gore

and Bush Strategists Analyze Their Campaigns," *New York Times*, February 12, 2001, A9. On the 2000 congressional election, see Adam Clymer, "Sharply Split Congress Grapples with How to Keep Things Going," *New York Times*, December 3, 2000, 1.

12. For examples of NRLC's advocacy against McCain-Feingold in the period, see Letter to Senator, Draft 1 (March 26, 2001), JBP, Matter Boxes, File 2264; Douglas Johnson to Member of the House of Representatives Re: Shays-Meehan Campaign-Finance Reform Substitute (June 13, 2001), JBP, Matter Boxes, File 2264. On Lott's efforts to prevent a vote on BCRA, see Alison Mitchell, "Senate Leader Sits on Campaign Finance Bill," *New York Times*, May 15, 2001, A18; Helen Dewar, "Lott Holds Campaign Finance Bill in Senate," *Washington Post*, May 15, 2001, A18. On the Senate vote, see Alison Mitchell, "Senate Passes Campaign Finance Bill," *New York Times*, April 2, 2001, https://www.nytimes.com/2001/04/02/politics/senate-passes-campaign-finance-bill.html, accessed April 7, 2020.
13. Chapter 4 discusses the first round of *Colorado Republican I* in greater depth. For the Court's decision in that case, see *Colorado Republican Federal Campaign Committee v. Federal Election Commission*, 518 U.S. 504 (1996). For the litigation in the lower courts after *Colorado Republican I*, see *Federal Election Commission v. Colorado Republican Federal Campaign Committee*, 41 F.Supp. 2d 1197 (D. Colo. 1999); *Federal Election Commission v. Colorado Republican Federal Campaign Committee*, 213 F.3d 1221 (10th Cir. 2000).
14. For the committee's argument, see Brief for the Respondent, 25–33, *Federal Election Commission v. Colorado Republican Campaign Finance Committee*, 533 U.S. 431 (2001) (No. 00-191). For the government's response, see Brief for the Petitioner, 16–39, *Federal Election Commission v. Colorado Republican Campaign Finance Committee*, 533 U.S. 431 (2001) (No. 00-191). For the lower courts' decisions, see *Federal Election Commission v. Colorado Republican Federal Campaign Committee*, 41 F.Supp. 2d 1197 (D. Colo. 1999); *Federal Election Commission v. Colorado Republican Federal Campaign Committee*, 213 F.3d 1221 (10th Cir. 2000).
15. See *Federal Election Commission v. Colorado Republican Campaign Finance Committee*, 533 U.S. 431, 447–461 (2001).
16. See ibid.
17. On efforts to keep a ban alive after *Stenberg*, see PBA Contingent Ban Draft 1 (January 8, 2001), JBP, Matter Boxes, File 2264; Doug Johnson to David O'Steen and Darla St. Martin (December 29, 2000), JBP, Matter Boxes, File 2264; David N. O'Steen et al. to Karl Rove (July 13, 2000), JBP, Matter Boxes, File 2264; National Right to Life Committee, Confidential Strategy Memo on Partial-Birth Abortion Ban (February 9, 2001), JBP, Matter Boxes, File 2264; Douglas Johnson to Pat Robertson (February 2001), JBP, Matter Boxes, File 2264.
18. On Cassidy, see Mary Ziegler, *Abortion and the Law:* Roe v. Wade *to the Present* (New York: Cambridge University Press, 2020), 173–175; see also "Trial to Determine Fate of Abortion Ban," *New York Times*, September 9, 1998, B6; Patrick Mullaney, "A Father's Trial and the Case for Personhood," *Human Life Review* 27

(2001): 85–100. On Cassidy's background as a litigator, see Harold J. Cassidy: Chief Counsel, http://haroldcassidy.com/bio.html, accessed July 31, 2017.

19. See the National Foundation for Life, The Global Project, Brochure (n.d., ca. 1998), PWP, Box 80, Folder 3; The National Foundation for Life Litigation Project to Indiana Citizens for Life (November 11, 1999), JBP, Matter Boxes, File 2264; Harold Cassidy to Gail Quinn, National Conference of Catholic Bishops (September 9, 1997), PWP, Box 80, Folder 10; Marilyn Ross of the National Foundation for Life to Cathy Deeds of the National Conference of Catholic Bishops (October 24, 1997), PWP, Box 80, Folder 10; Cathy Deeds to Gail Quinn et al. Re: National Foundation for Life Strategy Meeting (December 17, 1997), PWP, Box 80, Folder 10.
20. See National Foundation for Life, Brochure, 2; see also Deeds to Quinn et al., 3.
21. On Jay Sekulow, see Steven P. Brown, *Trumping Religion: The New Christian Right, the Free Speech Clause, and the Courts* (Tuscaloosa: University of Alabama Press, 2002), 37; Katherine Stewart, *The Good News Club: The Christian Right's Stealth Assault on America's Children* (New York: Hachette, 2012), 81. On NIFLA, see Steve Schwalm, "National Institute of Family and Life Advocates," *Human Events*, August 30, 1996, 9; Patty Pensa, "Pregnancy Centers Draw Tax Money," *Sun Sentinel*, August 28, 2006, 1A; Michael Alison Chandler, "Antiabortion Groups Offer Sonograms to Further Their Cause," *Washington Post*, September 9, 2006, A1.
22. National Foundation for Life, Brochure, 3.
23. James Bopp Jr. to Betsy DeVos (February 8, 2001), JBP, Matter Boxes, File 2264; see also Betsy DeVos to James Bopp Jr. (February 11, 2001), JBP, Matter Boxes, File 2264.
24. For examples of natural law scholarship, see John Finnis, *Natural Law and Natural Rights*, 2nd ed. (New York: Oxford University Press, 2011); Robert P. George, *Making Men Moral: Civil Liberties and Public Morality* (New York: Oxford University Press, 1993); Hadley Arkes, *Natural Rights and the Right to Choose* (New York: Cambridge University Press, 2003).
25. On Neuhaus's life, see Randy Boyagoda, *Richard John Neuhaus: A Life in the Public Square* (New York: Crown, 2015). For Arkes's memories of Neuhaus, see Hadley Arkes, "First Things First," *First Things*, April 9, 2009, https://www.firstthings.com/article/2009/04/001-first-things-first, accessed July 19, 2020. On Arkes's work on natural law, see "Arkes Inspires New Natural Law Institute," *Amherst College*, https://www.amherst.edu/academiclife/faculty_achievements/node/435597, accessed July 19, 2020; Hadley Arkes, "A New Natural Law Manifesto," *James Wilson Institute*, 2011, http://jwinst.org/about/a-natural-law-manifesto, accessed July 19, 2020.
26. Hadley Arkes, "Right to Choose, or License to Kill?" *Weekly Standard*, November 15, 1999, https://www.washingtonexaminer.com/weekly-standard/right-to-choose-or-license-to-kill, accessed April 7, 2020.
27. Hadley Arkes to Richard John Neuhaus (June 12, 1998), RJN, Box 3, Folder 27.
28. Ibid.; see also Hadley Arkes to Richard John Neuhaus (June 22, 1998), RJN, Box 3, Folder 27; Hadley Arkes to Richard John Neuhaus (May 17, 2002), RJN, Box 3,

Folder 28; Hadley Arkes to Richard John Neuhaus (March 29, 2002), RJN, Box 3, Folder 28.

29. See Press Release, "President Signs Born-Alive Act," *The White House*, August 2002, https://georgewbush-whitehouse.archives.gov/news/releases/2002/08/20020805-6.html, accessed April 7, 2020. For more on the roots of the language used in Bush's signing statement, see Mary Ziegler, *After* Roe: *The Lost History of the Abortion Debate* (Cambridge, MA: Harvard University Press, 2015), 42–65.

30. On the Enron scandal and its significance, see Kurt Eichenwald, *Conspiracy of Fools: A True Story* (New York: Random House, 2005); Jerry W. Markham, *A Financial History of Modern U.S. Corporate Scandals from Enron to Reform* (New York: Taylor and Francis, 2015), 20–123; Charles R. Geisst, *Wall Street: A History from Its Beginnings to the Fall of Enron* (New York: Oxford University Press, 2004), 399–407. On Enron's financial reach (including its donations to those who would later investigate the fallen corporation), see Don Van Natta Jr., "Enron or Andersen Made Donations to Almost All Their Congressional Investigators," *New York Times*, January 25, 2002, C4; William Brittain-Catlin, *Offshore: The Dark Side of the Global Economy* (New York: Farrar, Straus and Giroux, 2007), 83–84.

31. On the Senate vote, see David Rogers, "Senate Approves Measure to Curb Big Donations," *Wall Street Journal*, March 21, 2002, A24; Alison Mitchell, "Campaign Finance Bill Wins Final Approval in Congress and Bush Says He'll Sign It," *New York Times*, March 21, 2002, A1. For Bush's statement, see George W. Bush, "Statement on Senate Passage of Campaign Finance Reform Legislation," *Weekly Compilation of Presidential Documents*, March 25, 2002, 473–474.

32. See Bradley A. Smith, "Politics, Money, and Corruption: The Story of *McConnell v. Federal Election Commission*," in *Election Law Stories*, ed. Joshua A. Douglas and Eugene D. Mazo (New York: Foundation, 2016), 340–341.

33. On the effect of BCRA, see Richard Briffault, "The Future of Reform: Campaign Finance Reform After the Bipartisan Campaign Reform Act of 2002," *Arizona State Law Review* 32 (2002): 1179–1183; Gregory Comeau, "Bipartisan Campaign Reform Act," *Harvard Journal on Legislation* 40 (2003): 253–282. For the description of soft money: *McConnell v. Federal Election Commission*, 540 U.S. 93, 122 (2003).

34. For the text of BCRA, see 2 U.S.C. §§ 101 et seq.

35. See Brief for Appellants/Cross-Appellees Mitch McConnell et al., 10–27, 36–42, *McConnell v. Federal Election Commission*, 540 U.S. 93 (2003) (No. 02-1674).

36. Reply Brief of Plaintiffs-Appellees National Right to Life Committee, 7–9, *McConnell v. Federal Election Commission*, 540 U.S. 93 (2003) (No. 02-1674). For McConnell's statement: Brief for Appellants/Cross-Appellees Mitch McConnell et al., 22–23.

37. See Brief of Plaintiffs-Appellees National Right to Life Committee, 3–39, *McConnell v. Federal Election Commission*, 540 U.S. 93 (2003) (No. 02-1674); Brief for Appellants/Cross-Appellees Mitch McConnell et al., 42–50.

38. Brief for Intervenor-Defendants John McCain et al., 11–40, *McConnell v. Federal Election Commission*, 540 U.S. 93 (2003) (No. 02-1674).

39. Ibid., 42–73.

40. On the spread of soft money in the 2002 campaign, see Tom Hamburger, "With Soft Money on Way out, Firms Get in Last Binge," *Wall Street Journal*, November 5, 2002, A1; Adam Clymer, "Fund-raising Gives GOP Big Lead in Last Cycle," *New York Times*, March 19, 2003, A26. On the growth of soft money since 2000, see Federal Election Commission, "Party Fundraising Reaches $1.1 Billion in 2002 Election Cycle," December 18, 2002, https://www.fec.gov/updates/party-fundraising-reaches-11-billion-in-2002-election-cycle/, accessed April 7, 2020.
41. See National Right to Life Committee, "Recent Developments on Partial-Birth Abortion" (March 28, 2003), JBP, Matter Boxes, File 2270. On the results of the 2002 election, see Robin Toner and Carl Hulse, "Congress: By Acquiring Full Control of Congress, Republicans Gained New Responsibility," *New York Times*, November 10, 2002, https://www.nytimes.com/2002/11/10/us/2002-election-congress-acquiring-full-control-congress-republicans-gained-new.html, accessed April 7, 2021. On the record compiled in *McConnell*, see Smith, "Politics, Money, and Corruption," 340–345. Bopp sent extensive interrogatories to the intervenors, including Senators McCain and Feingold, seeking information on whether special interests had funded the push for BCRA—and whether reformers themselves received considerable sums from corporations and unions, violated election law, or involved themselves in anything that could be considered corruption. See Intervenors Response to Interrogatories, *McConnell v. Federal Election Commission et al.* (August 19, 2002) (Civ. No. 02-874), JBP, Matter Boxes, File 2734; Plaintiff Republican National Committee's Second Set of Interrogatories to Defendants, *McConnell v. Federal Election Commission et al.* (2002) (Civ. No 02-874), JBP, Matter Boxes, File 2734.
42. See Statement of Purpose and Executive Summary, "Planned Parenthood and the Right to Life: Comparison of Organization and an Outline of a New Strategy to Stop Abortion" (September 2002), JBP, Matter Boxes, File 2343; Charles Donovan, Executive Summary Notes (September 2002), JBP, Matter Boxes, File 2343. On the early work of the Culture of Life Leadership Coalition, see Letter to Culture of Life Leadership Coalition Leader (April 15, 2003), JBP, Matter Boxes, File 2343.
43. Presentation of Public Relations Group (April 29, 2003), 1–8, JBP, Matter Boxes, File 2343. For the conclusions of the Legal Working Group: Culture of Life Leadership Coalition Legal Working Group, Preliminary Report (2003), 1–14, JBP, Matter Boxes, File 2343.
44. On the role played by partial-birth abortion in the coalition's work, see Legal Working Group, Preliminary Report, 1–6.
45. *Federal Election Commission v. Beaumont*, 539 U.S. 146, 154 (2003).
46. Ibid., 160.
47. *McConnell v. Federal Election Commission*, 540 U.S. 93, 138–139 (2003). For more on the significance of *McConnell*, see Melvin Urofsky, *The Campaign Finance Cases:* Buckley, McConnell, Citizens United, *and* McCutcheon (Lawrence: University Press of Kansas, 2020), 102–115; Melvin Urofsky, *Money and Speech: Campaign Finance Reform and the Courts* (Ann Arbor: University of Michigan Press, 2005),

113–125; Timothy Kuhner, *Capitalism v. Democracy: Money in Politics and the Free Market Constitution* (Palo Alto: Stanford University Press, 2014), 101–115.

48. *McConnell v. Federal Election Commission*, 540 U.S. 93, 140–143 (2003).

49. Ibid., 189–191.

50. See Gail Russell Chaddock, "As Politics Flare, Judicial Appointments Take a 'Recess,' " *Christian Science Monitor*, April 6, 2004, 3. On the early days of the filibuster, see Jan Crawford Greenburg, "Democrats Vow Filibuster to Bar Judicial Nominee," *Chicago Tribune*, February 12, 2003, 1; Helen Dewar, "GOP Escalates Push for Nominees," *Washington Post*, July 26, 2003, A1. On the recess appointment issue, see Neil A. Lewis, "Bush Seats Judge After Long Fight, Bypassing Senate," *New York Times*, January 17, 2004, A1; Robert S. Greenberger, "Pickering Flap Widens Split on Court Nominees," *Wall Street Journal*, January 19, 2004, A4. For more on recess appointments, see Scott E. Graves and Robert M. Howard, *Justice Takes a Recess: Judicial Recess Appointments from George Washington to George W. Bush* (Lanham, MD: Lexington, 2009).

51. On Bush's contribution haul, see Richard Simon, "In Race for Funds, Bush Is the Winner," *Los Angeles Times*, January 8, 2004, A8.

52. See James Bopp Jr., "527 Rules: Tempting but Not Needed," *Roll Call*, February 2, 2004, 1. On the explosion of 527 spending, see Michael Janofsky, "Advocacy Groups Spend Record Amount on 2004 Election," *New York Times*, December 17, 2004, https://www.nytimes.com/2004/12/17/politics/advocacy-groups-spent-record-amount-on-2004-election.html, accessed April 7, 2004; Michael Dorf, "Why 527 Groups Can't Be Silenced," *CNN*, August 31, 2004, https://www.cnn.com/2004/LAW/08/31/dorf.527s/index.html, accessed April 7, 2020. For more on 527s, see Melissa Smith, Glenda Williams, Larry Powell, and Gary Copeland, *Campaign Finance Reform: The Political Shell Game* (Lanham, MD: Lexington, 2010), 105; Michael C. Dorf, *No Litmus Test: Law versus Politics in the Twenty-First Century* (Lanham, MD: Rowman and Littlefield, 2006), 73–76. For the FEC's fining of Swift Boat, see Peter Overby, "FEC Fines '527' Groups, Including Swift Boat Vets," *NPR*, December 14, 2006, https://www.npr.org/templates/story/story.php?storyId=6623828, accessed September 12, 2021.

53. James Bopp Jr. and Richard Coleson to Amici Curiae in *Wisconsin Right to Life* (October 25, 2005), JBP, Digital Records, *Citizens United* Folder.

54. See ibid. For the district court's decision, see *Wisconsin Right to Life v. Federal Election Commission*, 2004 WL 3622736 (D.D.C. 2004).

55. On the South Dakota campaign, Ziegler, *Abortion and the Law*, 175.

56. Roger Rieger to Pro-Life Colleagues (December 21, 2004), JBP, Matter Boxes, Harold Cassidy File. For the report, see Report of the South Dakota Commission to Study Abortion (December 2005), JBP, Matter Boxes, Harold Cassidy File. For a criticism of the approach, see Paul Benjamin Linton to Harold Cassidy (July 15, 2004), JBP, Matter Boxes, Harold Cassidy File.

57. See Peter Baker, "Bush Nominates Roberts as Chief Justice," *Washington Post*, September 6, 2005, A1; Richard Stevenson, "A Surprise Move: Critical Swing Vote—Bush's First Chance to Pick Justice," *New York Times*, July 2, 2005, A1;

Linda Greenhouse, "Despite Rumors, Rehnquist Has No Plans to Retire Now," *New York Times,* July 15, 2005, A10. On O'Connor's retirement, see Elisabeth Bumiller and Carl Hulse, "Bush Picks U.S. Appeals Judge to Take O'Connor's Court Seat," *New York Times,* November 1, 2005, A1; Sheryl Gay Stolberg and Elizabeth Bumiller, "Senate Confirms Roberts as 17th Chief Justice," *New York Times,* September 30, 2005, A1, https://www.nytimes.com/2005/09/30/politics/politicsspecial1/senate-confirms-roberts-as-17th-chief-justice.html, accessed April 8, 2020; Adam Liptak, "Alito Vote May Be Decisive in Marquee Cases This Term," *New York Times,* February 1, 2006, A1.

58. See Michael J. Klarman, *From the Closet to the Altar: Courts, Backlash and the Struggle for Same-Sex Marriage* (New York: Oxford University Press, 2013), 75–119; Daniel R. Pinello, *America's Struggle for Same-Sex Marriage* (New York: Cambridge University Press, 2006), 145–187; George Chauncey, *Why Marriage? The History Shaping Today's Debate over Gay Equality* (New York: Basic Books, 2004), 137–189. For the decision in *Goodridge,* see *Goodridge v. Department of Public Health,* 798 N.E.2d 941 (Mass. 2003).

59. See E. J. Kessler, "Parley Exposing Rift among Types of Conservatives," *Forward,* March 4, 2005, 1. On the debate about same-sex marriage and the full faith and credit clause, see Joseph William Singer, "Same Sex Marriage, Full Faith and Credit, and the Evasion of Obligation," *Stanford Journal of Civil Rights and Civil Liberties* 1 (2005): 1–12; William A. Reppy Jr., "The Framework of Full Faith and Credit and Interstate Recognition of Same-Sex Marriages," *Ava Maria Law Review* 3 (2005): 393–403; Patrick J. Borchers, "The Essential Irrelevance of the Full Faith and Credit Clause to the Same Sex Marriage Debate," *Creighton Law Review* 38:353–364 (2004–5); William N. Eskridge, "Credit Is Due," *New Republic,* June 16, 1996, https://newrepublic.com/article/103798/credit-due, accessed April 8, 2020. On social conservatives' threat to withhold support for Social Security, see David D. Kirkpatrick and Sheryl Gay Stolberg, "Backers of Gay Marriage Ban Use Social Security as a Cudgel," *New York Times,* January 25, 2005, A17; Janet Hook, "Social Security Overhaul Splinters GOP," *Los Angeles Times,* March 6, 2005, A30.

60. See Nicole Hemmer, *Messengers of the Right: Conservative Media and the Transformation of American Politics* (Philadelphia: University of Pennsylvania Press, 2016), 150–164; Brian Rosenwald, *Talk Radio's America: How an Industry Took over a Party That Took over the United States* (Cambridge, MA: Harvard University Press, 2019), 134–173.

61. Gail Russell Chaddock, "Court Nominees Will Trigger Rapid Response," *Christian Science Monitor,* July 7, 2005, 2; Tom Hamburger, "Vacancy on the Supreme Court: Process Won't Be Business as Usual," *Los Angeles Times,* July 2, 2005, A29; Jess Bravin and Jean Cummings, "Divided Ranks: In High Court Battle, First Phase Plays out among Conservatives," *Wall Street Journal,* July 5, 2005, A1.

62. On Justice Sundays, see Edward Chen and Peter Wallsten, "A Supreme Court Nominee; Conservatives, Pleased with Pick, Say Bush Kept Promise," *Los Angeles Times,* July 20, 2005, A18; David Kirkpatrick, "Christian Conservatives Will Take Aim at the Supreme Court in New Telecast," *New York Times,* July 15, 2005, A15.

63. On Roberts's self-portrayal as a neutral arbiter, see Jan Crawford Greenburg, "Roberts Testifies 'I Have No Agenda,'" *Chicago Tribune*, September 13, 2005, 1; Linda Greenhouse, "An Opening Performance Worthy of an Experienced Lawyer," *New York Times*, September 13, 2005, A29. On Roberts's earlier dealings with the abortion issue, see Jan Crawford Greenburg, "Bush Nominates Roberts," *Chicago Tribune*, July 25, 2005, 1; "Scrutinizing John Roberts," *New York Times*, July 20, 2005, A22. On Roberts's confirmation, see Stolberg and Bumiller, "Senate Confirms Roberts."
64. See David Rexrode, Republican National Committee, Re: New Information on Harriet Miers (October 3, 2005), JBP, Matter Boxes, File 2411; White House Talking Points: Harriet Miers (October 3, 2005), JBP, Matter Boxes, File 2411; Fred Barnes, Clipping, "The Nominee You Know," *Weekly Standard*, October 3, 2005, JBP, Matter Boxes, File 2411.
65. On conservative opposition to Miers, see Patrick Buchanan, Clipping, "Miers' Qualifications Are Non-existent," *Human Events*, October 3, 2005, JBP, Matter Boxes, File 2411; Richard Viguerie, Press Release, "Conservatives Feel Betrayed by the Miers Nomination" (October 3, 2005), JBP, Matter Boxes, File 2411; Amanda Carpenter, "Conservatives Unconvinced That Miers Belongs on the Court," *Human Events*, October 17, 2005, 1.
66. Robert H. Bork, "Slouching towards Miers," *Wall Street Journal*, October 19, 2005, A12. For more on the Federalist Society's opposition to Miers, see Jan Crawford Greenburg and Jeffrey Zeleny, "Push Is on to Salvage Bush Pick," *Chicago Tribune*, October 13, 2005, 1; Al Kamen, "Miers' Long-Ago Federalist Slap Still Stings," *Washington Post*, October 21, 2005, A21.
67. Leonard Leo, Memorandum to Interested Parties (October 3, 2005), JBP, Matter Boxes, File 2411; see also Charlie Savage, "Bush's Pick Has Leaned Left and Right," *Knight Ridder Tribune Business News*, October 4, 2005, 1. On conservatives' misgivings about Miers, see Jennifer Loven, "Bush Dismisses Howls from the Right, Says Miers Will Win Confirmation," *Chicago Tribune*, October 8, 2005, 1; Peter Baker and Dan Balz, "Bush Rejects Calls to Withdraw Miers," *Washington Post*, October 8, 2005, A8; Colbert I. King, "The Right on Fire over Miers," *Washington Post*, October 8, 2005, A21. On Leo, see Jeffrey Toobin, "The Conservative Pipeline to the Supreme Court," *New Yorker*, April 17, 2017, https://www.newyorker.com/magazine/2017/04/17/the-conservative-pipeline-to-the-supreme-court, accessed September 11, 2020; Melissa Quinn, "Inside the Mind of Leonard Leo, Trump's Right-hand Man on the Supreme Court," *Washington Monthly*, January 28, 2018, https://www.washingtonexaminer.com/inside-the-mind-of-leonard-leo-trumps-supreme-court-right-hand-man, accessed September 11, 2020.
68. National Right to Life Committee, Press Release (October 4, 2005), JBP, Matter Boxes, File 2411.
69. "ACLJ Calls Harriet Miers—President Bush's Supreme Court Nominee—an 'Excellent' Choice Who Embraces the Constitution and the Rule of Law," *Business Insider*, October 3, 2005, 1; see also Tom Marzen to James Bopp Jr. (October 3, 2005), JBP, Matter Boxes, File 2411.

70. See David Goldstein, "Brownback Prepared to Vote against Miers," *Knight Ridder Tribune Business News*, October 8, 2005, 1; Marcia Davis, "From the Oval Office to the Doghouse: It's Family Counseling Time for the GOP," *Washington Post*, October 8, 2005, C1; Charles Babington and Michael Fletcher, "Senators Assail Miers' Replies, Ask for Details," *Washington Post*, October 20, 2005, A1.
71. On the land deal, see Jack Douglas Jr. and Steven Henderson, "Miers' Family Received 'Excessive' Sum in Land Condemnation Case," *Knight Ridder Tribune Business News*, October 23, 2005, 1. On the website and campaign to sink Miers, see "Coalition of Conservative Groups Launch WithdrawMiers.Org," *U.S. Newswire*, October 24, 2005, 1; Michael A. Fletcher and Charles Babington, "Conservatives Escalate Opposition to Miers," *Washington Post*, October 25, 2005, A2. On the possibility that sexism had colored debate about Miers, see Jim VandeHei, "Laura Bush Echoes Sexism Charge in Miers Debate," *Washington Post*, October 12, 2005, A5.
72. On Bush's efforts to reassure social conservatives with the Alito pick, see Jeanne Cummings and Jess Bravin, "New Round: Choice of Alito for High Court Sets Stage for Ideological Battle," *Wall Street Journal*, November 1, 2005, https://www.wsj.com/articles/SB113075736648684085, accessed April 8, 2020; Rebecca Traister, "Conservative Women's Groups React to Alito Pick," *Salon*, October 31, 2005, https://www.salon.com/2005/10/31/conservative_women/, accessed April 8, 2020.
73. For the version of the law under consideration in *Randall*, see Vt. Stat. Ann., Tit. 17, § 2801 et seq. (2002). On the litigation of *Randall* in the lower courts, see *Landell v. Sorrell*, 118 F.Supp. 2d 459 (D.Vt. 2000); *Landell v. Sorrell*, 382 F.3d 91 (2d Cir. 2004).
74. On the changing meanings of *Roe*, see Ziegler, *After* Roe, 132–144.
75. Amici List (n.d., ca. 2005), JBP, Digital Records, *Citizens United* Folder; see also James Bopp Jr. and Richard Coleson, "Amici Curiae in *Wisconsin Right to Life* and *Randall v. Sorrell*" (October 10, 2005), JBP, Digital Records, *Citizens United* Folder; Amicus Conference Agenda, *Wisconsin Right to Life* and *Randall v. Sorrell* (2005), JBP, Digital Records, *Citizens United* Folder.
76. See Brief for Petitioners, 29–30, *Randall v. Sorrell*, 548 U.S. 230 (2006) (No. 04-1528). For Vermont's brief, see Brief of Respondents-Cross-Petitioners William Sorrell et al., 15–31, *Randall v. Sorrell*, 548 U.S. 230 (2006) (No. 04-1528).
77. See Brief for Petitioners, 40–50.
78. See *Randall v. Sorrell*, 548 U.S. 230, 248–250 (2006).
79. Ibid., 245–252.
80. Ibid., 244. For coverage of the decision, see "Campaign Finance Bellwether," *Washington Post*, July 3, 2006, A20; David Savage, "Supreme Court Rejects Campaign Finance Limits," *Los Angeles Times*, June 27, 2006, A14.
81. For the lower court's decision, see *Wisconsin Right to Life v. Federal Election Commission*, 2006 WL 2666017 (D.D.C. 2006).
82. See James Bopp and Richard Coleson to Amici Curiae in *Wisconsin Right to Life v. Federal Election Commission* (October 10, 2005), 1–3, JBP, Digital Records, *Citizens*

United Folder; Amici List, 1–6; Rich Coleson to Counsel for Amici Curiae in *FEC v. WRTL* and *McCain v. WRTL* (February 16, 2007), JBP, Digital Records, *Citizens United* Folder.

83. See Bopp and Coleson to Amici Curiae, 1–3; Coleson to Counsel, 2–3.
84. Bopp and Coleson to Amici Curiae, 1.
85. Ibid., 2, 5. For the Court's decision in *Austin*, see *Austin v. Michigan Chamber of Commerce*, 494 U.S. 652 (1990).
86. Bopp and Coleson to Amici, 1.
87. See Brief for Appellee, 24–25, *Wisconsin Right to Life v. Federal Election Commission*, 551 U.S. 449 (2007) (Nos. 06-969, 06-970).
88. Ibid., 55–60.
89. Memo, "Jim: Supplemental Suggested Issues for PBA Conference from Clarke Forsythe" (n.d., ca. 2006), JBP, Matter Boxes, File 2548; see also Paul Linton to Thomas Marzen (February 22, 2006), JBP, Digital Records, Partial Birth Abortion Project File. For more on the amicus conference: Walter Weber to Thomas Marzen (February 24, 2006), JBP, Matter Boxes, File 2548; "Partial Birth Abortion Amici Conference Agenda" (March 6, 2006), JBP, Matter Boxes, File 2548. On the expansion of Liberty Counsel and ACLJ, see Amanda Hollis-Brusky and Joshua C. Wilson, "Playing for the Rules: How and Why New Christian Right Public Interest Law Firms Invest in Secular Litigation," *Law and Policy* 39 (2017): 121–125.
90. On McCorvey, see Joshua Prager, *The Family Roe: An American Story* (New York: Norton, 2021); Joshua Praeger, "The Accidental Activist," *Vanity Fair*, January 18, 2013, https://www.vanityfair.com/news/politics/2013/02/norma-mccorvey-roe-v-wade-abortion, accessed July 19, 2020; Joshua Prager, "Exclusive: *Roe v. Wade*'s Secret Heroine Tells Her Story," *Vanity Fair*, January 2017, https://www.vanityfair.com/news/2017/01/roe-v-wades-secret-heroine-tells-her-story, accessed July 19, 2020. On Sandra Cano, see "Sandra Cano, the 'Mary Doe' of Landmark Abortion Case, Dies," *Washington Times*, October 1, 2014, https://www.washingtontimes.com/news/2014/oct/1/sandra-cano-mary-doe-landmark-abortion-case-dies/, accessed July 19, 2020. On Parker, see "Allan Parker," *The Justice Foundation*, https://thejusticefoundation.org/mission-statement/who-we-are/allan-parker/, accessed July 19, 2020; see also Kathleen Cassidy, "Post-abortive Women Attack *Roe v. Wade*," *At the Center*, January 2001, www.atcmag.com/Issues/ID/16/Post-Abortive-Women-Attack-Roe-v-Wade, accessed July 24, 2018.
91. See Brief for Amici Curiae Jill Stanek et al. at 20–21, *Gonzales v. Carhart*, 550 U.S. 124 (2007) (No. 05-380, 05-1382). For Operation Outcry's brief, see Brief of Sandra Cano et al. at 6–30, *Gonzales v. Carhart*, 550 U.S. 124 (2007) (No. 05-380, 05-1382). For the abortion rights response, see Brief for Institute for Reproductive Health Access et al. at 2–27, *Gonzales v. Carhart*, 550 U.S. 124 (2007) (Nos. 05-380, 05-1382). For the American Center for Law and Justice's brief, see Amicus Brief of the American Center for Law and Justice et al. at 3–26, *Gonzales v. Carhart*, 550 U.S. 124 (2007) (Nos. 05-380, 05-1382).

92. On the divisions produced by the 2008 GOP candidates, see Linda Feldmann, "In Bellwether States, Mitt Romney Surges Ahead," *Christian Science Monitor*, June 15, 2007, 1; Robin Toner, "Political Memo: Anti-Abortion Leaders Size Up G.O.P. Candidates," *New York Times*, July 30, 2007, A13.
93. See *Gonzales v. Carhart*, 550 U.S. 124, 134–150 (2007).
94. Ibid., 157–165.
95. Ibid. For contemporary coverage of *Gonzales*, see Jess Bravin, "Ruling to Shift Abortion Fight," *Wall Street Journal*, April 19, 2007, A4; Mary Beckman, "A Closer Look: 'Partial-Birth Abortion,' " *Los Angeles Times*, May 7, 2007, A3; Peter Steinfels, "Moral Plots and Subplots in Latest Court Decision on Abortion," *New York Times*, April 28, 2007, B8.
96. *See Federal Election Commission v. Wisconsin Right to Life*, 551 U.S. 449, 465–467 (2007).
97. Ibid., 469–472.
98. Ibid., 476–481.
99. See ibid., 504–536 (Souter, J., dissenting).
100. See James Bopp Jr. and Richard Coleson to David N. Bossie and Michael Boos Re: Media Exception (December 6, 2007), JBP, Digital Records, *Citizens United* Folder. For more on the background and ambitions of the organization, see Winkler, *We the Corporations*, 250–342; Richard L. Hasen, *Plutocrats United: Campaign Money, the Supreme Court, and the Distortion of American Elections* (New Haven: Yale University Press, 2016), 127–138.
101. On Boos, see "Who We Are: Michael Boos," *Citizens United*, http://www.citizensunited.org/about-michael-boos.aspx, accessed July 19, 2020; Chip Berlet and Matthew Lyons, *Right-Wing Populism in America: Too Close for Comfort* (New York: Guilford, 2000), 317. For the Supreme Court case, see *Boos v. Barry*, 485 U.S. 312 (1988).
102. On Bossie, see "David Bossie," *Ballotpedia*, https://ballotpedia.org/David_Bossie, accessed July 19, 2020; Lloyd Grove, "A Firefighter's Blazing Trail," *Washington Post*, November 13, 1997, https://www.washingtonpost.com/archive/lifestyle/1997/11/13/a-firefighters-blazing-trail/b9beb874-fd7b-4dfeb285-ffcd385501a2/, accessed July 19, 2020; Lauren Gambino, "Trump's New Hire David Bossie Has a Decades-Long History of Attacking the Clintons," *Guardian*, September 3, 2016, https://www.theguardian.com/us-news/2016/sep/03/citizens-united-david-bossie-trump-campaign, accessed July 16, 2020.
103. Bopp and Coleson to Bossie and Boos, 1–4; see also Michael Boos to James Bopp Jr. (December 4, 2007), JBP, Digital Records, *Citizens United* Folder; Michael Boos to David Bossie (January 4, 2007), JBP, Digital Records, *Citizens United* Folder. For the media exemption: 2 U.S.C. § 431(9)(B)(i) (excluding media distribution from the definition of "expenditure").
104. See Stephanie Simon, "The Nation: Iowa Crowds Give an Amen to Huckabee," *Los Angeles Times*, November 9, 2007, A13; Stephanie Simon, "The Nation: Key Antiabortion Group Supports Thompson," *Los Angeles Times*, November 13, 2007, A9; Peter Wallison and Peter Nicholas, "God, Gaming in the Political

Mix," *Los Angeles Times*, January 18, 2008, A1. On McCain's status as the presumptive nominee, see Michael Cooper, "For Republicans, It's McCain (and Others)," *New York Times*, May 7, 2008, https://www.nytimes.com/2008/05/07/us/politics/07repubs.html, accessed April 8, 2020.

105. On McCain's fundraising struggles, see Michael Luo and Mike McIntyre, "McCain to Rely on Party Money against Obama," *New York Times*, May 19, 2008, https://www.nytimes.com/2008/05/19/us/politics/19donate.html, accessed April 8, 2020; Jim Rutenberg, "Nearing Record, Obama's Ad Effort Swamps McCain," *New York Times*, October 17, 2008, https://www.nytimes.com/2008/10/18/us/politics/18ads.html, accessed April 8, 2008. On the effect of Palin on McCain's campaign, see Christal Hayes, "Sarah Palin: McCain Admitting That He'd Rather Have Had Joe Lieberman as a Running Mate 'Gut Punch,' " *USA Today*, May 11, 2018, https://www.usatoday.com/story/news/politics/onpolitics/2018/05/11/sarah-palin-mccain-regret-running-mate-gut-punch/602569002/, accessed April 8, 2020; Jonathan Chait, "Did Palin Hurt McCain?" *New Republic*, October 14, 2010, https://newrepublic.com/article/78407/did-palin-hurt-mccain, accessed April 8, 2020; Martin Longman, "Sarah Palin Broke the Republican Party," *Washington Monthly*, March 21, 2019, https://washingtonmonthly.com/2019/03/21/sarah-palin-broke-the-republican-party/, accessed April 8, 2020.

106. On Jack Davis, see Rachel Weiner, "Who Is Jack Davis?" *Washington Post*, May 12, 2011, https://www.washingtonpost.com/blogs/the-fix/post/who-is-jack-davis/2011/05/11/AFPOfcyG_blog.html, accessed September 11, 2020; Robert J. McCarthy, "Davis Would Caucus with GOP if He Wins Congressional Race," *Buffalo News*, April 29, 2011, https://buffalonews.com/news/davis-would-caucus-with-gop-if-he-wins-congressional-race/article_939da182–8b82–5b6a-99ff-335df5f42a8b.html, accessed September 11, 2020; Raymond Hernandez, "A Maverick Who Worries Both Parties," *New York Times*, October 16, 2006, https://www.nytimes.com/2006/10/16/nyregion/16davis.html, accessed September 11, 2020.

107. For the Court's decision in *Davis*, see *Davis v. Federal Election Commission*, 554 U.S. 724 (2008); see also Memorandum of Points and Authorities in Support of Plaintiff Jack Davis's Motion for Summary Judgment (2006) (Civil Action 06-01185), 3, JBP, Matter Boxes, File 2782. Bopp also organized an amicus conference for Davis. Amicus Conference Notes (January 2008), JBP, Matter Boxes, File 2782.

108. On the Democrats' momentum in the 2008 election, see Mike Dorning, "Democrats Weigh How Hard to Hit Agenda," *Chicago Tribune*, November 16, 2008, 1; Frank Green, "Obama, New Senate May Shape Appeals Courts Nationwide," *Daily News*, November 11, 2008, C4.

109. On Obama's fundraising, see Peter Overby, "Obama Finished the Campaign with Money to Spare," *NPR*, December 5, 2008, https://www.npr.org/templates/story/story.php?storyId=97877948, accessed March 1, 2021; Tom Cole, "Obama's $745 Million Campaign Ended Public Financing," *US News and World Report*, April 11, 2011, https://www.usnews.com/opinion/articles/2011/04/11/barack-obamas-745-million-2008-campaign-ended-public-financing, accessed

March 1, 2021. On the top outside spenders in 2008, see Center for Responsive Politics, "2008 Outside Spending, by Group," *Open Secrets*, https://www.opensecrets.org/outsidespending/summ.php?cycle=2008, accessed June 21, 2021. For Smith's piece, see Bradley Smith, "Outlook: Obama and the End of Fundraising Limits," *Washington Post*, October 24, 2008, http://www.washingtonpost.com/wp-dyn/content/discussion/2008/10/24/DI2008102402766.htm, accessed September 13, 2021.

110. See Michael Sokolove, "The Transformation of Levittown," *New York Times*, November 9, 2008, https://www.nytimes.com/2008/11/09/weekinreview/09sokolove.html, accessed July 15, 2020. On the 2008 floods, see Howard Greninger, "2008: Flooding Like Vigo County Had Never Seen Before," *Tribune Star*, June 8, 2018, https://www.tribstar.com/news/local_news/2008-flooding-like-vigo-county-had-never-seen-before/article_a3528d36-8501-58c7-9d04-1546892653ad.html#:~:text=A%20decade%20ago%20this%20week,then%20again%20in%20the%20spring., accessed June 21, 2021.

111. Republican National Committee, "Rebuild the Party: A 20-Point Action Plan to Strengthen and Modernize the *Republican Party*" (November 6, 2008), JBP, Matter Boxes, File 2629.

112. Michael Steele, "Blueprint for Tomorrow: En Route to a Republican Revolution" (December 2008), JBP, Matter Boxes, File 2695. On Steele's competitors, see Mass Email, Ken Blackwell 2009 to James Bopp (December 16, 2008), JBP, Matter Boxes, File 2629; Mary Jean Jeltsen to RNC Members (January 26, 2009), JBP, Matter Box 2629; Kate Dawson to RNC Members (January 19, 2009), JBP, Matter Boxes, File 2629.

113. Steele, "Blueprint," 14–16. On Project REDMAP, see "Project REDMAP," 2010, http://www.redistrictingmajorityproject.com/, accessed July 15, 2020. For more on Project REDMAP, see "Memos Reveal Scope of GOP Gerrymandering Ambitions," *The Intercept*, September 27, 2019, https://theintercept.com/2019/09/27/gerrymandering-gop-hofeller-memos/, accessed July 15, 2020; Jane Mayer, "State for Sale," *New Yorker*, October 10, 2011, https://www.newyorker.com/magazine/2011/10/10/state-for-sale, accessed September 12, 2021.

114. For the early litigation of *Reed*, see *Doe v. Reed*, 661 F.Supp. 2d 1194 (W.D. Wa. 2009); *Doe v. Reed*, 586 F.3d 671 (9th Cir. 2009). For coverage of the issue, see David Savage and Carol J. Williams, "Outing Your Political Foes," *Los Angeles Times*, October 25, 2009, A1; Abby Goodnough, "Setback for Group Fighting Gay Marriage in Maine," *New York Times*, October 30, 2009, A22.

115. For BCRA's disclosure requirement, see 2 U.S.C. §§ 201, 311 (2003).

116. James Bopp Jr. et al. to Potential Amici in *Citizens United* (November 19, 2008), JBP, Digital Records, *Citizens United* Folder; see also James Bopp Jr. et al. to Potential Amici in *Citizens United* Re: Briefing Recommendations (November 19, 2008), JBP, Digital Records, *Citizens United* Folder; Memo, "*Citizens United:* What Is This Case About?" (November 2008), JBP, Digital Records, *Citizens United* Folder; Kaylan Lytle Phillips to Potential Amici (July 24, 2008), JBP, Digital Records, *Citizens United* Folder.

117. James Bopp Jr. to Sean Cairncross et al. (November 9, 2008), JBP, Matter Boxes, File 2750; see also James Bopp Jr. to Charles Bell (November 8, 2008), JBP, Matter Boxes, File 2750; Republican National Committee, "Campaign Finance Reform, Top Line Talking Points" (n.d., ca. 2008), JBP, Matter Boxes, File 2750.
118. On the decision to replace Bopp for the oral argument in *Citizens United*, see James Bopp Jr. to David Bossie (November 26, 2008), JBP, Digital Records, *Citizens United* Folder. For more on the switch to Olson, see Heather Gerken and Erica J. Newland, "The *Citizens United* Trilogy: The Myth, the True Tale, and the Story Still to Come," in Douglas and Mazo, *Election Law Stories*, 346.
119. See Brief for the Appellant, 16–29, 21–44, *Citizens United v. Federal Election Commission*, 558 U.S. 310 (2010) (No. 08-205).
120. See Jeffrey Toobin, "Money Unlimited: How Chief Justice John Roberts Orchestrated the *Citizens United* Decision," *New Yorker*, May 21, 2012, https://www.newyorker.com/magazine/2012/05/21/money-unlimited, accessed April 9, 2020.
121. See Brief Amici Curiae of Seven Former Chairmen and One Former Commissioner of the Federal Election Commission on Supplemental Question, 5–8, *Citizens United v. Federal Election Commission*, 558 U.S. 310 (2010) (No. 08-205).
122. See ibid., 13.
123. For the ACLU's brief, see Supplemental Brief of the American Civil Liberties Union in Support of Appellant Citizens United, 1–17, *Citizens United v. Federal Election Commission*, 558 U.S. 310 (2010) (No. 08-205); Amicus Curiae Brief of the American Civil Liberties Union in Support of Appellant Citizens United, 1–8, *Citizens United v. Federal Election Commission*, 558 U.S. 310 (2010) (No. 08-205). For the center's brief, see Brief Amicus Curiae of the Center for Constitutional Jurisprudence, 2–9, *Citizens United v. Federal Election Commission*, 558 U.S. 310 (2010) (No. 08-205). For the NRA's statement: Brief of Amicus Curiae National Rifle Association, 3–17, *Citizens United v. Federal Election Commission*, 558 U.S. 310 (2010) (No. 08-205). For the Alliance Defense Fund's argument: Brief of Amicus Curiae Alliance Defense Fund in Support of Appellant, 19, *Citizens United v. Federal Election Commission*, 558 U.S. 310 (2010) (No. 08-205).
124. *Citizens United v. Federal Election Commission*, 558 U.S. 310, 366–367 (2010).
125. See ibid., 326–329.
126. Ibid., 325.
127. Ibid., 337–339.
128. Ibid., 340–341.
129. See ibid., 354.
130. Ibid., 359.

Chapter 6. The Rise of Trump

1. On the early advocacy in *Speech Now*, see Brief of Appellants, 24–41, *SpeechNow.org v. Federal Election Commission*, 599 F.3d 686 (D.C. Cir. 2010) (Nos. 08-5223, 09-5342). On Keating, see "Meet the Reformer: David Keating, Leader for the

Right on Money in Politics," *Fulcrum*, September 25, 2020, https://thefulcrum.us/campaign-finance/david-keating, accessed January 12, 2021; Alex Altman, "Meet the Man Who Invented the Super PAC," *Time*, May 13, 2015, https://time.com/3856427/super-pac-david-keating/, accessed January 12, 2021.

2. See *SpeechNow.org v. Federal Election Commission*, 599 F.3d 686, 692–696, 697–702 (D.C. Cir. 2010).
3. For the Supreme Court's decision, see *John Doe Number One v. Reed*, 561 U.S. 186 (2010). For Bopp's statement: Brief of Respondent John Reed, 21–22, *John Doe Number One v. Reed*, 561 U.S. 186 (2010) (No. 09-559).
4. On the tools the party used to marginalize more extreme candidates, see Hans J. G. Hassell, *The Party's Primary: Control of Congressional Nominations* (New York: Cambridge University Press, 2018), 25–32; Katherine Gehl, Michael Porter, Mike Gallagher, and Chrissy Houlihan, *The Politics Industry: How Political Innovation Can Break Political Gridlock and Save Our Democracy* (Cambridge, MA: Harvard Business Review Press, 2020), 23–54; Michael S. Kang, "Campaign Finance Deregulation and the Hyperpolarization of Presidential Nominations in the Super PAC Era," in *The Best Candidate: Presidential Nominations in Polarized Times*, ed. Eugene Mazo (New York: Cambridge University Press, 2020), 273–275.
5. On Fox News' dominance in the period, see Dylan Stableford, "Fox News Utterly Destroys Cable News Competition in 2010," *The Wrap*, December 28, 2010, https://www.thewrap.com/fox-news-wins-2010-cable-news-ratings-war-23505/, accessed January 12, 2021; Ed Pilkington, "Fox Most Trusted News Channel in US, Poll Shows," *Guardian*, January 27, 2010, https://www.theguardian.com/world/2010/jan/27/fox-news-most-popular, accessed January 12, 2021. On Breitbart, see Michael Gonzalez, "Andrew Breitbart to the Rescue," *Examiner*, June 5, 2011, 37; Jeremy Peters, "The Right's Blogger Provocateur: Breitbart Blazes a Trail of Uproar," *New York Times*, June 27, 2011, B1. On the early days of the Daily Caller, see Howard Kurtz, "It's the Caller, Not the Holler: Tucker Carlson and Company Say Their Site Will Maintain Nonpartisan Civility," *Washington Post*, January 11, 2010, C1; Michael D. Shear, "Justice's Wife Joins *Daily Caller*," *New York Times*, March 23, 2011, A17. On the growth of Newsmax, see Keach Hagey, "Newsmax Hits the Heartland," *Politico*, May 7, 2011, https://www.politico.com/story/2011/05/newsmax-hits-the-heartland-054514, accessed January 12, 2021; Andrew Edgecliffe-Johnson, "Media Trend Defied by Rise of Newsmax," *Financial Times*, June 4, 2010.
6. See Theda Skocpol and Vanessa Williamson, *The Tea Party and the Remaking of Republican Conservatism* (New York: Oxford University Press, 2012), 10–31; Theda Skocpol, "The Elite and Popular Roots of Contemporary Republican Extremism," in *Upending American Politics: Polarizing Parties, Ideological Elites, and Citizen Activists from the Tea Party to the Anti-Trump Resistance*, ed. Theda Skocpol and Catherine Tero (New York: Oxford University Press, 2020), 3–29; Theda Skocpol and Michael Zoorab, "The Overlooked Organizational Basis of Trump's 2016 Victory," in ibid., 53–79.

7. On Martin, see Mark Davis, "Jenny Beth Martin: The Head Tea Party Patriot," *Atlanta Journal-Constitution*, May 9, 2010, https://www.ajc.com/news/local-govt--politics/jenny-beth-martin-the-head-tea-party-patriot/abe8qovCj2hk7mr2WgYVDL/, accessed July 15, 2020. On Meckler, see Jeff Ackerman, "Local Attorney Seeks Return to Founding Principles in Government," *The Union*, February 26, 2010, https://www.theunion.com/news/local-news/local-attorney-seeks-return-to-founding-principles-in-government/, accessed July 16, 2020; Gary Weiss, *Ayn Rand Nation: The Hidden Struggle for America's Soul* (New York: Macmillan, 2012), 180–210.
8. On Russo, see Ed Pilkington, "Sal Russo: From Establishment Politics to Tea Party Express," *Guardian*, October 20, 2010, https://www.theguardian.com/world/2010/oct/20/sal-russo-tea-party-expresss, accessed June 3, 2020; " 'Tea Party Express' Shakes Up the GOP and the Movement," *NPR*, October 25, 2010, https://www.npr.org/templates/story/story.php?storyId=130811390, accessed July 16, 2020.
9. On Americans for Prosperity, see Jane Mayer, *Dark Money: The Hidden History of The Billionaires behind the Radical Right* (New York: Penguin, 2016), 221–225, 265; Skocpol, "The Elite and Popular Roots of Contemporary Republican Extremism," 1–25. On FreedomWorks, see Skocpol and Williamson, *The Tea Party*, 83.
10. George McKenna, "Thinking about Tea Parties," *Human Life Review* 36 (2010): 41–51. On the early work of True the Vote, see Press Release, "Volunteers Expose Voter Fraud in Harris County," *PR Newswire*, August 24, 2010; Sandhya Somashekhar, "Conservatives to Step Up Presence at Polls across U.S. to Prevent Voter Fraud," *Washington Post*, October 30, 2010, A5; Chris Kromm, "Houston's Voting Problem," *Tennessee Tribune*, October 14, 2010, 6A. On Hecker and the Contract from America, see Patrik Johnsson, "Contract from America: 'Tea Party' Crafts Its Election Manifesto," *Christian Science Monitor*, February 2, 2010, 6; Kathleen Hennessey, "GOP, Tea Party Seek Party Line," *Chicago Tribune*, February 21, 2010, 22.
11. See Jim Routenberg and Adam Nagourney, "Conservatives Propose Checklist to Measure Candidates' Commitment to the GOP," *New York Times*, November 24, 2009, A23. For more on the Scozzafava race, see Paul Kane, "Tea Party Complicates Push to Take the Senate," *Washington Post*, December 11, 2013, A1; Patrik Jonsson, "Tea Party Express Jubilant as Scozzafava Exits in NY-23," *Christian Science Monitor*, October 31, 2009, 6.
12. Routenberg and Nagourney, "Conservatives Propose," A23.
13. Philip Rucker, "GOP Woos Wary Tea Party Activists," *Washington Post*, January 30, 2010, A4; Adam Nagourney, "As GOP Hits Its Stride, Pitfalls Await," *New York Times*, January 31, 2010, A1; Bill Steiden, "A New Revolution Brewing?" *Atlanta Journal-Constitution*, January 31, 2010, A14. On the fate of Bopp's purity test, see Adam Nagourney, "The Caucus: Muddying the Purity Test," *New York Times*, January 08, 2010, A10.
14. See James Bopp Jr., Joe La Rue, Anita Woudenberg, and Kayla Phillips to Republican National Committee (April 23, 2010), JBP, Digital Records, McCain-Feingold Combined.

15. See ibid., 1–36. On the increase in political party revenues, see Anthony Corrado, *Campaign Finance Reform: Beyond the Basics* (New York: Century Foundation, 2000), 170; Federal Election Commission, Press Release, "Party Committees Raise More than $1 Billion in 2001–2002," March 20, 2003, https://www.fec.gov/updates/party-committees-raise-more-than-1-billion-in-2001–2002/, accessed June 16, 2021. On soft money from the late 1980s to the early 2000s, see Brennan Center for Justice, *Political Parties and Soft Money*, 2000, https://www.brennancenter.org/sites/default/files/legacy/d/download_file_10672.pdf; accessed February 2, 2021; David Magleby, ed., "Election Advocacy: Soft Money and Issue Advocacy in the 2000 Congressional Elections" (paper prepared for the Pew Charitable Trusts), February 26, 2001, at 16, on file with the author. On parties' efforts to adjust to BCRA and expand their donor base, see Anthony Corrado, "Political Party Finance under BCRA: An Initial Assessment," *Brookings*, 2004, https://www.brookings.edu/wp-content/uploads/2016/06/0311campaignfinancereform_corrado.pdf, accessed June 16, 2021. On the role of party insiders in "outside spending," see Rodney Kolodny and Diana Dwyre, "Convergence or Divergence: Do Parties and Outside Candidates Spend on the Same Candidates, and Does It Matter?" *American Politics Research* 46 (2018): 375–401; Joseph Fishkin and Heather Gerken, "The Party's Over: *McCutcheon*, Shadow Parties, and the Future of the Party System," *Supreme Court Review* 2014 (2014): 175–212.
16. Bopp et al. to Republican National Committee, 8–13.
17. On Bolick and Mellor, see Nina J. Easton, *Gang of Five: Leaders at the Center of the Conservative Crusade* (New York: Simon and Schuster, 2000), 197–263; Jefferson Decker, *The Other Rights Revolution: Conservative Lawyers and the Remaking of American Government* (New York: Oxford University Press, 2016), 200–243; Steven Teles, *The Rise of the Conservative Legal Movement: The Battle for Control of the Law* (Princeton: Princeton University Press, 2008), 41–61.
18. On the lower-court litigation in *Arizona Free Enterprise*, see *McComish v. Brewer*, 2010 WL 2292213 (D. Ariz. 2008); *McComish v. Bennett*, 605 F.3d 720 (9th Cir. 2010); *McComish v. Bennett*, 605 F.3d 510 (9th Cir. 2010).
19. See Kenneth P. Vogel, "Rove-Linked Group Uses Secret Donors to Fund Attacks," *Politico*, July 20, 2010, https://www.politico.com/story/2010/07/rove-linked-group-uses-secret-donors-to-fund-attacks-039998, accessed July 16, 2020; Michael Luo, "G.O.P. Allies Outspending Their Rivals," *New York Times*, September 15, 2010, A1; Michael Luo, "Changes Have Money Talking Louder Than Ever in Midterms," *New York Times*, October 8, 2010, A13. On the lack of reporting on 501(c)(4)s after the 2010 election, see Peter H. Stone, "Fine Line between Politics and Issues: Spending by Secretive 501(c)(4) Groups," *Open Secrets*, May 19, 2011, https://publicintegrity.org/politics/fine-line-between-politics-and-issues-spending-by-secretive-501c4-groups/, accessed June 16, 2021.
20. See Center for Responsible Politics, "Election 2010 to Shatter Spending Records as Republicans Benefit from Late Cash Surge," *Open Secrets*, October 27, 2010, https://www.opensecrets.org/news/2010/10/election-2010-to-shatter-spending-r/, accessed July 16, 2010; Michael Luo and Stephanie Strom, "Donor Names

Remain Secret as Rules Shift," *New York Times*, September 20, 2010, https://www.nytimes.com/2010/09/21/us/politics/21money.html, accessed July 16, 2020. On the volume of secret spending, see Michael Beckel, "Nonprofits Outspent Super PACs in 2010, Trend May Continue," *Center for Public Integrity*, June 18, 2010, https://publicintegrity.org/politics/nonprofits-outspent-super-pacs-in-2010-trend-may-continue/, accessed July 16, 2020.

21. See Skocpol and Williamson, *The Tea Party*, 158; Rachel M. Blum, *How the Tea Party Captured the GOP: Insurgent Factions in American Politics* (Chicago: University of Chicago Press, 2020), 100–145; Christopher S. Parker and Matt A. Barreto, *Change They Can't Believe In: The Tea Party and Reactionary Politics in America* (Princeton: Princeton University Press, 2013), 269–275. On the shift in control of state legislatures, see Tyler Millhouse and Geoff Pallay, "A Look Back at the 2010 State Legislative Elections," *Ballotpedia*, January 11, 2011, https://ballotpedia.org/A_look_back_at_the_2010_state_legislative_elections, accessed June 16, 2021.

22. See "More State Abortion Restrictions Were Enacted in 2011–2013 Than in the Entire Previous Decade," *Guttmacher News in Depth*, January 2014, www.guttmacher.org/article/2014/01/more-state-abortion-restrictions-were-enacted-2011–2013-entire-previous-decade, accessed September 27, 2017; "In Just the Last Four Years, States Have Enacted 231 Restrictions," *Guttmacher News in Depth*, January 2015, www.guttmacher.org/article/2015/01/just-last-four-years-states-have-enacted231-abortion-restrictions, accessed September 27, 2017; Erik Eckholm, "Abortion-Rights Advocates Preparing for a New Surge of Federal and State Attacks," *New York Times*, November 6, 2014, A16.

23. See Mary Spaulding Balch, JD, Director, State Development Department to Whom It May Concern, Re: Constitutionality of the Model Pain-Capable Unborn Child Protection Act, National Right to Life, July 2013, www.nrlc.org/uploads/state leg/PCUCPAConstitutionality.pdf, accessed September 26, 2017; Monica Davey, "Nebraska, Citing Pain, Sets Limits on Abortion," *New York Times*, April 14, 2016, A16; Erik Eckholm, "Theory on Fetal Pain Is Driving Rules for Abortions," *New York Times*, August 2, 2013, www.nytimes.com/2013/08/02/us/theory-on-pain-is-drivingrules-for-abortions.html, accessed August 18, 2019.

24. See Laura Meckler, "The Spending Fight: Abortion Returns to Center Stage," *Wall Street Journal*, April 8, 2011, A4; Charmaine Yoest and Denise M. Burke, "Planned Parenthood Takes on the States," *Wall Street Journal*, June 27, 2011, A17.

25. See "Profile, Pro-Life Mississippi: Les Riley," *Pro-Life Mississippi*, http://prolifemississippi.org/Pages/Les_Riley.html, accessed February 2, 2021; Tim Murphy, "The Most Radical Anti-Abortion Measure in America," *Mother Jones*, September 27, 2011, https://www.motherjones.com/politics/2011/09/abortion-mississippi-les-riley/, accessed February 2, 2021. For Bazelon's statement: Emily Bazelon, "The Reincarnation of Pro-Life," *New York Times*, May 27, 2011, https://www.nytimes.com/2011/05/29/magazine/the-reincarnation-of-pro-life.html, accessed April 7, 2021.

26. "Les Riley"; Murphy, "The Most Radical."

27. See Erik Eckholm, "Voters in Mississippi to Weigh Amendment on Conception as Start of Life," *New York Times*, October 26, 2011, A16; Richard Fausset, "One State Personifies Personhood Push," *Orlando Sentinel*, November 6, 2011, A3; Elizabeth Williamson, "Abortion Resurfaces for GOP Field," *Wall Street Journal*, November 7, 2011.
28. On Yue, see "Promises Made, Promises Kept: Solomon Yue for ORP National Committeeman" (2020), SYP; Solomon Yue, email interview with Mary Ziegler, January 30, 2021.
29. James Bopp Jr., Solomon Yue, and Dick Armey, "The Freedom Manifesto: It's Once Again Time to Choose Freedom over Tyranny" (2010), JBP, Digital Records, Republican National Conservative Caucus Folder; see also Organizational Actions of the Board of Directors of Republican National Conservative Caucus (2010), JBP, Digital Records, Republican National Conservative Caucus Folder. On Armey, see Peter Appelbome, "Six Texas Republicans Hope to Show They're No Fluke," *New York Times*, October 13, 1986, https://www.nytimes.com/1986/10/13/us/6-texas-republicans-hope-to-show-they-re-no-fluke.html, accessed July 16, 2020; Kate Zernike and Jennifer Steinhauer, "Years Later, Armey Once Again a Power in Congress," *New York Times*, November 14, 2010, https://www.nytimes.com/2010/11/15/us/politics/15armey.html, accessed July 16, 2020.
30. See Reid Wilson, "Next RNC Leader Will Inherit an Organization in Crisis," *National Journal*, November 6, 2010, 26; Nicholas Confessore, "Outside Groups Eclipsing GOP as Hubs of Campaigns," *New York Times*, October 29, 2011, https://www.nytimes.com/2011/10/30/us/politics/outside-groups-eclipsing-gop-as-hub-of-campaigns-next-year.html, accessed July 16, 2020; Grace Wyler, "Michael Steele Left GOP $23 Million in Debt," *Business Insider*, February 1, 2011, https://www.businessinsider.com/michael-steele-left-gop-23-million-debt-2011-2, accessed June 16, 2021.
31. On Priebus, see Patricia Mazzei, "Before Making His Name in Politics, Reince Priebus Was a Force at Miami Law School," *Tampa Bay Times*, November 20, 2016, https://www.tampabay.com/news/politics/stateroundup/before-making-his-name-in-politics-reince-priebus-was-a-force-at-miami-law/2303415/, accessed July 16, 2020; Cameron Joseph, "Chairman Priebus Leads RNC Revival," *The Hill*, February 16, 2012, https://thehill.com/homenews/campaign/211051-priebus-rnc-revival-from-23m-in-the-red-to-7m-in-the-black, accessed July 16, 2020.
32. James Bopp to RNC Members (December 21, 2010), JBP, Matter Boxes, File 2941; see also James Bopp to Reince Priebus (February 26, 2011), JBP, Matter Boxes, File 2941; Maria Cino to RNC Members (December 30, 2010), JBP, Matter Boxes, File 2941.
33. *Arizona Free Enterprise Freedom's Club PAC v. Bennett*, 564 U.S. 721, 732–750 (2011); ibid., 756–773 (Kagan, J., dissenting).
34. Kim Geiger and Melanie Mason, "Stephen Colbert Makes Case before FEC for 'Colbert Super PAC,'" *Los Angeles Times*, June 30, 2012, https://www.latimes.com/nation/la-xpm-2011-jun-30-la-pn-colbert-fec-20110630-story.html, accessed June 28, 2021. On Colbert's super PAC, see Trevor Potter, "Here's What I Learned

When I Helped Stephen Colbert Set Up His Super PAC," *Washington Post*, January 21, 2015, https://www.washingtonpost.com/posteverything/wp/2015/01/21/heres-what-i-learned-when-i-helped-stephen-colbert-set-up-his-super-pac/, accessed June 16, 2021; Andrew Prokop, "Here's How Stephen Colbert Taught Americans about Super PACs," *Vox*, May 15, 2015, https://www.vox.com/2014/6/4/5776676/stephen-colbert-super-pac-study, accessed June 16, 2021.

35. See Robert Barnes, "Campaign-Contribution Law Remains Unsettled," *Washington Post*, May 23, 2011, A17; T. W. Farnam, " 'Super PACs' Could Test Campaign Finance Law," *Washington Post*, May 26, 2011, A21; Eliza Newlin Carney, "Rules of the Game: Super PACs Multiply, Head to Hill," *Roll Call*, October 17, 2011, https://www.rollcall.com/2011/10/17/rules-of-the-game-super-pacs-multiply-head-to-hill/, accessed July 16, 2020. On spending by Carey Committees in 2016, see Open Secrets, "2016 Outside Spending, by Group: Carey Committees," 2016, https://www.opensecrets.org/outsidespending/summ.php?cycle=2016&chrt=P&disp=O&type=H, accessed September 13, 2021.

36. Pema Levy, "Moment of Conception," *American Prospect*, October 27, 2011, https://prospect.org/health/moment-conception/, accessed February 2, 2022. On Rohrbough, see "Dad's Inscription Ties Columbine Deaths to Abortion, Immorality," *Denver Post*, September 21, 2007, https://www.denverpost.com/2007/09/21/dads-inscription-ties-columbine-deaths-to-abortion-immorality/, accessed February 2, 2021; Anita Crane, "Brian Rohrbough: An Uncompromising Pro-Lifer," *Celebrate Life Magazine*, May/June 2007, https://clmagazine.org/topic/pro-life-champions/brian-rohrbough-an-uncompromising-pro-lifer/, accessed February 2, 2021.

37. Daniel C. Becker, *Personhood: A Pragmatic Guide to Prolife Victory in the Twenty-First Century and the Return to First Principles in Politics* (Alpharetta, GA: TKS, 2011), 28. For Becker's recollections: Dan Becker, interview with Mary Ziegler, November 29, 2017. For more on Becker, see Aaron Gould Sheinen, "Dan Becker Moves on as Georgia Right to Life Names New Leader," *Atlanta Journal-Constitution*, August 28, 2016, https://www.ajc.com/news/state—regional-govt—politics/dan-becker-moves-georgia-right-life-names-new-leader/XJYERgnHCZ8Q56IfJNB05M/, accessed February 2, 2021.

38. Levy, "Moment of Conception"; see also Nia-Malika Henderson, "DNC Highlights Romney's Support of 'Personhood' Bill," *Washington Post*, November 3, 2011, https://www.washingtonpost.com/blogs/election-2012/post/dnc-highlights-romneys-support-of-personhood-bill/2011/11/03/gIQAjYyWkM_blog.html, accessed February 2, 2021; Kate Sheppard, "Romney Tries to Have It Both Ways on Personhood," *Mother Jones*, November 22, 2011, https://www.motherjones.com/politics/2011/11/romney-human-life-amendment-personhood/, accessed February 2, 2021.

39. On the failure of the Mississippi vote, see Frank James, "Mississippi Voters Reject Personhood by Wide Margin," *NPR*, November 8, 2011, https://www.npr.org/sections/itsallpolitics/2011/11/08/142159280/mississippi-voters-reject-personhood-amendment, accessed February 2, 2021; "Mississippi Anti-Abortion 'Personhood'

Amendment Fails at Ballot Box," *Washington Post*, November 9, 2011, https://www.washingtonpost.com/politics/mississippi-anti-abortion-personhood-amendment-fails-at-ballot-box/2011/11/09/gIQAzQl95M_story.html, accessed February 2, 2021; Kate Sheppard, "Why Mississippi's Personhood Amendment Failed," *Mother Jones*, November 9, 2011, https://www.motherjones.com/politics/2011/11/why-mississippis-personhood-measure-failed/, accessed February 2, 2021.

40. See Mary Morgan Edwards, "Abortion Foe Janet Porter's Zealous Tactics Inspire, Divide," *Canton Repository*, December 10, 2016, https://www.dispatch.com/content/stories/local/2016/12/11/1-janet-porter-abortion-foes-zealous-tactics-divide-inspire.html, accessed July 16, 2020; Jessica Glenza, "The Anti-gay Extremist behind America's Fiercely Strict Anti-Abortion Laws," *Guardian*, April 25, 2019, https://www.theguardian.com/world/2019/apr/25/the-anti-abortion-crusader-hopes-her-heartbeat-law-will-test-roe-v-wade, accessed July 16, 2020.

41. See Edwards, "Abortion Foe's Zealous Tactics"; Miranda Blue, "Janet Porter's New Antiabortion Rom-Com Featuring Mike Huckabee and Steve King Is Sure to Be an Oscar Contender," *Right Wing Watch*, November 23, 2016, https://www.rightwingwatch.org/post/janet-porters-new-anti-abortion-rom-com-featuring-mike-huckabee-steve-king-is-sure-to-be-an-oscar-contender/, accessed February 2, 2021.

42. Erik Eckholm, "Anti-Abortion Groups Are Split on Legal Tactics," *New York Times*, December 5, 2011, A1. For more on Porter, see Glenza, "The Anti-gay Extremist"; Joseph D. Lyons, "Meet the Woman Quietly Driving the Republicans' Push to Ban Abortion at Six Weeks," *Bustle*, November 1, 2017, https://www.bustle.com/p/who-is-janet-porter-the-gops-heartbeat-bill-is-backed-by-a-zealous-anti-choice-activist-3196015, accessed July 16, 2020.

43. Eckholm, "Anti-Abortion Groups." On the rise in abortion restrictions in 2011, see Guttmacher Institute, "States Enact Record Number of Abortion Restrictions in 2011," January 5, 2012, https://www.guttmacher.org/article/2012/01/states-enact-record-number-abortion-restrictions-2011, accessed September 14, 2021; see also "More State Restrictions."

44. See *American Tradition Partnership v. Bullock, Attorney General*, 271 P.3d 1 (Mont. 2011). For the text of the law, see § 13-35-227(1), MCA. For more on the case, see "Montana Supreme Court Defies *Citizens United* Decision," *Dow Jones Industrial News*, January 3, 2012; Jess Bravin, "Montana Tests Supreme Court Political-Spending Ruling," *Wall Street Journal*, January 3, 2012.

45. Steve Hoersting to James Bopp and Richard Coleson (April 30, 2012), JBP, Matter Boxes, File 3168.

46. See *Buckley v. Valeo*, 424 U.S. 1, 23–38 (1976).

47. See Hoersting to Bopp and Coleson, 1–8.

48. James Bopp to RNC (February 7, 2012), JBP, Digital Records, Romney 2012 Folder. For more on Romney, see Andrew Romano, "Who and What Is Mitt Romney?" *Newsweek*, September 25, 2011, https://www.newsweek.com/who-and-what-mitt-romney-67497, accessed July 16, 2020; Ta-Nehisi Coates, "The Socially Awkward

Yet Underrated Mitt Romney," *Atlantic*, August 23, 2012, https://www.theatlantic.com/politics/archive/2012/08/the-socially-awkward-yet-underrated-mitt-romney/261512/, accessed July 16, 2020; David Javerbaum, "A Quantum Theory of Mitt Romney," *New York Times*, April 1, 2012, https://www.nytimes.com/2012/04/01/opinion/sunday/a-quantum-theory-of-mitt-romney.html, accessed July 16, 2020. On True the Vote's activities in 2012, see "Will the 2012 Elections Be Tainted by Voter Fraud?" *Washington Examiner*, February 11, 2012, 1; "True the Vote Holds Two-Day Summit to Strengthen the Election Process," *PR Newswire*, April 20, 2012; Matt Rhoades, "Political Operatives," *Politico*, July 12, 2012, https://www.politico.com/story/2012/07/political-operatives-078301, accessed June 21, 2021. For Romney's statement about being "severely conservative," see David A. Farenthold, "Mitt Romney Reframes Himself as a 'Severely Conservative' Governor," *Washington Post*, February 14, 2012, https://www.washingtonpost.com/politics/mitt-romney-reframes-himself-as-a-severely-conservative-governor/2012/02/14/gIQAaMiqHR_story.html, accessed June 28, 2021.

49. For Romney's position on abortion, see Josh Hicks, "Romney's Official Stance on Abortion," *Washington Post*, October 22, 2012, https://www.washingtonpost.com/blogs/fact-checker/post/romneys-official-stance-on-abortion/2012/10/20/f7bd00dc-1a3d-11e2-aa6f-3b636fecb829_blog.html, accessed September 15, 2021. On the 2012 election, see William J. Miller, "The 2012 Republican Nomination Season: Clown Car or Feuding Conservatives?" in *The 2012 Nomination and the Future of the Republican Party*, ed. William J. Miller (Lanham, MD: Rowman and Littlefield, 2013), 1–12. On Romney's fundraising prowess, see Abby Phillip and Kenneth Vogel, "Mitt's Burn Rate a Boon for Obama," *Politico*, February 21, 2012, https://www.politico.com/story/2012/02/romneys-burn-rate-boon-for-obama-073100, accessed September 15, 2021; Michael Barbaro and Jeremy Peters, "Romney Reopens 'Whatever-It-Takes' Playbook," *New York Times*, March 1, 2012, A1.

50. Asawin Suebsaeng, "Anti-Abortion Groups on Romney: Sigh, He'll Have to Do," *Mother Jones*, April 12, 2012, https://www.motherjones.com/politics/2012/04/national-right-life-endorses-avowed-convert-mitt-romney/, accessed September 15, 2021; Nicholas Cafardi, "Which Presidential Candidate Is Truly Pro-Life?" *National Catholic Reporter*, August 10, 2012, https://www.ncronline.org/news/politics/which-presidential-candidate-truly-pro-life, accessed September 15, 2021.

51. See *American Tradition Partnership, Inc. v. Bullock*, 567 U.S. 516 (2012) (per curiam). For the poll on *Citizens United*, see "Public Approval of Major Supreme Court Decisions," *New York Times*, July 19, 2012, https://archive.nytimes.com/www.nytimes.com/interactive/2012/07/19/us/public-approval-of-major-court-decisions.html?action=click&module=RelatedCoverage&pgtype=Article®ion=Footer, accessed July 16, 2020. On the influence of *Citizens United* on the 2012 election, see "Outside Spending for 2012 Election Already Beats 2010," *Reuters*, September 24, 2012, https://www.reuters.com/article/idUS306856210320120924, accessed July 16, 2012. On the polarization furthered by outside spending, see Raymond La Raja and Brian Schaffner, *Campaign Finance and Political Polarization: When Purists Prevail* (Ann Arbor: University of Michigan Press, 2015), 1–23. On the total

amount of outside spending in the 2012 cycle, see Adam Lioz and Blair Bowie, "Election Spending 2012: Post-election Analysis of Federal Election Commission Data," *Demos Policy Briefs*, November 9, 2012, https://www.demos.org/policy-briefs/election-spending-2012-post-election-analysis-federal-election-commission-data, accessed June 16, 2021. On the amount contributed by megadonors to super PACs, see ibid. On the money spent by Americans for Prosperity, see Nicholas Confessore, "$122 Million in Spending by Koch Group," *New York Times*, November 14, 2013, https://www.nytimes.com/2013/11/15/us/politics/122-million-in-2012-spending-by-koch-group.html, accessed September 14, 2021.

52. On Bopp's support for Romney in 2012, see "Romney Endorsed by Super PAC Lawyer Bopp," *Reuters*, February 7, 2012, https://www.reuters.com/article/idIN627619698201202O7, accessed January 13, 2021.

53. On Ginsberg, see Allison Hoffman, "The Tea Party's Enemy No. 1," *Tablet Magazine*, August 29, 2012, https://www.tabletmag.com/sections/news/articles/the-tea-partys-enemy-no-1, accessed July 16, 2020; Dylan Stableford, "Who Is Ben Ginsberg, the GOP Lawyer Facilitating the GOP's Attempt to Regain 'Leverage' in the Debate?" *Yahoo News*, November 2, 2015, https://news.yahoo.com/who-is-ben-ginsberg-the-lawyer-facilitating-the-185531804.html, accessed July 16, 2020; Paul Harris, "How Ron Paul's Far-Reaching Delegate Strategy Is Finally Starting to Pay Off," *Guardian*, May 4, 2012, https://www.theguardian.com/world/2012/may/04/ron-paul-delegate-strategy-gop-nomination, accessed July 16, 2020.

54. On Paul's delegate strategy and Ginsburg's efforts to overcome it, see Alexander Bolton, "Convention Rules Fight Flares Despite Reports of a Deal," *The Hill*, August 28, 2012, https://thehill.com/conventions-2012/gop-convention-tampa/246051-convention-rules-fight-flares-despite-reports-of-a-deal, accessed January 13, 2021; James Hoffman, "No Paul Revolution at Convention," *Politico*, August 23, 2012, https://www.politico.com/story/2012/08/no-paul-revolution-at-convention-080067, accessed January 13, 2021. On the rules changes proposed by Ginsberg, see Gwynn Guilford, "How the Republican Elite Tried to Fix the Presidency and Instead Got Donald Trump," *Quartz*, June 15, 2016, https://qz.com/685831/the-republican-crackdown-on-2012s-ron-paul-insurgency-boosted-donald-trumps-delegate-math-and-changed-how-the-party-connects-with-its-supporters/, accessed June 27, 2021.

55. For Bopp's letter to Barbour: James Bopp Jr. to Haley Barbour (August 27, 2012), JBP, Matter Boxes, File 3007; see also James Bopp Jr. to Haley Barbour (August 26, 2012), JBP, Matter Boxes, File 3007. On Paul's delegate strategy, see Paul Harris, "Ron Paul Delegates Continue Dissent over Failed 'Delegate Strategy,'" *Guardian*, August 29, 2012, https://www.theguardian.com/world/2012/aug/30/ron-paul-dele gates-convention-dissent, accessed July 16, 2020; Seema Mehta, "Ron Paul Supporters Walk out of GOP Convention," *Los Angeles Times*, August 28, 2012, https://www.latimes.com/archives/la-xpm-2012-aug-28-la-pn-ron-paul-supporters-walk-out-of-gop-convention-20120828-story.html, accessed July 17, 2020; David Weigel, "The Last Gasp of Ron Paul's Movement," *Slate*, August 29, 2012, https://slate.com/news-and-politics/2012/08/as-ron-pauls-presidential-bid-ends-the-gop-puts-in-new-rules-

to-prevent-a-future-republican-party-challenger.html, accessed July 17, 2020. On the rules vote, see Guilford, "How the Republican Elite."

56. James Bopp Jr. to Solomon Yue (September 3, 2012), JBP, Matter Boxes, File 3007; see also James Bopp Jr. to Republican National Committee (August 27, 2020), JBP, Matter Boxes, File 3007.
57. James Bopp Jr. to Reince Priebus et al. (February 22, 2012), JBP, Matter Boxes, File 3168; see also James Bopp Jr. to James Holcomb (February 24, 2012), JBP, Matter Boxes, File 3168. On the workings of JFCs, see Open Secrets, "Joint Fundraising Committees," https://www.opensecrets.org/jfc/, accessed September 14, 2021; Federal Election Commission, "Joint Fundraising with Other Candidates and Political Committees," https://www.fec.gov/help-candidates-and-committees/joint-fundraising-candidates-political-committees/, accessed September 14, 2021.
58. Ashley Stowe to Rich Coleson et al. (May 23, 2012), JBP, Matter Boxes, File 3086.
59. On the lower-court litigation in *McCutcheon*, see *McCutcheon v. Federal Election Commission*, 893 F.3d 113 (D.D.C. 2012).
60. See James Bopp Jr. to Richard Coleson (May 2012), JBP, Matter Boxes, File 2827.
61. On the rift between Bopp's firm and McCutcheon, see Dan Backer to James Bopp Jr. (September 20, 2013), JBP, Matter Boxes, File 3086; Dan Backer to James Bopp Jr. et al. (September 26, 2013), JBP, Matter Boxes, File 3086. On Bopp's Montana case, see *Laird v. Murry*, 903 F. Supp.2d 1077 (D. Mont. 2012). For Bopp's case on the FEC definition of express advocacy, see *The Real Truth about Abortion, Inc. v. Federal Election Commission*, 681 F.3d 544 (4th Cir. 2012). On the West Virginia case, see *Center for Individual Freedom v. Tennant*, 706 F.3d 270 (4th Cir. 2013). For the Vermont case, see *Vermont Right to Life Committee, Inc. v. Sorrell*, 875 F.Supp.2d 376 (D. Vt. 2012).
62. James Bopp Jr. to Solomon Yue (November 8, 2012), JBP, Matter Boxes, File 3007; see also Solomon Yue to James Bopp Jr. (November 11, 2012), JBP, Matter Boxes, File 3007; James Bopp to Solomon Yue (November 14, 2012), JBP, Matter Boxes, File 3007. On the result of the 2012 election and its significance, see Larry Sabato, "The Obama Encore That Broke Some Rules," in *Barack Obama and the New America: The 2012 Election and the Changing Face of America*, ed. Larry J. Sabato (Lanham, MD: Rowman and Littlefield, 2013), 10–45; John Sides and Lynn Vavreck, *The Gamble: Choice and Chance in the 2012 Election* (Princeton: Princeton University Press 2013), 174–200.
63. Republican National Committee, *The Growth and Opportunity Project Report* 8 (2013), https://online.wsj.com/public/resources/documents/RNCreport03182013.pdf, accessed July 17, 2020.
64. David Freedlander, "Is the Cult of Karl Over?" *Daily Beast*, November 10, 2012, https://www.thedailybeast.com/is-the-cult-of-karl-over, accessed July 17, 2020; see also Nia-Malika Henderson, "Internal GOP Clash Pits Tea Party Conservatives against Karl Rove," *Washington Post*, February 11, 2013, https://www.washingtonpost.com/politics/internal-gop-clash-pits-tea-party-conservatives-against-karl-rove/2013/02/11/10e9d512-7141-11e2-8b8d-e0b59a1b8e2a_story.html, accessed

July 17, 2020; Kenneth Vogel, Alexander Burns, and Tarini Parti, "Karl Rove vs. Tea Party," *Politico*, February 7, 2013, https://www.politico.com/story/2013/02/rove-vs-tea-party-for-gops-future-087296, accessed July 17, 2020.

65. Thomas Edsall, "The Republican Autopsy Report," *New York Times*, March 20, 2013, https://opinionator.blogs.nytimes.com/2013/03/20/the-republican-autopsy-report/, accessed September 15, 2021; see also La Raja and Schaffner, *Campaign Finance and Polarization*, 36–72; Glenn Thrush, "Losing the Battle, Winning the War," *Politico*, November 11, 2014, https://www.politico.com/magazine/story/2014/11/ed-gillespie-losing-the-battle-winning-the-war-112785, accessed January 13, 2021. For Collegio's statement and the statement made by Bossie and the other eighteen conservatives: Edsall, "The Republican Autopsy Report."

66. For AUL's statement: "AUL Launches the 'New Frontier' in Protecting Women from Abortion Industry Abuses," Americans United for Life, December 9, 2013, https://aul.org/2013/12/09/aul-launches-the-new-frontier-in-protecting-women-from-abortion-industry-abuses/, accessed July 17, 2020. For more on Porter's radio program, see Zoe Carpenter, "Meet the Fringe Activist behind One of the Country's Most Extreme Anti-Abortion Measures," *Nation*, December 3, 2019, https://www.thenation.com/article/archive/janet-porter-abortion-ban/, accessed February 2, 2021. This chapter later focuses on the heartbeat campaign in greater depth.

67. See Brief on the Merits for the Republican National Committee, 7–52, *McCutcheon v. Federal Election Commission*, 572 U.S. 185 (2014) (No. 12-536); see also Anita Woudenberg to James Bopp Jr. et al. (February 21, 2013), JBP, Matter Boxes, File 3086.

68. Brief for Appellant Shaun McCutcheon, 20–41, *McCutcheon v. Federal Election Commission*, 572 U.S. 185 (2014) (No. 12-536).

69. *McCutcheon v. Federal Election Commission*, 572 U.S. 185, 204 (2014).

70. Ibid., 204–210.

71. See ibid.

72. See ibid., 237.

73. See Molly McDonough, "Watchdog Group Questions Tax-Exempt Status of James Bopp's Madison Center for Free Speech," *American Bar Association Journal*, July 10, 2013, https://www.abajournal.com/news/article/watchdog_group_questions_tax_status_of_jim_bopps_james_madison_center, accessed June 23, 2021; Peter J. Reilly, "Claims *Citizens United* Attorney Broke Charity Law Don't Hold Up," *Forbes*, July 10, 2013, https://www.forbes.com/sites/peterjreilly/2013/07/10/crew-embarrasses-itself-with-bopp-whistleblower-claim/?sh=7113e491586d, accessed September 14, 2021.

74. See Michael Scherer, Pratheek Rebala, and Chris Wilson, "The Incredible Rise in Campaign Spending," *Time*, October 23, 2014, https://time.com/3534117/the-incredible-rise-in-campaign-spending/, accessed January 13, 2021; Andrew Prokop, "40 Charts That Explain Money in Politics," *Vox*, July 30, 2014, https://www.vox.com/2014/7/30/5949581/money-in-politics-charts-explain, accessed January 13, 2021; Lynn Vavreck, "A Campaign Dollar Is More Valuable to a Challenger Than an

Incumbent," *New York Times*, October 8, 2014, https://www.nytimes.com/2014/10/08/upshot/a-campaign-dollars-power-is-more-valuable-to-a-challenger.html, accessed January 13, 2021. On the cost of the 2014 election, see Russ Choma, "2014: Final Tally: Midterm Was Most Expensive, with Fewer Donors," *Open Secrets*, February 18, 2015, https://www.opensecrets.org/news/2015/02/final-tally-2014s-midterm-was-most-expensive-with-fewer-donors/, accessed June 16, 2021; Open Secrets, "Total Outside Spending by Election Cycle," https://www.opensecrets.org/outsidespending/cycle_tots.php, accessed September 14, 2021.

75. On the Continuing Appropriations Act, see 52 U.S.C. §§ 30116(a)(1)(B), (a)(2)(B), (a)(9).

76. Marc Fisher, "One America (Hint: It's the Boss's)," *Washington Post*, July 6, 2017, C1; see also Asawaen Suebsang, "Trump Embraces Right-Wing One America News Network to Make Fox News Jealous," *Daily Beast*, May 28, 2019; Ellen Cranley, "How One America News Network Quickly Rose to the Top of Trump's Must-Watch TV List," *Business Insider*, October 14, 2019.

77. Sarah Kliff, "Lawmakers Debate Contraceptive Mandate," *Washington Post*, February 17, 2012, A3; Kim Geiger and Noam Levey, "The Nation: New Take on Birth Control," *Los Angeles Times*, February 16, 2012, A7. On the *Manhattan Declaration*, see *Manhattan Declaration: A Christian Call to Conscience*, November 20, 2009, www.manhattandeclaration.org, accessed September 20, 2017. For interfaith organizing in the movement, see Neil J. Young, *We Gather Together: The Religious Right and the Problem of Interfaith Politics* (New York: Oxford University Press, 2016), 176–190; Daniel K. Williams, *God's Own Party: The Making of the Christian Right* (New York: Oxford University Press, 2010), 120–176. On the declining number of Americans who identified as Christian, see Pew Forum, "In U.S., Decline of Christianity Continues at Rapid Pace," October 17, 2019, https://www.pewforum.org/2019/10/17/in-u-s-decline-of-christianity-continues-at-rapid-pace/, accessed January 13, 2021; Pew Forum, "U.S. Public Becoming Less Religious," November 3, 2015, https://www.pewforum.org/2015/11/03/u-s-public-becoming-less-religious/, accessed January 13, 2021.

78. For the Court's decision in *Obergefell*, see *Obergefell v. Hodges*, 576 U.S. 644 (2015). For DeSanctis's statement: Alexandra DeSanctis, "Religious Liberty After *Obergefell*," *National Review*, June 12, 2017, https://www.nationalreview.com/magazine/2017/06/12/religious-freedom-obergefell/, accessed January 13, 2021. For the *Federalist* quote: Daniel Payne, "The Big Gay Marriage Lie," *Federalist*, July 24, 2015, https://thefederalist.com/2015/07/24/the-big-gay-marriage-lie/, accessed January 13, 2021.

79. See Robert P. Jones, Daniel Cox, E. J. Dionne Jr., William Galston, Betsy Cooper, and Rachel Lienesch, *How Immigration and Concerns about Cultural Changes Are Shaping the 2016 Election: Findings from the PRRI/Brookings 2016 Immigration Survey*, 2016, 17, https://www.prri.org/wp-content/uploads/2016/06/PRRI-Brookings-2016-Immigration-survey-report.pdf, accessed January 14, 2021.

80. See Reid Epstein and Heather Haddon, "Donald Trump Vows to Disrupt Crowded GOP Presidential Race," *Wall Street Journal*, June 16, 2015, https://www.wsj.com/

articles/donald-trump-to-unveil-plans-for-2016-presidential-race-1434448982, accessed January 15, 2021; Dan Balz, "The Trump Circus Comes to Iowa," *Washington Post*, June 18, 2015, A4; Husna Haq, "Why Is Donald Trump Surging in Early Polls?" *Christian Science Monitor*, July 1, 2015, https://www.csmonitor.com/USA/Politics/2015/0701/Why-is-Donald-Trump-surging-in-early-polls, accessed June 27, 2021.

81. Susan B. Anthony List, "Pro-Life Women Sound the Alarm: Donald Trump Is Unacceptable," January 26, 2016, https://www.sba-list.org/home/pro-life-women-sound-the-alarmdonald-trump-is-unacceptable, accessed April 7, 2021; see also Kelefa Sanneh, "The Intensity Gap," *New Yorker*, October 20, 2014, https://www.newyorker.com/magazine/2014/10/27/intensity-gap, accessed January 15, 2021; Sandhya Raman, "Abortion Foe Goes from Trump Skeptic to Trump Champion," *Roll Call*, June 27, 2019, https://www.rollcall.com/2019/06/27/abortion-foe-goes-from-trump-skeptic-to-trump-champion/, accessed January 15, 2021; Jennifer Haberkorn, "Anti-Abortion Groups Say They Distrust Trump," *Politico*, January 26, 2016, https://www.politico.com/story/2016/01/donald-trump-anti-abortion-group-distrust-218258, accessed January 15, 2021; Eliza Collins, "Why an Anti-Abortion Group Is Applauding NARAL," *Politico*, February 9, 2016, https://www.politico.com/story/2016/02/naral-susan-b-anthony-support-219024, accessed January 15, 2021. On the Republicans attending the NRLC event, see "Republican Presidential Hopefuls Address 45th National Right to Life Convention," *Targeted News Service*, July 15, 2015.

82. See Matt Flegenheimer and Maggie Haberman, "Donald Trump, Abortion Foe, Eyes 'Punishment' for Women, Then Recants," *New York Times*, March 31, 2016, https://www.nytimes.com/2016/03/31/us/politics/donald-trump-abortion.html, accessed January 15, 2021; Jose A. Del Real, "Trump: If Abortions Are Banned, Women Who Seek Them Should Face 'Punishment,' " *Washington Post*, March 30, 2016, https://www.washingtonpost.com/news/post-politics/wp/2016/03/30/trump-if-abortions-were-banned-women-who-seek-them-would-face-punishment/, accessed January 15, 2021; Rebecca Ballhaus and Beth Reinhard, "Donald Trump's Abortion Comments Spark Furor from Both Sides," *Wall Street Journal*, April 4, 2016, https://www.wsj.com/articles/trumps-abortion-comments-spark-furor-from-both-sides-1459371715, accessed January 15, 2020. For NRLC's endorsement of Trump, see "Donald Trump Facing Test in Wisconsin Primary as Ted Cruz Gains Momentum," *Dow Jones Industrial News*, April 5, 2016. For True the Vote's statement: Asawin Suebsaeng, "Bully of the Week: Voter Intimidation Squad Claims That Hillary Clinton Wants to Steal the Presidency," *Daily Beast*, February 21, 2016, https://www.thedailybeast.com/bully-of-the-week-voter-intimidation-squad-claims-hillary-wants-to-steal-presidency, accessed June 21, 2021.

83. James Bopp Jr., Solomon Yue, and Russ Walker to David McIntosh and Chuck Pike (June 10, 2015), 2, JBP, Digital Records, RNC 2016 Convention Combined File; see also James Bopp Jr. and Solomon Yue to Whom It May Concern Re: RNC Convention Project Proposal (October 21, 2015), JBP, Digital Records, RNC 2016 Convention Combined File.

84. Memorandum, Re: Republican National Convention Impact Project (April 28, 2016), JBP, Digital Records, RNC 2016 Convention Combined File.
85. On the Indiana result and suspension of Cruz's campaign, see David Jackson, "Cruz Quits Race After Knockout Blow in Indiana," *USA Today*, May 4, 2016, A1. For AUL's model law, see Americans United for Life, "Women's Health Protection Act," in *Legislative and Policy Guide for the 2013 Legislative Year* (Washington, DC: Americans United for Life, 2013), 1–6. For anti-abortion advocacy in the case, see Amici Curiae Brief of Forty-Four State Legislators in Support of Defendants-Appellants, 15, *Whole Women's Health v. Cole*, 2014 WL 6647162 (5th Cir.) (2016) (No. 14-50928); Brief Amicus Curiae of the National Right to Life Committee, 18, *Whole Women's Health v. Cole*, 2014 WL 6647162 (5th Cir.) (2016) (No. 14-50928).
86. See *Whole Woman's Health v. Hellerstedt*, 136 S. Ct. 2292, 2309–2310 (2016). On Scalia's death, see Eva Ruth Moravec, Sari Horvitz, and Jerry Markon, "The Death of Antonin Scalia: Chaos, Confusion and Conflicting Reports," *Washington Post*, February 14, 2016, www.washingtonpost.com/politics/texas-tv-station-scalia-died-of-a-heart-attack/2016/ 02/14/938e2170-d332–11e5–9823–02b905009f99_story.html, accessed April 30, 2019; Nick Corasaniti, "Scalia's Death Jolts the 2016 Presidential Race," *New York Times*, February 13, 2016, www.nytimes.com/live/supreme-court-justice-antonin-scalia-dies-at-79/scalias-deathjolts-presidential-race, accessed April 30, 2019.
87. Erik Eckholm, "Anti-Abortion Group Presses Ahead Despite Recent Supreme Court Ruling," *New York Times*, July 10, 2016, A12. On the Garland nomination and its aftermath, see Ron Elving, "What Happened with Merrick Garland in 2016 and Why It Matters Now," *NPR*, June 29, 2018, www.npr.org/2018/06/29/624467256/what-happened-with-merrick-garland-in-2016-and-why-it-matters-now, accessed April 30, 2019. On Clinton and the platform, see Alan Rappeport, "Hillary Clinton Denounces Donald Trump as Untrustworthy on Women's Issues," *New York Times*, June 10, 2016, https://www.nytimes.com/2016/06/11/us/politics/elizabeth-warren-hillary-clinton.html, accessed January 15, 2021.
88. Solomon Yue to Fred Hawkins et al. (April 1, 2016), SYP. On the possible alternatives to Trump proposed within the GOP, see Steven M. Teles and Robert P. Saldin, *Never Trump: The Revolt of Conservative Elites* (New York: Oxford University Press, 2020), 107–112. For Rove's statement: Byron York, "Karl Rove: 'Fresh Face' Might Be Best GOP Nominee," *Washington Examiner*, March 31, 2016, https://www.washingtonexaminer.com/tag/donald-trump?source=%2Fkarl-rove-fresh-face-might-be-best-gop-nominee, accessed September 16, 2021.
89. Solomon Yue to Oregon State Republican Party Central Planning Committee Members (March 17, 2016), SYP; see also Bruce Ash to Jim Bopp et al. (April 16, 2016), SYP; Solomon Yue to RNC Standing Rules Committee Members (April 18, 2016), SYP; Bruce Ash to RNC Standing Rules Committee Members (April 16, 2016), SYP; Solomon Yue to Oregon State Republican Party Central Planning Committee Members (April 22, 2016), SYP; see also Ralph Hallow, "RNC Official Escalates Feud with Priebus, Accuses RNC Chair of 'Institutional Tyranny,'" *Washington Times*, April 18, 2016, https://www.washingtontimes.com/

news/2016/apr/18/rnc-official-escalates-feud-priebus-accuses-gop-bo/, accessed February 2, 2021.

90. James Bopp Jr., "Final Confidential After-Action Report on RNCC Platform Project on the 2016 Republican National Convention" (2016), JBP, Digital Records, 2016 Republican National Convention Folder. On factions within the Republican Party in 2016, see ibid., 2–3; see also Solomon Yue to Katie Kerschner, Ross Little, Bruce Ash, Jim Bopp, and Ken Cuccinelli (July 7, 2016), SYP.
91. James Bopp Jr. to Members of the RNC Standing Rules Committee, Re: Resolution of Controversy Surrounding Rule 15/16 (2012), on file with the author.
92. Bruce Ash, email interview with Mary Ziegler, February 1, 2021; Solomon Yue, email interview with Mary Ziegler, January 31, 2021; Solomon Yue to Jeff Grossman (June 18, 2016), SYP.
93. See Bopp, "Final Confidential After-Action Report," 3–14.
94. See Melanie Mason, "The Nation: Upstarts Organize to Block Trump," *Los Angeles Times*, June 30, 2016, A6; Ed O'Keefe, "Hundreds of GOP Delegates Join New Anti-Trump Effort," *Washington Post*, June 21, 2016, A4; Ed O'Keefe, "As 'Never Trump' Forces Make Last Stand, Compelling Scenarios Emerge," *Washington Post*, July 14, 2016, A6. On the walkout, see Kyle Cheney, "Chaos Erupts on GOP Convention Floor After Voice Vote Shuts Down Never Trump Forces," *Politico*, July 18, 2016, https://www.politico.com/story/2016/07/never-trump-delegates-have-support-needed-to-force-rules-vote-225716, accessed January 15, 2021.
95. On Trump's voter fraud arguments and Republican strategies around election integrity, see David Weigel, "Warning of Cheating, Trump Rallies Poll Watchers," *Washington Post*, August 14, 2016, A2.
96. See Jack Noland, "In the First Post-*McCutcheon* Election, More Big Donors Giving More," *Open Secrets*, November 10, 2016, https://www.opensecrets.org/news/2016/11/in-first-post-mccutcheon-presidential-election-more-big-donors-giving-more/, accessed January 15, 2021; Josh Stewart, "*McCutcheon* Decision Has Allowed $39 Million in Presidential Election So Far," *Sunlight Foundation*, August 29, 2016, https://sunlightfoundation.com/2016/08/29/mccutcheon-decision-has-allowed-at-least-39-million-more-in-presidential-election-so-far/, accessed January 15, 2021. On Adelson's impact, see Robert D. McFadden, "Sheldon Adelson, Billionaire Donor to GOP and Israel, Is Dead at 87," *New York Times*, January 12, 2021, https://www.nytimes.com/2021/01/12/business/sheldon-adelson-dead.html, accessed September 16, 2021.

Conclusion

1. On the Russia investigation and Comey firing, see Michael D. Shear and Matt Apuzzo, "FBI Director James Comey Is Fired by Trump," *New York Times*, May 9, 2017, https://www.nytimes.com/2017/05/09/us/politics/james-comey-fired-fbi.html, accessed February 3, 2021; "Giuliani: Trump Fired Comey Because Former FBI Director Wouldn't Say He Wasn't a Target in the Investigation," *Politico*, May 3, 2018, https://www.politico.com/story/2018/05/03/trump-fire-comey-reason-rudy-

giuliani-566043, accessed February 3, 2021. On the so-called Muslim ban and the Supreme Court decision on it, see Aysha Khan, "American Muslims Welcome End of Trump's Travel Ban," *Washington Post*, January 22, 2018, https://www.washingtonpost.com/religion/muslim-travel-ban-end-trump-biden/2021/01/22/d09b42de-5c10–11eb-b8bd-ee36b1cd18bf_story.html, accessed February 3, 2021; Adam Liptak and Michael D. Shear, "Trump Travel Ban Is Upheld by Supreme Court," *New York Times*, June 26, 2018, https://www.nytimes.com/2018/06/26/us/politics/supreme-court-trump-travel-ban.html, accessed February 3, 2021.

2. Angie Drobnic Holan, "In Context: Donald Trump's 'Very Fine People on Both Sides' Remarks," *Politifact*, April 26, 2019, https://www.politifact.com/article/2019/apr/26/context-trumps-very-fine-people-both-sides-remarks/, accessed March 2, 2021; see also Michael D. Shear and Maggie Haberman, "Trump Defends Initial Remarks on Charlottesville; Again, Blames 'Both Sides,' " *New York Times*, August 15, 2017, https://www.nytimes.com/2017/08/15/us/politics/trump-press-conference-charlottesville.html, accessed March 2, 2021; Glenn Thrush and Maggie Haberman, "Trump Gives White Supremacists an Unequivocal Boost," *New York Times*, August 15, 2017, https://www.nytimes.com/2017/08/15/us/politics/trump-charlottesville-white-nationalists.html, accessed March 2, 2021.

3. On Trump's immigration policy, see Zolan Kanno-Youngs, "Trump Tried to Blur Responsibility for His Family Separation Policy in Final Debate," *New York Times*, October 23, 2020, https://www.nytimes.com/2020/10/23/us/politics/trump-child-separation.html, accessed February 18, 2021; "Trump Migrant Separation Policy: Children 'in Cages' in Texas," *BBC*, June 18, 2018, https://www.bbc.com/news/world-us-canada-44518942, accessed February 18, 2021; "U.S. Border: Who Decided to Separate Families?" *BBC*, June 26, 2019, https://www.bbc.com/news/world-us-canada-44303556, accessed February 18, 2021. On Trump's handling of COVID, see Steffie Woolhandler et al., "Public Policy and Health in the Trump Era," *Lancet*, February 10, 2021, https://www.thelancet.com/journals/lancet/article/PIIS0140–6736(20)32545–9/fulltext, accessed February 18, 2021; Jorge Ortiz, " 'Blood on His Hands': As US Surpasses 400,000 Deaths, Experts Blame Trump Administration for a 'Preventable' Loss of Life," *USA Today*, January 17, 2021, https://www.usatoday.com/story/news/nation/2021/01/17/covid-19-us-400–000-deaths-experts-blame-trump-administration/6642685002/, accessed February 18, 2021. On the effect of COVID on Trump's reelection chances, see Veronica Stracqualursi and Jim Acosta, "Trump Pollster Says COVID 19, Not Voter Fraud, to Blame on Reelection Loss," *CNN*, February 2, 2021, https://www.cnn.com/2021/02/02/politics/trump-2020-reelection-loss-covid/index.html, accessed June 25, 2021. On the impeachment and acquittal, see Noah Bookbinder and Kristin Amerling, "Senate Impeachment Trial: Weigh Trump's Repeated Obstruction Offenses to Protect Himself," *USA Today*, January 17, 2020, https://www.usatoday.com/story/opinion/2020/01/17/senate-impeachment-trial-trump-repeat-offender-obstruction-column/4482554002/, accessed September 14, 2021; "Trump Impeachment: The Short, Medium, and Long Story," *BBC*, February 5, 2020, https://www.bbc.com/news/world-us-canada-49800181, accessed September 14, 2021; Philip Ewing,

" 'Not Guilty:' Trump Acquitted on Two Articles of Impeachment as Historic Trial Closes," *NPR*, February 5, 2020, https://www.npr.org/2020/02/05/801429948/not-guilty-trump-acquitted-on-2-articles-of-impeachment-as-historic-trial-closes, accessed September 14, 2021.

4. On George Floyd's murder and Trump's handling of racial issues in its aftermath, see Matthew Impelli, "Nearly 70 Percent of All Americans Disapprove of Trump's Handling of George Floyd's Death, New Poll Shows," *Newsweek*, June 5, 2020, https://www.newsweek.com/nearly-70-percent-americans-disapprove-trumps-handling-george-floyds-death-new-poll-shows-1508999, accessed June 5, 2020; Matthew Mosk and Katherine Faulders, "Trump's Quest to 'Dominate' amid George Floyd Protests Sparks New Concerns about Presidential Powers," *ABC News*, June 8, 2020, https://abcnews.go.com/US/trumps-quest-dominate-amid-george-floyd-protests-sparks/story?id=71126346, accessed February 18, 2021.
5. On the March for Life, see Lauren Egan, "Trump Becomes First Sitting President to Attend March for Life," *NBC*, January 24, 2020, https://www.nbcnews.com/politics/donald-trump/trump-becomes-first-sitting-president-attend-march-life-rally-n1122246, accessed February 19, 2021. On Trump's conscience efforts, see Alison Kodjak, "New Trump Rule Protects Health Care Workers Who Refuse Care for Religious Reasons," *NPR*, May 2, 2019, https://www.npr.org/sections/health-shots/2019/05/02/688260025/new-trump-rule-protects-health-care-workers-who-refuse-care-for-religious-reason, accessed February 19, 2021; Benjamin Weiser and Margot Sanger-Katz, "Judge Voids Trump-Backed 'Conscience Rule' for Health Workers," *New York Times*, November 6, 2019, https://www.nytimes.com/2019/11/06/upshot/trump-conscience-rule-overturned.html, accessed February 19, 2021. On Trump's Title X regulations, see Sarah McCammon, "Planned Parenthood Leaves Title X Program over Trump Abortion Rule," *NPR*, August 19, 2019, https://www.npr.org/2019/08/19/752438119/planned-parenthood-out-of-title-x-over-trump-rule, accessed February 19, 2021.
6. On Trump's impact on the courts, see Richard Wolf, "Biden's Influence on Federal Judiciary May Be Limited Despite Liberals' Talk of 'Court-Packing,'" *USA Today*, December 20, 2020, https://www.usatoday.com/story/news/politics/2020/12/20/trumps-impact-federal-judiciary-may-hard-biden-reverse/6541264002/, accessed February 19, 2021; Elena Mejia and Amelia Thompson-Devaux, "It Will Be Hard for Biden to Reverse Trump's Legacy of a Whiter, More Conservative Judiciary," *538*, January 21, 2021, https://fivethirtyeight.com/features/trump-made-the-federal-courts-whiter-and-more-conservative-and-that-will-be-tough-for-biden-to-reverse/, accessed February 19, 2021; Moiz Syed, "Charting the Long-Term Impact of Trump's Judicial Appointments," *Propublica*, October 30, 2020, https://projects.propublica.org/trump-young-judges/, accessed February 19, 2021.
7. For the Court's decision in *June Medical*, see *June Medical Services v. Russo*, 140 S. Ct. 2103 (2020). For a sample of early responses to the decision, see Mary Ziegler, "How Not to Outlaw Abortion," *New York Times*, June 29, 2020, https://www.nytimes.com/2020/06/29/opinion/abortion-supreme-court-roberts.html, accessed

February 19, 2021; Mary Ziegler, "Courts Are Already Cutting off Abortion Access, without Saying a Word about *Roe*," *Washington Post*, August 17, 2020, https://www.washingtonpost.com/outlook/2020/08/17/jegley-undue-burden-roe/, accessed February 19, 2021; Melissa Murray, "The Supreme Court's Decision Seems Pulled from the '*Casey*' Playbook," *Washington Post*, June 29, 2020, https://www.washingtonpost.com/opinions/2020/06/29/problem-with-relying-precedent-protect-abortion-rights/, accessed February 19, 2021; Laurence Tribe, "Roberts' Opinion Could End Up Being More Protective of Abortion Law, Not Less," *Washington Post*, July 1, 2020, https://www.washingtonpost.com/opinions/2020/07/01/robertss-approach-could-end-up-being-more-protective-abortion-rights-not-less/, accessed February 19, 2021; Marc Spindelman, "Embracing *Casey: June Medical Services, LLC v. Russo* and the Constitutionality of Reasons-Based Abortion Bans," *Georgetown Law Journal Online* 109 (2020): 115–132. On the issue of whether Roberts's concurrence was the controlling opinion, see Dov Fox, I. Glenn Cohen, and Eli Adashi, "*June Medical Services v. Russo* and the Future of Abortion in the United States," *Journal of the American Medical Association Health Forum*, September 14, 2020, https://jamanetwork.com/channels/health-forum/fullarticle/2770774, accessed April 8, 2021. For the lower court's ruling in *Dobbs*, see *Dobbs v. Jackson Women's Health Organization*, 945 F.3d 465 (5th Cir. 2019). For predictions of what *Dobbs* could mean, see Leah Litman and Melissa Murray, "The Conservative Supreme Court Is about to Show Us Its True Colors," *Washington Post*, May 17, 2021, https://www.washingtonpost.com/opinions/2021/05/17/supreme-court-mississippi-abortion-restrictions-roe-v-wade/; accessed September 16, 2021; Mary Ziegler, "The Abortion Fight Has Never Been about Just *Roe v. Wade*," *Atlantic*, May 20, 2021, https://www.theatlantic.com/ideas/archive/2021/05/abortion-fight-roe-v-wade/618930/, accessed June 17, 2021.

8. See Sean McMinn, "Money Tracker: How Much Have Trump and Biden Raised in the 2020 Election," *NPR*, December 4, 2020, https://www.npr.org/2020/05/20/858347477/money-tracker-how-much-trump-and-biden-have-raised-in-the-2020-election, accessed February 19, 2021. On the record outside spending seen in 2020, see Eliana Miller, "Record Outside Spending Reaches Record $3.2 Billion," *Open Secrets*, December 21, 2020, https://www.opensecrets.org/news/2020/12/outside-spending-reaches-record-in-2020/, accessed February 19, 2021.
9. Margaret Menge, "Top Elections Lawyer: Vote-by-Mail 'the Most Massive Fraud Scheme in the History of America,'" *Inside Sources*, April 23, 2020, https://insidesources.com/top-elections-lawyer-vote-by-mail-the-most-massive-fraud-scheme-in-the-history-of-america/, accessed February 19, 2021. Bopp had worked with other Republicans on voter fraud claims since at least 2012. See Eliza Newlin Carney, "Conservative Veterans of Voting Wars Cite Ballot Integrity to Justify Fight," *Roll Call*, September 25, 2012, https://www.rollcall.com/2012/09/25/conservative-veterans-of-voting-wars-cite-ballot-integrity-to-justify-fight/, accessed February 19, 2021. On the origins of True the Vote, see Abby Rapoport, "What's the Truth behind True the Vote?" *American Prospect*, October 10, 2012, https://

prospect.org/power/truth-true-vote/, accessed February 19, 2021. On Bopp's involvement with True the Vote, see *True the Vote, Inc. v. Internal Revenue Service*, 2017 WL 1956929 (D.D.C. 2017); David Saleh Rauf, "*Citizens United* Lawyer Targets Campaign Finance Laws," *Valley Morning Star*, February 8, 2017, 9; *True the Vote v. Internal Revenue Service*, 2020 WL 5656694 (D.D.C. 2020). On Trump's effort to subvert the election, see Phillip Bump, "What We Know about Trump's Efforts to Subvert the 2020 Election," *Washington Post*, January 25, 2021, https://www.washingtonpost.com/politics/2021/01/25/what-we-know-about-trumps-efforts-subvert-2020-election/, accessed February 2, 2021; Jeremy Herb, Clare Foran, Manu Raju, and Phil Mattingly, "Congress Completes Electoral Count, Finalizing Result After Violent Delay from Pro-Trump Mob," *CNN*, January 6, 2021, https://www.cnn.com/2021/01/06/politics/2020-election-congress-electoral-college-vote-count/index.html, accessed February 2, 2021; Jim Rutenberg, Jo Becker, Eric Lipton, Maggie Haberman, Johnathan Martin, Matthew Rosenberg, and Michael S. Schmidt, "77 Days: Trump's Campaign to Subvert the Election," *New York Times*, January 31, 2021, https://www.nytimes.com/2021/01/31/us/trump-election-lie.html, accessed February 2, 2021.

10. For Bopp's recollections: James Bopp Jr., interview with Mary Ziegler, January 15, 2021; James Bopp Jr., interview with Mary Ziegler, February 5, 2021. For more on Trump's quest, see Bump, "What We Know"; "77 Days."
11. Bump, "What We Know"; "77 Days." For Eshelman's argument: Verified Complaint, 3, *Eshelman v. True the Vote*, Case No. 4:20-cv-04034 (S.D. Tex., Nov. 2020). On the order of dismissal, see *Fredric N. Eshelman v. True the Vote, Inc., et al.*, No. 2021V-0015, Order Granting Defendants' Pleas to the Jurisdiction (April 14, 2021).
12. Herb et al., "Congress Completes."
13. On the 2021 March for Life, see Michelle Boorstein and Samantha Schmidt, "Facing a Post-Trump World, Abortion Opponents at March for Life Strike a Less Partisan Tone," *Washington Post*, January 29, 2021, https://www.washingtonpost.com/religion/2021/01/29/march-for-life-roe-wade-abortion-trump-biden/, accessed February 19, 2021. On the criminal investigation of the insurrection, see Ed Pilkington, "Seditionaries: FBI Net Closes on MAGA Mob That Stormed the Capitol," *Guardian*, February 6, 2021, https://www.theguardian.com/us-news/2021/feb/06/us-capitol-insurrection-fbi-investigation, accessed February 19, 2021. On the failed effort to impeach Trump, see Domenica Montanaro, "Senate Acquits Trump in Impeachment Trial—Again," *NPR*, February 13, 2021, https://www.npr.org/sections/trump-impeachment-trial-live-updates/2021/02/13/967098840/senate-acquits-trump-in-impeachment-trial-again, accessed February 19, 2021; Nicholas Fandos, "Trump Impeached for Inciting Insurrection," *New York Times*, January 13, 2021, https://www.nytimes.com/2021/01/13/us/politics/trump-impeached.html, accessed February 19, 2021.
14. Bopp, January 15, 2021 interview; Bopp, February 5, 2021 interview. On the debate about Trump's removal from Twitter, see Billy Perrigo, "Big Tech's Crackdown on Donald Trump and Parler Won't Fix the Real Problem with Social Media,"

Time, January 12, 2021, https://time.com/5928982/deplatforming-trump-parler/, accessed February 19, 2021; Spencer Bokat-Lindell, "Deplatforming Could Work, but at What Cost?" *New York Times*, January 14, 2021, https://www.nytimes.com/2021/01/14/opinion/trump-deplatform-twitter.html, accessed February 19, 2021. On the suspension of donations to politicians who refused to certify the election, see Jemima McCoy and Andrew Solender, "Amazon, Intel Join Other Major Companies Suspending Donations to Republicans Involved in Biden Certification Challenge," *Forbes*, January 12, 2021, https://www.forbes.com/sites/jemimamcevoy/2021/01/12/amazon-intel-join-other-major-companies-suspending-donations-to-republicans-involved-in-biden-certification-challenge/?sh=7cc6e34c6425, accessed June 28, 2021. Some companies subsequently resumed donations to these Republicans. See Bill Allison, "Boeing PAC Resumes Giving to Republicans Who Opposed Certifying the Election," *Seattle Times*, June 14, 2021, https://www.seattletimes.com/business/boeing-pac-resumes-giving-to-republicans-who-opposed-certifying-election/, accessed June 28, 2021.

15. On the disclosure case in the lower courts, see *Americans for Prosperity et al. v. Becerra*, 903 F.3d 1000 (9th Cir. 2018). On the decision in *Americans for Prosperity*, see *Americans for Prosperity et al. v. Bonta*, 594 U.S. __, 12–15 (2021).
16. On the role played by white identity politics in the GOP, see Angie Maxwell and Todd Shields, *The Long Southern Strategy: How Chasing White Voters in the South Changed American Politics* (New York: Oxford University Press, 2019); Ashley Jardina, *White Identity Politics* (New York: Cambridge University Press, 2019); Alan I. Abramowitz, *The Great Alignment: Race, Party Transformation, and the Rise of Donald Trump* (New Haven: Yale University Press, 2018), 3–16. On the influence of Christian nationalism and the transformation of evangelical Protestantism, see Kristin Kobes Du Mez, *Jesus and John Wayne: How White Evangelicals Corrupted a Faith and Fractured a Nation* (New York: Liveright, 2020); Andrew L. Whitehead and Samuel L. Perry, *Taking America Back for God: Christian Nationalism in the United States* (New York: Oxford University Press, 2020); Katherine Stewart, *The Power Worshippers: Inside the Dangerous Rise of Religious Nationalism* (London: Bloomsbury, 2020). For Posner's argument: Sarah Posner, *Unholy: How White Christian Nationalists Powered the Trump Presidency, and the Devastating Legacy They Left Behind* (New York: Random House, 2021), 3–9.
17. See Geoffrey Kabaservice, *Rule and Ruin: The Downfall of Moderation and the Destruction of the Republican Party, from Eisenhower to the Tea Party* (New York: Oxford University Press, 2012), 150–172.
18. On the changing model of Supreme Court nominations, see Neal Devins and Lawrence Baum, "Split Definitive: How Party Polarization Turned the Supreme Court into a Partisan Court," *Supreme Court Review* 2017 (2017): 301–364; see also Ann Southworth, *Lawyers of the Right: Professionalizing the Conservative Coalition* (Chicago: University of Chicago Press, 2008), 135, 141.
19. See Alex Badas and Elizabeth Simas, "The Supreme Court as an Electoral Issue: Evidence from Three Studies," *Political Science Research and Methods* (2021): 1–19. On candidates' historic tendency not to prioritize the Court, see Christopher W.

Schmidt, "The Forgotten Issue? The Supreme Court and the 2016 Presidential Election Campaign," *Chicago Kent Law Review* 93 (2018): 411–460; William G. Ross, "The Supreme Court as an Issue in Presidential Election Campaigns," *Journal of Supreme Court History* 37 (2012): 329–335; Donald Grier Stephenson, *Campaigns and the Court: The US Supreme Court in Presidential Elections* (New York: Columbia University Press, 1999), 1–14 (arguing that the Court has played a significant role in roughly one-fifth of presidential elections in the years between 1800 and 1992).

20. See Pew Research Center, "Important Issues in the 2020 Election," August 13, 2020, https://www.pewresearch.org/politics/2020/08/13/important-issues-in-the-2020-election/, accessed June 17, 2021. On Trump's frequent mention of the Supreme Court on the campaign trail, see Brian Bennett, " 'Fill That Seat!' How Trump Is Weaponizing His Supreme Court Pick," *Time*, September 21, 2020, https://time.com/5891404/trump-weaponizing-supreme-court-pick/, accessed June 17, 2021; Tom McCarthy, " 'Fill That Seat!' Trump's Weaponizing of the Courts Will Be His Lasting Legacy," *Guardian*, September 22, 2020, https://www.theguardian.com/us-news/2020/sep/22/trump-judges-supreme-court-pick-ruth-bader-ginsburg, accessed June 17, 2021.

21. On the relationship between voter ideology and partisan affiliation, see Matthew Levendusky, *The Big Sort: How Liberals Became Democrats and Conservatives Became Republicans* (Chicago: University of Chicago Press, 2009); Morris Fiorina, Samuel Abrams, and Jeremy Pope, *Culture War? The Myth of a Polarized America*, 3rd ed. (New York: Longman, 2010); Alan Abramowitz, *The Disappearing Center: Engaged Citizens, Polarization, and American Democracy* (New Haven: Yale University Press, 2010); Manabu Saeki, "Anatomy of Partisan Sorting: Partisan Polarization of Voters and Party Switching," *Politics and Policy* 47 (2019): 699–747; Nolan McCarty, *Polarization: What Everyone Needs to Know* (New York: Oxford University Press, 2019), 15–32. For more debate on the source and extent of party polarization, see Gregory Martin and Steven Webster, "Does Residential Sorting Explain Geographic Polarization?" *Political Science Research and Methods* 8 (2020): 215–231.

22. On the spread and consequences of negative partisanship, see Lilliana Mason, *Uncivil Agreement: How Politics Became Our Identity* (Chicago: University of Chicago Press, 2018); Abramowitz, *The Great Alignment*, 3–16; Stephen W. Webster, *American Rage: How Anger Shapes Our Politics* (New York: Cambridge University Press, 2020), 3–19.

23. On the spread of conservative media, see Nicole Hemmer, *Messengers of the Right: Conservative Media and the Transformation of American Politics* (Philadelphia: University of Pennsylvania Press, 2016); Brian Rosenwald, *Talk Radio's America: How an Industry Took over a Party That Took over the United States* (Cambridge, MA: Harvard University Press, 2019).

24. See Bipartisan Policy Center, "Campaign Finance in the United States: Assessing an Era of Fundamental Change," January 2018, https://bipartisanpolicy.org/wp-content/uploads/2019/03/BPC-Democracy-Campaign-Finance-in-the-United-States.pdf, accessed February 22, 2021.

25. On the relationship between parties and outside spending, see Joseph K. Fishkin and Heather Gerken, "The Party's Over: *McCutcheon*, Shadow Parties, and the Future of the Party System," *Supreme Court Review* 2014 (2014): 191–195; Heather K. Gerken, "The Real Problem with *Citizens United:* Campaign Finance, Dark Money, and Shadow Parties," *Marquette Law Review* 97 (2013): 918–921.
26. On Roberts's seeming preference for a slow approach to dismantling abortion rights, see Ziegler, "How Not to Outlaw Abortion"; Murray, "The Supreme Court's Decision Seems Pulled from the *Casey* Playbook." For an estimate of how many states would ban abortion if *Roe* were gone, see "Abortion Policy in the Absence of *Roe*," *Guttmacher Institute*, February 1, 2021, https://www.guttmacher.org/state-policy/explore/abortion-policy-absence-roe, accessed February 22, 2021.
27. On Trump's increased support among voters of color, see Musa al-Gharbi, "White Men Swung to Biden. Trump Made Gains with Blacks and Latinos. Why?" *Guardian*, November 14, 2020, https://www.theguardian.com/commentisfree/2020/nov/14/joe-biden-trump-black-latino-republicans, accessed February 22, 2021; Leila Fadel, "How Did President Trump Appeal to Voters of Color?" *NPR*, November 5, 2020, https://www.npr.org/2020/11/05/931643022/how-did-president-trump-appeal-to-voters-of-color, accessed February 22, 2021. On Black voters' views of abortion, see Frank Newport, "Black Voters and Abortion," *Gallup*, September 3, 2020, https://news.gallup.com/opinion/polling-matters/318932/black-americans-abortion.aspx, accessed June 26, 2021. Although Latinos are more likely to be against legal abortion than some other groups, overall opposition has dropped in recent years, with U.S.-born Latinx voters supporting legal abortion at the highest rates. See Public Religion Research Institute, "The State of Abortion and Contraception Attitudes in All Fifty States," August 13, 2019, https://www.prri.org/research/legal-in-most-cases-the-impact-of-the-abortion-debate-in-2019-america/, accessed February 22, 2021. Asian/Pacific Islanders tend to strongly support abortion, although the numbers have decreased in recent years, particularly among GOP voters. Ibid.
28. On Trump's effect on turnout and participation for the GOP, see Drew Desilver, "Turnout Soared in 2020 as Nearly 2/3 of Eligible US Voters Cast Ballots for President," *Pew Research Center*, January 28, 2021, https://www.pewresearch.org/fact-tank/2021/01/28/turnout-soared-in-2020-as-nearly-two-thirds-of-eligible-u-s-voters-cast-ballots-for-president, accessed September 16, 2021/; Tufts Center for Research and Learning on Civic Engagement, "Election Week 2020: Young People Increase Turnout, Lead Biden to Victory," November 25, 2020, https://circle.tufts.edu/latest-research/election-week-2020, accessed February 22, 2021.
29. For evidence that campaign spending increases turnout, see David Primo and Jeffrey Milyo, *Campaign Finance and American Democracy: What the Public Really Thinks and Why It Matters* (Chicago: University of Chicago Press, 2020), 124–130; Joao Cancelo and Benny Geys, "Explaining Voter Turnout: A Meta-analysis of National and Subnational Elections," *Electoral Studies* 42 (2016): 265–274. On the role of small donors in Sanders's campaign, see Shane Goldmacher, "Bernie Sanders Raised $46 Million in February, a Record for 2020," *New York Times*, March 1, 2020, https://www.nytimes.com/2020/03/01/us/politics/bernie-sanders-

money.html, accessed June 28, 2021. On the polarization of small donors, see Raymond La Raja and Brian Schaffner, *Campaign Finance and Political Polarization: When Purists Prevail* (Ann Arbor: University of Michigan Press, 2015), 138, 166; Richard Pildes, "Participation and Polarization," *University of Pennsylvania Journal of Constitutional Law* 22 (2019): 341–366.

30. See David Hopkins and David Grossman, *Asymmetric Politics: Ideological Republicans and Group Interest Democrats* (New York: Oxford University Press, 2016), 23; Thomas Mann and Norman Ornstein, *It's Even Worse Than It Looks: How the American Constitutional System Collided with the New Politics of Extremism* (New York: Basic Books, 2016), 44–49; Rosenwald, *Talk Radio's America*, 8–10.
31. See Stephen Fowler, Abigail Censky, Ben Giles, and Brett Neely, "After Record 2020 Turnout, State Republicans Weigh Laws Making It Harder to Vote," *NPR*, February 7, 2021, https://www.npr.org/2021/02/07/964598941/after-record-2020-turnout-state-republicans-weigh-making-it-harder-to-vote, accessed February 23, 2021; Jane C. Timm, "Republicans Advance More Than 100 Bills That Would Restrict Voting in Wake of Trump's Defeat," *NBC*, February 5, 2021, https://www.nbcnews.com/politics/elections/republicans-advance-more-100-bills-would-restrict-voting-wake-trump-n1256821, accessed February 23, 2021.
32. Janet Folger Porter, Mass Email, "This Is Our 1775. Enlist in the Battle for Liberty" (November 22, 2020), on file with the author. For Bopp's perspective: Bopp, February 5 interview; Bopp, January 15, 2021 interview. On anti-abortion excitement over *Dobbs*, see Autumn Schimmer, "The Pro-Life Generation Is Thrilled over the Future Hearing of *Jackson v. Women's Health Organization*," *Students for Life*, May 20, 2021, https://studentsforlifeaction.org/the-pro-life-generation-is-thrilled-over-the-future-hearing-of-dobbs-v-jackson-womens-health-organization/?utm_source=rss&utm_medium=rss&utm_campaign=the-pro-life-generation-is-thrilled-over-the-future-hearing-of-dobbs-v-jackson-womens-health-organization, accessed June 28, 2021.
33. See Ziegler, "The Abortion Fight."
34. See Domenico Montanaro, "Poll: Majority Want to Keep Abortion Legal, but They Also Want Restrictions," *NPR*, June 7, 2019, https://www.npr.org/2019/06/07/730183531/poll-majority-want-to-keep-abortion-legal-but-they-also-want-restrictions, accessed June 28, 2021; Lydia Saad, "Americans' Abortion Views Steady in Past Year," *Gallup*, June 29, 2020, https://news.gallup.com/poll/313094/americans-abortion-views-steady-past-year.aspx, accessed June 28, 2021; Megan Brenan, "Gallup: Record-High 47% in US Think Abortion Is Morally Acceptable," *Gallup*, June 9, 2021, https://news.gallup.com/poll/350756/record-high-think-abortion-morally-acceptable.aspx, accessed June 28, 2021.
35. For arguments that the Fourteenth Amendment treats a fetus or unborn child as a person, see John Finnis, "Abortion Is Unconstitutional," *First Things*, April 2021, https://www.firstthings.com/article/2021/04/abortion-is-unconstitution al, accessed June 28, 2021; Josh Craddock, "John Finnis Is Right," *First Things*, March 2021, https://www.firstthings.com/web-exclusives/2021/03/john-finnis-is-right, accessed June 28, 2021. On the extent to which the Supreme Court

reflects popular opinion, see Michael Klarman, *From Jim Crow to Civil Rights: The Supreme Court and the Struggle for Racial Equality* (New York: Oxford University Press, 2004); Barry Friedman, *The Will of the People: How Public Opinion Has Influenced the Supreme Court and Shaped the Meaning of the Constitution* (New York: Farrar, Straus and Giroux, 2009).

INDEX